140-154 2

Public Relations Writing
and Media Techniques

233-244
394-402

Public Relations Writing and Media Techniques

THIRD EDITION

Dennis L. Wilcox
San Jose State University

Lawrence W. Nolte
Public Relations Consultant, Williamsburg, Virginia

Foreword by
Patrick Jackson
Senior Counsel, Jackson, Jackson & Wagner
Editor, PR Reporter

 LONGMAN

An imprint of Addison Wesley Longman, Inc.

New York • Reading, Massachusetts • Menlo Park, California • Harlow, England
Don Mills, Ontario • Sydney • Mexico City • Madrid • Amsterdam

Senior Editor: Deirdre Cavanaugh
Editorial Assistant: Kwon Chong
Project Coordination and Text Design: Ruttle, Shaw & Wetherill, Inc.
Cover Designer: Kay Petronio
Cover Photograph: Photo Disk, Inc.
Photo Researcher: Diane Kraut
Electronic Production Manager: Christine Pearson
Manufacturing Manager: Helene G. Landers
Electronic Page Makeup: Ruttle, Shaw & Wetherill, Inc.
Printer and Binder: R. R. Donnelley & Sons Company
Cover Printer: The Lehigh Press, Inc.

Library of Congress Cataloging-in-Publication Data

Wilcox, Dennis L.
    Public relations writing and media techniques / Dennis L. Wilcox,
Lawrence W. Nolte; foreword by Patrick Jackson—3rd ed.
        p.   cm.
    Includes index.
    ISBN 0-673-98083-9
    1. Public relations—United States.   2. Public relations—United
States—Authorship.   I. Nolte, Lawrence W.   II. Title.
HM263.W494 1997
659.2—dc20   96–26402
                                                         CIP

ISBN 0-673-98083-9

    45678910–DOC–9998

*Dedicated to
Marianne, Anne-Marie, and Dorothy,
whose love and support have made
this book possible*

Contents

Foreword

If one book can help us learn to write, to think, to plan, and to use various media and methods, it is a superior text. A person who knows and can apply what's in this book is ready for a career in public relations.

This text originated as the product of several developments in the emerging profession of public relations. The third edition continues this up-to-the-minute overview by adding significant material on advances in technology that affect the processes of writing and communicating.

Writing and media techniques receive here the balanced view that a student must develop to enter the field today. Recent research is emphatic that a majority of people lack the sophisticated reading and writing skills necessary to cope with the information explosion. Whether a consumer or a purveyor of goods, services, or information, one's ability to deal effectively with information overload is of paramount importance. Effective media communication skills are more important than ever because only the most precisely targeted and easiest to understand messages will get through to their intended audiences.

Writing is a thought-recovery process. We have thoughts in response to some mental or visual stimulus. We capture them at a keyboard or on the back of an envelope on the last flight from Dallas. This book teaches how to capture sound thinking in persuasive writing.

What makes this text so valuable is that it goes beyond telling *how* to write to examine the reasons *why* we write. The driving force in effective public relations practice is to see beyond what we do (the process) in order to focus on why (the expected outcomes). Most valuable are the examples that illustrate this point. By analytically teaching why we write, and the strategy and planning that go into persuasive writing, this book helps us think better. The first step to better writing is better thinking—and the combination leads to better public relations practice.

It is no overstatement that mastering the material covered in this comprehensive book is essential to a career in the field, or even to being able to use the principles of public relations as a manager, board member, or committee volunteer. A thorough understanding of this material would significantly enhance most managers' organizational effectiveness and ensure that customer satisfaction would increase a hundredfold.

Writing and media are only part of public relations, of course. The text recognizes this by also illuminating such subjects as events, conferences, meetings of various kinds, presentations, ethics, and, most important, *planning*. Still, a public relations practitioner without a thorough understanding of persuasive writing and efficient media networks would be like a doctor without a basic grounding in anatomy or physiology.

This third edition is particularly useful by presenting important material on the everyday forms that, in the aggregate, constitute the majority of public relations writing—letters, memos, direct mail, brochures, aids to accompany audiovisual materials.

Dennis Wilcox, a knowledgeable, questing, and contributing scholar of the field, is a spokesman not only for what public relations is but also for what it can and should be. Larry Nolte, who in his consulting puts the topics of this book into practice, has paved the way for the behavioral science approach that is widely accepted today.

In a society whose very size ensures that communication and interpersonal skills must be recognized as the basis of democracy, these authors demonstrate in this valuable volume the insight students need to succeed.

PATRICK JACKSON, FELLOW PRSA
SENIOR COUNSEL, JACKSON, JACKSON & WAGNER
EDITOR, PR REPORTER

Preface

The third edition of *Public Relations Writing and Media Techniques,* like its previous editions, is designed to be a comprehensive, highly readable text. It emphasizes how public relations specialists gather, produce, and distribute material on what is now known as the "information highway."

Consequently, there is expanded and new material showing public relations writers how to use the new technologies of electronic wire services, E-mail, satellite media tours, computer graphics, CD-ROM, the Internet, and the World Wide Web.

But gee-whiz advances in technology are not the only focus of this book. It also builds a framework in Part 1 that helps students understand the laws and regulations that affect public relations practice, the ethics of persuasion, what constitutes news, and how to generate news.

Above all, the text is a "how-to" manual for effective public relations writing. Writing, we believe, is the most essential skill for all public relations work. The chapters in Part 2 emphasize the writing of news releases and features for both print and broadcast. It also covers the fine art of writing pitch letters. Part 3 emphasizes writing for a variety of media—newsletters, brochures, advertising, speeches, letters and reports, even slide presentations.

Distribution and effective media relations are also important. Consequently, entire chapters detail the techniques of media placement and the basics of media relations. Finally, Part 4 puts it all together by thoroughly discussing event planning, program planning, and evaluation.

The major strengths of the book, according to reviewers, are:

- Comprehensive coverage of many topics.
- Excellent practical examples, illustrations, and checklists that show students how to produce and distribute quality materials.
- New and updated information on all aspects of current public relations practice.
- High readability, clear presentation of ideas, and excellent writing style.
- Summaries and exercises at the end of every chapter.
- The ability to mix and match chapters depending on the course and the time available.

An Instructor's Manual with test questions is available for this edition. Please contact your local Addison Wesley Longman sales representative.

We are grateful to the following reviewers for comments and suggestions in the second edition: William Baxter, Marquette University; E. W. Brody, Memphis State University; Cathy Morton, Texas Tech University; Susan Pendleton, Mansfield University; Bruce Renfro, Southwest Texas State University; Ed Romanoff, University of Pittsburgh; and Susanne A. Roschwalb, American University.

Our special thanks to the reviewers who helped us revise and update the third edition: Janice Barrett, Boston University; Lena Chau, California State University at Los Angeles; Jan Elliott, University of North Carolina; Terry Rentner, Bowling Green State University; Susanne A. Roschwalb, American University; and Joseph Zappala, Utica College.

Public Relations Writing and Media Techniques is for students who want to learn how to write, prepare, and distribute public relations materials. It is for professors who want a comprehensive, up-to-date text that accurately reflects public relations practice in the "real world."

DENNIS L. WILCOX, FELLOW PRSA
LAWRENCE W. NOLTE, FELLOW PRSA

PART 1

The Basics of Public Relations Writing

Public relations writing has four basic building blocks: (1) the proper use of the English language; (2) an understanding of the legal and ethical context for shaping messages; (3) knowledge of how people are influenced by messages and (4) creativity. Part 1 uses these building blocks to lay the foundation for in-depth instruction on how to master media techniques.

- ☐ *Chapter 1, "Preparing for Writing,"* discusses the purpose of public relations writing, the equipment needed, basic references, on-line retrieval services and networks, surfing the Internet and the basics of good writing.

- ☐ *Chapter 2, "Legal and Ethical Considerations,"* covers potential liability, libel, invasion of privacy, regulatory agencies, copyright, trademarks, codes of conduct and ethical standards.

- ☐ *Chapter 3, "Persuasive Writing,"* explores writing to change opinions and attitudes, appealing to self-interest, communication theories, basic persuasion concepts and message design.

- ☐ *Chapter 4, "Finding and Generating News,"* describes basic news values, the competition for space, where to find stories, ideas for making news, brainstorming and creativity.

1 | *Preparing for Writing*

Public relations writing is part of a process that requires writing tools, use of basic references, the ability to gather information and knowledge of basic English composition. From this standpoint, both the public relations writer and the journalist share a common approach to writing. For both, it's an exacting job that doesn't allow careless, sloppy work. Facts must be assembled and checked before the actual writing is started. The writing itself is an intense process of wrestling with word choice, sentence structure and thematic development.

This chapter sets the stage for good public relations writing. It tells you what equipment you need, how to use print and electronic references and the basic elements of composition.

THE PUBLIC RELATIONS WRITER

Although the public relations writer and the journalist share a number of common characteristics in their approach to writing, the public relations writer differs in objectives, audiences and channels.

Objectives

A journalist is usually employed by a news organization to gather, process and synthesize information for the primary purpose of providing news to the organization's subscribers, viewers or listeners. A hallmark of professional reporting is to present information in an objective manner. A reporter's personal preference may affect the choice of words and the news angle of the story, but in general, the reporter tries to maintain an attitude of strict neutrality.

The public relations writer, in contrast, is usually employed by an organization that wants to communicate with a variety of audiences, either through the news media or through other channels of communication. These organizations may include corporations, government agencies, environmental groups, labor unions, trade associations or public relations firms who provide information on behalf of clients. The writer's purpose is advocacy, not objectivity. The goal is not only to inform but also to persuade and motivate. Edward M. Stanton, former chairman of the Manning, Selvage & Lee public relations firm, defined public relations in *Public Relations Quarterly* (Spring 1991) as "working with clients on strategy and messages, and then delivering these messages to target audiences in order to persuade them to do something that is beneficial to the client."

Harold Burson, chairman of Burson-Marsteller and a longtime leader in the public relations profession, defines public relations activity, including writing, as "advanced information in the public forum for the purpose of contributing to public opinion." To be effective and credible, public relations messages must be based on facts. "Nevertheless," Burson continues,

> We are advocates, and we need to remember that. We are advocates of a particular point of view—our client's or our employer's point of view. And while we recognize that serving the public interest best serves our client's interest, we are not journalists. That's not our job. (*O'Dwyer PR Services Report,* November 1990).

Professor Robert Heath, co-author of *Rhetorical and Critical Approaches to Public Relations,* points out that the role of advocate is a time-honored one. It goes back 2,000 years to Aristotle, who conceptualized the term "rhetoric"—the ability to determine what needs to be said and how it should be said to achieve desired outcomes. Heath writes that rhetoric "entails the ability and obligation to demonstrate to an audience facts and arguments available to bring insight into an important issue."

Hence all public relations writing should begin with the question, How does this help the organization attain its objectives? For example, does a product news release point out the advantages of the company's new product and how it can benefit a potential customer? The editor of a company employee newsletter must also consider company objectives when planning various articles. If the company wants to increase employee productivity, the editor may decide to run several features about employees who are outstanding workers. A good example of how a company newspaper interprets corporate objectives is the excerpt from the Weyerhaeuser Corporation newspaper (see Figure 1.1).

Audiences

The journalist writes for one audience—readers, listeners or viewers of the medium for which he or she works. Newspapers, magazines, radio and television are usually defined as "mass media" because the audience is numerous and unknown to the communicator, and its members have little in common. A suburban daily newspaper, for example, circulates primarily among people who share a common residential area but have a broad range of backgrounds and interests. Such mass media, by definition, usually present material written at the fourth- to sixth-grade level and offer a wide variety of stories and features to satisfy almost any interest, be it sports, local news or the daily horoscope.

In contrast, the readers of a special interest magazine share a strong interest in only one subject—a particular hobby, a specific industry or a highly specialized occupation. Reporters for such magazines write about just one subject for a limited and intensely interested audience.

The public relations writer, however, may write for numerous and radically different audiences—employees, constituents, customers, business people, homemakers, travelers, bankers, stockholders, farmers and many others. Effective public relations writing is based on carefully defining the audience and its composition so that you can tailor your information to its interests and concerns. A public relations writer does research constantly to determine these audience needs, concerns, and interests. Armed with this information, you can write a more persuasive message. The concepts of public opinion and persuasion are discussed in Chapter 3.

Channels

Journalists, by nature of their employment, reach their audiences through one channel, the medium that publishes or broadcasts their work. The public relations writer, with many specific audiences to reach, will probably use many channels. Indeed, public relations writers must not only determine the message but must also select the most effective channel of communication. In many cases, the channel may not be any of the traditional mass media—newspapers, magazines, radio and television. The most effective channel for the tailored message may be direct mail, a pamphlet, an organizational newsletter, a videotape, a poster, a special event or even E-mail messages. Any combination of channels may be selected to achieve message penetration and maximum understanding.

W E Y E R H A E U S E R

Today

Mission statement:

To enhance and protect Weyerhaeuser's standing with its employees. To develop employees' understanding of Weyerhaeuser's business issues and motivate them to help the company achieve its vision and values.

■ **Making Total Quality the Weyerhaeuser way of doing business**

Today *will help Weyerhaeuser create a Total Quality culture through stories that relate to:*
teamwork
reliable processes
continuous improvement
use of Total Quality tools

■ **Relentless pursuit of full customer satisfaction**

Today *will encourage a customer-driven approach through stories about:*
excellence in customer service
customers
anticipating customer needs

■ **Empowering Weyerhaeuser people**

Today *will build employee loyalty and commitment through stories that relate to:*
role models
contributions to Weyerhaeuser's
success
benefits of working for Weyerhaeuser

■ **Leading the industry in forest management and manufacturing excellence**

Today *will improve the understanding of internal and selected external audiences concerning Weyerhaeuser's record of forest stewardship. Today will help Weyerhaeuser continuously improve its manufacturing capabilities through stories that emphasize:*
innovation
safety/housekeeping/preventive maintenance
productivity
standardization
benchmarking
sharing best practices

■ **Producing superior returns for our shareholder**

Today *will help Weyerhaeuser achieve top-quartile results by increasing employee understanding of:*
Weyerhaeuser financial performances
corporate/business strategies
economic trends
our competitors
industry developments

Today *also will support Weyerhaeuser's values with the following types of stories:*

■ *Customers*
  (see above)
■ *People*
  diversity
  development
  superior performance
  (also see above)
■ *Citizenship*
  company environmental policy
  environmental excellence

opportunities to improve environmental
  performance
integrity/ethics
community involvement/volunteering
Weyerhaeuser's heritage
■ *Accountability*
  business strategies & results
  business-improvement plans
■ *Financial Responsibility*
  affordability/cost-consciousness
  wise use of capital

Figure 1.1 Publication objectives are linked to overall organizational objectives. This is the mission statement for the employee newspaper of Weyerhaeuser Corporation, a large timber and paper company. (*Courtesy of Weyerhaeuser Corporation, Tacoma, WA.*)

PREPARATION FOR WRITING

In writing for public relations, you will need certain basic equipment, references and files.

Equipment

Today's professional writing is done on a word processor, commonly called a personal computer (PC). In fact, an informal survey by the Public Relations Society of America (PRSA) and Mead Data Corporation showed that more than 90 percent of public relations practitioners use PCs.

Public relations people spend a median of five hours per day on their PCs, according to a 1995 survey by Tim McIntyre at Boston University's School of Mass Communication. In comparison, a survey by Porter/Novelli Public Relations showed that the average American only spends about nine hours a week using a PC compared to more than 20 hours watching television. Word processing, according to the McIntyre study, is the software application public relations professionals use most. This application is followed in descending order by databases, graphic/art programs, spreadsheets, games and Internet access.

Indeed, the personal computer allows you to use sophisticated word processing software programs that permit maximum flexibility to write, edit, format, insert artwork and merge information into a complete document. Word processing packages such as *Microsoft Word* or *MacWrite* also have built-in dictionaries for checking spelling and grammar, plus other features such as a thesaurus, page previews, search and replace, word count, pagination and editing functions. Your time is substantially reduced for revisions and rewrites.

As to the type of computer or word processor public relations writers choose, both IBM-compatible machines and Apple have their advocates. One survey of membership in the International Association of Business Communicators (IABC), for example, showed a "horse race" between the two systems. *Communication World* (January-February 1993) reported that 48 percent of the respondents worked with the Apple Macintosh and 38 percent with IBM or IBM-compatible equipment. Another 11 percent used Macs for graphics and IBMs for text.

McIntyre, however, found that almost 60 percent of his respondents used IBM-compatible computers as compared to 24 percent using Apple machines. Another 12 percent used both systems. In general, experts tend to recommend IBM-compatible computers, for three reasons:

- New developments in Windows applications have made IBM-compatible machines more similar to Apple's user-friendly approach.
- IBM-compatible machines are the industry standard. According to a *New York Times* article (January 16, 1996), "For every Macintosh sold in 1996, nine new Windows computers will be sold."
- There are more software programs on the market that run on IBM-compatible machines.

Figure 1.2   A computer, a printer and a modem are now basic equipment for a public relations writer. This photo is an example of product publicity distributed by a manufacturer of computers. (*Courtesy of Hewlett-Packard Company, Palo Alto, CA.*)

Computer manufacturers and software publishers are continually improving their products, making them even more powerful and versatile. That's the good news. The bad news is that anything recommended today is out of date in about six months.

Today, computers typically have 1.2 gigabyte hard drives and 16 megabytes of memory. *Microsoft Windows 95* doesn't even run on a machine with less than eight megabytes of memory. Newer machines also have 150MHZ processors, CD-ROM drives, fax/modems, sound cards, stereo speakers and a number of factory-installed software applications. Access to the Internet is discussed later in the chapter.

College students often have access to well-stocked computer labs and may not need all these features on their own computers. On the other hand, if you're a working professional, you might find that the most powerful computer available that you can afford is a better investment in the long run because you won't have to replace equipment so often.

In terms of software, a panel of experts interviewed in the *Wall Street Journal* (November 13, 1995) highly recommended a package of *Microsoft Works* and *Microsoft Bookshelf*. *Microsoft Works* includes a word processor, spreadsheet and a drawing package. *Microsoft Bookshelf* includes an atlas, the *American Heritage Dictionary, Roget's Thesaurus,* the *Columbia Dictionary of Quotations, Columbia Encyclopedia, World Almanac* and *People's Chronology.* Another recommendation is *Microsoft Publisher,* a desktop publishing program (see Chapters 12 and 13).

Fortunately, printer technology doesn't change as rapidly as computers and software. You should buy an inkjet or laser printer to ensure that the quality of your documents is high. Black-ink printers are less expensive than color printers, but experts say the trend is toward full-color printers.

References

A reference library is a must for any writer. Basic sources, located close to your PC or part of a software application, will enable you to answer questions about the proper use of words, grammar and style and to confirm basic factual information.

Dictionary   The most common reference book is an up-to-date dictionary. Most daily newspapers, including the *Wall Street Journal,* use *Webster's New World Dictionary,* college edition. Another popular dictionary is Houghton Mifflin's *American Heritage Dictionary of the English Language,* known for its inclusion of up-to-date slang and regional expressions, its lively word histories and extensive use of photography.

Dictionaries are also available on software and are built into such programs as *Microsoft Word.* In addition, the software may include a thesaurus, an etymological dictionary and even a collection of familiar quotations that can be accessed through a computer's hard disk.

Dictionaries also appear on CD-ROM. Two examples are the 180,000-word *Webster's Electronic Dictionary* from Random House and Houghton Mifflin's 116,000-word *American Heritage Electronic Dictionary.* These dictionaries are commonly used for spell-checking, but they are also able to supply writers with words they don't even know. Type "Mexican" and "dog," and the dictionary gives you "chihuahua."

Although the above dictionaries are adequate for most writing assignments, many writers also use an unabridged dictionary, which often contains almost twice as many entries as the standard dictionary. An unabridged dictionary weighs about 12 pounds, but you can also get it on a CD-ROM disk that weighs about two ounces. An example is the *Random House Unabridged Dictionary,* 2nd edition, which has 315,000 entries and allows the writer to access it directly while another document is on the computer screen. In this edition, which updates the 1987 version, more than a thousand new words have been added, including such terms as "glass ceiling" and "Generation X."

Encyclopedia   Encyclopedias offer a galaxy of basic information on almost any subject. Although they are still sold in multivolume sets that take up nearly an entire bookcase, the trend is toward encyclopedias on CD-ROM.

The *Microsoft Encarta Encyclopedia* is a popular choice and gets high marks from reference librarians for its wealth of multimedia items and graphic interfaces. It contains 26,000 articles; 8,000 photos; 9.5 hours of audio; and more than 100 minutes of video and animation. Comparable CD-ROM encyclopedias are *Compton's Interactive Encyclopedia* and the *Grolier Multimedia Encyclopedia.* A dictionary and a thesaurus are built into the *Compton* product, which is a nice bonus for students. On the other hand, the *Grolier* encyclopedia gets high marks for its maps and extensive musical clips.

Stylebook   A writer's reference library should contain two kinds of stylebooks; one for general reference and another that deals with the specific styles of various publications.

All writers, on occasion, puzzle over a matter of punctuation, subject–verb agreement, or the use of passive or active voice. Strunk and White's *The Elements of Style* has saved writers embarrassment over a number of years, but there are several other grammar and style texts available. One popular text, in softback or spiral bound, is *When Words Collide* by Lauren Kessler and Duncan McDonald; published by Wadsworth.

In terms of journalistic writing, the most widely used stylebook is the *Associated Press Stylebook and Libel Manual.* It is used by an overwhelming majority of the weekly and daily newspapers. The *New York Times Stylebook* is also widely used. Writers who cover business or prepare news releases about business topics often use the *Wall Street Journal Stylebook.*

These manuals enable you, as a public relations writer, to prepare materials in the writing style of most newspapers. They cover such topics as capitalization, abbreviations, punctuation, titles and general word usage. For example, there is a trend in the media to combine words that were once written separately or hyphenated; hence, the proper style is now "software," "database," "lifestyle," "teenager" and "spreadsheet."

Thesaurus   A book of synonyms, antonyms and idiomatic phrases is often helpful in finding the word that best conveys your meaning. *Roget's Thesaurus* is also available on CD-ROM.

Atlas   A current world atlas is an important resource for spelling place names and obtaining vital statistics about various nations. The emphasis here is on the word "current," especially in light of the many changes that have taken place in recent years: Germany has been reunited, the former Soviet Union is now a series of independent nations, Czechoslovakia has divided into two nation-states and Yugoslavia is now Bosnia and Croatia.

The current edition of the *National Geographic Atlas of the World,* for example, includes 20 new countries and 14,000 name changes. And a good atlas is more than a collection of maps; it is often a comprehensive encyclopedia of geographic and demographic information, illustrated with multicolored maps and comparative graphs. A public relations writer working for a multinational corporation will find a current atlas indispensable.

Press Directory   If you're in the business of sending news releases to the media, it is important to have lists of publications, names of editors and addresses readily available. Local directories of media outlets are often available from the chamber of commerce, the United Way or other civic groups. State or regional directories also exist.

18B – General Interest – continued

P C MAGAZINE (18B-1520)
One Park Avenue
New York, NY 10016-5802

T
(212) 503-3500
Fax: (212) 503-5799
Home Page: http://www.ziff.com/pcmag
E-Mail: 157.9301@mcimail.com

Circ: 1,039,720; **Freq:** Bi-Weekly; **Pub:** Ziff-Davis Publishing Co., Inc.;
Uses: New Prod, By-line, Staff, Letters, Books, No Photos; **Online:** Compuserve, Dialog, Lexis/Nexis; **Sub Rate:** $49.97; **Ad Rate:** $36,940.
Profile: Written for buyers of IBM/MS DOS standard personal computers, software, peripherals, and accessories. Highlights include extensive, comparative, lab-based product reviews, productivity enhancement, and new analysis columns.

News Executives/Editors:

Publisher	Daniel Rosensweig	(212) 503-5277
Editor In Chief	Michael J. Miller	(212) 503-5694
Executive Editor	Rick Ayre	(212) 503-5523
Executive Editor	Don Willmott	(212) 503-5571
Executive Editor	Bill Howard	(212) 503-5293
Editor	Jake Kirchner	(212) 503-5255
Managing Editor	Paul B. Ross	(212) 503-5254
Online Associate Editor	Jenny Donelan	(212) 503-5295
Advertising Sales Director	Vickie Pinsky	(212) 503-4453
Book Review Staff Editor	Tin Albano	(212) 503-5013
Business Editor	Jake Kirchner	(212) 503-5255

Computers/High Tech:
Telecommunications Associate Editor	Leon Erlanger	(212) 503-5205

Communications:
Senior Editor	David Greenfield	(212) 503-5642
Associate Editor	Gail Shaffer	(212) 503-5059

Personal Computers:
Senior Editor	Thomas Mace	(212) 503-5039
Associate Editor	John Clyman	(212) 503-3975

Hardware:
Executive Editor	Bill Howard	(212) 503-5293
Associate Editor	Leon Erlanger	(212) 503-5205
Software Senior Editor	Thomas Mace	(212) 503-5039

Networking:
Senior Editor	David Greenfield	(212) 503-5642
Associate Editor	Gail Shaffer	(212) 503-5059
Graphics Associate Editor	Lance Ulanhoff	(212) 503-5566
Features Executive Editor	Bill Howard	(212) 503-5293

New Products:
Senior Editor	Brian Nadel	(212) 503-5267
New Product Review Assistant Editor	Melissa Perenson	(212) 503-5689

Technical:
Executive Editor	Rick Ayre	(212) 503-5523
Senior Associate Editor	Sharon Terdeman	(212) 503-5069

General Columnist:
"After Hours"	Gayle Ehrenman	(212) 503-5667
"Trends"	Carol Levin	(212) 503-5486

Selected Editorial Offices/Bureaus

P C MAGAZINE (18B-1520B)
539 Key Royale Dr.
Holmes Beach, FL 34217
(813) 778-1077

Senior Editor	Frank Derfler
Networking Senior Editor	Frank Derfler

Figure 1.3 Media directories are important reference tools. Directories provide addresses, names of editors, phone numbers and other important information. This is the entry for a popular computer magazine. (*Courtesy of Bacon's Information, Inc., Chicago, Il.*)

For media listings on the national level, popular sources are *Editor and Publisher International Yearbook, Bacon's Media Directories* and *Working Press of the Nation.* Another popular reference source is *Standard Rate and Data,* a six-volume set that contains details of a media outlet's market, audience, demographics and advertising rates. Press directories are also available on CD-ROM. We will discuss press directories further in Chapter 10.

Professional Periodicals   Standard references should be supplemented with subscriptions to professional periodicals. It is important for the professional writer to keep up with developments in the field and to learn about new techniques that can improve the writing, production, and distribution of public relations material.

A number of newsletters and magazines cover the public relations field. Newsletters include *PR Reporter, PR News, Jack O'Dwyer's Newsletter,* the *Ragan Report* and *Communication Briefings.* The last one is an excellent source of information about writing techniques. The Public Relations Society of America (PRSA) also produces a monthly tabloid newspaper, *Tactics,* filled with many "how-to-" articles.

In addition, several public relations newsletters are now exclusively devoted to how cyberspace (the Internet and World Wide Web) can be used for public relations. Two such newsletters are Ragan's *Interactive PR* and PRSA's *Cyberspace.* The newsletters carry case studies, product reviews, "how-to" articles and lists of new web sites.

Magazines about the public relations field include the *Public Relations Strategist,* published by the Public Relations Society of America (PRSA), and *Communication World,* published by the International Association of Business Communicators (IABC). You can subscribe to these publications or receive them as part of your annual membership fees. Some other magazines are *Public Relations Quarterly, Reputation Management* and *O'Dwyer's PR Services Report.* The two major scholarly publications in the field are *Public Relations Review* and the *Journal of Public Relations Research.*

In addition to articles about trends and issues in the field, these magazines also carry advertisements for companies specializing in services such as news release distribution, media monitoring, photography and video news releases.

Current Events and Trends   Writing often starts with a creative idea and a good understanding of the world around you. Many public relations employers screen job applicants by administering a current events quiz to ascertain the scope of an individual's interests and intellectual curiosity. Employers require outstanding writing skills, but they are also looking for a second dimension in a public relations writer: knowing what to write about.

Thus aspiring public relations writers should make it a habit to read at least one weekly newsmagazine (*Time, Newsweek, U.S. News & World Report*), a local daily newspaper and a daily newspaper with national circulation such as the *New York Times* or *Wall Street Journal.* Nationally syndicated public affairs programs on radio and television are also good sources of current events knowledge and interpretative analysis.

Public Relations Quarterly

VOLUME 40   NUMBER 2   SUMMER 1995

"Building Cathedrals" — Reflections on Three Decades in Corporate PR and a Peek at the Future
Carole M. Howard

Figure 1.4 Trade newsletters and magazines are an important source of continuing education for the public relations writer. This is a sample cover from one such publication. (*Courtesy of* Public Relations Quarterly, *Rhinebeck, NY.*)

Increasingly, alternative magazines such as the *Utne Reader* and *E-Magazine* are considered required reading for public relations professionals. According to an article in the *Public Relations Journal* (October, 1990), "Alternative publications offer a point of view on social issues ranging from animal rights to waste disposal that are not part of the diet served by the mainstream press." These publications often function as "trend incubators" and help public relations personnel detect early signs of trends that may become major public issues.

Current nonfiction best sellers should also be part of your reading program. A popular book is an indication of public interest, and often media interest, in a particular topic. In the 1990s, books about gender issues continually make the best seller lists. For example, John Gray's *Men Are from Mars, Women Are from Venus,* about ways to improve communication and relationships between the sexes, dominated the best-seller list for more than two years. Deepak Chopra's *The Seven Spiritual Laws of Success,* about how to generate wealth, also became a #1 best seller.

Many people get all their news and entertainment from television. You should know what is being presented to the public for several reasons. First, media coverage sets the agenda for people's thinking. Second, watching the news will show you what kinds of stories are used and how they are handled. Other programs, especially talk shows, will teach you what sorts of stories get on the air and indicate the kind of audience that tends to watch such programs.

In sum, paying attention to current events and the thoughts of opinion leaders pays several dividends. First, it makes you a well-informed person and hence more attractive to employers for public relations writing jobs. Second, knowing the concerns of the public helps you construct more salient messages for your target audience. Third, current events often provide a "news hook" for obtaining media acceptance of your material. For example, a company making security locks for computer files was virtually ignored by the media until news stories about computer hackers breaking into national security systems made national headlines. We will return to the environmental context of public relations writing in Chapter 4.

Research

Because the purpose of writing is to convey information, the first step is to get the facts. In some cases all the facts will be readily available, but most of the time you'll have to dig for them. For example, an announcement that Jane Smith has been elected president of the school board would not be interesting unless it included some information about her personally.

Research may yield the facts that she is a vice president of a local bank; a graduate of Bryn Mawr, where she majored in American history; the mother of 10-year-old twins named Henry and Philip; the wife of John Smith, a real estate broker; and a member of Soroptimists and the First Presbyterian Church.

Such facts, which make Jane Smith more interesting to the reader, can be learned by making a few phone calls. But what if the person is a stranger? Suppose that Dr. James White is to speak at the commencement exercise of Putnam College. Initial information may state that he teaches sociology at Fareastern University, is head of the department and has written numerous books. These facts won't make a very interesting announcement, but research can provide some meat for these bare bones.

The news bureau of Fareastern University would be the first source to tap. It should provide information about Dr. White's education, experience, family and length of service; other jobs he has held; and books and scholarly papers he has written. A trip to the library might turn up copies of the books and professional journals that carry some of Dr. White's writings. Reading or at least scanning some of these can give you an idea of what Dr. White has said and how others have responded to him. With this backlog of information, you should be able to write an interesting news story that will make the readers want to hear Dr. White speak.

These illustrations are perhaps oversimplified, but they indicate the value of research in any kind of writing. In general, research for this purpose is divided into several categories:

Inquiries   The telephone is one of your best research tools. Call experts in the field or people who are knowledgeable about the subject. Although you may think that this is an intrusion, most people will be flattered and pleased to provide information. In addition, they can supply names, places and examples that will add flavor to your writing.

Interviews   Before the interview, review your information about the subject of the interview. This should reveal what is not known and suggest questions to be asked. Prepare a list of specific questions, and ask them one at a time. If the answers are not clear, continue to probe until they are.

If the interviewee goes off on a tangent, this may contribute information that you hadn't thought of. Pursuing these unexpected leads may yield valuable ideas, so digressions should not be squelched. Taking notes is a must, and a tape recorder can help you keep an accurate account of what was said. As the interview progresses, it is important to watch the interviewee and to pay attention to tone of voice. Tone, facial expressions and gestures often reveal more than words alone.

Library Resources   The reference section of a library can be a valuable source of information. Periodical indexes, in particular, can help you research current information about any topic. Several indexes are now on CD-ROM. They include *ABI/INFORM,* which indexes more than 300 business journals; *ERIC,* which lists academic papers and reports; and *INFOTRAC,* which indexes more than 950 magazines and seven national newspapers.

Periodical indexes, in print form, are also available. Here is a list of sources public relations writers commonly use:

> *Business Periodicals Index.* Arranged alphabetically by subject. Public relations periodicals are included in this index.
> *Communications Abstracts.* Covers major communications-related articles, reports, and books. Abstracts follow each citation.

Consumer's Index to Product Evaluations and Information Sources. Complete indexing to product recall and product information articles appearing in various periodicals.

Funk and Scott. Gives an alphabetical listing of companies and what has been written about them.

The Gallup Poll and *The Gallup Report.* Both list opinion polls and interpretations of them.

Reader's Guide to Periodical Literature. Indexes periodicals of general interest dating back to the 1890s by author and subject.

Simmon's Study of Media and Markets. Extensive annual survey of households in terms of product usage by brand and exposure to media. Media reports cover the demographics of viewers, listeners and readers.

Social Science Index. Indexes social issues and their influences.

Work Related Abstracts. Gives information from more than 250 management, labor, government, professional and university periodicals.

The indexes of many daily newspapers are available in most libraries. The most commonly used are *The Official Washington Post Index,* the *New York Times Index* and the *Wall Street Journal Index.*

If you're looking for information on the background of prominent people, a good reference source is *Who's Who in America.* Similar "Who's Who" reference books are prepared on a regional basis or for specific professional fields such as medicine, science and law.

For basic demographic data, a good resource is the *Statistical Abstract of the United States,* based on the latest census. It provides a wealth of information about the composition of the American population from almost every conceivable angle. A good resource for the names and addresses of trade groups and professional associations is the *Encyclopedia of Associations.*

On-line Retrieval Services   Although the library offers numerous sources of information and remains the primary resource for university students, the information revolution has made it possible for working professionals to access much of this information through a personal computer and a modem from any location.

With fact finding and research essential in sophisticated public relations practice today, a computer with a modem is becoming as important as a dictionary to the public relations writer. Using a modem, you can extract information from an estimated 1,500 electronic databases that store an enormous amount of current and historical information. Here are some of the best-known databases:

Dialog—A Knight-Ridder service, it provides more than 45 databases with 2,500 magazines, journals and newsletters.

Dow Jones News/Retrieval—A massive business library with more than 45 million documents drawn from nearly 3,000 key business and financial publications, including the *Wall Street Journal* and the *New York Times.*

Nexis/Lexis—Includes 8 million full-text articles from more than 125 magazines, newspapers, and news services; contains the full text of the *New York*

Times and the *Washington Post.* Also contains abstracts from leading international publications.

You get information from these databases by using a combination of search words. If you want information about the sponsorship of sporting events, you might use the search words "sports/sponsorships/corporations." A computer program will then search through thousands of articles looking for articles in which these words appear. The result may be a list of 50 to 100 articles. You will no doubt find what you're looking for within this list.

A survey conducted by the Public Relations Society of America (PRSA) and Nexis/Lexis found that public relations counselors spent 20 percent of their work week using on-line retrieval services. The purpose was primarily for identifying trends, as well as searching for information on clients' competitors. The most common issues counselors track, in descending order, are (1) education/workforce training, (2) environmental topics, (3) health-care costs/reform, (4) international trade and (5) occupational health/safety issues.

On-line Networks

The use of on-line networks has skyrocketed in recent years. They not only have many of the same services that commercial on-line databases provide, but they also enable you to send E-mail, participate in chat groups on specific subjects, post notes on computer bulletin boards and fully access millions of documents on the Internet, including the World Wide Web containing thousands of "home" pages for various organizations.

The two largest commercial networks are America Online, with 4.5 million subscribers, and CompuServe, with 3.9 million subscribers. In early 1996, America Online (AOL) was adding 60,000 new users a week. CompuServe was experiencing a similar growth curve.

Both networks offer many of the same services—full access to the Internet, E-mail, a monthly magazine, and so on—and both have their advocates. AOL has a reputation for being more user-friendly and having more extensive software support, but CompuServe has a better reputation for providing more databases and business information.

In addition, CompuServe has a discussion group dedicated to public relations and marketing (PR/Marketing Forum). It's also where you'll find a forum for journalists that allows press releases. If you're a member, you can upload news releases as text files. Over 3,000 journalists belong to this forum. Indeed, a survey of journalists showed that 35 percent use CompuServe, as compared to 19 percent using America Online.

Other commercial services include Prodigy (1.6 million subscribers), e-World (126,000 subscribers), and GEnie (75,000 subscribers). A newcomer is the Microsoft Network (MSN), which is part of the *Windows 95* software. Experts estimate that if only 20 percent of the people who purchase *Windows 95* sign up for the service, this would equal 9 million subscribers.

The Internet and World Wide Web

Commercial networks, such as those described above, provide access to the Internet as part of their services. However, you can also directly access the Internet and the World Wide Web (110,000 sites as of October 1995) simply by subscribing to other commercial services or by getting software that allows you to make a telephone connection to the vast array of computer networks around the globe. As of mid-1995, there were more than 6 million host computers.

One access program is *Gopher,* which was developed by the University of Minnesota. There are also software programs called "browsers" that allow you to view documents created specifically for the Internet's World Wide Web and other Internet services. Two popular browsers are *Netscape* and *Mosaic.*

The Internet, as well as the commercial information retrieval companies and the on-line commercial networks, provides a powerful research tool for the public relations writer. See the box for a partial list of files that are readily available to the "net surfer." How public relations personnel use the Internet and the World Wide Web for dissemination of messages is discussed in Chapter 10.

Another aspect of the Internet is Usenet—an international meeting place where people gather (but not in real time) to meet friends, discuss events, keep up with trends, seek information or just talk. More than 10,000 newsgroups exist on Usenet, including PRFORUM, which is dedicated to communications.

PRFORUM is a place where you can request information that you are looking for; people who know something about the subject can respond by sending you an E-mail message. One public relations professional, for example, asked for information on how to go about developing a communication strategy for one of her clients. Within a day, several replies offered valuable tips, including:

- Linking the communications strategy to the organization's goals;
- Techniques for segmenting publics;
- Six strategies for linking organizational goals to communication goals; and
- Learning about what the audience wants.

To subscribe to PRFORUM, which is free, send the following message via E-mail: SUBSCRIBE PRFORUM (your real name) to the following Internet E-mail address:

LISTSERV@INDYCMS.IUPUI.EDU

WRITING GUIDELINES

The ability to write well is a necessity for work in public relations. J. Ronald Kelly, senior vice president of Cohn & Wolfe public relations, echoed the feelings of many professionals when he wrote in the *Public Relations Quarterly* (Winter 1994–95):

> The majority of our entry level work requires good, basic writing skills. I simply do not have the time to teach grammar, spelling, punctuation, subject–verb agreement, use of

SURFING THE INTERNET

Public relations writing requires research and fact finding. Here's a sampling of sites on the Internet where you might find information:

Public Relations Firms (list of home pages):
http://www.yahoo.com/Business.Corporations/Corpor

Philanthropy:
http://www.duke.edu/~ptavern/Pete.Philanthropic.html

Statistical Abstract of the US:
http://www.census.gov/stat_abstract

Bureau Labor Statistics:
http://stats.bls.gov/blshome.html

Environmental News Network:
http://www.enn.com/

Reporter's Internet Survival Guide:
http://www.gns.com/~casey/crystll.gif

Newslink (web sites of newspapers, magazines, etc.):
http://www.newslink.org

Consumer Market Research:
http://www.npd.com

Electronic Newsstand (magazines, newspapers):
http://enews.com

***Time* Magazine:**
http:www.timeinc.com/time/magazine/magazine.html

Yahoo (directory of the World Wide Web):
http://www.yahoo.com

Yellow Pages of the World Wide Web:
http://www.index.org

***Wall Street Journal* Update:**
http://update.wsj.com

International Association of Business Communicators (IABC):
http://www.hooked.net/iabc.com/welcome.html

(continued)

Public Relations Society of America (PRSA):

http:www.prsa.org

Business Wire (hyperlinked to corporate home pages):

http://www.hnt.com/bizwire

PR Gopher (information and links to other sources):

gopher://iam41.arcade.uiowa.edu:2270

United States Information Agency (information on nations):

gopher://198.80.36.82

Humor and Jokes:

http://www.tc.cornell.edu/~ckline/humor/maillist.html

Light Bulb Jokes:

http:/www.infi.net/~cashman/humor/canonical/lightbulb.html

active verbs, lead writing, inverted pyramid style, etc. And as you know, time is money in an agency setting. Therefore, I seek graduates who can contribute to the bottom line from the first day. I need people who have good mastery of basic writing skills.

Outlining the Purpose

Before beginning any writing assignment, take the time to ask yourself some key questions. Public relations counselors Kerry Tucker and Doris Derelian, writing in *Public Relations Journal* (February, 1991), suggest six basic questions

1. What is the desired communication outcome? In other words, what do we want our audience to do or not do?
2. Who is our target audience? (The more specific the segment, the better.)
3. What are our target audience's needs, concerns, and interests?
4. What is our message?
5. What communication channel is most effective?
6. Who is our most believable spokesperson?

Answering these questions goes a long way toward helping you determine the content and structure of your message.

The next step is to more fully outline question 4—what is the message. Usually an outline includes major topics, and minor topics within each major topic. One approach to outlining is to list the major message points as major topics. There may be two or three key messages, for example, that you want to communicate in a news release or a feature story. Under each of these headings, jot down a list of what facts, statistics and examples you will give to support the major point.

Sentences

Sentences should be clear and concise. Long, compound sentences slow the reader down and are often hard to understand. In general, a sentence containing 25 to 30 words is difficult even for a college-educated audience. This doesn't mean that all sentences should be eight to 10 words long; you should strive for a variety of lengths with the average sentence about 15 to 17 words.

In many cases, a complex sentence simply contains more words than necessary. Take this bloated sentence, for example: "They have assisted numerous companies in the development of a system that can be used in the monitoring of their customer service operations." Revised, this sentence is more concise and easier to understand: "They have helped many companies develop systems for monitoring their customer services operations."

Communication Briefings has compiled a list of word savers that can help keep sentences concise and on course. Shorten the common wordy phrases on the left to the single words on the right when writing or editing copy:

a great number of	many
at this point in time	now
come to a realization	realize
despite the fact that	although
due to the fact that	because
for the purpose of	for, to
give approval of	approve
of the opinion that	believe
owing to the fact that	because
since the time when	since
take under consideration	consider
until such time as	until
with the exception of	except for
would appear that	seems

Paragraphs

Short paragraphs are better than long ones. A review of a daily newspaper page shows that the journalistic style is short paragraphs averaging about six to eight typeset lines. Lead paragraphs in news stories are even shorter—about two or three lines.

Public relations writing should follow the same guidelines. Short paragraphs give the reader a chance to catch a breath, so to speak, and continue reading. Long paragraphs not only tax the reader's concentration but also encourage the reader to "tune out."

Remember that the paragraph on your computer screen is even longer when set in a newspaper column only 2 inches wide. Your eight lines become 12 lines in a newspaper or magazine. A typical paragraph contains only one basic idea. When another idea is introduced, it's time for a new paragraph.

Word Choice

College-educated writers often forget that words common to their vocabulary are not readily understood by large segments of the general public. General circulation newspapers, for example, aware that the majority of their readers have not been to college, strive to write news stories at the fourth- to sixth-grade level. A writer's word choice is further complicated by the fact that an estimated 27 million adults in the United States lack basic reading skills and often can't comprehend messages written beyond the second-grade level.

If your target audience is the general public, remember that a short word—one with fewer syllables—is more easily understood than a longer one. The words on the right illustrate the point:

purchase	buy
residence	home
employ	hire
endeavor	try
assistance	help, aid
experiment	test
requirements	needs
responsibility	duty, task
accumulate	gather, collect
economize	save
sufficient	enough
utilize	use

More complex words, of course, can be used if the target audience is well educated. Most readers of the *Wall Street Journal*, for example, are college graduates, so the writing is more complex than that found in a small-town daily.

Also, if the target audience is professionals in a field such as law, education, science or engineering, the standard for word choice is different. Educators, for example, seem to like elaborate expressions such as "multiethnic individualized learning" or "continuum."

Scientific writing, too, is loaded with esoteric words. Newspaper editors often complain that they receive news releases from high-technology companies that are so full of jargon that neither they nor their readers can grasp what is being said.

If your audience is engineers, of course, you can use specialized words and phrases. Good writing, however, requires that you simplify the message as much as possible. Eric Hatch, writing in the March 1991 issue of *Communication World,* gives an example of the "engineering style" of writing:

A plan will be implemented to incorporate performance database already available from previous NASA 8 × 6 and BTWT tests on the various UDF® models with the code cur-

---

GUIDELINES FOR EFFECTIVE WRITING

Use Short Sentences

Your sentences should not exceed 15 to 17 words. Avoid compound and run-on sentences.

Use Good Paragraphing

A paragraph should express one central idea. For readability, it should not run more than six to eight lines. A lead paragraph to an article or news release should be even shorter.

Use Simple Words

Don't use a multisyllabic word when a simple word can express the same idea. Be aware of your audience.

Use Familiar Words

Don't use jargon from specialized fields and occupations that won't be familiar to the general public.

Make Your Message Personal

Use personal pronouns such as "you." Tailor the message to the audience's concerns and needs.

Illustrate Concepts with Examples

A concrete example helps clarify an abstract idea. Make ideas tangible to the reader or listener.

---

rently under development to yield more accurate spanwise Cd (drag coefficients) distributions and velocity diagrams between blade-rows for our acoustics prediction use.

In this example, notes Hatch, "the author has jammed everything into one polysyllabic elephant of a sentence." He suggests the following rewrite; though still complex, it is more readable to an educated audience:

A database compiled during earlier wind tunnel tests on the various UDF® blade models will be incorporated into the new code. This should give us more accurate drag coefficients and velocity diagrams between the blade rows, resulting in better predictions of the engine's acoustical behavior.

Active Verbs

Verbs vitalize your writing. Don't sacrifice verbs by burying the action in nouns or adjectives. You will boost clarity and add vigor to your writing by stripping away excess words around a verb. Here are some examples:

ORIGINAL STATEMENT:	The annual report produced a disappointed reaction among the board of directors.
REVISED STATEMENT:	The annual report disappointed the board of directors.
ORIGINAL STATEMENT:	Our consultants can assist you in answering questions about floor treatments.
REVISED STATEMENT:	Our consultants can answer your floor treatment questions.

Imagery

Strong visual descriptions are better than generalized statements. Writing that Coca-Cola is sold in many nations or marketed internationally doesn't have much impact on the reader. A stronger image is created if you write that Coca-Cola is now sold on all continents and is readily available to two-thirds of the earth's population. Or, as Coca-Cola stated in a recent annual report to stockholders, if "all the system's customers lined up along the equator, a thirsty consumer could purchase a Coca-Cola every 16 feet."

ERRORS TO AVOID

Errors in your writing will brand you as careless, unprofessional and inconsiderate of your audience. Errors also call into question the credibility of the entire message. Professional writing requires attention to detail and repeated review of your draft to catch all potential errors.

Spelling

Credibility is sacrificed when spelling errors appear in public relations materials. For example, one news release for a company that manufactured a spell-checking program for a word processor included the nonwords "tradmark" and "publishere." Naturally, the company was embarrassed about the "typos"—especially after the *Wall Street Journal* poked fun at the company on page 1. We can only guess at how much these typos cost the company in sales and consumer confidence.

Time magazine does know the actual cost of a spelling error. Some years ago, *Time* ran a cover headline reading "New Plan for Arms Control." More than 200,000 covers were printed without the "r" in the word "control" before the error was discovered. The presses were stopped, and the error was corrected; putting the "r" back in "control" cost the magazine $100,000.

Gobbledygook and Jargon

"Gobbledygook" consists of ponderous words and phrases that obscure simple ideas. For example, to the user of gobbledygook, things don't get "finished," they get "finalized." Events didn't happen "then," they happened "at that point in time." The child isn't "failing" but rather is "motivationally deprived."

"Jargon" consists of words that are known almost exclusively to insiders. Some examples: A "four on the floor" is a four-speed hand-shifted automobile transmission. A "no show" is a person who fails to use a ticket for an event or a trip.

Gobbledygook and jargon are often seen in news releases about high-tech products, giving the uninitiated reader a baffling message. Here is an example:

> Novell, Inc., announced today it is shipping its powerful asynchronous communication software, NetWare Asynchronous Communication Services (NACS), as a NetWare Loadable Module (NLM). NACS v3.0, which supports Novell's Asynchronous I/O (AIO) and NetWare Asynchronous Support Interface (NASI) programming interfaces, enables NetWare users to access and share communication resources such as modems, asynchronous hosts, and X.25 network services.

Poor Sentence Structure

The subject and the words that modify it often become separated in a sentence, causing some confusion as to what exactly is being discussed. Here are some examples from news stories:

> Police will be looking for people driving under the influence of alcohol and distributing pamphlets that spell out the dangers of drunken driving.
>
> The proposed budget provides salary increases for faculty and staff performing at a satisfactory level of two percent.
>
> The student was charged with possession and consumption of an opened beer can, which is against university rules.

Poor sentence structure can also lead to embarrassment. A company newsletter, detailing an employee's illness, once reported: "Jeff was taken to the hospital with what was thought to be thrombus phlebitis. After spending a restless night with a nurse at the hospital, the results were negative."

DEVICES FOR ACHIEVING CLEAR WRITING

Example
Say something—then use an example or a statistic to illustrate it.

Definition
Uncommon words call for a dictionary definition or a simple explanation of what you mean.

Comparison
If the reader is unfamiliar with the concept or thing written about, compare it with something familiar.

Restatement
Say the same thing in different words. This reinforces the concept.

Wrong Words

A good dictionary serves not only to check spelling but also to verify the meaning of a word.

An Associated Press (AP) story once told about a man who had inherited a small scenic railroad from his "descendants," who had started it in the nineteenth century. The writer meant "ancestors" but used the wrong word. Another publication also used the wrong word when it reported "Windows 95 a High-Tech Coupe for Consumers." The actual word is "coup."

More common mistakes involve the usage of "it's" and "its," "effect" and "affect," "there" and "their" and "presume and "assume." Other frequently confused words are listed in the next section. When in doubt, take the time to use the dictionary. It will save you embarrassment later.

"Sound-alike" Words

Many words sound alike and are similar in spelling but have very different meanings. Although it may be somewhat humorous to read that a survey is "chalk full" of information (instead of "chock-full"), a company's management team is doing some "sole" searching (instead of "soul searching"), or an employee was in a "comma" (instead of a "coma") after a car accident, such mistakes are the mark of a careless writer.

A spell-checking program for your personal computer is extremely efficient at catching misspelled words but often can't catch homonyms because they are correctly spelled words. Therefore, it is always important to proofread your copy, even after it has been corrected by a spell-checker program.

Here is a list of words that are frequently confused:

adapt, adept, adopt	implicit, explicit
callow, callous	lose, loose
canvas, canvass	negligent, negligible
compliment, complement	peak, peek, pique
dominant, dominate	pore, pour
desert, dessert	principle, principal
ensure, insure, assure	stationary, stationery
imply, infer	there, their

Redundancies

Another gross error in writing is redundancy. It is not necessary to use the word "totally" to modify a word such as "destroyed" or "completely" to modify "demolished." A lot of writers also say that something is "somewhat" or "very" unique. "Unique," by definition, means one of a kind; either something is unique or it isn't. The following redundancy appeared in a news release: "In addition, the company lists $50 million in receivables that it hopes to collect. These are unpaid bills, largely from customers, that have yet to be paid."

Too Many Numbers

People can digest a few figures but not a mass of statistics. Use numbers sparingly in your writing, and keep in mind the following points:

- It is better to write "$92 million" than "92,000,000 dollars."
- It is better to give a readily understood comparison than a massive number. For example, you could say that 500 million pounds of garbage are produced in the United States every day, but it would be more effective to express that as 10 pounds per citizen. (Again, this demonstrates our earlier point about the use of imagery in writing.)
- Check your math. The price of something can go up more than 100 percent, but it can never go down more than 100 percent.

Hype

You can ruin the credibility and believability of your message by using exaggerated words and phrases. When Sharp Electronics Corporation introduced a new hand-held computer, the news release called it "the next true revolution in man's conquest of information." Other companies often describe their products as "first of its kind," "unique" and even "revolutionary," which tends to raise suspicion among media gatekeepers as well as readers.

High-tech companies were singled out by the *Wall Street Journal* (January 12, 1989) for overusing adjectives. After analyzing 201 news releases, reporter Michael Miller issued a "hype hit parade." In descending order of overuse were the following words: leading, enhanced, unique, significant, solution, integrated, powerful, innovative, advanced, high-performance and sophisticated.

Bias and Stereotypes

Stereotypes often creep in as a writer struggles to describe a situation, group or person. How often have you read a description of a woman in an employee newsletter that used such adjectives as "pert," "petite," "fragile," "feminine," "stunning," "gorgeous," "statuesque" or "full-figured"? How about "blond and blue-eyed"? Would you also write "brown-haired and brown-eyed"? Would you describe a man in similar terms?

In general, avoid descriptive terms of beauty or physical attributes and mannerisms whenever possible. In most cases, such descriptions have no bearing on the story and can be considered sexist. For example, here's how one Chicago company described its president in a news release: "A tall, attractive blonde who could easily turn heads on Main Street is instead turning heads on Wall Street." Or consider the news release from a Los Angeles firm about the appointment of the head of a Japanese company's consumer electronics division: "Demure, naturally pretty and conservative in her dress and manner, Miho Suda could easily pass as a college student."

You should also avoid any suggestion that all members of any group have the same personal characteristic, be it ambition, laziness, shrewdness, guile or intelligence. Don't suggest that some characteristic sets an individual apart from a stereotyped norm either. For example, it is inappropriate to write, "John Williams, who is black, was promoted to senior vice president." Nor would you write, "Linda Gonzales, a U.S. citizen, will serve as assistant treasurer." In both cases, you're implying that these individuals are exceptions to some norm for their ethnic group.

Avoid gender bias by using non–gender-related words. Awareness of the irrelevance of an employee's gender is why airlines now have "flight attendants" instead of "stewardesses" and why the postal service hires "mail carriers" instead of "mailmen." It also is unnecessary to write that something is "man-made" when a neutral word such as "synthetic" or "artificial" is just as good. "Employees" is better than "manpower," and "chairperson" is more acceptable than "chairman." Some terms may seem difficult to neutralize—"congressperson," "businessperson," and "waitperson" don't exactly trip off the tongue. However, with a little thought, you can come up with appropriate titles, such as "legislator," "executive," and "server."

The problem of avoiding gender bias is particularly difficult because much of our language is geared to the use of the word "man" as a generic term for both males and females. Attempts to avoid this lead to such usages as "he/she" or "his/her" that make for difficult reading. However, another word can be used in most cases. If you pluralize the noun in question, the pronoun "their" will serve nicely. In other cases, you can use words such as "personnel," "staff," "employee," "worker," "person" or "practitioner" to describe both men and women in the workplace.

Politically Incorrect Language

Beyond avoidance of stereotypes, there is an ongoing controversy about what constitutes "politically correct" (commonly called "PC") language. In today's world of diversity at all levels of national life, there is increased sensitivity about what words and images are used to describe minorities and other groups of people.

For example, the Alliance for the Mentally Ill of New York State picketed a Daffy's discount clothing store because of a billboard showing an empty straitjacket with the headline, "If you're paying over $100 for a dress shirt, may we suggest a jacket to go with it?"

Such concern has merit, and writers should be sensitive to words and images that may offend individuals or groups. However, critics charge that a flood of euphemisms can cause a loss of clarity and may result in a kind of nonsensical bureaucratic language that impedes effective communication.

For example, some groups think the word "civilization" is politically incorrect because it infers that some people are not civilized. Still others object to the word "disabled" and want to substitute "physically challenged" or "differently abled." In this situation, we no longer have short people, but "vertically challenged" people. Even the old term, "Dutch treat" is under attack because it implies that Dutch people are cheap.

On another level, similar suggestions seem quite logical. For example, in a global economy, American companies now refer to "international" markets because "foreign" sounds too ethnocentric. Today's writers use "Asian American" instead of the now pejorative "Oriental." And the term "Hispanic" is now more acceptable than the politically charged "Spanish-speaking." The term "Latino," however, raises some controversy; some women say it is sexist because the "o" in Spanish is male.

The term "black" seems to be making a comeback, according to the U.S. Department of Labor, which surveyed 60,000 households about the names of race and ethnic categories to use in job statistics. Forty-four percent of the blacks preferred this designation, while another 28 percent preferred "African American" and 12 percent liked "Afro-American." As a matter of policy, many newspapers use African American on first reference and black as the noun of second reference. Headlines almost always use black because it is short.

The University of Missouri School of Journalism has produced the *Dictionary of Cautionary Words and Phrases* to make writers more aware of particular words and phrases in particular contexts. In many cases, it helps make the language more specific. For example, the dictionary suggests that the term "senior citizen" not be applied to anyone under age 65, that "girl" is appropriate only for females under 17 and that "gay" be applied only to men (the term "homosexual" can refer to both men and women).

Language, and its connotations, is constantly changing. The professional public relations writer must be aware of the charges and must make decisions on the basis of such factors as sensitivity to the audience, accuracy and clarity of communication.

SUMMARY

1. Public relations writers should always strive for clarity, brevity and accuracy.
2. Public relations writing requires a thorough knowledge of grammar, punctuation, sentence structure and so on. Writers must be aware of objectives, audiences and various channels of communication.
3. The computer is the major tool of the public relations writer.
4. A good library of reference works is necessary.
5. Research is essential before beginning any writing assignment.
6. On-line databases, networks and the Internet are rapidly becoming the primary mode of research for public relations people.
7. Errors in style and mechanics can destroy the effectiveness of your writing.
8. Avoid stereotypes in writing, and be sensitive to the contextual meaning of words in today's society.

EXERCISES

1. Find an article in a newspaper or magazine that you think is outstanding. Write a 500-word report explaining how the article illustrates the concepts of good writing outlined in this chapter.

2. The student government is sponsoring a noon rock concert on your campus. List all the communication channels you could use to publicize this concert. Do all of them require some sort of writing? In what ways?

3. Visit a local computer store. Interview salespeople and do some research on what kinds of computer equipment and software would be best for a professional writer. Write a report explaining your recommendations.

4. Most newspapers use *The Associated Press Stylebook.* Use the book to look up the following. Which are correct according to AP style?
   A. Hudson Bay or Hudson bay?
   B. ball point pen or ballpoint pen?
   C. employe or employee?
   D. all right or alright?
   E. A.M. or a.m.?
   F. February 2nd or Feb. 2?
   G. John Jones, vice president, or John Jones, Vice President?

5. Review a copy of IABC's *Communication World, Public Relations Quarterly,* or another publication in the public relations field. Write a report on something you read and how it applies to public relations writing.

6. Current events and issues often provide a "news hook" to get media coverage for a product or service. Review the daily newspaper for a week or so; what news event or issue could be used as a "news hook" to get the owner of a construction company mentioned in the local newspaper?

7. You are assigned to write a story for the college newspaper on how students are using the Internet to do term papers. Write an outline of what primary sources (interviews) and secondary sources (articles, reports, books) you would use to develop this story.

8. This chapter lists some Internet sites that a public relations writer might use. Do some "surfing" on the net from the list on page 19. Write a report on what information would be of interest to a writer. How could a writer use some of this information?

9. The local chapter of the American Red Cross wants you to write a news release about a new campaign to increase participation in a first aid training program. Answer the six questions listed on page 20 before you begin any writing.

10. Rewrite the following sentences to improve their conciseness and clarity:
    • The researchers are of the opinion that this test produces biased results a great number of times owing to the fact that subjects exhibit a tendency to misinterpret the questions.
    • A combination of the proper orientation to take full advantage of the site's natural amenities and a unique asymmetrical floor plan to maximize the numbers of windows and offices serve to distinguish the building.
    • Although forecasters had predicted a drop in interest rates in this quarter, they still see no long-term effect on growth.

11. Although the content of a message may remain the same, the nature of the audience often determines the writing style. A public health agency, for example,

wants to tell people how to avoid winter colds and the flu. To this end, three kinds of messages will be prepared:

- A simple note distributed to children in grade school.
- A news item for the neighborhood newspaper.
- A news item in a hospital newsletter that provides medical information in lay terms.

Write a 75-word article for each of these audiences. To complete this assignment, you may want to do some additional research on what causes colds and the flu.

12. Research is an important factor in public relations writing. Using the various sources cited in this chapter, find the answers and cite the source for the following questions:
    - What is the capital of Botswana?
    - What country is the leading exporter of rice?
    - What is the population of Florida?
    - Do U.S. citizens pay more taxes than citizens in the nations of Western Europe?
    - How many pounds of chicken does the average American eat every year?
    - What percent of the adult population in the United States has a four-year college degree?
    - How many people, on a worldwide basis, use the Internet?
    - Who said "There are two times in a man's life when he should not speculate: when he can't afford it and when he can"?

2 | *Legal and Ethical Considerations*

A writer, once he or she has mastered the basics of good writing, also has the responsibility to work within the law and adhere to high professional standards. This chapter establishes that framework, and it appears early in the text for good reasons.

First, you must understand legal concepts to know what you may do and what you must avoid doing. Careless work can lead to costly litigation for you and your employer. Second, you cannot produce and distribute publicity materials that are credible and believable unless you have a strong ethical sense of right and wrong. Employers may come and go, but your reputation stays with you.

EXAMPLES OF LEGAL PROBLEMS

As a public relations writer, you represent the management of your organization. What you release is interpreted as the voice of management. Nevertheless, you can be held personally liable for any statements that cause defamation or violate the guidelines of state or federal regulatory agencies. Actions are ordinarily brought against the top officials of an organization, but remember that you can be named as a co-defendant.

To protect yourself, you should be sure that the facts you are given are accurate. It is no excuse to say, "The boss told me that this was so." In court, you must be able to prove that you made a reasonable effort to verify information.

Among the actions for which you might be liable are the following:

- Disseminating information that a court or regulatory agency finds misleading, untrue or damaging;
- Participating in an illegal action;
- Counseling or guiding policy to accomplish an illegal action; or
- Setting up an organization whose real identity is concealed.

To emphasize the importance of how the law can affect your work, here is a sampling of legal problems that involved public relations and advertising activities of various organizations:

- A Kentucky couple filed a complaint against Merrill Lynch for $240,000 for invasion of privacy, claiming that they were in the background of a photograph used in an advertisement.
- The Church of Scientology filed a libel suit against the vice president of corporate affairs for Eli Lilly and Company after he called the church a "commercial enterprise" in an article that appeared in *USA Today*.
- General Electric was forced to change the promotion of its Energy Choice light bulbs and pay a $165,000 settlement after the Federal Trade Commission charged GE with failing to disclose that the bulbs were more energy-efficient only because they provided less light than the standard product.
- An artist sued the American Family Association for copyright infringement after the association used portions of his work in a mass mailing.
- The vice president of public affairs for Beneficial Corporation and her two brothers were charged with insider trading after trading stock the day before a public announcement about the company's finances.
- The United Way of America was sued by an 81-year-old man featured on a campaign poster who charged that the picture had been used without his permission.
- Eight female employees of Stroh's brewery, charging that the firm's advertising campaign featuring the Swedish Bikini Team was sexist and demeaning to women, filed a sexual harassment suit against the beer maker.

LIBEL AND SLANDER

Review

Any false statement about a person that is printed or broadcast and tends to bring public hatred, contempt or ridicule on this person or to inflict injury on his or her business or occupation may be libel. If the statement is broadcast, it may constitute either libel or slander. If it is made to a third person but neither printed nor broadcast, it may be slander.

Any plaintiff in a libel suit must prove four points: (1) that the statement was published to others by print or broadcast; (2) that the plaintiff was identified or is identifiable; (3) that there was actual injury in the form of money losses, impairment of reputation, humiliation, or mental anguish and suffering; and (4) that the publisher of the statement was malicious or negligent.

With public figures—people in government or politics or who are much in the news—the test is whether the publisher of the statement knew that it was false or had a reckless disregard for its truth. The question of who is a public figure cannot be answered arbitrarily, and the courts are inconsistent on this. It often depends on the context. With private figures—people who are not officials or prominent in the news—the test is whether the publisher of the statement was negligent in checking the truth of it. In quoting someone, for instance, be sure you state exactly what was said.

These few highlights only hint at the ramifications of libel law. For your protection and for the protection of your organization, you need to dig deeper into this subject. To understand the nature of libel, you should read the chapter on libel in the *Associated Press Stylebook and Libel Manual.* Another book on this subject is *Synopsis of the Law of Libel and the Right of Privacy,* published by World Almanac Publications.

In thinking of libel, you should not confine your precautions to the mass media. An item in an organization's newsletter saying that "Jack was feeling no pain" at the office party could be construed as libel. An unflattering picture of a disheveled employee walking out the door could also be libelous.

Remember that you needn't use a name to commit libel. A recognizable description serves the same purpose. If the subject remains unnamed but the public knows who is being talked about, there may be grounds for a libel case.

In recent years, several lawsuits have been filed because of news releases. In one case, a man sued his former employer after a news release announced that he had been let go after having been investigated for accepting kickbacks from suppliers. In another case, a medical center was sued by another medical facility for implying in a news release that the number of patient deaths at the competing medical center was the highest in the region.

The Fair Comment Defense

These examples provide a warning of what can happen, but that doesn't mean that an organization has to avoid statements of opinion in public relations materials. Truth is the traditional defense against libel charges, but opinions also have a degree of legal protection under the First Amendment to the U.S. Constitution, which protects the freedom of speech and establishes the legal concept known as *fair comment privilege.*

In one case, the owner of the New York Yankees was sued for libel by an umpire when a news release from the team called him a "scab" who "had it in" for the Yankees and "misjudged" plays. A lower court awarded the umpire libel damages, but the New York Supreme Court overturned the judgment by ruling that the comments in the news release constituted protected statements of opinion. A judge also found the Genesis One Computer Corporation innocent of libel when it characterized another firm's breach of contract as a "device" to avoid payment of commissions due Genesis.

If you ever have occasion to write a news release that makes critical comments about another individual or organization, you could use the fair comment defense. However, take several precautionary measures. Experts suggest that (1) opinion statements be accompanied by the facts on which the opinions are based; (2) opinion statements be clearly labeled as such; and (3) the context of the language surrounding the expressions of opinion be reviewed for possible libel implications.

A poor choice of words can literally cost a company millions of dollars. ABC-TV said in a news story that Philip Morris "spiked" cigarettes with nicotine. The unfortunate use of that term resulted in ABC-TV making a public apology and agreeing to pay $15 million to Philip Morris for its legal expenses in bringing the libel suit.

INVASION OF PRIVACY

In recent years, there has been increased sensitivity to invasion of privacy. Laws have been passed and lawsuits have been filed in an effort to protect the privacy of individuals. In general, laws and lawsuits strive to prevent anyone from knowing anything about an individual that the individual does not want known.

Protection of employee privacy can create problems. People are interested in people, and most people are willing to have favorable things said about them. The trick is to include the good things and avoid the others. If John Doe is promoted to a new job, he will be pleased if others know about it. He may be willing to reveal considerable personal detail about himself to help you write an engaging story.

If Doe has two children, he may approve mention of that fact. If one of them is retarded, he may not want that published. If he is married, he may be willing to have that known. If he is in the middle of a divorce, he is likely to prefer no mention.

You can obtain information to flesh out a story by asking questions of each person involved. Elicit facts that are interesting and favorable. After the story is written, show it to the person mentioned. If he or she objects to anything, take it out. Once the material has been approved, get the subject to sign it. A simple "OK— John Doe" on the story will suffice.

There may be times when a reporter will ask you for information about an employee. In general, most companies have adopted a policy of merely confirming that a person is employed and in what position. You can also tell a reporter the date on which the employee first joined the firm.

Under no circumstances should you tell a reporter an employee's home address, marital status or number of children, nor should you reveal any aspect of a job performance record. If the reporter wants to know such things, the best approach is to say that you will ask the employee to call. In this way, the employee knows that an inquiry has been made and can determine what information is to be divulged. It also lets you and the company off the hook in terms of protecting the employee's privacy.

Another way for a company to protect itself against employees' invasion-of-privacy suits is to have a standard biographical form that each one fills out. At the top of this form should be a clear-cut statement that the information provided may be used in company publicity and employee newsletters.

Releases for Advertising and Promotion

Using names and photos of people in advertising, product publicity and promotions requires special handling and extra legal attention. These situations are not the same as the "implied consent" that is given when someone poses for a news story in the organization's employee magazine or newsletter.

The courts have consistently ruled that a person's right to privacy is violated when photos or names of individuals are published without prior *written* consent for commercial purposes or purposes of trade. Chemical Bank of New York, for example, used pictures of employees in advertisements without their written permission and was promptly sued for $600,000 in damages for invasion of privacy and "misappropriation of personality."

This situation reinforces the point that everyone whose picture, quote or name is being used in an advertisement or a sales brochure must give explicit written consent. Courts have also ruled that product news releases are primarily for "purposes of trade" and are covered under many of the same guidelines applied to advertising.

In addition to a signed consent form, individuals are usually offered a cash payment to establish the legal concept of "due consideration." If the person is prominent, the fee may be large, perhaps thousands of dollars. Celebrities and professional models, who are often used in advertisements, usually have agents who negotiate substantial fees. At the other end of the spectrum, consumers, employees, and "average citizens" may receive only a nominal payment of $10 or $25.

Signed consent forms and releases usually cover a specified period of time that the person's name or photo image can be used—as little as only six months or as long as 10 years. In the case of employees, it's always wise to have materials dated. For example, publishing an old picture that shows an employee with a full head of hair when he is now bald might hold him up to ridicule and hence result in a lawsuit.

Consent forms for advertising can be complex. For most public relations purposes, however, a simple release will probably suffice, and pads of standard photo releases can be purchased at camera stores. Your legal counsel may be able to provide forms tailored to your organization.

You do not need a release when the photo records a public event and a considerable number of people are involved. But if that picture is later used for promotional purposes and individuals are identifiable, you should have releases.

A STANDARD RELEASE FORM

Lockheed Missiles & Space Company, Inc.
A Subsidiary of Lockheed Aircraft Corporation
Sunnyvale, California

The undersigned, having previously consented to being photographed, does hereby authorize Lockheed Aircraft Corporation and Lockheed Missiles & Space Company, Inc., to use and reproduce the said photograph and copy for Lockheed publicity and promotional purposes.

_____
Date

_____
Name

_____
Address

REGULATIONS OF GOVERNMENT AGENCIES

Releasing false or misleading information can get you in trouble with government regulatory agencies. Federal and state agencies are empowered by law to enforce regulations about the distribution and content of financial and product information. They may issue cease-and-desist orders or injunctions. Fines can be levied, and adverse publicity can appear in the media. Also, people who feel that they have been injured or deceived can file lawsuits and collect damages.

False information can involve either misrepresenting facts or misleading someone into believing something that is not quite true. Writers who prepare financial and marketing communications in particular must be thoroughly familiar with the guidelines of federal regulatory agencies such as the Securities and Exchange Commission and the Federal Trade Commission.

Securities and Exchange Commission

The Securities and Exchange Commission (SEC) requires that any information affecting the value of a security be made known to the owners and to the SEC. This is done by filing certain annual and quarterly reports, highlights of which are often included in news releases. The SEC also requires "full and prompt disclosure" of any changes or developments that might affect the value of securities.

In general, a company whose stock is publicly traded must immediately release the following kinds of news:

1. Dividends or their deletion;
2. Annual or quarterly earnings;
3. Preliminary but audited interim earnings;
4. Stock splits;
5. Mergers;
6. Changes in top management;
7. Major product developments;
8. Major expansion plans;
9. Change of business purposes;
10. Defaults;
11. Dispositions of major assets;
12. Proxy materials; and
13. Purchases of its own stock.

In financial information, accuracy is imperative. Public relations firms have been held responsible for releasing false and misleading information even though they were told by their clients that the supplied facts were correct. The SEC has ruled that anyone preparing or releasing financial news is responsible for making a reasonable effort to ascertain that the information is accurate. You don't have to be an accountant, but you should know how to read a balance sheet and determine whether the information presented is logical and reasonable.

Often a company is tempted to report only the good news and bury the bad news. Although this sounds like a good idea to executives interested in the image of the corporation, it is a dangerous practice when it comes to financial news.

Increasingly, courts are applying the "mosaic doctrine" to financial information. Maureen Rubin, an attorney, writes in the *Public Relations Journal* (March 1991):

> Under this doctrine, a court may examine *all* information released by a company, including press releases, to determine whether taken as a whole, they combine to create an "overall misleading impression," whether by omission of material information or by inclusion of false information.

Thus a company and its public relations firm may be held liable even if each individual release or other statement is literally true when examined separately.

In other words, companies should avoid the temptation to paint a rosy picture of financial stability if in fact there are problems that stockholders and potential investors need to know in order to make an informed judgment. For example, a company should not announce a new product that is still in the research stage and will not be available to the public for another year.

Writers of financial news releases should also be aware of the fact that they have information not yet available to the public. If they use this advantage to buy or sell stock in the company in question, they are violating SEC rules on insider trading.

Tony Franco, owner of his own public relations firm in Detroit, got into trouble with the SEC several years for alleged insider trading. One of his clients gave him advance information to write a news release about its proposed acquisition by another company at $50 a share. The SEC suit charged that Franco used this advance information, before any public disclosure was made, to have his broker purchase shares in the company at the current price of $41 a share.

Federal Trade Commission

The Federal Trade Commission (FTC) deals with "unfair methods of competition in commerce, and unfair acts and practices," all of which are illegal. Both advertising and publicity are subject to FTC scrutiny. Also, false advertising and false publicity may be the subject of lawsuits from individuals who may claim injury or deception.

Any product information you release to the public is subject to FTC scrutiny. At first you may think mainly of news releases and feature stories, but you should also include letters, booklets, leaflets, brochures, pictures, drawings, audiovisual materials, speeches and any other type of communication that can reach the public.

Among the areas where deception can occur are these:

1. Unsubstantiated claims—statements that you cannot prove;
2. Ambiguous claims—statements that are confusing;

FTC SETS STANDARDS FOR "GREEN" MARKETING

The Federal Trade Commission, in an effort to reduce consumer confusion about the environmental claims of various products, established a new set of guidelines in mid-1992. They outline how various environmental terms can be used in product publicity, advertising, and package labels. Here is an excerpt from the guidelines:

- *Recycled content.* An advertiser should be able to prove and quantify the amount of material in a product or package that has been kept from a landfill or retrieved as manufacturing scraps. Unqualified claims can be made only when the entire product or package—excluding minor, incidental components—is made of recycled material.
- *Recyclable.* This should be used only if the product or package can be reused as raw material in making a new product or package.
- *Ozone-safe* and *ozone-friendly.* These should not be used if the product contains any ozone-depleting chemical. Claims that a product has reduced ozone-depleting potential must be substantiated.
- *Degradable, biodegradable and photodegradable.* These should mean that the product will "decompose into elements found in nature within a reasonably short period of time after customary disposal." Otherwise, the claim must be qualified, as in the case of products that might degrade quickly in open air but not in landfills, where they commonly end up.

Source: *San Jose* (California) *News,* July 29, 1992, p. 1.

3. Fraudulent testimonials—statements that were never actually made;
4. Puffery and exaggeration—stretching the truth;
5. Deceptive pricing—concealment of true cost;
6. Deceptive demonstrations—apparent proof that is not really proof;
7. Deceptive surveys—for example, "independent" surveys that you have paid for;
8. Unsound surveys—surveys that are not statistically valid;
9. Fraudulent contests—contests that were rigged in some way;
10. Deceptive illustrations—pictures that convey a false impression;
11. Nonexistent authority—for example, "Doctors recommend . . . ";
12. Nonexistent surveys—interpretation of a few comments as surveys; and
13. Unfair or misleading comparisons—inaccurate portrayals of superiority over other products.

The FTC interpretation of publicity will be based on the "net impression received by the consumer," not just on the bald facts. Among the types of statements that have been found false or deceptive are these:

1. That the product or service is original or the first in the field;
2. That it is approved by a government agency;
3. That the product is patented;
4. That it was developed in a research laboratory;
5. That the product contained nutritional substances;
6. That its life or effectiveness was not as claimed;
7. That a nonexistent or warped survey proved some point; and
8. That the product was misbranded in some way.

There are a number of "red-flag" words that the FTC looks for in product advertisements and news releases. They include: authentic, certified, cure, custom-made, exclusive, famous, first-class, natural, reliable, safe, slightly used, unbreakable and wrinkle-proof.

Other Regulatory Agencies

Although the SEC and the FTC are the major federal agencies concerned with the content of advertising and publicity materials, you should also be aware of guidelines used by the Food and Drug Administration (FDA) and the Bureau of Alcohol, Tobacco and Firearms (BATF).

The FDA oversees the advertising and promotion of prescription drugs, over-the-counter medicines and cosmetics. Under the Federal Food, Drug and Cosmetic Act, any person who "causes misbranding" and provides misleading or inaccurate information is liable.

Prescription drugs, in particular, have major FDA curbs on advertising and promotion, so the drug companies sidestep the regulations by publicizing diseases. Eli Lilly & Co., the maker of Prozac, is a good example; the company sponsors ads telling the public about depression. And the Glaxo Institute for Digestive Health conducts information campaigns about the fact that stomach pains can be an indication of major problems. Of course, Glaxo also makes the ulcer drug Zantac.

If you're writing publicity or advertising copy for a product containing alcohol, you should be aware of the laws and regulations under the Federal Alcohol Administration Act. One section prohibits "any statement that is false or untrue in any particular or that, irrespective of falsity, directly, or by ambiguity, omission, or inference, or by the addition of irrelevant, scientific, or technical matter tends to create a misleading impression."

Wineries, for example, have run into problems with the BATF by implying health benefits associated with drinking wine. Geyser Peak winery was told to pull advertisements that included the statement "As age enhances wine, wine enhances age." Even if this statement could be proved, the BATF took the attitude that such claims for alcoholic products should not be allowed.

In summary, a public relations firm and its writers have a responsibility to know all pertinent regulatory guidelines. A number of court cases have determined that you, as the writer, can be held liable for disseminating false and misleading information on behalf of a client. Be cautious about the information and documentation supplied to you by employers or clients.

COPYRIGHT LAW

Review

The purpose of a copyright is to secure for the creator of original material all the benefits earned by creating it. Copyrights apply not only to written words but also to illustrations, plays, musical works, motion pictures, sound recordings, graphics, sculptures, pantomimes and dances.

The copyright law protects original material during the life of the author plus 50 years. This applies to material published during and after the author's lifetime as well as to unpublished material. Material does not have to be printed or distributed to have copyright protection. As soon as it is created in a concrete form, it is protected, regardless of whether it bears a copyright notice.

If you want the most unassailable copyright protection, you should take formal steps to acquire it as soon as any material is published. There is a five-year grace period after publication before formal notice is required. However, you should avoid this delay whenever possible. It is easier and safer to file the formal notice as soon as your material appears.

To do this, you must place on the material, before publication, any one of three permissible statements:

1. © 19XX
2. Copyright 19XX
3. Copr. 19XX

The actual year shown is the year of publication. Two copies of the copyrighted item must be sent to the Register of Copyrights, Library of Congress, Washington,

DC 20559, together with an "Application for Copyright Registration" form and a fee. Instructions, fee schedule and forms can be obtained from the copyright office.

News releases, features and illustrations accompanying them are not normally copyrighted. Booklets, leaflets, books and similar publications usually are copyrighted unless there is a desire to allow others to reproduce them. In that case, it is customary to place a notice in the publication stating that reproduction and distribution of copies is permissible without charge.

The Rights of Free-lancers

If you work full-time for an employer, your status is considered "work-for-hire." This means that the employer owns your work and the copyright.

Different rules apply, however, for free-lancers and those who work on commission. Under the 1976 U.S. Copyright Act (enacted in 1978), free-lancers retain copyright if they are paid to write a particular feature article, compile a brochure or even take pictures or create graphics. This means that the original buyer has one-time use of the material and the free-lancer is free to resell the material to others.

The concept of one-time rights is important. Traditionally, employers used a particular piece of writing or a photograph in multiple ways without paying the creator any additional money. A picture, for example, might be on the cover of the corporate annual report, show up in the company newsletter, become part of the company calendar and even be used as part of an advertising campaign.

Now, under the Copyright Act, employers have to pay the creator each time they want to use the material. This allows free-lancers the opportunity to earn income from the repeated use of their created work.

If an employer wants unlimited rights to use the material, it is necessary to have a separate "work-for-hire" agreement signed. Such an agreement transfers all ownership and copyright rights to the employer. Another approach is to sign a licensing agreement with the creator of the work, which would cover any other use of the material.

In general, employers want maximum flexibility and free-lancers want to retain as many rights as possible. To avoid misunderstandings, it is important for both employers and free-lancers to sign agreements before the work begins so that both parties know exactly what rights are being given up and retained. (See also Chapter 7.)

Free-lance writers and photographers are also pressing for additional compensation from newspapers and magazines that routinely provide published articles to on-line databases such as Nexis/Lexis and on the Internet. The free-lancers claim that their agreements only covered one-time *print* publication rights.

The advent of the World Wide Web, and the extensive corporate use of home pages, means that agreements with free-lancers will also need to cover the electronic dissemination of materials in cyberspace.

Fair Use and Infringement

As a public relations writer, you will also use information and materials from a variety of sources. Therefore, it is important for you to understand thoroughly the dividing line between fair use and copyright infringement.

Fair use of materials, in general, applies for purposes of criticism, comment, news reporting, teaching, scholarship or research. If you are writing something and want to use a quotation from a copyrighted article or book, you may do so as long as you give proper credit to the author and the source.

If you quote a lengthy passage from an article or a book, however, it is best to get permission. In general, using a paragraph from a 1,000-word article is acceptable, but using several paragraphs might constitute copyright infringement if permission has not been obtained. Writers should also be careful about using whole paragraphs of copyrighted material with only a few words changed. If the content and structure of the sentences are virtually the same, this not only constitutes copyright infringement but also *plagiarism,* a form of theft.

GUIDELINES FOR USING COPYRIGHTED MATERIALS

Public relations personnel can avoid costly lawsuits by observing the following guidelines:

- Ideas cannot be copyrighted, but expression of those ideas can be.
- Be careful about using the titles of movies, books and songs as themes for public relations materials and programs.
- News releases and publicity photographs are not ordinarily copyrighted because their purpose is widespread distribution and use by the media.
- Major public relations materials (brochures, pamphlets, newsletters, videotapes and position papers) should be copyrighted, if only to prevent unauthorized use and copying of the format by competitors.
- Copyrighted material intended to advance the sales and profits of an organization should not be used unless permission is obtained.
- Copyrighted material should not be taken out of context, particularly if such usage implies endorsement of the organization's products or services.
- Reprints of an article should be ordered from the publisher.
- Permission must be obtained from the copyright owner to use segments of popular songs (written verses or sound recordings).
- Permission is required to use segments of television programs or motion pictures.
- Photographers retain rights to negatives, and permission must be obtained to reprint photos for uses other than those originally agreed on.
- Photographs of celebrities, living or dead, cannot be used for promotion and publicity purposes without permission.
- Permission is required to reprint cartoons and cartoon characters. Cartoons, like other artwork and illustrations, are copyrighted.
- Government documents are not copyrighted, but caution is necessary if the material is used in such a way as to imply endorsement of products or services.
- Private letters, or excerpts from them, cannot be published or used in sales and publicity materials without the permission of the letter writer.

Source: Adapted from Dennis L. Wilcox, Phillip H. Ault, and Warren K. Agee, *Public Relations Strategies and Tactics,* 4th ed. (New York: HarperCollins, 1995), p. 332.

Writers of company newsletters and magazines, primarily using information for news reporting purposes, are generally within the boundaries of the fair use concept. Writers who prepare materials directly supporting the sales of a product or service (news releases, advertisements, promotional brochures), however, need to be more concerned about copyright infringement.

The use of a selected quotation from an outside source in a product news release or sales brochure, for example, should be cleared with the source. The reason is that you're directly profiting from using someone else's material to sell goods and services.

In addition, using selected quotes may distort the author's meaning. For example, a research report may give a new computer product an overall poor performance rating but mention some good things about the product too. To use only the favorable quote from the review in a news release or advertisement, the computer company should clear the quote with the report's authors to avoid possible lawsuits.

Titles of books and plays cannot be copyrighted, but the principle of unfair competition applies nevertheless. Lawyers say that a public relations staff should not copy anything if the intent is to capitalize on or take advantage of its current renown. The key to a lawsuit is whether an organization is in some way obtaining commercial advantage by implying that a service or product has the endorsement of or is closely allied with the literary property. This is also a problem in using names and logos that closely resemble registered trademarks of well-known companies.

The use of cartoons, illustrations and photographs from outside sources (either previously published or unpublished) always requires permission. Copyright infringement also extends to videotaping television documentaries or news programs if the intent is for widespread use of the material to internal or external audiences.

Another category that always requires copyright permission is musical material. The holders of musical copyrights do not permit use of *any* part of their compositions without prior written permission. Quoting even part of a lyric or playing only a few bars of a tune is forbidden. But also keep in mind that most classical music, especially that of the seventeenth and eighteenth centuries, is in the public domain and can be used without permission.

Article reprints also require written permission and, in many cases, the payment of fees. If your company or organization is profiled in a magazine or newspaper, for example, order reprints from the publisher. If you make your own copies for widespread distribution, you are violating the copyright of the publication. Magazines and certain newspapers, such as the *Wall Street Journal,* have special departments set up to handle reprint requests.

Even the unauthorized photocopying of newsletters can cost the organization large sums of money. A U.S. district court ordered Labtest International, a New Jersey firm, to pay $111,000 to Washington Business Information, Inc., for reproducing copies of the company's weekly *Product Safety Letter.*

Although an organization may invoke the fair use doctrine, recent court cases have shown that the doctrine does not give companies the right to use published articles without permission. For example, Texaco lost a lawsuit filed by publishers of scientific journals who claimed that the oil company was photocopying articles for internal use without permission or compensation to the authors.

Texaco, as well as Labtest International, could have avoided legal problems if they had paid a licensing fee to the Copyright Clearance Center (CCC). This office,

---

COPYRIGHT COPS SURF THE NET

The problem of copyright infringement has also reached the Internet. Copyright holders are increasingly patrolling the Internet and its World Wide Web segment to stop the unauthorized use of material.

- Dutton Children's Books threatened a lawsuit against a New Mexico State University student for using Winnie-the-Pooh illustrations on his home page.
- Paramount pictures sent warning notes to Star Trek fans who were using the Internet to disseminate photos from the TV series.
- Elvis Presley Enterprises, Inc., ordered the removal of sound clips from "Blue Suede Shoes" and "Hound Dog" from a home page that also displayed images from Graceland postcards.

Publishers are also pushing Congress to pass copyright law changes that would better define digital transmission as a form of publication.

Source: *Wall Street Journal,* "Vigilant Copyright Holders Patrol the Internet," Dec. 13, 1995, p. B1.

---

set up by publishers, licenses the photocopying of materials. The cost of a college course pack, a combination of photocopied articles and book chapters, usually includes a licensing fee levied by the CCC.

Not all publishers, however, are members of the CCC, so it is often necessary to contact a publisher directly for the right to distribute a photocopied article to students, a sales force, or employees.

U.S. government documents are in the public domain and can be used in whole or in part without permission. You could get into legal trouble, however, if government reports were used out of context to imply endorsement of a product.

TRADEMARK LAW Review

An organization's name, products, slogans and manufacturing processes are usually trademarked. This means that these things are officially registered with the U.S. government (or another national government) and their use is restricted to the owner or manufacturer. A trademark is legally protected and should be capitalized whenever it is used.

A trademark is a valuable asset zealously guarded by its owners. Sony, Coca-Cola, IBM, Porsche, McDonald's and Reebok are all registered trademarks. So is the Mercedes-Benz star symbol, as well as slogans such as AT&T's "Reach Out and Touch Someone." High-technology systems may also be trademarked. The term "PhoneMail," for example, is a registered trademark of the Rolm Corporation.

Organizations and corporations protect their trademarks in various ways. One method is to establish standard policies on how the organization should use and display its trademarked names. You must know the registered trademarks of your company and how they may be used. For example, at General Foods, the word "Jell-O" is never used alone. Such use would imply that Jell-O is a generic product

TRADEMARKED NAMES ALWAYS START WITH A CAPITAL LETTER

Trademarked names are like proper nouns; they are capitalized and should be followed by a generic noun or phrase. The International Trademark Association also recommends that trademarks should never be pluralized, used in possessive form, or used as verbs. Currently, there are more than 700,000 trademarks registered with the U.S. government. Here's a sampling of trademarks that are often assumed to be generic words:

AstroTurf	No Doz
Band-aid	NutraSweet
Chap Stick	Plexiglas
Day-Timer	Post-It
DeskJet	Rolodex
Fiberglas	Stairmaster
Gatorade	Teflon
Hula Hoop	Walkman
Kleenex	Ziploc
Muzak	

Source: International Trademark Association, 1133 Avenue of the Americas, New York, NY 10036–6710.

and that other companies can use the same word. Instead, the usage at GF is always "Jell-O brand" gelatin dessert or pudding.

When you write a news release or brochure about your company's product, you not only capitalize trademarked names and slogans, but you also indicate they are trademarked by placing the symbol ®, TM, or SM next to them. The ® symbol means that the trademark is registered by the U.S. Patent and Trademark Office, TM indicates that trademark registration is pending, and SM means that the mark designates a service rather than a product.

Many companies also list trademarked names at the end of any news release in which they appear. Be certain of the rules that apply to the products for which you are responsible. If you worked for the Hewlett-Packard Company, for example, you would have to know whether the company made a "laser jet," "Laser-Jet," or "LaserJet" printer.

Companies also guard their trademarks by continually using them, sending advisories to media outlets about proper use of these trademarks, placing advertisements in journalism publications reminding readers of trademarked names (see Figure 2.1) and monitoring publications to ensure that other organizations are not infringing on a trademark. If they are, legal action is threatened or taken.

Be extremely careful not to use another company's trademark improperly or to infringe on it in any way. You may like Garfield and Snoopy, but don't put them on posters advertising the company picnic. They are registered trademarks, like all cartoon characters. If you want to use such characters in company promotions and publicity, you must request permission and pay a licensing fee. Also, you cannot use

THE WORD FRIGIDAIRE ALWAYS ENDS WITH A CAPITAL "R."

The capital "R" has a circle around it, too. Because Frigidaire® is more than an ordinary word, it's our registered trademark.

To many, it means the finest quality refrigerator available. It's a name that's so popular some people call every refrigerator a Frigidaire® Unfortunately, that's wrong.

Only Frigidaire® refrigerators have the quality, engineering and heritage to bear the name.

So if a refrigerator really is a Frigidaire® say so.

If it's not, use the other word that ends with an "R". Refrigerator. We would appreciate it. **Frigidaire®**

HERE TODAY. HERE TOMORROW.

Figure 2.1 Brand names are important assets. An "R" with a circle around it tells you that it is a registered trademark. This advertisement was placed in a journalism magazine to remind reporters of the trademark. (*Courtesy of White Consolidated Industries, Inc.*)

the logos or names of amateur or professional athletic teams without obtaining permission and paying a fee.

Payment is also required if you want to use stock photos of current, retired or deceased actors or entertainers. A company cannot use a picture of W. C. Fields, the Marx Brothers or Elvis Presley—or even dress someone up to look like them for publicity and promotional purposes—without first paying the heirs or the movie studios a licensing fee.

In legal terms, using images of popular personalities without permission is called *misappropriation of personality*. For example, a $400,000 award given to Bette Midler was upheld by the U.S. Supreme Court. She had brought charges against an advertising agency that used a "sound-alike" singer for a TV commercial. The courts found that Midler's exclusive right to her vocal style had been violated. In another case, lawyers for actress Catherine Deneuve filed a trademark infringement suit against a lesbian magazine named *Deneuve*. The magazine changed its name.

A take-off on a registered trademark can also get you into trouble. A student at the University of North Carolina found this out the hard way when he decided to produce and sell T-shirts that said "Nags Head, N.C.—King of Beaches" on the front and "This Beach Is for You" on the back. Anheuser-Busch was not amused and slapped him with a lawsuit for infringement on their trademarks "King of Beers" and "This Bud's for You." The student was eventually vindicated in the federal appeals court, which ruled that his parody couldn't possibly be confused with company trademarks. However, the lawsuit cost the student a lot of money and four years of nerve-racking litigation.

SiliconGraphics
Computer Systems

For information, contact: FOR IMMEDIATE RELEASE
Susan Austin, 415-390-3233
saustin@corp.sgi.com

SILICON GRAPHICS PIONEERS NEW ERA IN DESKTOP REALISM WITH INDIGO^2 IMPACT WORKSTATIONS

**Powerful New Systems Developed with Team
of Leading-Edge Customers, Software Developers**

MOUNTAIN VIEW, Calif. (July 10, 1995)–Silicon Graphics, Inc. (NYSE:SGI) today unveiled Indigo^2 IMPACT™, a new line of powerful 3D graphics and imaging workstations that bring unequalled capabilities to the power desktop. Introduced with new customized third-party software solutions, Indigo^2 IMPACT is the result of a new strategy for accelerated collaboration between Silicon Graphics engineers and the company's leading-edge customers and software developers.

Third-party applications written to take advantage of these workstations provide the foundation for a new breed of solutions in the most demanding visual computing environments, including computer-aided design and engineering, geographic information systems, film and video production, chemistry, game development and visual simulation.

"The demand of our visual computing customers consistently outruns the evolutionary curt makes traditional computing technology," said Edwarirman and CEO of SiliconGraphics"By h Indigsolutio

-end-

Silicon Graphics, the Silicon Graphics logo and Indigo are registered trademarks, and Indigo^2, POWER Indigo^2, Indigo^2 IMPACT, Indigo^2 High IMPACT, Indigo^2 Maximum IMPACT and POWER Indigo^2 Maximum IMPACT, are trademarks, of Silicon Graphics, Inc. Extreme is a trademark used under license. MIPS is a registered trademark, and R4400 and R8000 are trademarks, of MIPS Technologies, Inc. Rambus and RDRAM are trademarks of Rambus, Inc.

Figure 2.2 Trademarked names are often listed in the text and at the end of a news release to alert media gatekeepers about the need for capitalization. (*Courtesy of Silicon Graphics, Inc., Mountain View, CA.*)

Everyday, irregardless of his homework, Jeffrey went "rollerblading" because it was to nice to lay around with his nose in a english book.

Of the 7 errors in this headline, "rollerblading" as a verb strikes us as most extreme. Other common misuses of the Rollerblade brand name include "rollerblades, rollerbladers, blades, bladers and blading." Remember, the careful writer skates on in-line skates known as Rollerblade® skates.

⚡⚡⚡.Rollerblade.

Figure 2.3 Trademarked names can lose their protection if people use them as verbs. This advertisement cautions people that they can't go "rollerblading." (*Courtesy of Rollerblade, Inc.*)

Nike, Inc., also knows the cost of trademark infringement. The company had paid millions in the Barcelona Olympics to have its name on the U.S. and Algerian track and field uniforms and on a new line of clothing, only to find out that it could not use its name in Spain because it violated the trademark of a Barcelona sock company that had registered the name in 1932. Nike, Inc., estimated its loss at more than $20 million in Spain and several times that figure worldwide. In another case, Levi Strauss asked Jordache to drop its 101 mark because it infringed on Levi's 501 trademark.

Social service organizations are not exempt from charges of infringement on registered trademarks. The U.S. Olympic Committee filed suit against the March of Dimes for sponsoring the "Reading Olympics." Under U.S. law, no one can use the word "Olympic" or related words and symbols without the U.S. Olympic Committee's consent.

In sum, become familiar with what might be considered trademark infringement. Even if you are innocent, the money and time spent fighting a lawsuit are rarely worthwhile. Here are some guidelines the courts use to determine if a trademark has been infringed upon:

1. Has the defendant used a name as a way of capitalizing on the reputation of another organization's trademark?

2. Is there an intent to create confusion in the public mind? Is there an intent to imply a connection between the defendant's product and the item identified by the trademark?
3. How similar are the two organizations? Are they providing the same kinds of services or products?
4. Has the original organization actively protected the trademark by publicizing it and using it?
5. Is the trademark unique? A trademark that merely describes a common product might be in trouble. Microsoft, for example, lost a bid to trademark the word "windows" for its exclusive use.

WORKING WITH LAWYERS

You now have an overview of how various laws and government regulations affect your work as a public relations writer and specialist. A basic knowledge of the law should help you do your work in a responsible and appropriate manner, but you also should realize that a smattering of knowledge can be dangerous.

Laws and regulations can be complex. You are not a trained attorney, so you should consult lawyers who are qualified to answer specialized questions regarding libel, copyright, trademarks, government regulation and invasion of privacy. Your organization's own staff attorneys or outside legal counselors are your first source of information.

At the same time, remember that lawyers can tell you what to do or not do; they should not tell you what to say or how to say it. They are experts on the law but not on effective communication. They don't understand that the media want information now or that "no comment" is perceived as a guilty plea in the court of public opinion.

Indeed, a major area of friction in any organization is the clash between the legal and public relations departments. Lawyers generally prefer to say little or nothing in most situations, whereas the public relations staff perceives its role as providing a steady flow of information and news about the organization to multiple publics. It is a never-ending tug-of-war. At the same time, it is essential that the legal and public relations staffs cooperate in the best interests of the organization.

Great care must be taken in releasing information about litigation, labor negotiations, complex financial transactions, product recalls and plant accidents. Numerous laws and regulations, to say nothing of liability considerations, affect what should or should not be said.

The courts have consistently ruled that an organization's statements and news releases can be used in a court of law. For example, a news release by Getty Oil about an impending merger with Pennzoil became a significant document in the court case charging Texaco with illegally interfering with Pennzoil's move to purchase Getty. The result was a $3 billion judgment against Texaco.

This is why it is often important to draft a proposed statement or release and submit it to legal counsel for approval. The release should give as much information as possible and should be phrased clearly and concisely. The object of such a release is to convince the public that the organization is not hiding behind legal technicalities but, at the same time, must protect itself from possible lawsuits and litigation.

Your relations with legal counsel will be more pleasant and more productive if you keep abreast of new developments. To do this, you should maintain a file of newspaper and magazine articles that report on legal developments and decisions relating to public relations. This might include new regulatory guidelines, consent decrees, libel awards, trademark infringement suits, product recalls and court decisions on employee privacy. For example, it is your responsibility to know that the FTC has posted new guidelines on how to use environmental terms in "green" marketing (see p. 39).

To ensure the best cooperation and mutual respect between the legal and public relations functions, here are some guidelines:

1. Each department should have a written definition of its responsibilities.
2. The heads of both departments should be equal in rank and should report to the organization's chief executive officer or executive vice president.
3. Both departments should be represented on key committees.
4. The legal counsel should keep the public relations staff up to date on legal problems involving the organization.
5. The public relations staff should keep the legal staff up to date on public issues and media concerns that will require an organizational response.
6. The departments should regard each other as allies, not opponents.

ETHICS AND PROFESSIONALISM

So far, this chapter has concentrated on the legal aspects of public relations writing. Equally important, however, are the ethical and professional values that you bring to your work.

Ethical considerations, like the law, are often ambiguous and subject to interpretation. Most situations are neither black nor white but rather various shades of gray. Although the public relations writer is an advocate and must convey information in a persuasive way, this does not excuse the presentation of false or misleading information. In sum, you have to ask not only whether something is legal but also whether it is the right thing to do.

Thomas Bivins, writing in the Winter 1992 *Public Relations Review*, asserts that public relations practitioners have five moral obligations:

1. *To ourselves*—to preserve our own integrity;
2. *To our clients*—to honor our contracts and to use our professional expertise on our clients' behalf;
3. *To our organization or employer*—to adhere to organizational goals and policies;
4. *To our profession and our professional colleagues*—to uphold the standards of the profession and, by extension, the reputation of our fellow practitioners; and
5. *To society*—to consider social needs and claims.

Unfortunately, trying to serve the needs of these groups often involves personal conflict. An employer or a client, for example, may think it in the organization's interest to hide information that may be detrimental to its reputation or sales. As a public relations writer and practitioner, do you go along with the organization's wishes, or do you adhere to your own personal values and the standards of the public relations profession?

The answer depends in large part on how you view your role. Some writers consider themselves technicians whose responsibility is to prepare materials as the organization or client wants them, even if the result is dishonest or misleading. They are the literary equivalent of "hired guns," available for any and every cause. Professionalism to them means writing good, persuasive copy even if they don't believe in what they are writing.

Other writers feel that they serve as lawyers in the court of public opinion. All parties, they believe, are entitled to tell their side of the story and be represented by public relations counsel. In this mode, the writer's obligation is to present the best possible defense of the client. Thus a public relations firm should have no qualms about representing a foreign government accused of human rights violations, a racist hate group, or a cigarette company. After all, the First Amendment to the U.S. Constitution guarantees freedom of speech.

Although both views are common in the public relations industry, organizations such as the Public Relations Society of America and the International Association of Business Communicators argue that these approaches are self-defeating and lead to widespread public distrust of public relations activities. Professionalism and public credibility hinge on other considerations. Long-term public relations educator Scott Cutlip asks, "Is the legality of a product all that matters to a corporation or a counselor?"

Fraser Seitel, former vice president for public relations at Chase Manhattan Bank, would say "no." He contends that public relations people should stand up for something, maintain high communications standards, and never compromise their standards. "We must take pride in the communications products for which we are responsible. If the trend continues of PR people becoming image mercenaries, accepting any client regardless of character or conscience, as long as he or she pays the freight, then all of us lose," Seitel warns. "We aren't in the business of confusing or distorting or obfuscating or lying."

As for being a lawyer in the court of public opinion, there is widespread disagreement. Jack O'Dwyer, editor of a public relations newsletter, holds that public relations is not like the law:

> The public accepts the fact that disreputable interests have the right to legal counsel but the public does not believe they also have the right to PR. A courtroom is a highly controlled setting where one legal counsel will battle it out with another under supervision by an expert judge who enforces ground rules. But PR people usually work for organizations and there may be no expert PR help on the other side.

In other words, although all parties have the right to express their side of the story, you are under no obligation to work on behalf of any organization or cause. Public relations firms, like attorneys, may turn down clients if they feel that such representation violates their own values and professional standards.

A nationwide survey of leading public relations firms conducted by Art Stevens of Lobsenz-Stevens public relations in New York, for example, found that two-thirds of the firms would not take a tobacco company account. And most firms would not work for repressive countries or indicted criminals.

Making an ethical decision on the kind of organization or cause that you want to have as an employer or a client, however, is only one part of the equation. Moral and ethical decisions also have to be made almost daily about the content and structure of various messages. Do you say that an executive has resigned "for personal reasons" even though you know that the person was fired for incompetence? Do you exaggerate the number of people attending an event? Do you say that a product is safe even though tests have revealed a potentially dangerous design flaw? Do you write about a company's restructuring to be more profitable without mentioning the layoff of 1,500 employees?

There are no easy answers to such questions. The simple axiom "Always tell the truth" understates the complexity of the decision process. For example, Chapter 1 makes it clear that public relations writing is not journalistic reporting of all the unvarnished facts about a situation; that information should be placed in a context

THE ETHICS OF FRONT GROUPS

What do the Coalition for Vehicle Choice, Americans for Medical Progress, People for the West and the Princeton Dental Resource Center have in common? They are all front groups formed and funded by special interests but designed to create the impression that they are organized by citizens and volunteers to promote the general public welfare. People for the West, for example, is a coalition of cities and mining companies that are lobbying to open up more public land for development.

The use of front groups raises some ethical questions regarding the public's right to know who funds and organizes such groups.

A good example is the Coalition to Protect Communities' and States' Rights. Although the name is high-sounding, the actual purpose of the group is to mobilize opposition to Indian-operated gambling casinos in several states. One member of the coalition is the Nevada Resort Association, made up of casino operators, who don't want competition from Indian-operated establishments. Owners of horse-racing interests also fund the coalition.

Burson-Marsteller public relations represents the coalition but refused to reveal its members to *Jack O'Dwyer's Newsletter.* The newsletter cited Article 7 of the Public Relations Society of America code, which states, "A member shall be prepared to identify publicly the name of the client or employer on whose behalf any public communication is made," and Article 8, which says, "A member shall not use any individual or organization professing to serve or represent an announced cause, or professing to be independent or unbiased, but actually serving another or undisclosed interest."

A representative of Burson-Marsteller who is also a member of PRSA then cited Article 13 of the code, which says, "A member shall scrupulously safeguard the confidences and privacy rights of present . . . employers."

Who's right? Is Burson-Marsteller in violation of the PRSA code? Is the firm operating in a fair and ethical manner by not disclosing the coalition's membership and funding?

GUIDELINES FOR ETHICAL CONDUCT

Various professional organizations such as the International Public Relations Association (IPRA), the International Association of Business Communicators (IABC) and the Public Relations Society of America (PRSA) have set standards for ethical conduct in public relations. Here are some excerpts from the 17-item PRSA code that apply to public relations writing and media relations:

- A member shall conduct his or her professional life in accord with the public interest.
- A member shall adhere to the highest standards of accuracy and truth, avoiding extravagant claims or unfair comparisons and giving credit for ideas and words borrowed from others.
- A member shall not knowingly disseminate false or misleading information and shall act promptly to correct erroneous communications for which he or she is responsible.
- A member shall not engage in any practice which has the purpose of corrupting the integrity of channels of communications or the processes of government.
- A member shall be prepared to identify publicly the name of any client or employer on whose behalf any public communication is made.
- A member shall not use any individual or organization professing to serve or represent an announced cause, or professing to be independent or unbiased, but actually serving another or undisclosed interest.
- A member shall not guarantee the achievement of specified results beyond the member's direct control.

Source: *Public Relations Journal,* June 1995, pp. 22–25. (Annual Membership Register)

that helps the organization achieve its objectives. In addition, it is often impossible to say everything about a particular subject in a single message.

David Martinson, a professor of public relations at Florida International University, puts the ethical dilemma succinctly: How, he asks, "does the practitioner respond when trying to determine whether or not to release information—or how much of it to release?" Then he answers, "By determining whether the information should be communicated. The practitioner must have an objective standard to use in determining which information should be released to all seriously interested parties." He suggests that public relations personnel should apply the concept of *substantial completeness,* defined as "the point at which a reasonable reader's requirements for information are satisfied."

Martinson continues:

A practitioner adopting a policy of substantial completeness will release that information which the public needs to make an informed decision. In conceding that all information regarding a particular matter might not be released because in many cases that is impossible, no suggestion is made that only that information most favorable should be released. Those who release only favorable information may not be lying in a formal sense, but they certainly are not contributing to a process whereby concerned publics can make an informed decision—they clearly have not adopted a policy of substantial completeness.

At times there also are competitive, legal and proprietary reasons why an organization doesn't want to distribute information or answer press questions. In this case, the best approach is to be candid. Jerry Dalton, former national president of the PRSA, says that organizations "should state that they will not discuss what they are doing and then give an honest reason why they have taken this seemingly hard-line decision."

Simply refusing to comment, for good reason, is not considered lying by journalists who responded to a survey conducted by Professors Michael Ryan and David Martinson (*Journalism Quarterly*, Spring 1994). However, both journalists and public relations people consider it lying if (1) you give evasive answers to questions or (2) say that rumors about a situation are wrong when they are in fact correct.

Questions of ethics and professionalism are raised throughout this textbook as they relate to various aspects of public relations writing and media techniques. Chapter 7, on photographs and artwork, for example, discusses the ethical implications of altering photos through computer manipulation. Later, in Chapter 11, ethical dealings with the media are discussed.

Providing a framework for many of these discussions are the codes of ethics for various organizations. The box on page 54 highlights the code of professional practice for the Public Relations Society of America. Take the time to read and understand it.

SUMMARY

1. You are legally and ethically responsible for the information that you produce and distribute.

2. You should know the dividing lines between libel, slander and the concept of fair comment.

3. Employees, as well as outsiders, have a right to privacy that can be violated through the careless release of personal information.

4. You must have written permission to use an individual's quotes and photographs for promotional or advertising purposes.

5. Regulatory agencies such as the SEC and the FTC have guidelines and rules concerning the content and release of information about products and services.

6. Copyrights are simple, easy to get and dangerous to infringe. Don't plagiarize. Understand thoroughly the limitations of fair use.

7. Trademarks are valuable assets. It is your responsibility to protect and use them correctly.

8. The use of trademarked names and cartoon characters often requires the payment of licensing fees.

9. Written contracts or letters of agreement are necessary for the employment of freelance writers and other outside consultants.

10. Lawyers and legal staff members are valuable resources for understanding the various legal implications of public relations activities. They are allies, not enemies.

11. Public relations writers are more than wordsmiths and technicians; they have a moral and ethical responsibility to communicate in a fair and truthful manner.

12. Ethics are vital for professionalism. You must do more than just obey the law. You must consider the public interest.

EXERCISES

1. Expresso Unlimited, a chain of coffee shops, hires you as director of public relations and marketing. Your promotion plans for the first year include the following:
   - Develop a series of advertisements showing pictures and quotes from employees who make and serve the coffee.
   - Develop a series of advertisements showing customers enjoying the atmosphere and flavorful coffee.
   - Hire a free-lance photographer to build up a photo file for use in possible magazine articles, brochures, newsletters and advertising.
   - Reprint and distribute various magazine articles about the company and its philosophy.
   - Start an employee newsletter with emphasis on employee features and "personals."
   - Reprint cartoons about coffee drinking from various publications, including the *New Yorker,* in the newsletter.
   - Cite a government study that rates the quality of coffee beans from around the world, and point out that Expresso Unlimited only uses the highest rated beans.
   - Distribute news releases that quote surveys showing that the majority of serious coffee drinkers prefer Expresso Unlimited in comparison to other chains.
   - Establish a home page on the Internet that would include pictures of famous people drinking a cup of coffee.

   Prepare a memo outlining the legal and regulatory factors that should be considered in implementing these plans.

2. Conduct an interview with the editor of an employee newspaper or magazine. What is the policy regarding the use of employee personals such as birthdays, anniversaries and vacation trips? What procedures are in place to ensure that employee privacy is preserved?

3. Conduct an interview with someone in the public relations or human resources department of an organization. What policies does the organization have regarding the release of employee information to the news media or to others who may request such information?

4. Do some research in the library or on-line. Find some examples of lawsuits stemming from copyright or trademark infringement. In what ways do the cases

deal with the production and distribution of public relations and promotional materials?

5. A survey by Art Stevens (page 53) found that the majority of public relations firms won't work for a tobacco company, a repressive government or an indicted criminal. Would you agree? Would you work on behalf of an organization involved in such issues as right-to-life, pro-choice, alcohol, euthanasia, animal rights, anti-gay rights or pro-gay rights? Explain your answers.

6. The issue of using front groups for public relations purposes was discussed in the box on page 53. Answer the questions about ethics that appear at the end of the box and give your rationale.

7. You work for a company that is having a down-turn in its stock price. The president of the company suggests that the stock might go up if you write a news release about a new, highly advanced product. The R&D department, however, says a lot of research and development remains—and the product may not be ready to market for 12 to 16 months. Does writing a news release about the new product raise any ethical problems? If there are ethical problems, how might the news release be structured to avoid them?

3 | *Persuasive Writing*

*M*essages are designed to change attitudes and opinions, reinforce existing predispositions and influence people to use a product or a service. At other times, the organizational objective is to simply create a favorable impression and help people better understand a situation.

To be an effective writer, you need to understand how public opinion is formed and how people absorb messages. In an age of information overload, writers must constantly analyze public attitudes and shape messages that cut through the clutter. How do you appeal to self-interests? Which spokesperson has the most credibility? What information is most salient to the target audience? What is the most effective communication channel? This chapter provides answers to these questions and discusses your responsibilities as a persuader.

PUBLIC OPINION

Public opinion is not just mass opinion. It is the sum of individuals' opinions on a subject that affects them. For example, the stockholders of a factory (a public) may favor moving to another location, while the employees (a public) may vigorously oppose the idea. Meanwhile, the general public may be unaware of the controversy or indifferent. The reason for these differing opinions is variance in who is affected and in what way.

Attitudes and Opinions

An opinion is an expression of attitude. It may be expressed by writing, by speaking, by acting or by not acting. People who fail to express their opinions may do so because their attitudes are weak or because they don't believe that expressing themselves will do any good.

An attitude is a predisposition to think, speak or act in a given way about a specific subject. No one is born with an attitude—all attitudes are learned. Some attitudes are deeply rooted, when tied into other attitudes, beliefs and values, they may be hard to change.

In the case of the proposed factory move, the opinion of the stockholders is probably based on an attitude concerned with costs and profits. The opinion of the employees is probably based on a concern for their jobs or the inconvenience of moving to a new location.

In public relations writing, it is necessary to think about the attitudes of the particular public you are trying to influence. You must also know how public opinion is built.

Building Public Opinion

Public opinion doesn't really exist until something affects a number of people who have similar attitudes. The people must be aware of the issue or they will not have any opinion about it. Usually the awareness results from some event. When something happens or is likely to happen, people become concerned—if they know about it. People have to express their opinions to others with similar attitudes. Someone must call for action, and the action must be possible. People are much more certain about what they want than they are about how to get it. Public opinion isn't evident unless it can expect to get results. The disagreement about abortion is a good example. Both sides have strong attitudes, and each side expresses its opinion vociferously because each really expects its actions to rally supporters and lead to favorable legislation and court decisions.

BASICS OF COMMUNICATION

David Therkelsen, director of marketing for the American Red Cross in St. Paul, Minnesota, conceptualizes the process of effective communication as follows:

To be successful, a message must be *received* by the intended individual or audience. It must get the audience's *attention*. It must be *understood*. It must be *believed*. It must be *remembered*. And ultimately, in some fashion, it must be *acted upon*. Failure to accomplish any of these tasks means the entire message fails.

To communicate is to make known—to project ideas into the minds of others. This process depends on four elements: a sender, a message, a medium and a receiver. If all these elements are operating, there will be communication. If any one fails, there will be no communication. Since your purpose is to persuade, you want to communicate your ideas to a particular group of people—those who can help or hinder your organization in attaining its objectives. In describing the process of communication, it is normal to list the elements as sender, message, medium and receiver, but it may be better to think of the process in reverse order: whom to reach, how to reach them, what to say and on whose behalf.

Receiver

This is the target audience, the people you must reach. You must learn about the characteristics and attitudes of your projected receivers if you are to communicate effectively and persuasively. Such factors as educational level, economic status, occupation, place of residence, religious affiliation, national origin, social class and political affiliation affect how a target audience receives and perceives your message.

As business becomes more global, there is also a growing need to understand the attitudes, customs and cultures of people in other nations. Faulty translations of publicity materials can cause a number of gaffes if one does not understand the language and culture of a nation. A baby formula manufacturer discovered that in its product introductions in one Spanish-speaking country, the term used for "nipple" was a vulgar expression. A publicist would be wise not to send product publicity photos of women driving cars to Saudi Arabia. In that nation, women are not allowed to drive.

Your responsibility is to research your audience. Reference books, surveys and polls, on-line databases and conversations with members of the target audience are good approaches. Armed with such knowledge, you can give information in such a way that the recipients will accept the message, absorb it, and eventually act on it.

Media

The media are the physical channels that carry the message to the receiver. They may include newspapers, magazines, radio, television, letters, speeches, audiovisuals, pictures, newsletters, leaflets, brochures and the telephone. Every medium has advantages and disadvantages.

Your job is to determine which medium or combination of media will be most effective in reaching the target audience. It is also important to know the message format that each media requires. Television, for example, requires highly visual material and short "sound bites." Home pages on the World Wide Web (Internet) require strong graphics and interactive mechanisms. A newspaper story requires a strong lead paragraph that attracts the reader.

TAILORING MESSAGES TO AMERICAN LIFESTYLES

Public relations writers increasingly use psychographics to tailor messages to specific audiences. SRI International, a research organization in Menlo Park, California, has developed a values and lifestyles program known as VALS.

Through extensive research, SRI was able to come up with several lifestyle typologies:

Survivors and sustainers are at the bottom of the hierarchy. Generally they have low incomes, are poorly educated, and are often elderly. These people eat at erratic hours, consume inexpensive foods, and seldom patronize restaurants.

Belongers are family-oriented and traditional and tend to be lower- or middle-income people.

Achievers, at the uppermost level of the VALS scale, are often college-educated professionals with high incomes. They are also more experimental and open to new ideas.

A good example of how public relations writing can be tailored to each group is provided by Burson-Marsteller, a public relations firm that handled the National Turkey Federation account. The objective was to increase the consumption of turkey on a year-round basis.

By segmenting the consumer public into various VALS lifestyles, Burson-Marsteller was able to select the appropriate media for specific story ideas. An article placed in *True Experience,* a publication reaching the "survivors and sustainers" group, was headlined "A Terrific Budget-Stretching Meal" and emphasized bargain cuts of turkey. *Better Homes & Gardens* was used to reach the "belongers" with articles that emphasized tradition, like barbecued turkey as a "summer classic" on the Fourth of July. The "achievers" were reached through *Food and Wine* and *Gourmet* magazines, with recipes for turkey salad and turkey tetrazzini.

By identifying the magazines that catered to these three lifestyle groups and tailoring the information to fit each magazine's demographics, Burson-Marsteller was able to send an appropriate message to each audience. The result was increased turkey sales on a year-round basis.

Message

Planning the message starts with a determination of exactly what ideas you want your receivers to have: what you want them to think, believe or do. Then you must acquire a solid knowledge of what your audience currently knows and believes. If you want to affect attitudes and opinions, you must find out about those that already exist. This calls for research—possibly surveys.

Your message must be applicable, believable, realistic and convincing. It must be expressed clearly and understandably in familiar words and phrases. Above all, you must convince the receivers that the idea you are presenting can be beneficial to them.

EFFECTIVE COMMUNICATION

Philip Lesly, president of Philip Lesly Company, provides the following guidelines for effective, persuasive communication.

1. Approach everything from the viewpoint of the audience's interest. What is on its mind? What is in it for each person?

2. Make the subject matter part of the atmosphere in which audience members live—what they talk about, what they hear from others. That means tailoring the message to their channels of communication.

3. Communicate *with* people, not *at* them. Communication that approaches the audience as a target makes people put up defenses against it.

4. Localize—get the message conveyed as close to the individual's own setting as possible.

5. Use a number of communication channels, not just one or two. The impact is far greater when a message reaches people in a number of diferent forms.

6. Maintain consistency so that the basic content is the same regardless of audience or context. Then tailor that content to the specific audience as much as possible.

7. Don't propagandize, but be sure you make your point. Drawing conclusions in the information itself is more effective than letting the audience draw its own conclusions.

8. Maintain credibility—which is essential for all these points to be effective.

Source: Adapted from a speech by Phillip Lesly as part of the Vern C. Schranz Distinguished Lecturership series at Ball State University.

Sender

The sender is the organization from which the message comes. Every organization has different publics, divergent interests, dissimilar objectives, unique problems, distinctive beliefs and peculiarities. As a writer, you must know and understand the organization so that the messages you prepare will be not only effective but also truly representative of the organization. In addition, you must be sure that what you send out is the truth, the whole truth, and nothing but the truth.

THEORIES OF COMMUNICATION

A message may move from the sender through the media to the receiver without necessarily conveying ideas and getting them accepted. Yet ideas do get accepted, and there are several theories about how this is accomplished.

Two-Step Flow Theory

The flow of communication might be described as a series of expanding contacts. It assumes that opinion leaders first pay attention to messages in the media, analyze it, interpret it and then pass on the information to their friends and associates.

There are formal opinion leaders, such as an elected official or the president of a company, but there are also informal opinion leaders. All of us rely on various people for information and guidance because we perceive that they know about a particular subject.

Later research has shown that the two-step flow theory is really a multistep model—communication going from opinion leaders to an attentive public and ultimately to an inattentive public. However, the basic idea about the role of opinion leaders in communication remains intact. High-technology companies, for example, often design their marketing strategy to first reach the respected journalists and experts who really know the industry. They are the opinion leaders who will ultimately tell the public whether to buy the product. A later section discusses adoption theory.

Media Uses and Gratification

Recipients of communication are not passive couch potatoes. The basic premise of uses and gratification theory is that the communication process is interactive. The communicator wants to inform, even motivate, people. Recipients want to be entertained, informed, or alerted to opportunities that can fulfill their needs.

Thus, people make highly intelligent choices about what messages require their attention and meet their needs. The role of the public relations writer, then, is to tailor messages that are meaningful to the audience. Maslow's hierarchy of needs is discussed on pages 65–66.

Cognitive Dissonance

People will not believe a message, or act on it, if it is contrary to their predispositions. A public relations writer must, in this instance, introduce information that causes them to question their beliefs.

This can be done in several ways. First, you can introduce information that says it's okay to change; perhaps the situation has changed because of new discoveries, and so on. Second, you can use sources or testimonials from people the audience trusts.

Media Effects

One theory postulates that the mass media have limited effects. The media may set the agenda in terms of what people think about, but it has limited influence in telling them what to think.

There's also the theory of moderate and powerful media effects. This theory postulates that the media are influential in shaping public opinion when the public has little or no opinion on a subject, the subject is non–ego threatening and the reader or viewer has no firsthand knowledge of the event or situation. In a highly urbanized and global society, the public is increasingly dependent on the media for information.

Diffusion and Adoption

The diffusion theory was developed in the 1930s and expanded on by Professor Everett Rogers of Stanford University. It holds that there are five steps in the process of acquiring new ideas:

1. *Awareness*—the person discovers the idea or product.
2. *Interest*—the person tries to get more information.
3. *Trial*—the person tries the idea on others or samples the product.
4. *Evaluation*—the person decides whether the idea works for his or her own self-interest.
5. *Adoption*—the person incorporates the idea into his or her opinion or begins to use the product.

In this model, the public relations writer is most influential at the *awareness* and *interest* stages of the process. People often become aware of a product, service or idea through traditional mass outlets such as newspapers, magazines, radio and television. Indeed, the primary purpose of advertising in the mass media is to create awareness, the first step in moving people toward the purchase of a product or support of an idea.

At the interest stage, people seek more detailed information from such sources as pamphlets, brochures, direct mail, videotape presentations, meetings and symposiums. That's why initial publicity to create awareness often includes an 800 number or an address that people can use to request more information.

Family, peers and associates become influential in the trial and evaluation stages of the adoption model. Mass media, at this point, primarily serves to reinforce messages and predispositions.

It is important to realize that a person does not necessarily go through all five stages of adoption with any given idea or product. A number of factors affect the adoption process. Rogers lists at least five.

- *Relative advantage*—is the idea better than the one it replaces?
- *Compatibility*—is the idea consistent with the person's existing values and needs?
- *Complexity*—is the innovation difficult to understand and use?
- *Trialability*—can the innovation be used on a trial basis?
- *Observability*—are the results of the innovation visible to others?

You should be aware of these factors and try to overcome as many of them as possible. Repeating a message in various ways, reducing its complexity, taking com-

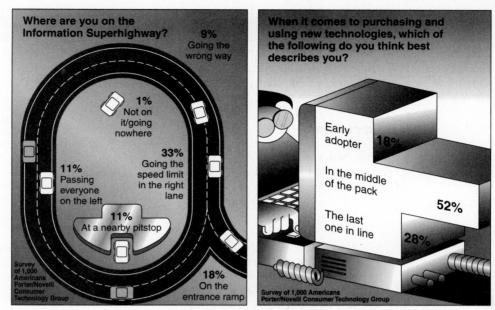

Figure 3.1 People adopt new products and ideas at varying rates. Persuasive writers try to identify and target "early adopters" because they are opinion leaders. This graphic shows the results of a survey about acceptance of new technologies. (*Courtesy of Porter/Novelli Public Relations, New York.*)

peting messages into account and structuring the message to the needs of the audience are ways to do this.

Hierarchy-of-Needs Theory

The hierarchy-of-needs theory has been applied in a number of disciplines, including communication. It is based on the work of Abraham H. Maslow, who listed basic human needs on a scale from basic survival to more complex ones:

1. *Physiological needs.* These involve self-preservation. They include air, water, food, clothing, shelter, rest and health—the minimum necessities of life.
2. *Safety needs.* These comprise protection against danger, loss of life or property, restriction of activity and loss of freedom.
3. *Social needs.* These include acceptance by others, belonging to groups, and enjoying both friendship and love.
4. *Ego needs.* These include self-esteem, self-confidence, accomplishment, status, recognition, appreciation and the respect of others.
5. *Self-fulfillment needs.* These represent the need to grow to one's full stature—simply as a human being or in terms of some special talent, gift or interest.

A BEHAVIORAL COMMUNICATION MODEL

Awareness ——▶ Latent readiness ——▶ Triggering event ——▶ Behavior

Most theories of communication end with the receipt of the message by the receiver. The assumption is that the reader will be persuaded and that the sender's objective will be accomplished.

The behavioral communication model, suggests *PR Reporter,* is better because it forces practitioners to think in terms of what causes people to pay attention to a message or take action. The four-step sequential process is as follows:

1. *Awareness.* The basic purpose of communication is to create awareness, which is the start of any behavioral process.
2. *Latent readiness.* An individual's attitudes and predispositions have a great deal of influence on whether the person is mentally prepared to pay attention to the message and take action on it. There is considerable evidence that receivers don't always respond. They may hear the message but do nothing with it.
3. *Triggering event.* This step gives people a chance to act on their latent readiness. A triggering event is something that stimulates action. It may be a telephone call from a charitable agency asking for a donation, a series of accidents on a stretch of road that makes voters finally vote for costly improvements, or the announcement of a new product on the market. Public relations people should build triggering events into their planning; this moves the emphasis from communication to behavior motivation.
4. *Behavior.* Although the ultimate goal is to motivate people to buy something or act in a certain way, they may adopt intermediate behaviors such as requesting more literature, visiting a showroom, or trying the product or idea on a limited basis.

The key is determining exactly what triggering event will cause a reaction on the part of the target audience.

Source: *PR Reporter,* August 13, 1990, p. 1.

The campaign for the National Turkey Federation mentioned earlier in the chapter is a good example of applying Maslow's concepts. Low-income people got an economical recipe that satisfied basic physiological needs. However, the fancy recipes in upscale magazines were designed to meet the ego and social needs of people who were not worried about food costs.

At times, a public relations or advertising writer can appeal to several needs at once. An ad for a new car, for example, often emphasizes economic, safety, social and ego needs. For the Baby Boomer who just turned 50, a red sports car may even satisfy self-fulfillment needs.

The main point is to understand that your audience is looking for messages that satisfy needs. If you can identify and articulate those needs, you're well on your way to being a persuasive writer.

Applying Theory to Practice

Understanding the concepts of opinion formation, the process of information diffusion and the psychological needs of audiences has a great deal of practical application for the public relations writer.

The diffusion model, for example, points out that mass and direct media are most important in the beginning stages of the process. Although the writer's goal is ultimately to change attitudes and behavior, this is difficult to accomplish unless the audience (1) is highly interested in the message, (2) is predisposed to accept it and (3) receives reinforcement of the message through their opinion leaders and peer groups.

Consequently, most writers are realistic enough to have the limited objectives of message exposure and accurate dissemination of the message, which coincide with the interest and awareness stages of the diffusion model.

Professor James Grunig at the University of Maryland further applies the diffusion model by saying that the writer has two kinds of audience: passive and active.

Passive audiences have to be lured into accepting your message. Consequently, messages directed to them need to be highly visual, use catchy themes and slogans, and contain short messages. A number of communication tools provide this format: dramatic pictures and graphics, billboards, radio and television announcements, posters, bumper stickers, buttons and special events that emphasize entertainment.

Active audiences, by contrast, are usually aware of the product, service or idea. They have reached the second stage of the diffusion process, *interest,* and are seeking more detailed information. Appropriate communication tools for them include brochures, in-depth newspaper and magazine stories, slide presentations, videotape

APPEALS THAT MOVE PEOPLE TO ACT

Persuasive messages often include information that appeals to an audience's self-interest. Here is a list of persuasive message themes:

- Make money
- Save money
- Save time
- Avoid effort
- More comfort
- Better health
- Cleaner
- Escape pain
- Gain praise
- Be popular
- Be loved/accepted
- Keep possessions
- More enjoyment
- Satisfy curiosity
- Protect family
- Be stylish
- Have beautiful things
- Satisfy appetite
- Be like others
- Avoid trouble
- Avoid criticism
- Be individual
- Protect reputation
- Be safe
- Make work easier
- Be secure

Source: Charles Marsh, "Fly Too Close to the Sun," *Communication World,* September 1992, p. 24.

demonstrations, short films, symposiums and conferences, speeches and display booths at trade shows.

In most cases, the competent communicator acknowledges the existence of both passive and active audiences by preparing a number of messages that vary in content and structure. A daily newspaper may receive an attractive publicity photo with a short caption, while a specialized trade publication might get an in-depth news release detailing the product's features. The potential customer who calls the company's toll-free number may receive a full-color brochure. The strategy of developing multiple messages for a variety of channels is detailed in Chapter 19.

PERSUASIVE WRITING

Your purpose is to persuade your target audience. Your message may be delivered in one way, a few ways, or many ways. Techniques for getting your messages into the mass media are detailed in later chapters. As you work on message content, however, keep in mind the concepts of audience analysis; source credibility; appeal to self-interest; clarity of the message; timing and context; symbols, slogans, and acronyms, semantics; suggestions for action and content and structure.

A PERSUASION SAMPLER

A number of research studies have contributed to our understanding of the persuasion process. Here are some basic ideas:

- Positive appeals are generally more effective than negative appeals, in terms of both retention of the message and actual compliance with it.
- Messages presented on radio and television tend to be more persuasive than those seen in print. If the message is complex, however, better comprehension is achieved through print media.
- The print media are more appropriate for conveying detailed, lengthy information; broadcast channels are best for presenting brief, simple ideas. Television and radio messages tend to be consumed passively, whereas the print media allow for review and contemplation.
- Strong emotional appeals and the arousal of fear are most effective when the audience has some minimal concern about or interest in the topic.
- Highly fear-arousing appeals are effective only when some immediate action can be taken to eliminate the threat.
- With highly educated, sophisticated audiences, logical appeals, using facts and figures, work better than strong emotional appeals.
- Like self-interest, altruistic need can be a strong motivator. Men are more willing to get physical checkups for the sake of their families than for themselves.
- A celebrity or an attractive model is most effective when the audience has low involvement, the theme is simple, and broadcast channels are used. An exciting spokesperson attracts attention to a message that would otherwise be ignored.

Source: Adapted from Ronald E. Rice and William J. Paisley, eds., *Public Communication Campaigns* (Newbury Park, Calif.: Sage, 1982).

Audience Analysis

A message must be compatible with group values and beliefs. Taxpayers, for example, get more interested in recycling when the message points out that trash collection costs millions of tax dollars annually or that recycling will generate revenues to keep taxes down.

Tapping a group's attitudes and values in order to structure a meaningful message is called *channeling*. It is the technique of recognizing a general audience's beliefs and suggesting a specific course of action related to audience members' self-interests. In this example, the incentive to participate in recycling programs is given a strong push by the prospect of tax savings.

However, taxpayers are only one target audience. A message to members of hiking clubs might emphasize that overflowing landfills and mountains of trash are despoiling scenic areas. Always keep in mind that the more you can segment various audiences, the more you can tailor your message to specific group attitudes.

Source Credibility

A message is more believable to an audience if the source has credibility, which is why writers try to attribute information and quotes to perceived experts. Indeed, expertise is a key element in credibility. The other two elements are sincerity and charisma. Ideally, a source will have all three attributes.

Lee Iacocca, former chairman of Chrysler Corporation, is a good example. As chairman of the auto company, he was highly credible as an expert on Chrysler products. In countless advertisements and speeches, he also came across as a candid, no-nonsense individual who sincerely believed that Chrysler products were the best on the market. Third, Iacocca had that elusive element of charisma—he was self-assured, confident, and articulate. He became a household name.

Not every company has a Lee Iacocca for its president, nor is that necessary. Depending on the message and the audience, various spokespersons can be used and quoted for source credibility. For example, if you are writing a news release about a new product for a trade magazine, perhaps the best source to quote would be the company's director of research and development. This person is a credible source primarily because of personal knowledge and expertise. If the news release is about the fourth-quarter earnings of the company, the most credible person to quote in the news release would be either the chief executive officer or the vice president for finance, both experts by virtue of their position.

Source credibility also can be hired. The California Strawberry Advisory Board, for example, arranges for a home economist to appear on television talk shows to discuss nutrition and demonstrate easy-to-follow strawberry recipes. The audience for these programs, primarily homemakers, not only identifies with the representative but also perceives the spokesperson to be an expert. Additional credibility is gained if the spokesperson comes across as being sincere about the message.

Sincerity is an important component in celebrity endorsements. Bill Cosby may not be an expert on all the products he endorses, but he sounds like he truly believes what he is saying. Sincerity and charisma are the key elements of using celebrities to provide source credibility.

Celebrities are used primarily to call attention to a product, service, or idea. The sponsor's intent is to associate the person's popularity with the product. This is called *transfer*.

On occasion, however, celebrities lose source credibility because of scandal or negative publicity. Florida orange juice producers immediately dropped Burt Reynolds as a spokesperson because of his bitter breakup with Loni Anderson. The producers thought his marital problem was at odds with the image of orange juice as a healthy, happy, family product.

In sum, the use of various sources for credibility depends in large part on the type of audience being reached. That is why audience analysis is the first step in formulating effective public relations messages.

Appeal to Self-interest

Self-interest was mentioned in connection with both Maslow's hierarchy of needs and audience analysis. A public relations writer must at all times be aware of what the audience wants to know.

Writing publicity for a new food product can serve as an example. A news release to the trade press serving the food industry (grocery stores, suppliers, wholesalers, distributors) might focus on how the product was developed, distributed, and made available to the public, the manufacturer's pricing policies, or the results of marketing studies that show consumers want the product. This audience is interested in the technical aspects of distribution, pricing and market niche.

You would prepare quite a different news release or feature article for the food section of a daily newspaper. The consumer wants information about the food product's nutritional value, convenience and cost, and wants to know why the item is superior to similar products. The reader is also looking for menu ideas and recipes using the product.

Clarity of the Message

Communication, as already stated, doesn't occur if the audience doesn't understand your message. It is important to produce messages that match the characteristics of your target audience in content and structure.

A bar association once thought it was a great idea to produce a brochure to help motorists understand liability in an accident. However, by the time the committee of lawyers added all their legalese, the brochure became useless as an aid to the general public.

One solution to this problem is to copy-test all public relations materials on the target audience. Another solution is to apply readability and comprehension formulas to materials before they are produced and disseminated. Most formulas are based on the number of words per sentence and the number of one-syllable words per 100 words.

In general, standard writing should average about 140 to 150 syllables per 100 words and the average sentence length should be about 17 words. This is the level of newspapers and weekly news magazines such as *Time*.

Timing and Context

Your message must arrive at a time when it can conveniently be considered. If it is too early, your audience may not be ready to think about it. April is not the time to talk about winter sports or sports equipment, but October might be just right. Information about income taxes is especially interesting just before the April 15 deadline, but it's "old hat" a few days later. News about a cure for male baldness gets full attention from middle-aged bald-headed men at almost any time.

Symbols, Slogans and Acronyms

The Red Cross is the best-known humanitarian organization in the world. The name is totally unenlightening, but the symbol is recognized and associated with the care and help given by the organization. Flags are symbols. Smokey the Bear is a symbol. The Christian cross, the Jewish Star of David, and the Muslim crescent are familiar symbols around the globe. You aren't likely to produce a symbol that will become world-famous, but if at all possible, you should try to find something graphic that helps individualize and identify a given organization. Trademarks and logos are examples, but even unregistered visual symbols can help.

Slogans can be highly persuasive. They state something important in a few memorable and easily pronounceable words: "Remember the Alamo," "Remember the *Maine*," "Don't give up the ship," "Votes for women," "Equal rights," "No taxation without representation," "Don't leave home without it," "Balanced budget," and so on. If you can coin a slogan that expresses the basic idea of what you are trying to promote, it will help you attain your objective.

Acronyms range from the effective to the ridiculous. Coined from the initial letters of the name of some organization or cause, an acronym can be highly useful in some cases. A good acronym is NOW, for the National Organization for Women. It is pronounceable and memorable, and it makes a succinct political point. These women are striving for equality, and they want it "NOW." Another good reason for using acronyms is to shorten a lengthy name. AIDS is much easier to comprehend and write about than "acquired immune deficiency syndrome."

PERSUASION BY REPETITION

Amateur publicists often make the mistake of failing to reinforce messages. They simply put up one poster or send one news release and call it a day. Remember that repeating the message in various forms is essential for the following reasons:

- Not all members of your audience use the same media channels to get their information.
- Repetition of the message, in various forms, reminds the audience about an idea or product.
- Repetition helps break down earlier resistance to the message.
- Repetition helps overcome competing messages and distractions.

Semantics

The dictionary definition of words may be clear and concise, but there is another dimension to words—their connotative meaning to various individuals and groups of people. The study of meaning given to words and the changes that occur in these meanings as time goes on is the branch of linguistics called *semantics*.

For example, consider the evolution of the word "gay" in American society. The word is traditionally defined as merry, joyous, and lively. Thus, in the nineteenth century, we had the "Gay Nineties" and people often referred to bright colors or sprightly music as "gay." By the 1920s and 1930s, however, "gay" started being applied as a code word for prostitutes who were said to be in the "gay life." From there, it was just a short step for the word to be applied to the "underground" world of homosexuals.

By the same token, the terms "pro-life" and "pro-choice" have very definite connotations to certain groups of people. "Affirmative action" means opportunity to some and exclusion to others. The controversy over politically correct language was cited in Chapter 1. Even the expression "politically correct" has different connotations to different groups of people. To some, it is derogatory, an attempt by radical groups to censor freedom of expression. To others, the concept stands for equality and an effort to eliminate sexism and racism.

To write persuasively and to influence target audiences, you must be sensitive to semantics. The protracted argument of the Republican Congress and President Clinton over medicare funding is a good example. The Republicans said they wanted to "preserve, protect, and strengthen" the program, while the President, and much of the press, portrayed the Republican plan as meaning major "cuts" in funding.

Suggestions for Action

Persuasive writing must give people information on how to take action, and the suggestions must be feasible.

A campaign by a utility provides a good example. If the company really wants people to conserve energy, it must provide them with information on how to do so. The suggestions may be as simple as turning the thermostat down to 68 degrees, wearing sweaters in the house during the winter months, or purchasing a roll of weather stripping to place around the windows and doors. All these suggestions are within the capability of the utility's customers.

However, if the suggestion is to insulate your house thoroughly, this may not be feasible for consumers with limited incomes. In this case, the utility may accompany the suggestion with a special program of interest-free loans or a discount coupon to make it easier for customers to take the recommended action. In this way, the suggestion becomes feasible to thousands of homeowners.

Environmental organizations, to use another example, make a point of providing information on how to write to your legislator. They provide not only the legislator's address but also a sample letter that you can copy. Greenpeace simply mails its members postcards with preprinted messages. All you have to do is sign the postcard and affix a stamp.

Content and Structure

People are motivated by theatrics and a good story. They are moved by bold action and human drama. Your message should go beyond cold facts or even eloquent phrases. If you can vividly describe what you are talking about—if you can paint word pictures—your message will be more persuasive.

A number of techniques can make a message more persuasive; many of them have already been discussed. Here is a summary of additional writing devices.

Drama   Everyone likes a good story. This is often accomplished by graphically illustrating an event or a situation. Newspapers often dramatize a story to boost reader interest. Thus we read about the daily life of someone with AIDS, the family on welfare who is suffering because of state cuts in spending, or the frustrations of a middle manager who is unemployed for the first time in her career. In the newsroom, this is called *humanizing an issue.*

Dramatizing is also used in public relations. Relief organizations, in particular, attempt to galvanize public concern to attract donations. The idea is to personalize suffering and tragedy. Saying that 3 million Africans are starving isn't as persuasive as describing a young mother in Somalia sobbing over the lifeless form of her skeletal baby. Readers and viewers can identify with the mother's loss, which graphically illustrates the need for aid. Large numbers alone are cold and impersonal and generate little or no emotional involvement.

A more mundane use of dramatizing is the application story, sent to the trade press. This is sometimes called the *case study technique,* in which a manufacturer prepares an article on how an individual or a company is using the product. Honeywell Corporation, for example, provides a number of application stories about how offices and businesses have saved money by installing Honeywell temperature control systems.

Statistics   For some reason, people are awed by statistics. The use of numbers, which appear so precise, seems to convey objectivity, largeness and importance in a credible way.

Toyota, seeking to portray itself as an important contributor to the American economy, placed ads in major metropolitan dailies that used impressive numbers. One ad stated, "Over the last five years Toyota in America has purchased $20 billion in parts and materials from 510 U.S. suppliers. Today, more than half the Toyota vehicles sold in America are built at our plants in Kentucky and California."

Numbers can be effective, but a writer should use them sparingly. A news release crammed with statistics tends to overwhelm the reader.

Surveys and Polls   The public and the media express a great deal of interest in what might be called popularity ratings. During a presidential election campaign, various polls and surveys about who's ahead and why seem to dominate coverage. People are also interested in what product ranks number one in cost or satisfaction or what airline is first in service or leg room.

Polls and surveys, which also use numbers, are related to the persuasion technique called the *bandwagon*. The idea is to show overwhelming support for your idea or product by saying that "four out of five doctors recommend . . . . " or that "65 percent of the voters support . . . . " Consequently, everyone should get on the "bandwagon." Using a poll or survey is a good device for getting audience attention and, as explained in Chapter 4, for generating news.

Examples   A statement or an opinion is more persuasive if some examples are given. The basic approach in this book is to make a statement and then give an example of the concept. In this way, generalized statements become clear and more understandable. Examples can clarify, elaborate on and reinforce basic messages.

Testimonials   The testimonial is a form of source credibility that can be either explicit or implied. The American Cancer Society may use a woman in her 50s who is dying of lung cancer as explicit testimony about the dangers of smoking. A good example of an implied testimonial is the *Washington Post*'s report that President Clinton's favorite burger was a soy-bean based veggie product made by Boca Burger Company. Sales of the product immediately boomed. Testimonials are usually given by people or organizations not formally connected with the product, service or cause.

Endorsements   The endorsement is a variant of the testimonial. Endorsements may be made by individuals, organizations or media outlets. Star athletes make millions endorsing everything from footwear to soft drinks. Organizations such as the American Dental Association endorse toothpaste brands, and daily newspapers regularly endorse political candidates and community causes.

Emotional Appeals   Persuasive messages often play on our emotions. Fund-raising letters from nonprofit groups use this writing device. Amnesty International, an organization dedicated to protecting human rights and fighting state terrorism, started one direct mail letter with the following message printed in big red type:

"We Are God in Here . . . "

That's what the guards taunted the prisoner with as they applied electrical shocks to her body while she lay handcuffed to the springs of a metal bed. Her cries were echoed by the screams of other victims and the laughter of their torturers.

An institutional advertisement for a local food bank simply showed a picture of a sad child with the headline "It's Hard to Smile When You're Hungry."

Emotional appeals can do much to galvanize public opinion, but they can also backfire. If the appeal is too strong or shocking, it tends to raise people's ego defenses, and they tune out the unpleasant message. Sometimes, the emotional appeal is designed to make people feel guilty. This kind of approach, research studies suggest, is not very effective.

United States Committee for

unicef

United Nations Children's Fund
333 East 38th St., New York, NY 10016

Hugh Downs
Chair

Dear Friend,

You couldn't tell which one at birth. . .

. . . yet one out of every five children born in some of the developing world's poorest countries will die before reaching his or her fifth birthday.

Which child will it be?

Each one is just like a child you know in your own life. Each one has unique talents and a particular potential that no other human being will ever duplicate. Each child's life is a miraculous event that will happen only once in eternity.

But all of these children are in danger, because they were born in the wrong place — a place where there isn't enough food or medicine to keep children healthy.

One of them will soon starve to death or die of a childhood disease like measles or pneumonia, and we'll lose one of these priceless treasures. And once again, a supreme tragedy will occur that will profoundly affect all of humanity.

The tragedy becomes sharper when you realize that the child's death could be prevented by a few dollars worth of food and medicine.

When confronted with this child's plight, many people turn a deaf ear . . . and ignore the fact that <u>most of the 40,000 children who will die today could easily be saved</u>.

I'm writing to you today in the hope that you'll respond to the tragedy of these child deaths. I am appealing to you as a member of the human family and asking for your help to save our children.

The United Nations Children's Fund, UNICEF, is the way you and I can help children in Mozambique, Liberia, Cambodia, and dozens of other developing countries around the world.

over, please...

Figure 3.2 Emotional appeal, combined with statistics, makes a persuasive message. Hugh Downs, a television personality, adds source credibility. Key messages are underlined. A suggestion for action (a donation) is provided on the second page, which is not shown. (*Courtesy of UNICEF.*)

Fear arousal is another form of emotional appeal. An example is "What would happen if your child were thrown through the windshield in an accident?" What makes the question effective is the fact that the message goes on to suggest that a baby, for safety, should be placed in a car seat. Moderate fear arousal, accompanied by a relatively simple suggestion for avoiding the situation, is considered an effective persuasive technique.

THE ETHICS OF PERSUASION

Robert Heath, co-author of *Rhetorical and Critical Approaches of Public Relations,* writes, "A theme that runs throughout the practice and criticism of public relations is its ability to influence what people think and how they act." He continues:

> Even when practitioners' efforts fail to establish their point of view or to foster the interests of their sponsors and influence stakeholders, their comments become part of the fabric of thought and over time add to societal beliefs and actions. Practitioners create opinions, reinforce them, or draw on them to advocate new opinions and actions.

To many observers, persuasion is a somewhat unsavory activity that distorts the truth and manipulates people. The public distrusts professional "persuaders," and the media often refer to public relations people and political consultants as "spin doctors." Yet persuasion is an integral part of society. Everyone uses words and visual symbols to share and evaluate information, shape beliefs and convince others to do or think things. The ancient Greeks recognized rhetoric, the "science of persuasion," as worthy of study and an essential part of public discourse.

In sum, persuasion is not a nasty concept. It doesn't have to be manipulative, propagandistic, or full of half-truths. Thomas Collins, manager of public affairs for Mobil Oil Company, sounded this theme when he addressed the annual meeting of the Public Relations Association of Indonesia. He said:

> PR counselors must ensure the messages we create, package, and target are efficient and cost-effective, but they must also be believable. This requires that the images we engineer reflect the reality of our clients' existence. We reject deliberate fabrication because bogus images pollute the public mind and do not serve the public interest, and ultimately undermine the trust we seek. . . . The essential ingredient underlying any successful relationship is trust.

Although public relations writers are, by definition, advocates, they also have responsibilities as professional communicators. Professor Richard L. Johannesen of Northern Illinois University lists the following ethical criteria for using persuasive devices that every public relations professional should keep in mind:

- Do not use false, fabricated, misrepresented, distorted or irrelevant evidence to support arguments or claims.
- Do not intentionally use specious, unsupported or illogical reasoning.
- Do not represent yourself as informed or as an "expert" on a subject when you are not.

- Do not use irrelevant appeals to divert attention or scrutiny from the issue at hand. Among the appeals that commonly serve such a purpose are "smear" attacks on an opponent's character, appeals to hatred and bigotry, innuendo and "God" or "devil" terms that cause intense but unreflective positive or negative reactions.
- Do not ask your audience to link your idea or proposal to emotion-laden values, motives or goals to which it is not actually related.
- Do not deceive your audience by concealing your real purpose, your self-interest, the group you represent or your position as an advocate of a viewpoint.
- Do not distort, hide or misrepresent the number, scope, intensity or undesirable features of consequences.
- Do not use emotional appeals that lack a supporting basis of evidence or reasoning and would therefore not be accepted if the audience had time and opportunity to examine the subject itself.
- Do not oversimplify complex situations into simplistic, two-valued, either/or, polar views or choices.
- Do not pretend certainty when tentativeness and degrees of probability would be more accurate.
- Do not advocate something in which you do not believe yourself.

It is clear that as a writer of persuasive messages, the public relations writer is more than a technician or a "hired gun." Responsibility to client or employer should never override responsibility to the profession and the public interest.

However, writers often lack the technical and legal expertise to know whether information provided to them is accurate. Heath explains, "In this regard, they are uneasy partners in the public relations process. They are often given information regarding managerial or operating decisions or practices that they are expected to report as though it were true and just."

This doesn't excuse writers from ethical responsibility. Heath continues:

> The problem of reporting information that they cannot personally verify does not excuse them from being responsible communicators. Their responsibility is to demand that the most accurate information be provided and the evaluation be the best available.

SUMMARY

1. Public opinion is the sum of individual opinions on a subject of importance to those individuals. The purpose of persuasive communication is to sway the opinions of individuals or to motivate them to a specific action.

2. Opinions are expressions of attitudes. Individuals get their attitudes from a variety of social, economic, cultural, educational, religious and political sources and experiences.

3. The audience's self-interest is the basis for persuasion. Self-interest includes economic, social and psychological needs.

4. The basic communication model has four elements—sender, message, channel (medium), and receiver.

5. Opinion leaders are important in the communication process. They pass on information to their followers and influence the acceptance or rejection of a message.

6. People adopt new ideas in a five-stage diffusion process—awareness, interest, trial, evaluation and adoption.

7. Mass and directed media messages are most influential in the awareness and interest stages of the adoption process. Opinion leaders and peers are influential in the later stages.

8. People are often galvanized to form opinions and take action after a "triggering event" has called their attention to an idea or a concept.

9. According to Abraham Maslow, people have a hierarchy of needs—physiological, safety, social, ego and self-fulfillment needs.

10. A communicator recognizes that there are two kinds of audiences—passive and active (information-seeking)—and plans messages and communication channels accordingly.

11. The tactics of persuasion are based on psychology. It is vital to understand why your audience thinks as it does and how and when to present your ideas.

12. The tactics of persuasive writing include concepts of audience analysis, source credibility, appeal to self-interest, clarity of message, timing and context, use of symbols and slogans, semantics, suggestions for action, and content and structure—including drama, emotional appeal and the use of examples.

13. Persuasion should not be manipulative and propagandistic; it should be based on truthful information and the presentation of ideas in the marketplace of public discussion.

EXERCISES

1. The box on page 61 describes how knowledge of American lifestyles (VALS) enabled the National Turkey Federation to structure messages to various groups. Apply the same concept to structuring messages for a chamber of commerce in a Southwestern city that wants to attract more visitors. What would the message theme be for (1) survivors and sustainers, (2) belongers and (3) achievers? Do some research in media directories. What magazines would be best to carry an article reaching each of the three groups?

2. A company wants to introduce a new 35 mm. camera to the market. Using the concept of opinion leaders, compile a list of individuals and organizations that could be targeted for initial publicity before the general public. In what ways could these individuals and groups be used for testimonials and endorsements?

3. The camera manufacturer also has to use the concepts of diffusion and adoption theory to promote the new camera. Such factors as (1) relative advantage,

(2) compatibility, (3) complexity, (4) trialability and (5) observability must be addressed in designing a persuasive message. How would you address each of these factors in terms of message content?

4. Many people have a strong belief that aid to "welfare mothers" takes too many tax dollars and only encourages women to have more babies. You work for a group that is fighting cuts in welfare spending. What information and message could you formulate to cause "cognitive dissonance" among the opponents of welfare aid?

5. The behavioral communication model states that people don't pay attention to messages unless there is some triggering event. Propose some possible "triggering events" for the following items:
   • A Red Cross campaign for more blood donations.
   • The introduction of a new, low-cost laptop computer.
   • The opening of a new flower shop.

6. Maslow's hierarchy of needs is used in public relations and advertising. Do an analysis of advertisements that appear in a magazine. What "needs" are expressed in the ads? Next, analyze the ads on the basis of what persuasive message themes are used.

7. The concept of channeling is discussed in terms of tailoring messages to audience self-interests. A city zoo wants to increase memberships and donations. What message theme would be developed for the following audiences:
   • business and industry,
   • teachers,
   • parents and
   • environmental and conservation groups.

8. Product publicity often uses experts and celebrities to build credibility and acceptance for the product. Select an expert endorser *and* a celebrity for each of the following:
   • lightweight luggage,
   • suntan lotion,
   • a campaign for literacy training,
   • hiking boots and
   • an expensive outdoor gas grill.
   Explain your rationale for selecting each individual.

9. The writing level should be geared to the audience. Standard writing contains about 140 to 150 syllables per 100 words and an average sentence length of 17 words. Select a page from a textbook and one from a weekly news magazine. Do they reflect standard writing, or are they more difficult or easier than the average?

10. One way of attracting attention is to dramatize the message. How could you dramatize the following:
   • a new four-wheel drive utility vehicle on the market;
   • a campaign to increase public school funding;
   • an information campaign to prevent AIDS.

11. After five years of limited profits and some losses, your company has had an extremely profitable year. The employees' union, which showed commendable restraint at the bargaining table, is now looking to the company for an increase in wages. Management, however, feels that all available funds must be used to repair equipment and install new and more efficient machinery if the company wants to ensure future profitability and survival. The company president asks you to draft a statement to the employees. It must be a persuasive statement explaining why there will be no wage increases this year. What would you write to persuade the employees that the company's decision is correct?

4 | *Finding and Generating News*

A major purpose of many public relations programs is to provide information to the media in the hope that it will be published or
broadcast. The resulting coverage is called publicity. *The public relations
writer who writes and places stories in the media is commonly referred
to as a* publicist.

An effective publicist needs to know three things, which are discussed
in this chapter. First, you need to be thoroughly familiar with journalistic
news values and tailor your stories accordingly. Second, you must know
where to find news in the organization and how to extract the angle that
would be most interesting to journalists and the public. Third, you must
be a problem solver and come up with creative publicity tactics that effectively break through the forest of competing messages.

BARRIERS TO MEDIA COVERAGE

Review

The purpose of media coverage, from an organization's standpoint, goes beyond news and information. Publicity is designed to advance the organization's goals. It may be used to create favorable attitudes and opinions about the organization, its products or its services. In many cases, publicity is strongly marketing oriented and designed to generate sales.

There are several barriers to getting publicity in the media, including the following:

Fight for Space

1. *Publicity Versus Advertising.* Reporters and editors ultimately decide whether an organization's information qualifies as news and is worthy of being published or broadcast. They may choose to change the order of the information, delete parts of it or even completely rewrite it. Thus a two-page news release from a company may be published as a full story, a one-paragraph news item or not at all. Advertising copy has no such barrier. The organization buys the space in which the advertisement will run, and the ad appears exactly as submitted. The material is handled by the advertising or sales department of the newspaper or broadcast station, not the news department.

2. *Shrinking News Holes.* Economic downturns and a proliferation of competition have left many publications scrambling for advertising dollars, which directly affects the news space available. Many periodicals have cut back on pages and have consequently reduced the news hole. The result is increased competition for getting your publicity accepted and published. A newspaper or trade magazine editor, for example, has hundreds of news releases and story ideas for every edition, and can use only a few. Much of this book is designed to improve your ability to generate the kind of news that editors will use.

3. *Changing Nature of the Mass Media.* The mass media are becoming increasingly fragmented, meaning that they no longer offer the opportunity to reach large numbers of people in a single effort. The "one size fits all" news release is dead. In addition, evening papers have died in many cities, morning papers have lost circulation and the three major networks (ABC, NBC, CBS) find their audiences shrinking.

4. *Information Overload.* Our society is experiencing widespread information clutter. The decline of the mass media has been accompanied by a proliferation of more specialized media—suburban weeklies, trade newspapers and magazines, cable channels, on-line networks and the Internet—all of which compete for the individual's attention. As a consequence, your organization's news, even if it does get published or broadcast, may never get the audience's attention.

Despite these barriers, the news media are indispensable if the organization's objective is to inform, persuade, and motivate various audiences. You, however, must recognize the barriers and take several steps to make your efforts more effective. They include (1) targeting the right media with your information, (2) thinking continuously about the interests of the readers or listeners, (3) keeping in mind the objectives of the client or employer and (4) exercising creativity in thinking about how to present information that will meet the requirements of media gatekeepers. Don't try to blanket the media with a blizzard of news items.

To work effectively, you must understand what makes news and how to find or create news.

WHAT MAKES NEWS

Students in newswriting classes are taught the basic components of what constitutes "news." Public relations writers, or publicists, must also be familiar with these components if they are to generate the kind of information that appeals to media gatekeepers. Aspects of news include timeliness, prominence, proximity, significance, unusualness, human interest, conflict and newness.

Timeliness

Timeliness may be the most important characteristic of news. By definition, news must be current and timely.

One way to make news timely is to announce something when it happens. An organization usually contacts the press as soon as an event occurs—the issuing of the quarterly earnings report, the appointment of a chief executive, the layoff of workers. Any delay in conveying this information could result in its being rejected as "old news."

A second aspect of timeliness is offering information linked to events and holidays that are already on the public agenda. Auto clubs and insurance companies, for example, have excellent placement success with articles about safe driving just before a long holiday weekend. Christmas is a major season for purchasing children's toys, so the media are receptive to news releases from toy manufacturers about new products on the market and what kinds of toys are setting sales records. Watchmaker TAG Heurer even received publicity by simply asking a sample of people what they would do with the extra hour when daylight savings time ended. The answer? Rest.

A third approach to timeliness relates to ongoing and current issues that are on the public's mind. Any research study relating to cancer usually gets extensive play in the media. There's also great public debate about the cost of health care, so pharmaceutical firms tailor their news releases around the idea that new "wonder drugs" are a cost-effective way of reducing long hospital stays.

Prominence

The news media rarely cover the grand opening of a store unless a celebrity is involved. For example, an electronics store generated a front-page story in the local daily simply because Vanna White, a television personality, was on hand to cut the ribbon. In smaller communities, the mere presence of a beauty queen or a local radio or television personality is often enough to attract coverage.

The presence of movie stars, rock stars and professional athletes at special events invariably draws crowds and the media to special events, but an organization can attract media coverage by using other kinds of prominent people as well. An immunization clinic for low-income children usually gets first-page coverage if a former First Lady such as Roslyn Carter pays a visit. A former astronaut visiting a local high school also generates media interest.

Giving an issue celebrity status is one way of cutting through the clutter of competing cause and less-than-exciting news. Take the issue of obesity and good health. Former surgeon general Everett Koop was tapped by a consortium of food manufacturers to talk about the importance of exercise and a healthy diet—and was immediately overwhelmed by requests for talks and media interviews.

Routine news, of course, doesn't have the glamour of a Vanna White or the public esteem of a former First Lady. But you can still gain from the use of names as much as possible in your material. For example, compare these two ways of reporting an energy conservation program at Glutz Manufacturing Company:

- The Glutz Company announced today that it is installing a new heat exchanger that will save a million barrels of oil a year.
- Henry Glutz, president of the Glutz Manufacturing Company, announced today that the company is installing . . .

The release may go on to paraphrase or quote other company executives, the head of the U.S. Department of Energy or even the leader of a national trade association who would comment on the company's decision. The idea is that names make a story more interesting. Quoting well-known or prominent people on the local, state or national level also makes the story more credible.

Note that prominence is not restricted to people; it extends also to organizations. Large multinational corporations such as IBM or Exxon automatically get more media attention because they control so many resources and affect so many lives. If you work for a smaller, less prominent company, you will have to try much harder to get media coverage.

Proximity — HomeTowner (localizer, it)

Surveys have shown that the news releases most acceptable to media gatekeepers are those with a local angle. These stories, often called "hometowners," are custom tailored for an organization or an individual's local newspaper. Typically, the local angle is in the lead and top half of the release.

Professors Linda Morton and John Warren, for example, conducted a survey of hometown releases from a major university and found a 36 percent acceptance rate by newspapers (*Public Relations Review*, Winter 1992). In contrast, generalized news releases generally get a 3 to 8 percent acceptance rate. They conclude, "Because a primary goal is to bring the writer's work before the general public through the media, hometowners are clearly an effective tool to bring this about."

PR Data Systems, a distribution service, did a content analysis of seven dailies in Illinois and Wisconsin and came to the same conclusion. Almost 70 percent of all news coverage in the business and financial sections of these newspapers, according to a report in *O'Dwyer's Public Relations Newsletter,* was devoted to local companies.

"Company-supplied national news releases fared poorly," according to Ed Harrington, director of midwestern operations for PR Data Systems. He continues, "One business editor reported he used only three of 150 releases received during the study period because all of the others lacked a local angle."

Obviously, the local angle—proximity—has strong news value. Whenever possible, it is important to "localize" information. Publicists should take the time and effort to tailor national information by including the names of local dealers, retailers and other area representatives for the news media serving a particular city or the surrounding area. According to PR Data Systems, you can achieve 700 percent more pickup by taking this extra step.

Localizing news releases and tailoring them to specific kinds of media is easily done today through computer programs that can automatically merge local people into a news release. An insurance company, for example, may have a national meeting for its agents. You would localize this event by having the computer insert the names of individual agents into the standard format of the news release. The newspaper editor in Lexington, Kentucky, would receive a news release that began, "John Smith of Lexington, an agent for Northwestern Mutual Insurance Company, has returned from the company's annual conference in New York." Hometown news releases are discussed in Chapter 5.

A more specialized form of localizing is highlighting various aspects of a person's background. If John Smith is inducted into the President's Round Table for selling $50 million of life insurance in one year, various audiences would be interested in this achievement.

For example, the weekly newspaper in the small town where John graduated from high school needs a news release that mentions John's parents, his graduation year and the fact that he was president of the senior class. In contrast, the suburban weekly in the town where John currently resides would appreciate a paragraph giving his business address, the names of his wife and children and the fact that he is the past president of the local Lions Club. A trade newspaper covering the insurance industry would be more interested in a news release that detailed his professional career.

In sum, always keep the local angle, or proximity, in mind when you write a news release. This often requires more research and writing, but the resulting media coverage is worth the effort. As news correspondent Mort Rosenblum once wrote, "A dogfight in Brooklyn is bigger than a revolution in China."

Significance

Remi… Any situation or event that is likely to affect a substantial number of people is significant. An increase in the price of heating oil is significant in the Northeast, where many homes are heated by oil. However, this news is not very significant in the

West, where most homes are heated by gas. However, an increase in the price of gasoline receives a great deal of local, regional and national coverage because it affects almost everyone.

In judging significance, you must know not only how many people will be affected but also who will be affected. A requirement that filling stations install equipment to reduce the amount of gasoline vaporized into the atmosphere was of minor interest to the public, but it was extremely significant to the oil companies and service station owners because of added costs. Consequently, the general press gave the new requirement a few paragraphs, whereas it received extensive coverage in oil industry publications.

With a little creative thinking, you can find an angle that makes a story more significant to the general public. For example, the law requiring protected gas nozzles at filling stations becomes more newsworthy when Chevron or Shell points out that the cost of conversion to new pumps will increase the price of gasoline by 2 cents a gallon.

Unusualness

Anything out of the ordinary normally attracts press interest and public attention. The presence of a giant inflated King Kong hugging an office building in Portland was certainly unusual. So was the 75-foot-long birthday cake in the shape of a snake that the San Diego Zoo used to celebrate its seventy-fifth year of operation.

Activist groups like Greenpeace and animal rights advocates often generate news coverage by staging demonstrations with protesters wearing animal costumes or conducting a mock funeral procession.

Even celebrities who have died may be useful in generating news coverage. Polaroid Corporation, for example, sponsored a Marilyn Monroe look-alike contest on what would have been her sixty-fifth birthday. Polaroid, a camera manufacturer, thought the event was appropriate because Monroe was the "most photographed celebrity in history." The media also thought so: The event generated 127 print stories and 74 broadcast mentions.

Human Interest

People like to read about other people. That is why the news media often focus on the lives of the rich and famous or even the poor and downtrodden. Michael Jackson and Lisa Marie Presley got national attention when they married—and when they divorced 20 months later—but a family who survived for a week after their car got stuck in a Nevada snowstorm also got nationwide coverage.

A journalist may focus on the plight of one welfare family to illustrate the problems of the entire social services system. Television news, which tries to explain complex issues in a minute or two, often uses the vehicle of personalizing the problem or issue by letting one individual or family speak. Indeed, people would rather listen to the problems of a welfare mother in her own words than view a series of bar charts showing the decline in state and federal funding.

Public relations writers also have opportunities to humanize stories. Here are some examples.

Figure 4.1 The unusual creates news. Getting publicity for a brand of china is a tough assignment. However, a Nieman Marcus store in suburban Chicago solved the problem by using tea cups to support a Rolls Royce. Setting up the stunt took about two hours. Meanwhile, a store vice president takes a well-planned tea break. *(Courtesy of UPI/Bettmann.)*

- A university graduates 10,000 students every spring, but the news release focuses on an 80-year-old grandmother who is graduating with her daughter and her granddaughter.
- A company that manufactures a voice-activated cellular phone for disabled people prepares a feature article about how the phone helps one disabled Vietnam veteran.
- A brilliant research engineer for a computer company is the subject of a company feature story that is sent to the trade press.
- A food bank, after getting permission, gives the names of clients to a reporter who wants to interview some of them for a story on how the agency has helped them.
- A company public relations person convinces the business editor of the local daily to do a profile on the company CEO, who first came to this country as a Vietnamese refugee speaking no English.

Conflict

When two or more groups advocate different points of view on a topic of current interest, this creates news. Indeed, reporters often fuel the controversy by quoting one side and then asking the other side for a comment.

Organizations get coverage when they state a point of view that is contrary to other points of view. The Western Livestock Producers Association got news coverage, for example, when it spoke out against environmentalists who wanted to ban cattle grazing on public lands. Forest product companies also found themselves in the public limelight when environmental groups opposed the logging and clear-cutting of old forests.

The media's interest in conflict as news, on occasion, is taken to the point of silliness. In San Francisco, a group calling itself the Coalition Against *Fantasia's* Exploitation (CAFE) urged a boycott of Walt Disney's animated musical film *Fantasia* because, among other things, the film's sequence featuring hippos in tutus was offensive to overweight people. The coalition got national coverage, including mention in a *Time* magazine cover story. Media interest was so great, in fact, that the spokespersons for the coalition finally had to admit that there was no such organization and that it was all an April Fool's joke.

Newness

Advertising and marketing people say that the two words they find most useful are "new" and "free." You will seldom use "free," but you should constantly search for something "new." Any news release announcing a new product or service has a good chance of being published. Every year, automobile companies get major coverage in the media when they announce their new models.

New uses for old products are the basis of most food publicity. There is nothing new about potatoes, walnuts, yams or avocados, yet food editors steadily publish new recipes for these and scores of other foods. On occasion, there is a genuinely new food product; not only are genetically engineered tomatoes new, but they have also generated plenty of controversy and conflict among advocates and opponents.

One note of caution. The news media are getting somewhat distrustful of claims that a product or service is "new." In many cases, the only thing "new" about a product is the packaging; from an editor's point of view, that is not "new" enough. High-technology companies have also raised reporter suspicions about new products that often turn out to be what cynical reporters call "vaporware."

HOW TO FIND NEWS

Now that you understand what constitutes news, you should have a good framework as you approach the process of finding news.

Internal News Sources

The first step is to become totally familiar with the organization you represent. One way to learn about an organization is to do research. According to Professor Robert Kendall in his text *Public Relations Campaign Strategies*, this involves looking at a variety of sources, including these areas:

- *Important Papers*—Policy statements, annual reports, organizational charts, position papers, research reports, market share, sales projections and biographies of top managers.
- *Periodicals*—Current and past issues of employee newsletters and magazines.
- *Clipping Files*—Published articles about the organization and the industry. Review the local press as well as the national and international press.
- *Other Published Materials*—Copies of the organization's brochures, speeches, slide presentations, videotapes and sales material.

DOBISKY ASSOCIATES

Media Relations for Higher Education

181 Washington St. • Keene, NH 03431 • 603-352-8181
FAX 603-352-8529

July 25, 1995

Mr. Robert D. Chadbourne
Freelance
69 Lee Street
East Longmeadow, MA 01028

Dear Bob:

After police stopped him for nearly falling asleep while driving, University of Louisville engineering instructor Mark Rajai soon decided it takes a "cool" head to stay alert behind the wheel—so he and his students invented one. Two, in fact.

Both devices—which Rajai calls Anti-Sleeping/Sleep Alarms—make use of cool air and an alarm, and can help keep you and those long-haul truckers on the road with you wide awake.

"There is a direct correlation to cold air on the temple and staying awake," says Rajai, who teaches engineering graphics in the university's Speed Scientific School.

When Rajai began his research in 1992, he focused on the time-honored driver defenses against dozing off—cranking up the air conditioner and cranking down the car windows.

Cold air alone, he determined, is enough to keep 30 percent to 50 percent of drivers alert. However, most drivers don't relish having cold air blasting in their faces, he also found.

"I needed to find a way to blow air onto the temple which was relatively comfortable," Rajai says.

Students in his engineering-design class pitched in. Two groups of four took surveys and researched designs for the two devices, which he is about to patent.

(continued)

Figure 4.2 An interesting lead and the element of newness make this letter a good "pitch" to a freelance writer. News coverage is often generated as a result of such letters. (*Courtesy of John McLain of Dobisky Associates, Keene, NH.*)

PAGE TWO
Mr. Robert D. Chadbourne
July 25, 1995

Rajai believes there's nothing on the market, although car manufacturers and others are trying to develop devices themselves.

Rajai's Anti-Sleeping/Sleep Alarms are activated in different ways for the two general types of dozing drivers.

The first type, for people who lose muscle control and nod off, fits over the back of the driver's seat, with side panels sticking out over the driver's temples. Operated off the car's cigarette lighter, the panels channel cool, comfortable air toward the driver's temples.

It also incorporates a button on the steering wheel that will set off an alarm if the driver's thumb falls away from a magnet on the steering wheel.

"It's not a loud morning alarm. We made sure it doesn't scare the driver," Rajai says.

When the driver pushes the button to turn off the alarm, the device automatically is reset and ready to go again.

Type two device deals with a different kind of snoozer—one who doesn't move or who sleeps with his eyes open, Rajai says. For this, he designed an alarm that monitors the driver's eyelids. It's like a small phone headset with a magnet near the hairline. Another magnet, so tiny that the driver won't feel it, is stuck to an eyelid.

If the driver closes his eyes or doesn't blink for 3- to 5-seconds, the alarm goes off. The headset also pipes cool air to the driver's temples.

Mark Rajai is at 502/852-7129 (Office) or 615/892-7106 (Home). For help catching up with him, call me at 603/352-8181.

Cordially,

John McLain

John McLain

JM/jd

Figure 4.2   *(continued)*

In addition to reviewing all of these sources, primarily available in published form, you must also play the role of reporter by moving around in the organization. Talk to a variety of people, ask a lot of questions, and constantly be on the lookout for something new or different. News stories don't necessarily come to you; you may have to come to the stories. Other people may have no awareness of the news value of an event or a situation, so you must be alert to clues and hints as well as hard facts.

Figure 4.3 The pitch letter from Figure 4.2 resulted in this article for *Automobile Executive*. (*Courtesy of National Automobile Dealers Association, McLean, VA.*)

A new source of a raw material may represent merely costs and quantities to the purchasing agent but may lead you to several stories. For example, a new fiber might change the characteristics of a textile, with interesting consequences for clothing manufacturers, consumers, designers and fashion writers.

A change in work schedules may affect traffic and thus be important to the community. Personnel changes and promotions may interest editors of business and trade papers. A new contract, which means hiring new employees, might be important to the regional economy. By the same token, the loss of a major contract—and its implications for the employees and community—also qualifies as significant news.

External News Sources

Ideas on how to get your organization in the news can come from almost any source. You might attend a Rotary Club meeting and hear a speaker talk about the advantages and disadvantages of the flat income tax.

That might spur you to investigate how such a proposal might affect the amount of money that corporations pay in taxes. This, in turn, might lead to the idea that your company president could generate some media coverage by talking about how the flat tax would affect the company and other corporations. And, if income tax reform is a topic on the public agenda, the local or national press might be interested in his or her thoughts on the subject. You could present the information in the form of an interview or as an op-ed in the local paper, the *New York Times* or the *Wall Street Journal*. Op-eds are discussed in Chapter 9.

A good technique for publicists is to think about how you can use news to create news. In order to do this, you need to read, listen to and watch the news for events and situations that may affect your organization. As Michael Klepper, a New York publicist, says, "This requires becoming a media junkie, which is an absolute necessity for anyone wanting to be successful in the media relations part of the business."

A new ruling by the Environmental Protection Agency (EPA) could have a major effect on a manufacturing company. A reduction in state funding could create problems for a public health agency, and changes in Medicare affect hospitals.

All news events can be used to create news, but you must think of applications to your particular organization and industry. That's the hard part. To help you do this, we will discuss creativity and brainstorming later in this chapter.

Other external sources that you can tap for ideas are polls and surveys, census reports, trade media, financial analyst reports, findings of governmental commissions, sales figures for entire industries and updates on competitors.

Professional periodicals and newsletters serving the public relations industry should not be overlooked. They often include results of surveys indicating what the "hot" topics are in the media.

A national survey of newspaper editors by News USA, a news release and feature article distribution firm, illustrates the point. The survey, reported in *PR News*, found that the topic of health generated the most interest on the part of editors. In descending order were the topics of senior citizens, medicine, agriculture, environment, food, education, consumer issues, recreation and finance. A survey of food editors by another firm indicated that low-fat and fat-free recipes and information were "hot" topics.

Valerie Basheda, a reporter for the *Detroit News,* has also researched fad topics in the media. She wrote that medicine, environment and lifestyle-related topics are fertile ground for stories.

A newsletter published by Ketchum Public Relations sums it up well: "By looking at your client's agenda and activities, and applying them to each of these subjects, [you] may realize new placement and story opportunities."

Public relations newsletters also give tips about what specific publications and editors are seeking. For example, *Jack O'Dwyer's Newsletter* reported that the editor of *Interactive Age* "is interested in getting news about companies involved in Internet banking and financial services." Tip sheets are further discussed in Chapter 10.

HOW TO CREATE NEWS

There is no hard-and-fast definition of what is news. A Hearst editor once declared, probably with more truth than he realized, "News is what I say it is." At one time, "news" was defined as any natural occurrence or act of God.

In the late 20th century, historian Daniel Boorstin coined the term "pseudo-events" to describe events and situations that are primarily created for the sake of generating press coverage. An early example is the Miss America contest, which was started more than 75 years ago and is still going strong.

THIRTY-TWO WAYS TO CREATE NEWS FOR YOUR ORGANIZATION

1. Tie in with news events of the day.
2. Cooperate with another organization on a joint project.
3. Tie in with a newspaper or broadcast station on a mutual project.
4. Conduct a poll or survey.
5. Issue a report.
6. Arrange an interview with a celebrity.
7. Take part in a controversy.
8. Arrange for a testimonial.
9. Arrange for a speech.
10. Make an analysis or prediction.
11. Form and announce names for committees.
12. Hold an election.
13. Announce an appointment.
14. Celebrate an anniversary.
15. Issue a summary of facts.
16. Tie in with a holiday.
17. Make a trip.
18. Make an award.
19. Hold a contest.
20. Pass a resolution.
21. Appear before public bodies.
22. Stage a special event.
23. Write a letter.
24. Release a letter you received (with permission).
25. Adapt national reports and surveys for local use.
26. Stage a debate.
27. Tie in to a well-known week or day.
28. Honor an institution.
29. Organize a tour.
30. Inspect a project.
31. Issue a commendation.
32. Issue a protest.

Source: Dennis L. Wilcox, Phillip H. Ault, and Warren K. Agee, *Public Relations Strategies and Tactics,* 4th ed. (New York: HarperCollins, 1995), p. 300.

FOR IMMEDIATE RELEASE

CASUAL CLOTHES GAINING GROUND IN THE OFFICE

SAN FRANCISCO (MAY 21) — A new trend in office fashion has been quietly building during the past few years as more and more companies allow their employees to wear casual clothes to the office, according to a survey released today.

In a nationwide poll of 500 human resource managers, two-thirds agreed that there is a trend toward casual dress in the workplace. Sixty-seven percent of those surveyed also said that their company allows employees to dress casually, either every day (14 percent), most days (23 percent), one day per week (26 percent) or on special occasions (24 percent). Many of these companies — 38 percent — have made the switch to casual dress within the last five years.

(more)

Figure 4.4 Lifestyle trends are popular with editors. Levi Strauss, a manufacturer of leisure clothes, distributed this news release about a trend toward more casual dress in the workplace. (*Courtesy of Levi Strauss and Company, San Francisco, CA.*)

The original idea behind the Miss America contest was to extend the tourist season in Atlantic City after Labor Day. The contest was not only good for business, but it also provided the American public with a form of entertainment.

The Miss America competition was a creative solution to the question, "How do we extend the summer season past Labor Day?" Indeed, creativity and imagination are essential attributes for work in public relations, but such things are difficult

IF IT'S MAY, IT'S NATIONAL ASPARAGUS MONTH

National organizations and trade associations often designate a week or a month to focus on an industry or a product. May is a popular month, with such designations as National Barbecue Month, National Paint Month, National Physical Fitness and Sports Month, National High Blood Pressure Month, National Home Decorating Month and Correct Posture Month.

The National Asparagus Association selected May because it marks the peak of asparagus production. By promoting the month, the trade group hopes to encourage consumption of its product at home and in restaurants. Surveys show that more meals are eaten out on Mother's Day than on any other day, and the asparagus association encourages restaurants to use its product.

The warm weather in May also prompts the National Paint and Coating Association to sponsor National Paint Month. As a spokesman says, "It's the time of year when people begin thinking about home improvements, and hence it is the perfect month to alert the public to the 'power of paint.'"

Since 1968, the American Chiropractic Association has observed Correct Posture Month during May. Proclamations recognizing May as Correct Posture Month are distributed to chiropractors, who submit them for endorsement by local, state and national officials. This lends the event a shade of governmental legitimacy. Using prominent names often makes such items acceptable to the news media and generates local coverage for chiropractors.

During the month, chiropractors are urged to get involved in community service, including activities such as free spinal checkup clinics, which also generates publicity. During the restoration of the Statue of Liberty, chiropractors donated $1 per patient visit during May toward the landmark's restoration. The association chose this project because, as one spokesperson said, "The Statue of Liberty also had a back problem."

A listing of all the days, weeks and months designated by all kinds of organizations, including governments, is published annually in *Chase's Annual Events*. The publication, published by Contemporary Books in Chicago, has 10,000 entries listed in chronological order. By consulting this publication, you will find such sponsored events as the National Volunteer Blood Donor Month (January 1–31) and National Raisin Week (May 2–8).

to teach and even more difficult to learn. One learning approach is to use a creativity checklist. Judith Rich, creative director of Ketchum Public Relations in New York, gives her version of such a list:

- Be open to new experiences.
- Recognize and challenge your own creative ability.
- Don't negate the importance of right-brain thinking.
- Encourage your mind to work in different ways.
- Interesting comments are more creative than critical ones.
- Creativity depends more on motivation and mental effort than on any other factor.

- Our primary need is to try harder, to make use of our potential.
- Don't just look for information in the "normal" places.
- Kids are the most creative people around. Listen to them.
- Don't let the "habit" approach interfere with your natural urge to be creative.
- Listen to "outsiders"—they may give you the inside track on a creative solution.
- Draw heavily on personal resources—remember the content of your dreams. Your unconscious may sometimes solve your conscious concerns.

Brainstorming

Many public relations firms, such as Ketchum, come up with creative ideas by conducting brainstorming sessions. The point of such a session is to encourage everyone to express any idea that comes to mind. An idea may be totally impractical and off the wall, but no one is allowed to say "it won't work" or "that's a stupid idea." This inhibits creative thinking and people's willingness to participate.

All ideas, regardless of their merit, can be placed on a flip chart or white board. As the team looks at all the ideas, new ideas that combine and refine the original list are usually generated. Another approach is to give everyone three colored dots and ask them to place the dots next to the three ideas they believe are best, based on feasibility, cost-effectiveness and timeliness. Then you emphasize and shape the ideas receiving the most dots.

If you have a large team of people trying to come up with creative ideas, a similar approach is to give everyone 25 to 50 notecards and ask them to jot down one idea per card. By a system of sorting, you can come up with five or six common ideas that bear further discussion.

You can do problem solving and create news in a variety of ways. The next several pages highlight the creative tactics of (1) special events, (2) contests, (3) polls and surveys, (4) top 10 lists, (5) stunts, (6) product demonstrations, (7) rallies and protests and (8) personal appearances.

THE SUPER BOWL: THE ULTIMATE PSEUDOEVENT

"The Super Bowl is as phony as a tear rolling down a press agent's cheek, but how can you not like it anyhow?" This is how Russell Baker, a columnist for the *New York Times,* describes the created event that annually attracts a television audience of more than 100 million.

The Super Bowl is a win–win situation for many commercial interests. It extends the professional football season and generates millions more in revenue for the competing teams. The television networks charge up to $1 million for a 30-second commercial spot. And local bars and restaurants throughout the land have outstanding Sunday sales.

Of course, the media crank out reams of publicity about the event where two U.S. teams play for a "world" championship.

Special Events

There are two kinds of events: those that produce publicity as a byproduct and those planned primarily to generate publicity.

An example of the first kind is an annual convention that is held whether there is publicity value or not. Publicity, in this instance, is a byproduct of the media covering some of the speakers or panel discussions. Such meetings are discussed in more detail in Chapter 18.

At times, things that occur on a routine basis can become the focus of media coverage if some creativity is exercised. A new store may quietly open its doors for business, or it can have a "grand opening" with a celebrity cutting the ribbon.

Groundbreakings are similar. You can start construction on a new office building without fanfare, or you can have a groundbreaking ceremony with the mayor and other dignitaries attending. In both cases, the events would have happened

Figure 4.5 Special events and rallies make news. The Million Man March in Washington, D.C., to celebrate unity and commitment among Black men for a better society, made news around the world. (*Courtesy of Reuters/Ron Thomas/ Archive Photos.*)

even if there had been no publicity, but they benefit from the byproduct of media coverage.

The second situation is one where publicity and media coverage is the primary goal. The Marilyn Monroe look-alike contest mentioned earlier is a good example.

Bristol-Myers Squibb was also after publicity when it staged an event at income tax time for Excedrin, a pain remedy. The company created a "tax team" to cope with Excedrin Headache #1040. The team, clad in Excedrin sweat shirts and accompanied by an eight-foot inflated Excedrin bottle mascot, stood outside post offices on April 15th and distributed samples to harried taxpayers who were there to mail their returns. The stunt made all the local television newscasts.

Parker Brothers also opted for such an event to draw attention to its game, Monopoly, which was celebrating its 60th anniversary. One event was having the tuxedoed character from the game ring the opening bell at the American Stock Exchange and announce that it is scrapping the "luxury tax" in celebration of its sixth decade.

The game company also staged an event in Atlantic City by officially correcting a 60-year-old error in the spelling of Marvin Gardens. It actually should have been "Marven Gardens," the name of the street in Atlantic City where the game's originator got the name. A full-color 25 by 25–foot replica of the Monopoly board was laid out on the Boardwalk, and a bronze sign was placed in Marven Gardens acknowledging the spelling error. The event got national and international coverage.

Anniversaries of products, institutions and events are popular as "news hooks" that generate publicity. Publicists constantly use this technique.

Contests

The contest is a common device for creating news. In fact, it is often advised that "if all else fails, sponsor a contest."

There are contests of every kind. At the local level, the American Legion sponsors high school essay contests on citizenship and Ford Dealers enthusiastically sponsor safe-driving contests for teenagers. There are also numerous Elvis look-alike contests, tractor pulls and beauty pageants.

The news value of such events often depends on the size of the city and the scope of the local media. Most metropolitan newspapers and broadcast outlets ignore most of these contests, but weekly papers in smaller towns often thrive on such material.

If the event is highly visual and unusual, it stands a good chance of getting television coverage. A "World Record Pizza Toss" in New York City sponsored by a cheese company was covered by TV stations throughout the United States, Japan, and the Far East. The winner tossed a pizza 28 feet into the air. Another contest that got plenty of TV coverage was the "Wonderbra Model Search" with 18.4 million viewers nationwide. The coverage was quite uplifting, so to speak, for the models as well as the manufacturer.

The Pillsbury annual "Bake-Off" with $1 million in prizes is a classic. General Mills also launched a national contest to find the next "Betty Crocker"—the faces of 75 winners will be combined into a new portrait of the woman who has been around as corporate icon since 1921. Not to be outdone, Campbell Soup named an 11-year-old California boy as the winner of its "Art of Soup" contest that drew 10,000 competitors.

Cover Girl/YM Model Search Begins

Cover Girl Supermodels Tyra Banks (second from right) and Niki Taylor (second from left) celebrate the 1995 High School Cover Girl Model Search with three finalists. The contest is co-sponsored by YM Magazine and Cover Girl Cosmetics.

(NAPS)—Want to be the next Niki Taylor, Rachel Hunter, or Tyra Banks? Here's your chance! Once again, Cover Girl Cosmetics and Young & Modern (YM) Magazine have launched their annual search for a young woman with the personality, poise and clean, fresh natural beauty of a Cover Girl model. The High School Cover Girl Model Search is now in its 35th year and is open to teen-age girls in grades 7-12 in the United States, Puerto Rico and Canada. For those who have dreamed of becoming a model, the time to apply is now!

The prize:

• Ten lucky finalists will be selected for a dream-come-true trip to New York City (all expenses paid!) where they'll spend an exciting week filled with sightseeing and photo sessions. All ten finalists will appear in YM's November '96 issue.

• The winner will receive a $10,000 modeling contract, appear in a national ad for Cover Girl Cosmetics and on YM's November cover.

To enter:

• Submit an essay (75 words or less) that discusses your goals, accomplishments and interests, and include any previous modeling experience.

• Submit two recent photos (at least one in color) with name, address, telephone number, school name and grade, age, height, weight, and measurements on the back of each print.

Send to: High School Cover Girl Model Search, c/o Marina Maher Communications, Dept. IA, 400 Park Avenue, New York, NY 10022. Entries for this year's contest must be received by March 15, 1996. The ten finalists will be chosen in late April. Good luck!

Figure 4.6 Contests generate news coverage. This camera-ready article was distributed by North American Precis Syndicate on behalf of the contest sponsors. (*Courtesy of North American Precis Syndicate, New York.*)

Contests can also be held on a global basis. Visa International, as part of its sponsorship of the 1996 Olympics, held a global youth art contest that was conducted in the United States and 19 other nations. See Figure 5.2 for a copy of the news release.

Polls and Surveys

The media seem to be fascinated by polls and surveys of all kinds. Public opinion is highly valued, and much attention is given to what the public thinks about issues, political candidates, quality of products and so on.

Thus, organizations can sponsor polls and surveys for publicity purposes. Bausch & Lomb is a good example. It wanted to position itself as a new player in the dental field, so it commissioned a national periodontal awareness survey. The results were published in a front-page story in a leading medical journal and in the dental trade press. The general public was reached with articles such as "dumb about gums" in the *Chicago Tribune,* which was syndicated nationally.

In another example, a drug company sponsored a survey of cancer patients and found that they generally were not aware that infections were the most "life-threatening risk" of some chemotherapy treatments. Of course, the survey provided the perfect opportunity to showcase the company's infection-fighting drug.

In both cases, surveys and polls were used not only to create public awareness but also to help create a market for a product.

Nancy Hicks, a senior vice president of Hill & Knowlton, says surveys and polls can be marvelous publicity opportunities if a few guidelines are followed. In an article for PRSA's *Tactics* (November 1994), she suggested:

- *The topic.* It should be timely, have news value and fit the needs of the organization.
- *The research firm.* It should be one that has credibility with journalists. That's why many commissioned surveys are done by the Gallup Organization or similar nationally known firms.
- *The survey questions.* They should be framed to elicit newsworthy findings.

Hicks also suggests paying attention to how the material is packaged for the press. "The lead in the news release should feature the most newsworthy findings, not what is of most interest to the sponsoring organization," says Hicks.

Press kits should include background information on the organization and on the research firm, a summary of the major research findings and simple charts and graphs that can be easily reproduced as part of a news story. Press kits are further discussed in Chapter 9.

Top 10 Lists

Surveys and polls, although credible, take time and can be expensive. A less expensive way to create news of this sort is to simply compile a "Top 10 List."

Fashion Institutes issue lists of the "Top 10 Best Dressed Women," and environmental groups compile lists of the "Top 10 Polluters." Newspapers and maga-

Better Homes and Gardens ® **FAMILY NETWORK**

FOR: IMMEDIATE RELEASE   Contacts: Naomi Mintz
                                                 212/536-8832
                                                 Karen Frankel
                                                 212/536-8774

REUNIONS CAPTURE AMERICA'S RENEWED FAMILY SPIRIT

Survey Finds 70% Have Attended Reunions;
Over 1/3 Plan to Hold Them Regularly

America has rediscovered the family — not just on Madison Avenue and in prime-time television, but in real life. From small towns to big cities, the time-honored tradition of the family reunion is enjoying a renaissance.

The popularity of reunions was gauged recently by a <u>Better Homes and Gardens</u> Family Network survey. More than 70 percent of respondents said they had attended at least one reunion, and, on the average, they reported having gone to nearly four. The future of reunions looks promising as well: One-third of the respondents hold or plan to hold reunions on a regular basis.

- more -

Figure 4.7 Surveys make news. *Better Homes and Gardens* used a survey about the popularity of family reunions to reposition itself as a magazine for the entire family. A large number of weekly and daily newspapers used the news release. (*Courtesy of Ketchum Public Relations, New York.*)

zines also get into the act by compiling a list of the "Top 10 College Basketball Players," or the "Top 10 Newsmakers" of the year.

Blistex, Inc. created a variation on the top 10 list by compiling a list of newsmakers with the "world's most beautiful lips." Recent celebrities named to the "hall of fame" were Steven Spielberg for the "most prehistoric lips" and Joe Montana

PIZZA'S BEST TOPPING: PUBLICITY

Perhaps the most unusual survey is Domino's annual "Pizza Meter," a largely pepperoni-in-cheek survey of 500 delivery drivers and managers. The survey, first conducted in 1986, is billed as an index to the nation's appetite based on news events. Among the findings of the 1995 survey:

- On the day that Jerry Garcia died, mushroom-topped pizza orders to Domino's outlets increased nationwide by 61 percent.
- When Colin Powell announced he would not run for president, Domino's orders from the White House rose 18 percent.
- The 15 minutes before the jury announced the O.J. Simpson verdict was one of the busiest ordering periods in the company's history.
- The 1995 World Series was reported as the lowest in pizza orders for any World Series since the advent of the Pizza Meter.

Relating pizza orders to news events creates a barrage of media coverage every December when the Pizza Meter results are released.

The CNN news anchor broke into laughter as he read the report; Jay Leno devoted six minutes to the survey on the "Tonight Show"; and such publications as *Time, USA Today, Glamour, Playboy,* and *Cosmopolitan* gave space to it. In addition, many daily papers ran the story after it was distributed by Associated Press (AP).

for "lips too good to pass up." And, of course, David Letterman was named for having "top ten lips."

The company, through the assistance of Golin/Harris Communications, has been doing the "most beautiful lips" for more than a decade. The result is about 200 million impressions annually (circulation of publication or audience size of radio and television stations) for Blistex. The effort keeps Blistex a top-of-mind brand for consumers and also positions the company as an authority on lip care.

There are endless possibilities for top 10 lists. A San Francisco public relations firm even got eight inches in the *Wall Street Journal* for its "Top 10 most humiliating public relations gaffes of the year." First place went to the District of Columbia Housing Authority, which issued a news release about a drug bust the night before the raid was planned. The dealers heard about it on the radio and failed to make an appearance.

WINDOWS 95: HYPE AT ITS BEST

Microsoft Corporation pulled out all the stops in generating news for its improved product, *Windows 95*. The $200 million campaign, the most spent on any product introduction in recent history, was itself the subject of countless news stories.

Microsoft was able to generate publicity through the use of staged events, celebrities and stunts. Here is a sampling:

- The payment of a large fee to the Rolling Stones for permission to use their song, "Start Me Up." This was the first time that the band had allowed the commercial use of their music, which was news in itself.
- Jay Leno was commissioned to be the master of ceremonies at the official product launch at corporate headquarters. Jennifer Aniston and Matthew Perry, stars of "Friends," did a one-hour infomercial video.
- Sponsorship of one day's edition of the *London Times*. About 1.5 million copies, included was a large advertising supplement on Microsoft, were given away.
- Contest. The first person in the world to buy a *Windows 95* upgrade. The honor went to a New Zealand college student.
- Flood-lighted the Empire State Building in the colors of *Windows 95*.
- Local events in multiple nations. Stores stayed open past midnight, and hoards of computer junkies stood in long lines at special events for a chance to get a free copy.

Stunts

Journalists often disparage publicity stunts, but the fact is that these stunts do get coverage.

When President Bush banned broccoli from *Air Force One* and publicly admitted that he didn't like the dark green vegetable, growers and packers immediately sent a whole truckload to the White House and garnered massive publicity along the way. The news media not only followed the progress of the truck from California but spent a lot of time in humorous speculation on whether the President would accept the shipment.

As it turned out, Barbara Bush did accept the broccoli on the White House lawn with the press in full attendance. Back at the packing shed, orders for broccoli rolled in. "We could have spent $500,000 on ads in trade journals and not had anything like this," a packing house executive said.

On a smaller scale, the National Hot Dog and Sausage Council got press coverage when they took exception to the $1,000 fines levied against three Seattle Seahawks players for eating wieners on the sidelines during an exhibition game. The trade group sent the coach six pounds of hot dogs, daring him to resist their "great taste."

Stunts, however, can backfire. Mayor Frank Jordan of San Francisco, running for re-election, posed for photos in a shower with two local disc jockeys and got a lot of publicity. However, the public was not impressed and he lost the election.

Stunts are part of a publicist's inventory, but they should be used with caution. Stunts must fit the personality of the organization, be timely and not cause the public any inconvenience.

Product Demonstrations

The objective of a demonstration is to prove something. One computer company, for example, demonstrated its new laptop computer by taking reporters on a flight from New York to Los Angeles and letting each reporter use the new product during the trip.

Data General took another approach for demonstrating its computers. It arranged for Tom Brokaw to jog in New York's Central Park while experts critiqued his running form on the "Today Show" using the company's hardware.

A lighthearted but equally effective demonstration of proof was a "wedding kiss workshop" sponsored by a lipstick manufacturer. To demonstrate its smearproof lipstick, the company used the two stars of the off-Broadway hit *Tony and Tina's Wedding*, who were introduced as kissing experts. During the one-hour workshop, staged exclusively for media representatives, actors demonstrated kissing techniques and five brides-to-be competed for the title of "best kisser." The story made the *Wall Street Journal* and CNN News.

Hotels and resorts also do "product demonstrations" by inviting journalists to spend a weekend at the facility. Food companies do demonstrations by getting representatives on cooking and home shows. Weber Grills, for example, hired a well-known chef to give tips on talk shows about the proper way to barbecue.

CORPORATE NEWS BUREAUS GENERATE NEWS

A number of companies have formed corporate news bureaus and "institutes" to distribute research studies and lifestyle information as a method of generating media placements.

Reebok, for example, has the Aerobic Information Bureau, and Quaker Oats has organized the Gatorade Sports Science Institute. Schering Corporation, manufacturer of Chlor-Trimeton allergy tablets, serves the pollen-conscious public with its Allergy Season Index.

The allergy index relies on the forecasts of allergists in 35 metropolitan areas to let the public know what parts of the country will experience high concentrations of pollen and other allergy-provoking substances. "Local papers and news shows jump on it because they see it as a service to the public," says Chlor-Trimeton product manager Lauren Raabe. Such coverage also helps the visibility of the company.

Reebok, through its information bureau, distributes the results of scientific studies about aerobics and the use of proper gear for exercise. The information is factual and devoid of brand names, but it does position the company as an expert in the market when media stories attribute the study to the Reebok Aerobic Information Bureau.

The Kellogg Company, manufacturer of breakfast cereals, also gets a publicity dividend by providing general information about healthy diets under the banner of the Kellogg Nutrition Project.

Rallies and Protests

A rally or protest may be a large event such as the "Million Man March" that took place in Washington, D.C., or it could be as small as a group of high school students showing support for a fired coach.

Few television stations or newspapers can resist covering a rally or a protest demonstration, each of which has high news value from the standpoint of human interest and conflict. Moreover, a rally or protest is event oriented and has action, which is ideal for television coverage and newspaper photographs.

In almost all cases, a demonstration is planned in advance. The manuals of activist groups, for example, point out that supporters should be asked to participate and bring placards and signs. In addition, the media should be contacted in advance to assure coverage. Prominent people and celebrities, if possible, should be asked to join the march or give a talk at a rally. Prominence, as activists know, is another important news value.

Protests and rallies, however, aren't just a publicity tool of pro-life, animal rights, and environmental groups. They are also used by labor unions, candidates for elective office and corporations. In one situation, employees of a company held a protest rally in front of a newspaper office after the paper ran a story critical of the company's products and its lack of quality control. Other news media in the city as well as the offending newspaper covered the rally.

Figure 4.8 Demonstrations make news. Television, in particular, covers such events because they are highly visual, often portray conflict and involve human drama. (*Photo by Bob Daemmrich/Stock, Boston.*)

GENERATING NEWS: A ROAD MAP TO SUCCESS

How do you generate news and publicity for a road atlas that has been published 66 times before? That was the dilemma facing Rand McNally as it prepared to promote its new edition.

The Chicago office of Ketchum Public Relations was asked to apply its creative and strategic thinking to the problem. Reviewing the revisions to the atlas that were the result of consumer requests, Ketchum staffers found the creative solution they were looking for in the form of a handwritten letter from a 10-year-old boy in Mishawaka, Indiana.

Young Chris Muncy had written to Rand McNally asking that Parrott, Virginia, the home of his grandparents, be added to the road atlas. After company cartographers confirmed that the town of 800 citizens met their criteria, Chris was notified that his wish would be granted.

Ketchum believed that the story of a boy putting his grandparents' town "on the map" had tremendous publicity value as a human interest story. Ketchum worked with the citizens of Parrott to hold a Chris Muncy Day and a local parade. Ted McNally, vice president and great-great-grandson of the company's founder, presented the boy with the first copy of the new edition, which Chris then presented to the citizens of Parrott.

The boy's letter, parade, and presentation were the subject of national press and video releases. Special regional mailings were sent to media in Virginia and Indiana.

The result was the most effective publicity launch in the 67-year history of the road atlas. Exclusive stories appeared on ABC-TV *World News Tonight* and in *People* magazine, and an Associated Press story ran in more than 100 newspapers nationwide. The video news release was broadcast on more than 30 television stations across the nation.

A special news feature aired by CNN was also adapted for a special video presentation seen by passengers on American and United Airlines flights for two months. Chris was interviewed on such radio programs as the *Tom Snyder Show* and was even invited to appear on the game show *To Tell the Truth*.

Ketchum's efforts on behalf of Rand McNally earned it an award for creative public relations from *Inside PR* magazine, which explained its selection in this way: There are two keys to the success of a creative public relations idea: the first is that it must be inherently interesting, amusing, exciting, and newsworthy; the second is that there must be some logical connection between the creative idea and the strategic objectives of the program. Rand McNally's Parrott Makes the Map program fulfilled these two criteria perfectly.

Personal Appearances

Two kinds of personal appearances generate news. First is the kind where news is incidental to something else. Second is the appearance where news is the only objective. Most typical of the first type is the situation where someone makes a speech to an organization. If the president of the XYZ company addresses the local chamber of commerce, he will be heard by all who attend the meeting.

The audience for the speech, however, may be greatly increased if the media are supplied with copies of the speech or a news release summarizing what was said. As a general rule, every public appearance should be considered an opportunity for news both before and after the incident. And, of course, there should always be an effort to get reporters to attend the meeting and get the story themselves.

Appearances where publicity is the sole objective take several forms. One is the appearance on a radio or television talk show. There are numerous opportunities for appearing on such shows. For example, there are now more than 1,000 radio stations in the nation (out of 10,000) that emphasize talk instead of music.

Local TV stations and cable systems have their shows, and there are national shows such as *Meet the Press, Face the Nation* and *Larry King Live.* Reaching an even larger audience are the daytime syndicated shows such as *Oprah Winfrey,* which has about eight million viewers daily. Chapter 8 discusses how to get on such shows.

Another approach is the tour. Colin Powell went on the speaking circuit to promote his book and singer Tony Bennett did a series of personal appearances on behalf of WordPerfect's new line of software. Former surgeon general Everett Koop, mentioned earlier, did a number of personal appearances as part of his campaign to promote healthy diets.

The Internet also provides for a "personal appearance" of sorts. In one situation, the president of a company did a question and answer (Q&A) with a Usenet group.

SUMMARY

1. A major objective of many public relations programs is to get publicity for the employer or client.

2. Publicity is not an end in itself. It is a means to help achieve organizational goals and objectives.

3. Publicists should thoroughly understand the basic news values of (1) timeliness, (2) prominence, (3) proximity, (4) significance, (5) unusualness, (6) human interest, (7) conflict and (8) newness.

4. The first step in preparing publicity is to be thoroughly familiar with the company or organization.

5. A public relations writer should constantly monitor current events and situations that may affect the organization and provide opportunities for publicity.

6. Problem-solving skills and creativity are required to generate publicity.

7. Creative solutions can be developed through brainstorming sessions.

8. Some opportunities for generating publicity include (1) special events, (2) contests, (3) polls and surveys, (4) top 10 lists, (5) stunts, (6) product demonstrations, (7) rallies and protests and (8) personal appearances.

EXERCISES

1. It is important for public relations writers to know everything about a company or an organization to determine story angles that may be of interest to the news media. Select an organization to research. Find out the following things about it:
   a. Size
   b. Number of plants and where located
   c. Number of employees
   d. Products
   e. Competitive position in the marketplace
   f. Unique aspects
   g. Number of shareholders
   h. Possible medical or safety hazards of the company's products
   i. Names and background of key executives
   j. Use of trademarks
   k. Key publics
   l. Trends affecting the industry

   A variety of library sources as well as literature from the company can be of help. Once this material is assembled, what timely story angles about the company can you compile?

2. A Japanese restaurant chain in the United States is celebrating its twenty-fifth anniversary next year. The owners of the chain see this as an opportunity to garner publicity and perhaps motivate more Americans to patronize the local franchise. What activities and special events would you recommend that would attract media coverage?

3. Companies and retail outlets often generate publicity by associating with a holiday such as the Fourth of July, Thanksgiving, or Valentine's Day. Develop some ideas on how a delivery service such as Federal Express or United Parcel Service might tie in to a holiday.

4. Special events are often organized to generate publicity for an organization. Suggest a special event for each of the following:
   a. A manufacturer of computers
   b. A retail clothing store
   c. A hospital
   d. A charitable agency
   e. An insurance company
   f. A university

5. It is important to localize news if you want coverage in community newspapers. Suggest a way to localize each of the following items:
   a. A national airline has just compiled the number of flights, mileage, and total passengers carried last year.
   b. A computer company has introduced a new laptop computer.
   c. A national manufacturing company with plant sites in 100 different cities has just announced its annual earnings and stock dividend.

    d. A company has just developed a computerized map system for use in automobiles—a display on the dashboard portrays a map and shows the motorist's progress by means of a red light.

    e. A charitable agency has just released national figures on the number of Americans afflicted with AIDS.

6. Surveys indicate that the topic of health generates a lot of media interest. How could a manufacturer of vacuum cleaners use this topic to generate some publicity for the company?

7. A beer company is interested in doing some sort of poll or survey that would generate media coverage. What would you recommend?

8. An architectural firm likes the idea of creating a "top 10 list." What ideas do you have for such a list?

9. One company demonstrated a laptop computer on a plane trip for reporters. How else could you generate publicity for a new laptop computer on the market?

10. Organize a brainstorming session in the class on the question, "How can women's sports at the university generate more community awareness and support?"

PART
2

Writing for Mass Media

Each mass medium requires a different format and approach, and you must master all of them. Consequently, the next seven chapters describe a nuts-and-bolts approach to writing for various mass media as well as how to get your stories published or broadcast.

☐ *Chapter 5, "The News Release,"* explores the importance of news releases, planning the news release, formatting the release, types of releases, the parts of the release, writing effective lead paragraphs, maximizing publicity and mistakes to avoid.

☐ *Chapter 6, "The Feature Story,"* discusses the value of features, getting ideas and angles, types of features, the parts of a feature and placement opportunities.

☐ *Chapter 7, "Photos and Graphics,"* explains the elements of a good publicity photo, writing the photo caption, packaging and distribution, the advent of infographics and maintaining the artwork file.

☐ *Chapter 8, "Radio and Television,"* covers radio news releases, television news releases and VNRs and placement opportunities.

☐ *Chapter 9, "Pitch Letters, Advisories, News Conferences and Op-Ed,"* describes how to write effective pitch letters, media advisories, fact sheets, corporate backgrounders, press kits, media interviews, news conferences, satellite media tours, letters to the editor and op-ed articles.

☐ *Chapter 10, "Media Lists, Mailings and the Internet,"* examines using media directories, mailing lists, fax, electronic wire services, feature placement firms, CD-ROM, the Internet, the World Wide Web and Usenet.

☐ *Chapter 11, "The Basics of Media Relations,"* discusses how media and public relations depend on each other, areas of friction, guidelines for effective media relations and crisis communications.

5 | *The News Release*

A news release, or press release, is a basic element of almost every publicity plan. There are, however, two sobering thoughts about news releases. First, some studies estimate that between 55 to 97 percent of all news releases sent to media outlets are never used. Second, there is massive competition for the attention of media gatekeepers. Most publications receive about 300 to 500 news releases a month. The two major electronic distributors, Business Wire and PR Newswire, transmit an average of 900 releases a day.

Given the odds, this means that you must do three things if your release is to stand a chance of getting published. First, you must follow a standardized format. Second, you must provide information that will interest the audience of the medium that receives it. And third, your news release must be timely.

This chapter outlines how to prepare news releases that will meet these criteria. The emphasis is primarily on print media in this chapter. Chapter 8 deals with broadcast releases.

THE VALUE OF NEWS RELEASES

So why write a news release? The primary reason, of course, is to help achieve organizational objectives. The adoption theory model discussed in Chapter 3 points out that people start the process of decision making after awareness has been created.

News releases, when they form the basis of stories in the news columns of newspapers and magazines or are part of a television news show, create awareness about ideas, situations, services, and products. A new product on the market, or an appeal for Red Cross blood donations, is brought to the attention of the public. A manufacturer of a potato-chip maker, for example, sold out its entire stock after the *New York Times* included parts of a news release in an article about new kitchen gadgets.

News releases are also cost-effective. Almost any organization, from the garden club to IBM, can create and distribute news releases at nominal cost compared to the cost of buying advertising. There's also the factor of credibility. News releases appear in the news columns of newspapers, and studies consistently show that people consider information in a news story much more believable than an advertisement.

In one such study, the Wirthlin Group surveyed a sample of 1,023 adults. Almost 30 percent of the respondents said a news article would affect their buying decisions as opposed to only 8 percent who indicated the same for an advertisement.

PLANNING A NEWS RELEASE

Writing a news release requires the tools and equipment described in Chapter 1. The following sections discuss the selection of paper, some fundamentals about word processing a release, and the style you should follow. But before writing anything, the public relations writer should complete a planning worksheet.

The Basic Questions

Your planning worksheet should answer the following questions:

- What is the subject of the message? What is the specific focus of this release?
- Who is this message designed to reach? For example, is it aimed at local citizens, or is it mainly for executives in other companies who read the business page and might order the product?
- What is in it for this particular audience? What are the potential benefits and rewards?
- What goal is the organization pursuing? What is the organization's purpose? Is it to increase sales of a product? Position the company as a leader in the field? Show company concern for the environment?
- What do you want to achieve with the news release? Is the objective to inform, to change attitudes and behavior, to increase attendance at a local event?
- What themes should this news release highlight? How can they be tailored to the interests of the audience?

These questions enable you to select and structure the content of a news release from a public relations perspective. The release can still meet the journalistic goal of presenting information objectively and in proper newspaper or broadcast style, but it must also be carefully crafted to advance organizational objectives. This kind of planning is the major difference between writing as a journalist and writing as a public relations person.

You must, however, think like a journalist and do another checklist to ensure that you have covered the five Ws and H: who, what, when, where, why and how. If you have the answers to these questions written down and at your fingertips, you are ready to begin.

Selection of Paper

The standard paper for a news release is white, 8 1/2 by 11 inches and 20-pound weight. This is the usual grade sold in most office supply stores. The paper should be suitable for high-speed copiers, offset duplicators, ink jet printers and laser printers. This is because most news releases are now produced on a word processor and printed out on a laser printer. For the multiple copies that are usually needed, high-speed office copiers are used.

Some publicists suggest that paper costs can be reduced by using a legal-size sheet, 8 1/2 by 14 inches, for releases that run just a bit longer than the standard 8 1/2 by 11 sheet. A better idea, however, is first to see if the release can be edited to fit the smaller page size. Indeed, a good rule is always to try to reduce the length of your releases. You'll save in collating, paper and sometimes postage costs.

The use of colored paper for a news release doesn't get much support from experienced publicists, despite the argument that a colored release will stand out from the mass of white paper that piles up in a newsroom. Most editors say colored releases are treated like other releases and are evaluated only for their news value.

If color does strike your fancy, use pastel colors such as ivory, light blue, light green, or pale yellow. Don't use dark colors; they make words hard to read. The same goes for brilliant colors such as shocking pink, Day-Glo green, or bright yellow. The editor wants facts, not a rainbow.

Spacing and Margins

Double-spacing is the standard for news releases. Double-spaced copy is easier to read at the draft stage, and editors find that the extra space allows them to do editing and rewrites.

However, there is increasing use of single-spaced news releases. This has occurred because many releases today are transmitted to publications and broadcast outlets via E-mail or electronic networks (Business Wire or PR Newswire) that automatically place the news release in a newspaper's computer. Editors, by calling up the news release on their PCs, can change the format to anything they want.

In general, if your news releases are going to a variety of publications, it's still wise to double-space them. Many government agencies, however, have the standard practice of single-spacing news releases. Agency heads say its saves paper, trees, and postage when many news releases are distributed on a daily basis. This is true, but another solution is to write shorter news releases and fewer of them.

Some organizations have also started to put copy on both sides of the paper. This, however, is not widely accepted and you should check with media outlets before doing this.

Standard margins for a news release are two inches from the top of the page and about 1.5 inches on each side, plus the bottom of the page. If you are using letterhead, you would start writing copy about two inches below it.

Some other formatting rules:

- Use 10- or 12-point standard type. Courier is a popular font. Avoid "squeezing" copy to fit one page by reducing the size of type. It's self-defeating.
- Don't split sentences or paragraphs between pages.
- Never hyphenate a word at the end of a line. Unjustified right margins are acceptable.
- Number the pages of a news release.
- Place a slug line (short description) at the top of each page after the first one. This identifies the story in case the pages get separated.
- Write "more" at the end of each page if the news release continues.
- Write the old journalistic term "–30–," "end," or "###" at the end of your news release.

Use AP Style

The *Associated Press Stylebook* is the standard reference for writing news releases because most newspapers use "AP style" or some variation of it. If a news release conforms to AP style, it makes the work of reporters and editors much easier.

Lorry Lokey, general manager of Business Wire, says that thorough knowledge of AP style helps tailor your news release to the person who ultimately decides if it is published. He says, "Editors are your customers, to put it bluntly; you are trying to sell them on your 'story.' Put roadblocks in their way via faulty style and they are likely to take their business to someone else's release."

Lokey also complains that public relations writers don't seem to notice that most newspapers keep paragraphs limited to less than six typeset column lines. Instead, far too many news releases have paragraphs that are six to 10 typed lines, the equivalent of nine to 18 newspaper column lines. More aspects of style are discussed later in this chapter.

TYPES OF NEWS RELEASES

A news release can be prepared on virtually any subject that would affect or interest a general or specialized audience. Indeed, in the course of a year, an organization prepares and distributes news releases on a variety of subjects. There are five basic types of news releases, although the lines between them sometimes blur. They are (1) announcements, (2) spot announcements, (3) reaction stories, (4) bad news and (5) the "hometown" release.

NISSAN MOTOR CORPORATION
U.S.A.

NISSAN MOTOR CORPORATION AWARDS $100,000 TO NAACP

BALTIMORE MD, December 28, 1995—Nissan Motor Corporation U.S.A. today donated $100,000 to the National Association for the Advancement of Colored People (NAACP) on behalf of its employees in America to help the venerable civil rights organization get off to a fresh start under its new leader, Rep. Kweisi Mfume (D-MD).

"We as a corporation and individuals, will not stand on the sidelines and watch the parade go by," said Jerry Florence, Nissan Vice President, Brand and Consumer Marketing. "The NAACP has faced the future head-on and we want to help the organization become better, stronger and healthier. That's a tall order, and one that can only be fulfilled by a decisive leader, who can rally divergent constituencies around a common goal."

Florence presented the $100,000 check to Rep. Mfume during a news conference at NAACP headquarters in Baltimore. Mfume, who has been in Congress since 1987, plans to resign on Feb. 15 to become head of the 86-year-old civil rights organization.

"We applaud Nissan for taking this important step in helping the NAACP to achieve its goals," said Congressman Mfume. "This is surely a clear indication to the corporate community that it's all right to join again in the efforts of the NAACP."

In North America, Nissan's operations include styling, engineering, manufacturing, sales, consumer and corporate finance, and industrial and textile equipment. Nissan in North America employs more than 22,000 people in the United States, Canada and Mexico and generates nearly 75,000 jobs through its 1,594 Nissan and Infiniti dealerships across the continent.

# # #

Contacts:
Ed Lewis, Nissan North America (DC): 301-384-4312(h) 202-466-4471(o)
Dierdre Dickerson, Nissan North America (LA) 310-767-6461

Corporate Office 18501 South Figueroa St., Carson, California
Mailing Address: P.O. Box 191, Gardena, California 90248-0191 Telephone: (310)532-3111

Figure 5.1 A news release should be well written and follow a basic format. Good margins, short paragraphs, and quotes make it easy to read. Notice that the contact gives both his home and office telephone numbers so reporters can easily reach him. (*Courtesy of Nissan Motor Corporation, Gardena, CA.*)

Announcements

Announcements herald such occurrences as personnel appointments, promotions, and changes; new products or services (if they are really new and interesting); reports of sales, earnings, acquisitions, mergers, events, awards, honors, policy

CONTACT:
Sandra Stairs
Visa International
(415) 432-2416

Larry Koffler
Ann Wool
Edelman PR
(212) 704-8162/8118

**VISA OLYMPICS OF THE IMAGINATION
SPANS THE GLOBE FOR YOUNG ARTISTS
WITH A VISION OF THE FUTURE**

*Five Children from the United States Join an International
Team of 30 at the 1996 Olympic Summer Games in Atlanta*

SAN FRANCISCO, CA, October 10, 1995 -- An active imagination and artistic talent will be the key
ingredients for schoolchildren ages 11 through 13 who want to win a trip to the 1996 Olympic
Summer Games by entering the "Visa Olympics of the Imagination," a global youth art contest that
begins this week across the United States and in 19 other countries worldwide.

Schoolchildren from 20 countries will be challenged to create their vision of a futuristic
Olympic sport for a chance to win an Olympic package for two to the Centennial Olympic Games next
summer in Atlanta. All entries must include a written description of how the new Olympic sport
might promote world peace and unity.

"The future of the Olympic Games and the ideals of fair play and determination lie in the
hands of our children," said Ed Jensen, president and CEO of Visa International. "We are thrilled to
further these Olympic ideals and celebrate 100 years of the Modern Olympic Movement by bringing
children of the world together to share their visions of the Olympic Games."

Five children from the United States will be selected to the international team of 30 artists
who will be flown to Atlanta to attend five days of exciting Olympic events ranging from Track and
Field to Swimming. A parent or guardian will accompany each of the worldwide winners as part of
the prize. In addition, the children's winning artwork will be exhibited during the Olympic Games
and reproduced as commemorative postcards for the millions of visitors and athletes from around the
world. The overall grand prize winner of the 1994 Olympic Winter Games contest will join the 29 new
winners at the 1996 Games.

VISA INTERNATIONAL   Post Office Box 8999   San Francisco   California   94128

Figure 5.2 Visa International used a special letterhead for news releases about a
children's art contest related to the 1996 Olympics. This helped distinguish the event
from regular Visa mailings to the media. (*Courtesy of Visa International, San Francisco, CA.*)

changes, employment opportunities, anniversaries, price changes, hirings, layoffs, construction, openings and closings of facilities, contracts received (or canceled) and legal actions (these, of course, must be checked with the organization's legal counsel).

In general, it is a good idea to have announcements made by the highest-ranking person in the organization. As pointed out in Chapter 4, prominence is a news value. The president of a company making an announcement garners more news interest than a vice president or a department manager. However, when it comes to localizing news, the local plant manager is more prominent to the local press than the company president whose office is in a distant city.

Spot Announcements

When things that are due to some outside action or influence happen to an organization, a spot news release may be in order. When a storm disrupts the services of a public utility, a fire or an accident stops work, a flood closes roads, a strike closes a factory—all such incidents can lead to the issuance of a release that tells what has happened and what effect it is having.

If the affected organization doesn't give the news to the media, reporters will write their own stories and may do a poor job because they don't have all the facts. In many cases, follow-up stories must be released later. These may carry additional detailed information and report on progress in solving the problem.

Reaction Releases

Reaction releases are used when something is done or said that may harm an organization—for example, a charge that a factory has unsafe working conditions, a lawsuit claiming injury or a finding that a certain food additive may cause cancer.

When a government agency decides to stop funding a particular activity, the people affected by the cutback will issue reaction releases proclaiming that the project is essential and that no budget cuts should be made.

Another use of the reaction release is to hitch on to something that, though not harmful to the organization, has some bearing on it. For instance, if the Environmental Protection Agency announces an easing of controls, an affected company might issue a release stating that it will continue its policy of nonpollution and outline that policy.

Bad News

Some organizations try to suppress news that might reflect badly on them. This is a sure way to make things worse. People will talk, rumors will spread and investigative reporters will take a major interest in exposing the "cover-up."

The only way to make the best of such a situation is to tell the truth. A release giving the facts clearly and completely should be drafted immediately. If reporters ask for information, it should be given to them.

Some organizations try unsuccessfully to bury bad news within a story. One corporation started a news release about its year-end results by reporting "progress in our strategic program by divesting companies outside our core consumer business." In the second paragraph, the company said it had declared dividends on preferred stock. The news that the company had a loss of $109 million didn't come until the second page, and it wasn't until the fourth page that the company said it was omitting its dividend on common stock.

This approach to reporting bad news may slip by some journalists, but most alert reporters will detect the clumsy attempt and make a mental note that all future company news releases should be taken with a grain of salt. As discussed in Chapter 2, a professional public relations writer should convince the company that such a news release is not only unethical but also potentially embarrassing and self-defeating.

The "Hometown" Release

The most common reason that news releases don't get used is the absence of a local angle. Although there are many publications and broadcast outlets that serve a national audience, the reality is that most media outlets serve local audiences.

A case in point is the *Grosse Pointe* (MI) *News,* a weekly newspaper serving an affluent suburb of Detroit. John Minnis, news editor of the paper, and Cornelius Pratt, a professor of public relations at Michigan State University, found that the newspaper received 189 news releases in a single week. Of that number, 65 (34 percent) were selected for publication. Overall, 57 percent of the releases printed were chosen for their local angle.

The two researchers, who reported their findings in the Fall 1995 issue of *Public Relations Quarterly,* concluded, "Location, location, location is the axiom of real estate agents. In public relations, it should be localization, localization, localization."

There are two ways to localize. One is to use the names of local people; the other is to use information that is of local significance. The computer makes it possible to easily alter a basic news release by inserting information that emphasizes the local angle.

Suppose you were trying to publicize the annual meeting of agents from Universal Life Insurance Company. The fact that an insurance company held a meeting of its agents is not likely to strike a spark with the editor of the *Smalltown Sentinel.* But if the story begins with the fact that agent Jane Smith of Smalltown attended the meeting, the editor will probably take a greater interest. This is called the "hometown" angle.

Such a story, directed to hometown newspapers, could be developed for every agent attending the meeting. In most cases, the beginning paragraph is personalized with the name of the agent and the rest of the news release is standardized to give information about the company, type of insurance written, volume of business and even the highlights of the annual meeting. In this way, the company gets publicity in a number of media outlets (mostly weekly newspapers) across the country.

The technique of "hometown" releases is used by many organizations. Colleges and universities, for example, often prepare individualized releases about entering freshmen for newspapers in their hometowns. The Defense Department also sends releases about the positive accomplishments of enlisted men and women to their hometown media. In one recent year, the U.S. Navy prepared and distributed 1.13 million "hometown" releases.

Localizing information is another way to get releases published. An airline, for example, usually issues a quarterly summary giving the total number of passengers, the number of flights and other statistical details. This information, in itself, doesn't have much local interest except in the city where the airline is headquartered. You, however, gain more publicity by extracting local statistics from the general report. For example, the media outlets in Boise, Idaho, would get a "localized" release from the airline that would give the number of passengers boarding the plane in Boise and the most frequent destinations. The release might also give the number of flights per month out of Boise. The last part of the news release would give the overall statistics for the airline.

Any number of state and national organizations also "localize" information. The National Association of Realtors, for example, may break down national statistics by city. Editors in Tucson would get a release about the real estate market in their area while media outlets in Dayton get another "localized" version.

Localizing news releases takes a bit more time, but the resulting publicity makes it more cost-effective than the standard news release sent to everyone. Another example of how information is localized is the fill-in-the-blank approach shown in Figure 5.3.

PARTS OF A NEWS RELEASE

A news release has six basic components: (1) organization name, (2) contacts, (3) headline, (4) dateline, (5) lead paragraph and (6) body of text.

Organization Name

The first page of a news release is usually printed on an organization's letterhead. Letterheads give the name of the organization, its complete address, telephone numbers, fax numbers and even E-mail addresses. If the organization doesn't have a letterhead, you should use a larger or different font in your computer to create one.

Many organizations tailor a letterhead specifically for news releases. In addition to giving the organizational information, the term "News Release" or something similar will appear right after or as part of the letterhead.

The term "For Immediate Release" also appears near the letterhead of many releases, but many publicists say this is just a tradition and not really necessary. New York public relations counselor Alan Hirsch told *Jack O'Dwyer's Newsletter,* "Using 'for immediate release' on any news announcement is extreme ignorance because the term is obsolete and has no meaning. Media don't hold up the news any more. . . . "

That may be true in the age of instant global communication, but there are times that a writer will request a specific release time. For example, you may write: "For Release after 9 p.m. January 16." This often occurs when the release concerns a speech by someone or an award takes place at a certain time.

PRESS RELEASE

Chevron Community Concerts

_____ SYMPHONY ORCHESTRA
CELEBRATES AMERICA IN INNOVATIVE PRESENTATION OF
MUSIC AND PHOTOCHOREOGRAPHY

All Copland Concert on _____ at _____ p.m.
underwritten by Chevron U.S.A.

_____ Narrates *A Lincoln Portrait*
Murry Sidlin, guest conductor
James Westwater, photochoreographer

The _____ Symphony Orchestra under the baton of guest conductor Murry Sidlin presents an imaginative blend of music by America's pre-eminent composer Aaron Copland and photographs by James Westwater in _____ Auditorium on _____ at _____ p.m. The program includes "Appalachian Suite," Copland's *Appalachian Spring* enhanced by a photgraphic tribute to the beauty of the Appalachian highlands and "Western Suite," visual homage to the American cowboy and the rugged beauty of the West allied with Copland's music from the ballet *Billy the Kid*. The program also features _____ , narrating Copland's *A Lincoln Portrait*, with text from the President's letters and addresses. The concert is underwritten in part by Chevron U.S.A. as part of the company's nationwide Chevron Community Concerts program.

Developed by James Westwater nearly ten years ago, "photochoreography" utilizes three 10' x 14' screens suspended nine feet above the orchestra. Precisely synchronized images create a constantly changing scene in response to the music, sometimes with three separate images, at other times in a three-screen panorama.

Conductor Murry Sidlin is a nationally recognized and articulate advocate of American orchestral music. His association with the music of Copland is especially noteworthy. During the 1986-87 season, he conducted over 50 performances of his chamber ensemble transcription of Copland's only full length opera, *The Tender Land*, at New Haven's Long Wharf Theatre and Aspen Music Festival. Sidlin has served as music director of the New Haven and Long Beach (CA) Symphonies and been guest conductor with major American orchestras including the Atlanta, Baltimore, Houston, Milwaukee, Pittsburgh, St. Louis, and San Francisco Symphonies. Mr. Sidlin received enthusiastic praise from Time, Newsweek, The New York Times, and numerous music journals for his role as conductor host of the public television series "Music is. . . ."

In addition to his work as a Chevron Concert Artist, Mr. Westwater has produced photochoreographic performances in cooperation with the National Geographic Society and the Institute of Polar Studies. A recipient of the Antarctic Medal and a past fellow of the Explorers Club, James Westwater's initial photographic concerto received its premiere at Kennedy Center for the Performing Arts with the National Symphony Orchestra. In a departure from his usual subject matter, Mr. Westwater was commissioned by the Cincinnati Symphony Orchestra to produce a photographic concerto based on the life and music of John Lennon. "Tribute to John Lennon" was subsequently performed by the Cincinnati Symphony and singer Roberta Flack on an extensive American tour capped by a concert in New York City's Radio City Music Hall.

Messrs. Sidlin and Westwater have collaborated on a number of photographic concertos since they met in 1975. Other performances under the auspices of Chevron Community Concerts have included engagements with the Houston, Midland-Odessa (TX), Denver, New Mexico, Honolulu, and New Orleans Symphonies, and Philharmonic Orchestra of Florida.

Ticket information: _____

# # #

Figure 5.3 A concert tour allows each city to localize a standard news release by filling in the blanks. The entire release, however, should be retyped with the appropriate information inserted before being submitted to a media outlet. (*Courtesy of Chevron Corporation, San Francisco, CA.*)

The primary reason is that unplanned things happen. The speaker or award recipient, because of a plane delay or another emergency, may not show up. In such a case, the media would look foolish reporting a speech or an award that was never given.

At times, you may also wish to indicate that a particular news announcement is "embargoed" until the organization makes a formal announcement at a news conference. The idea behind this is that a particular news outlet won't "scoop" the opposition by broadcasting or publishing the announcement ahead of time. This approach, however, is risky unless you get the "promise" of the news organization to honor your request. In many cases, they won't.

Contacts

Place the date about two inches below the letterhead. Then double-space and identify the contact person for the particular release. This is often the writer of the news release, but it can also be the director of the public relations department or another executive.

Include the contact person's full name, telephone number, fax number or even E-mail address. Here is an example:

CONTACT: Rebecca Garcia

415–328–5555, ext. 117

rgarcial117@aol.com

If a public relations firm has prepared the release, the contacts for both the firm and the client organization are often given. It's also a good idea, if the news release is distributed nationally, to give an after-hours number where reporters can contact you.

Headline

Most news releases, particularly product-related ones, carry a brief headline. This usually appears in boldfaced and in a slightly larger type than that used in the body of the news release. Thus, if the body is in 12-point type, the headline often is in 14- or 16-point type.

The purpose of the headline is to give an editor or journalist a quick indication of what the news release is about. Headlines are supposed to give the "bottom line," the most newsworthy aspect of the story. Headlines should be factual, devoid of hype and to the point. Here are some examples:

- Merck Develops New Drug for Asthma Sufferers
- LSI Logic Selects New President
- HP Announces Its First Organizer
- Pacific Bell and Teleport Communications Group Reach Interconnect Agreement
- Theater Company Stages "Guys and Dolls"

Note that these headlines are all written in the active present tense. Avoid past tense; it gives the impression that the news item is not timely. If you do use a headline, place it two or three lines above the first line of the news release.

Dateline

This begins at the start of the lead paragraph, which is discussed in the next section. The dateline is simply the city and state where the release originated, plus the date. The location is usually all caps, and the date is cap lowercase. The dateline, in order to stand out, is usually boldfaced. This is an example:

> **SAN FRANCISCO, CA, November 15, 1996**—Fans of *Forrest Gump* and its sound track. . . .

Another approach to the dateline is simply to put the date on the release above the contact's name. Those who favor this approach say a dateline should not clutter up the lead paragraph.

The Lead

The most important part of any release is the lead paragraph. In one or two sentences, you must give the reader the basic details of the story or, in the case of the feature approach, motivate people to keep reading.

There are two basic types of leads. First is the summary lead, which includes the key information in a brief statement. For example:

- Coldwell Banker Corp., one of the nation's largest residential real estate brokerage firms, is re-entering the commercial real estate business. It plans to sell franchises in more than 100 U.S. markets.
- Vanderbilt University's Owen Graduate School of Management is the recipient of a $33.5 million gift. It is one of the biggest single donations ever given to a business school.
- The Molson Companies, Canada's biggest brewer, has agreed to sell most of its chemicals unit, the Diversey Corporation, to Unilever for $780 million.

The second type is the interest or feature lead, which raises the reader's curiosity. Essentially, the lead is a "hook" that encourages the reader to read the second paragraph for more information. For example:

- Lots of people are talking about a surge in business these days. Those people are not in commercial real estate.
- Want a newspaper? A sandwich? An umbrella? In a few years, if the Metropolitan Transportation Agency has its way, commuters may be buying them with the same cards they pass through the subway turnstiles to pay their fares.
- The patient was getting the best care the local doctors could provide. But this case needed outside expertise, and a long-distance phone call was not an option. (Story about a satellite medical service.)

Contacts: Rebecca Garcia, 415-328-5555, ext.117   Chris Iwamura
rgarcia117@aol.com   NewView, Inc.
Neale-May & Partners   415-299-9016
cji@newview.com

NEW VIEW INTRODUCES *iscreen!*™ INTERNET ACCESS SOLUTION TO PROTECT CYBERKIDS FROM PORNOGRAPHY, OBSCENITY AND OTHER OBJECTIONABLE ONLINE MATERIAL

Easy-to-Use New Service Allows Parents and Teachers to Customize Each Child's Internet Access; Sophisticated Client/Server Architecture Provides Most Current and Reliable Site Ratings Possible

REDWOOD CITY, CA, January 3, 1996-- The cyberworld will become a safer place for kids to play and learn because NewView, Inc. has launched *iscreen!*, a positive, choice-oriented Internet access management solution for homes and schools.

Developed in response to growing concern over sex, violence and other objectionable material on the Internet, *iscreen!'s* sophisticated client-server architecture provides parents and teachers with customizable selection, greater ease-of-use, wider range of rating criteria and more detailed reports than any other system on today's market -- all at a lower price.

"With an estimated 200 new Web sites per day being added to the Internet, *iscreen!* fills a void in the current Internet access management market," stated NewView president/CEO Woodson Hobbs, an information management thought leader and former CIO of the Charles Schwab Corporation. "Because the system's large directory of safe-rated sites resides on the server, the architecture is exceptionally scalable and can accommodate the rapid expansion of this important cyberspace destination."

-2-

Figure 5.4 A product news release. Notice the use of multiple headlines to give busy editors a summary of the release. Increasingly, contacts are giving E-mail addresses in addition to telephone numbers. (*Courtesy of Neale-May & Partners, Palo Alto, CA.*)

Inexperienced writers often have the mistaken impression that a lead should answer all six journalistic questions. However, trying to do this often results in a tangle of dependent clauses and convoluted sentences that are difficult to read. Michael Ryan, writing in *Public Relations Quarterly* (Summer 1995), gives an example of such a lead paragraph:

> A conference addressing the issue, "Maternal and Child Health: Making Indigent Health Programs Work," will be held on Thursday, March 20, 9:00 a.m. to 12:30 p.m. in the Jefferson Davis Hospital Board Room, 1801 Allen Parkway. The Houston conference is the fourth in a series of 20 regional meetings cosponsored by the March of Dimes and the Children's Defense Fund of Texas.

The solution, in this case and others, is to put only the most important element of the story in the lead paragraph. The other Ws, or the H, can be woven into the succeeding paragraphs. Here are examples of leads that emphasize only one element:

Who:	Recording artist Lisa Atkinson will lead a sing-along and entertain preschool children . . .
What:	"Fire, Earth, and Water," a major exhibit of pre-Columbian sculpture from the Land Collection, opens Friday . . .
When:	November 15 is the last date for filing claims for flood damage caused by . . .
Where:	A golden retriever has won Best of Show honors at the 90th Golden Gate Kennel Club Dog Show.
Why:	Farnell of Britain will merge with Premier Industrial of Cleveland. The deal, valued at $2.8 billion, is an effort to consolidate the worldwide distribution of electronics equipment.
How:	Flextime, the system that permits employees to set their own starting and stopping times, has reduced labor turnover at Kellogg Enterprises by . . .

The mechanics of a lead paragraph are relatively simple. Use strong declarative sentences, keep the number of dependent clauses to a minimum, keep it to four or five lines on your computer screen and rewrite if any sentence comes out more than three lines long. You should also avoid the following:

Prepositional phrases:	At a meeting held in the . . . or For the first time in history . . . . These phrases, used at the beginning of a lead paragraph, tend to weaken the force of the sentence.
Participial phrases:	Meeting in an atmosphere of confidence, . . .
Dependent clauses:	That all high school students be required to . . . .
Clutter:	Joe Gonzales, a veteran retailer and former mayor, at a meeting of the Chamber of Commerce to . . . .

TYPES OF NEWS RELEASE LEADS

Following are examples of several kinds of leads:

1. *Straight news lead* (who, what, when, where):

   The History Center of De Anza College will open the school year Sept. 21 with a barbecue at 11 a.m. in Martin Murphy Historical Park, 235 E. California Ave., Sunnyvale.

2. *Modified straight news lead* (stressing a major theme):

   A Chicago thoracic surgeon who plans to focus study on national health insurance programs has been named president of the Cook County Medical Society.

3. *Informal lead* (designed to arouse interest):

   The sky will be ablaze with the crackle of scale-model machine-gun fire this weekend at the Hill Country Air Museum here. (Story about a model airplane exhibit.)

4. *Feature lead* (often used in magazine articles or human interest newspaper features):

   Jan Talbott is into the bike craze in a big way. (Story about a custom bicycle built to accommodate a six-foot six-inch man.)

Body of Text

The lead paragraph is an integral and important part of the text. As such, it forms the apex of the journalistic "inverted pyramid" approach to writing. This means that the first paragraph succinctly summarizes the most important part of the story and succeeding paragraphs fill in the details.

There are three reasons for using the inverted pyramid structure. First, if the editor or reporter doesn't find something interesting in the first few lines, he or she won't use the story.

Second, editors often cut the length of an item, and they start at the bottom. In fact, Business Wire estimates that more than 90 percent of news releases printed are rewritten in much shorter form than the original text. So, if the main details of the story are at the beginning, the release will still be understandable and informative even if most of it ends up in the trash basket.

A third reason for using this structure is that the public doesn't always read the entire story. Statistics show, for example, that the average reader spends less than 30 minutes reading a metropolitan daily newspaper. This means that they read a lot of headlines, some beginning paragraphs, and a few stories in their entirety. If they read the headline and the first paragraph, readers should get the main facts.

Once the lead is written, you must add information until the story is complete. Ryan, professor of communication at the University of Houston, says a news release should have four basic paragraphs. His model:

- Paragraph One
  - A. Most important facts of release.
  - B. Attribution, less essential information.

- Paragraph Two
  - A. Essential background material, names of key characters or sources, a second important element.
  - B. Names of secondary characters or sources.

- Paragraph Three
  - A. Elaboration on material in 1A.
  - B. Background material, attribution.

- Paragraph Four
  - A. Most important material in sentence.
  - B. Background material, attribution.

This model doesn't mean that all news releases should be four paragraphs long. Ryan points out that there could be several paragraphs of the same kind in a news release. For example, your particular news release may require more background or include several important and interesting supporting quotations. Thus, in order to fully tell the story, you may use several "3" paragraphs.

The end of a news release often includes what is known in the trade as *boilerplate,* an old press term for a standardized text used over and over again. For example:

> Rolm Corporation, a unit of the Siemens Company, is a leading supplier of telecommunications products and applications. Rolm pioneered the development of digital telephones and switches, including automatic call distribution, voice messaging systems and integrated voice/data technologies. Rolm employs more than 30,000 people and has annual sales exceeding $4.5 billion.

The idea, however, is to keep in mind a structure that enables you to write a succinct news release that includes all the important and interesting information. There is no rule that news releases should be a specific length, but most writers strive to tell their stories in one or two pages. Journalists appreciate news releases that are short and to the point; they are busy and won't read a multiple-page news release. If you do need to provide a lot of background information, it's wise to place this information in a separate document such as a fact sheet or corporate backgrounder, discussed later in this chapter.

When the release is completed, it should be checked and double-checked. Facts, figures, spelling, punctuation, grammar, sentence and paragraph length, clarity and adherence to approved news style must be considered. Quotations and the spelling of names must be checked with extra care. A sure way to create ill will is to issue a release that is inaccurate.

FOR IMMEDIATE RELEASE   **CONTACT:** Julie Lee
                                                      (612) 431-9322

BUGS! OPENING AT THE MINNESOTA ZOO

APPLE VALLEY, Minn., April 18, 1994 -- Be one of the first to see and experience more than 70 different species of arthropods, and thousands of individual beetles, butterflies and moths, ants, bees, spiders, millipedes, centipedes, tarantulas and cockroaches when BUGS! opens at the Minnesota Zoo on May 28.

The BUGS! exhibit grand opening on Saturday, May 28, 9 a.m. to 6 p.m., sponsored by Target, includes free child admission with paid adult (with Target coupon), a free bug gift for children, entertainment and costumed characters.

The opening continues through Memorial Day, Monday, May 30, and includes a special concert by BUG! in the Weesner Family Amphitheater on Sunday, May 29, at 5:30 p.m.

The new summer exhibit BUGS! runs from May 28 through Labor Day and is free with regular zoo admission. The Minnesota Zoo is located just 10 minutes south of Mall of America off of Highway 77 or Cedar Avenue. For more information, call the Zoo-To-Do-Hotline at 612-432-9000.

-30-

13000 Zoo Boulevard, Apple Valley, MN 55124 • (612) 431-9200 • Fax (612) 431-9300
Recycled paper with a minimum of 10% postconsumer waste.

Figure 5.5 An attractive letterhead carries out the theme of a special exhibit at the Minnesota Zoo. Notice that the last paragraph contains directions and a phone number to call for more information. (*Courtesy of Julie Lee, Minnesota Zoo, Apple Valley, MN.*)

A NEWS RELEASE AUDIT

After you have written your news release, review it with the following questions in mind.

- Is it newsworthy? Is it something that people need to know in order to be informed, to make decisions or to understand what is going on in their community?
- Is the letterhead appropriate? Does it identify the source of the release?
- Is the contact person identified by name, title and phone number? Is the contact person knowledgeable enough to answer media inquiries and freely accessible?
- Is the dateline appropriate? Does it include place and time for use in media outlets?
- Is the lead complete? Are the five Ws and one H arranged in order of importance?
- Is the lead attention-getting? Does it summarize the story?
- Is the story attributed in the lead or second paragraph?
- Is the inverted pyramid structure used? Can the editor cut it after any paragraph without losing the essential information?
- Do the sentences vary in length and complexity? Are there enough simple, declarative sentences to balance compound sentences?
- Are paragraphs well designed? Is the thematic development natural, and are transitions from one ideal to another smooth?
- Is the style suitable for intended readers? Do you avoid excessive jargon? Have you used the subject-verb-object format? Active verbs? Have you omitted unnecessary words and phrases? Have you explained concepts that may be unfamiliar to your readers?
- Is the information suitably documented? Would a skeptic question any assertions or statements made without attribution?
- Are the subject and its treatment appropriate for intended readers? How can you improve the subject or treatment?
- Is the copy clean, neat and attractively formatted? Are there any errors in spelling and grammar?

FACT SHEETS

A fact sheet can accompany a news release, or it can be sent in lieu of a news release. It is essentially what the name implies—a list of facts that a reporter can use as a quick reference when writing a story.

The material is organized in outline form to enable journalists and editors to quickly scan it for information that can either be used to supplement the news release or, in some cases, to write their own news stories.

A fact sheet for an upcoming event may use boldface headings such as (1) name of event, (2) sponsor, (3) location, (4) date and time, (5) purpose of event, (6) expected attendance, (7) prominent people attending and (8) unique or unusual aspects of the event.

A fact sheet on an organization may use such headings as (1) name, (2) products or services produced, (3) annual revenues, (4) total employees, (5) names and short biography of top executives, (6) markets served, (7) position in the industry and (8) other pertinent details. Some organizations use the term "corporate back-grounder" to describe these aspects. See Figure 5.6 for the fact sheet on the Minnesota Zoo and Figure 5.7 for an example of a corporate backgrounder.

The third kind of fact sheet is simply a summary of a new product's characteristics. A fact sheet on a company's new snack product, for example, might give such details as (1) nutrition information, (2) manufacturing process, (3) pricing, (4) availability and (5) how it serves a consumer need.

A fact sheet can be compiled on almost anything. Even a simple one, covering the five Ws and H can be helpful to journalists who want a quick reference to basic information. Fact sheets and corporate backgrounders also accompany press kits, as discussed in Chapter 9.

PLACEMENT   *Review*

A news release does no good unless it is published. Getting anything published is called *placement*. Placement depends on delivering the story to the right gatekeeper through the right channels at the right time. The pros and cons of various distribution channels are discussed in Chapter 10.

Gatekeepers

Review You must get the story to the editor or reporter who is most likely to be interested in the particular subject. Thus anything about food would go to the food editor, and anything about entertainment would go to the entertainment editor or reporter. Large papers have many editors; smaller papers often have editors covering several subjects.

You can find editors' names in the media directories (see Chapter 10). For weekly newspapers and most magazines, your contact is the editor, although some large magazines have a large number of specialized editors.

There is much controversy about the practice of sending a news release to more than one person at a paper. If two editors or reporters come up with the same story, each may feel duped. One way to avoid this is to send the release to one gatekeeper and provide copies—marked "F.Y.I." ("for your information")—to any others who might be interested. The original would show who got copies, and copies would show to whom the original was sent.

Deadlines

Review News releases must be timely. The media thrive on late-breaking information and want to know about events when they happen, not a week later. If it is not possible to get routine information distributed right away, a common technique is to make sure that there are no references to specific dates in the release. The announcement

**MINNESOTA ZOO
1994 FACT SHEET**

Mission

The Minnesota Zoo exists to strengthen the bond between people and the living earth. To accomplish this, the zoo provides award-winning recreational, educational and conservation programs to the public.

General Information

Hours: The zoo is open year-round (every day except December 25).
                October-April: 9 a.m. to 4 p.m. daily
                May and September: 9 a.m. to 4 p.m. weekdays
                                        9 a.m. to 6 p.m. weekends
                Memorial Day-Labor Day: 9 a.m. to 6 p.m. Monday-Saturday
                                        9 a.m. to 8 p.m. Sunday

Size: The zoo is situated on 500 acres of land in Dakota County featuring many natural wetland and wooded areas as well as rolling hills.

Budget: The zoo finances its $13.7 million budget through an annual appropriation from the state legislature, memberships, admissions, private grants, donations and other enterprise activities. Nationally, zoos receive an average of 67 percent of their funding from public sources.

Staff: The zoo's staff totals approximately 200 in the winter, 250+ in the summer and 500+ volunteers year-round.

Animals: Of the 2,700 animals at the zoo, 54 animals representing 17 species are on the endangered species list. The Minnesota Zoo is involved with national and international programs to breed and preserve these species.

-more-

13000 Zoo Boulevard, Apple Valley, MN 55124 • (612) 431-9200 • Fax (612) 431-9300
♲ Recycled paper with a minimum of 10% postconsumer waste.

Figure 5.6   Fact sheets often accompany news releases. They give reporters additional information that they may wish to incorporate into their stories. This fact sheet accompanied the news release in Figure 5.5. (*Courtesy of Julie Lee, Minnesota Zoo, Apple Valley, MN.*)

Corporate Backgrounder

(www.newview.com)

Company

NewView is the newest entrant and most advanced software service provider in the Internet access solutions market. Drawing on the extensive experience, vision, and technical expertise of president/CEO Woodson Hobbs and co-founders, NewView offers homes and schools today's most comprehensive site-rating and access management solution for protecting children from objectionable material on the Internet.

NewView rates and indexes Internet site content according to a wide range of criteria. The company's innovative *iscreen!* software offers parents and educators the power to make access decisions based on sex, violence, and many other issues. Its Internet directory gateway provides children with safe, enjoyable, entertaining, and educational access to the Internet.

- A positive approach to Internet safety
- First Amendment friendly
- More rating categories and user options
- No maintenance and more affordable

iscreen!

Fills a Market Void – Safe, Personalized, Tamper-Proof

iscreen! is the most powerful, flexible and user friendly Internet access solution, enabling adults to decide on what they want their children to see, do or read. *iscreen!*'s sophisticated client-server technology:

- Supports individual user profiles,
- Offers a personalized, child oriented Internet Directory,
- Provides access only to *SafeSites* except for parental overrides,
- Allows the exclusion of picture files,
- Covers the widest range of rating categories and degrees of access,
- Provides parents with monitoring reports,
- Notifies parents and teachers of attempts to circumvent, and
- Eliminates the task of downloading and updating lists.

-1-

Figure 5.7 Organizations also send "corporate backgrounders" with news releases so reporters can get a better idea of the company producing a new product. This corporate backgrounder accompanied the news release in Figure 5.4. (*Courtesy of Neale-May & Partners, Palo Alto, CA.*)

of a new company president or a major contract, for example, would not say that the news is two weeks old.

Important late-breaking news can always be telephoned or faxed to a newspaper at the last minute and get published. Evening papers go to press around noon. The deadline for late-breaking news is variable but is usually early in the morning. Morning papers go to press in the evening, sometimes as late as 10 or 11 p.m., so you could get late-breaking news considered as late as 6 p.m.

Most news releases, however, deal with routine announcements that are not hot news. In this case, media outlets like to receive information with plenty of lead time. Publicity about an upcoming event, for example, should be sent to gatekeepers at least two weeks ahead of time so that editors can process the information and get it into the newspaper in a timely fashion. If a major event is planned, editors appreciate as much advance information as possible so that they can plan their coverage.

Monthly trade magazines usually need information six to eight weeks in advance, and monthly consumer magazines often work five or six months in advance. These publications often deal with feature-type stories rather than straight news releases; these are discussed further in Chapter 6.

News releases to local television and radio stations should arrive at least two or three days in advance. Public service announcements should be sent to radio and television stations at least six weeks in advance. These are discussed further in Chapter 8.

Getting Maximum Publicity

Whenever you take the time and energy to develop a news release, you should think of how you can produce several releases that can be sent to various media from the same information.

If Susan Chang has been appointed president of Mammoth Manufacturing Company, there are several media outlets for this story: local news media, the trade magazines serving the industry, her college alumni publication, and the publications of organizations to which she belongs.

In each case the release would be individualized, but all would contain information about the Mammoth Manufacturing Company. Individualizing requires writing the release to fit the medium to which it will be released. For a metropolitan daily, the release should be about one paragraph long—unless the company is of great importance, in which case the release may be longer and give more details. The release may also be longer for trade publications, hometown papers, and organizational publications.

Surveys also lend themselves to developing several releases from basic data. Dye Van Mol & Lawrence public relations of Nashville took this approach to publicize the results of a family values survey for Shoney's Restaurants. News releases were prepared emphasizing various findings of the survey. Some news release headlines were: "Mealtime Is Family Time for Most U.S. Households," "Households with Greater Income Have Less Time for Family," and "Regions Show Real Difference in Family Values."

供立即公佈，1995年5月

請洽：當地媒體經理＿＿＿＿＿＿

加州公用事業委員會放寬收入的合格標準，協助更多的客户獲得普濟電話服務資格

　　加州公用事業委員會(CPUC)最近放寬收入的合格標準，以協助收入有限的居民獲得加州優惠電話服務的資格。新的收入限制將每户申請普濟電話服務(Universal Lifeline Telephone Service)收入的標準提高2.6%，以因應到每年生活費的上升。加州所有的本地電話公司都提供普濟電話服務，包括Pacific Bell和GTE California Incorporated。

　　一人或兩人之家庭要符合這項計劃的資格，每年的總收入上限可達$16,100。以前的收入標準爲$15,700。三口之家的收入標準放寬到$18,900；。三口之家的收入標準爲22,700。家庭人數每增加一名，收入標準就放寬$3,800。

　　普濟電話服務的目的，是確保加州所有的居民家庭無論收入多寡，都能獲得基本的電話服務。Pacific Bell的居民客户中，大約有210萬人即22%擁有普濟電話服務。

　　普濟電話服務爲符合資格的客户提供同樣的基本電話服務，但只收一半月費。目前普濟電話服務的無限量通話服務Flat Rate Lifeline Service月費爲$5.62。普濟電話服務的有限量通話服務Measured Rate Lifeline Service月費則爲$3.00。其安裝手續費僅收$10。普濟電話服務的優待還包括在安裝第一個電話插座時，人工費減收50%。普濟電話服務客户在申請開户時無需繳納押金。

2

Figure 5.8 News releases are often produced in several languages to serve the ethnic media of a region. This is the Chinese version of a release that was also translated into Spanish, Korean and Vietnamese. (*Courtesy of Pacific Telesis, San Francisco.*)

MISTAKES TO AVOID

Media outlets receive a blizzard of news releases every week. Such a deluge makes editors highly critical of what they receive. One survey of city editors, for example, found that 54 percent thought news releases were written "slovenly" and another 65 to 75 percent believed that they frequently promoted "products, services, and other activities which do not legitimately deserve promotion."

The survey points to some basic rules of successful news release writing. Stick to the facts. Write clearly and succinctly. Keep the audience in mind at all times.

Remember the following don'ts about news release writing:

- Don't write lead paragraphs that are 14 lines long and loaded with compound sentences.

TEN CLASSIC NEWS RELEASE MISTAKES

Alan Caruba, a public relations consultant and publicist for three decades, has prepared this list of what he calls the ten "Classic News Release Mistakes":

1. Failure to provide a headline. "It's a news story and headlines articulate the theme. Sub-headlines, too, are useful."
2. Boiler-Plate. "A first paragraph that jams in the client's name, their title, the company, its location, etc., while ignoring the primary theme of the release, kills it."
3. Spelling and grammatical errors. "Very harmful to any release because it suggests its writer is either uneducated or the release was not proofread."
4. Punctuation errors. "Since editors and reporters, as well as broadcast news personnel, make their living writing, these mistakes are 'red flags' raising doubts about the source of the release."
5. Hyperbole. "The word from which we get the term 'hype' in which ordinary things are given extraordinary qualities. It's instantaneously recognizable, creating barriers to credibility."
6. Documentation. "Failure to attribute data to verifiable, independent sources diminishes credibility."
7. Contacts. "Failure to provide the names, phone and/or fax numbers of informed, articulate spokesperson(s) renders a release useless."
8. Too long. "The best releases are the briefest. Too much initial data can be a turn-off. If more is wanted, it will be requested."
9. Localize. "Whenever possible, 'localize' the release."
10. Be accessible at all times. "The best news release makes the media come to you. Opportunity ceases after the third ring of your phone."

Source: Reprinted from *O'Dwyer's PR Services Report*, September 1995, p. 44.

- Don't use flowery adjectives—stick to the facts.
- Don't place the name of the company or the product in all capital letters, even if it's trademarked that way.
- Don't use highly technical jargon that only a scientist or an engineer would understand.
- Don't make a news release so commercial that it sounds like an advertisement.
- Don't automatically distribute a news release to all media outlets; distinguish between the trade press and the consumer press and between regional and national publications.

SUMMARY

1. The majority of news releases are never used by media outlets. To beat the odds, your release must be newsworthy, timely and well written.

2. News releases are a basic element of almost every publicity plan. When published or broadcast, they can raise public awareness and influence decision making.

3. Planning worksheets and answering five Ws and H are basic presteps in writing a news release.

4. News releases are word processed, use standard paper and conform to Associated Press (AP) style.

5. There are several types of news releases: announcements, spot announcements, reaction stories, bad news and hometown releases.

6. The key to successful news release writing is to emphasize the local angle.

7. The news release has six components: organization name, contacts, headline, dateline, lead paragraph and body of text.

8. Lead paragraphs should summarize the basic story in four or five lines. Feature leads should arouse interest and encourage people to keep reading or listening.

9. Don't try to get all five Ws and H (who, what, when, where, why and how) in the lead paragraph. Choose the most important one or two elements.

10. Write news releases that will appeal to editors and their audiences. Too many releases please the client or employer, but violate journalistic standards.

11. News releases are highly structured pieces of writing. Use inverted pyramid style with the most important facts first.

12. Keep news releases factual. Avoid puffery and hype.

13. Fact sheets, or corporate backgrounders, are organized in outline form for easy reference.

14. Multiply a basic news release by tailoring it for various media.

EXERCISES

1. Select several issues of a daily newspaper and study the lead paragraph of various stories in the business or community news section. Find samples of (1) a straight news lead, (2) a modified straight news lead, (3) an informal lead and (4) a feature lead. See the box on page 127.

2. Make arrangements with a local newspaper to collect a number of news releases that the editors didn't use. Write short critiques of at least five of them from the standpoint of writing style and content as discussed in this chapter. Why do you think the editors didn't use these news releases?

3. The chapter begins by listing six questions that a writer should answer before writing a news release. Answer these questions as if you were preparing a news release for the following situations:
   • A new play is opening at the city's professional repertory theatre.
   • A food manufacturer is introducing a completely fat-free potato chip.

- The local Red Cross chapter is kicking off its annual drive for blood donations.

4. About 100 students on your campus are being inducted into a national scholastic honorary society. Prepare a news release format that will allow you to send tailored stories to every student's hometown. The basic format should allow you to insert names and other information into the general news release

5. Write a news release for your college newspaper about the upcoming meeting of a student organization that has invited a guest speaker.

6. Prepare a fact sheet on an organization or business in your community.

7. A news release must not be too commercial or sound like an advertisement for a product. Get a sales brochure from a local automobile dealership and, on the basis of the information, write an acceptable news release that doesn't contain puffery or hype.

8. The Balcor Corporation, a diversified commercial real estate company, has a new president. He is Harvey Wilson, formerly executive vice president of Knox Company, a developer of suburban shopping malls. He replaces Adam Smith, president of Balcor for the past 15 years, who has announced his retirement. Wilson's appointment was announced by Balcor's board of directors.

   Wilson's background is as follows:

   a. He is 52 years old.
   b. He is married and has two children in college.
   c. He has been the executive vice president of Knox Company for the past seven years. Prior to this, he served as the chief financial officer of several construction firms including Krupp Company, which builds hotels around the globe.
   d. He has a B.A. degree in accounting from the University of Washington and an M.B.A. from Stanford University.
   e. He is a member of the National Accounting Association and was formerly on its board; the Illinois Business Round Table, an organization of business executives; the Chicago Sailing Club; and the Chicago Athletic Club.
   f. He is respected in the construction and real estate industries for his quiet, efficient management style.
   g. He lives in Arlington Heights, Illinois.
   h. He will assume the presidency of Balcor, headquartered in Atlanta, next month.
   i. Balcor Corporation owns a number of office parks across the nation and manages 22 other business properties. Total revenue last year was $47 million.

   Write a news release announcing Wilson's appointment for the local and national real estate trade press.

9. A new 25-story office building will be built in downtown Minneapolis. The building, to cost an estimated $40 million, is part of a downtown redevelopment effort to keep major corporations in the central city.

   The office building will be the new headquarters of Kelso Industries, a diversified manufacturer of building products and the owner of a hardware chain,

Kelso Supplies, with more than 100 stores throughout Minnesota, Wisconsin, and Iowa.

The Minneapolis Redevelopment Agency is guaranteeing the financing of the building and contributing up to $5 million to landscape the public areas around the building and improve the surrounding streets. The architect is Weber and Associates, and the contractor is Rudolph and Sletten. The building will be completed in about 18 months. Company executives and city officials say the building is the cornerstone of the downtown revival.

Write a news release on behalf of Kelso Industries to announce the decision to locate its headquarters in downtown Minneapolis. Use appropriate quotations from company executives and city officials as you deem necessary. You can also elaborate on the facts given in this summary to describe the building.

10. The situation in question 9 lends itself to multiple news releases. How would you modify the basic local news release for the following purposes:
    - Trade magazines in the building product and hardware industry.
    - Professional and trade magazines for architects.
    - Trade newspapers and magazines in the construction industry.
    - The business editor of the *New York Times*.
    - The local communities where Kelso has hardware stores.

6 | *The Feature Story*

Feature writing requires writers to shift their thinking. News releases, discussed in the last chapter, require left brain skills emphasizing logical, sequential, analytical thinking. Feature writing, in contrast, requires right brain skills such as intuition, image making and conceptualization.

Facts form the basis of feature writing in public relations, just as they do in news release writing, but the approach is different. This time you are asked to write with more imagination and color. Feature stories should not only be informative but entertaining.

This chapter explores the various types of features that public relations writers can develop, and gives tips on writing and placing such features.

THE VALUE OF FEATURES

get reader or ready
interested
have Strong
open

Perhaps the best way to show the value of feature stories is to contrast them with basic news releases. The news release emphasizes the timely disclosure of basic information about situations and events. The feature article, in contrast, provides additional information and creates understanding in a more imaginative way.

Take, for example, the appointment of a new company president. The news release will give the basic information in one or two paragraphs. It will give the new president's name and perhaps a brief summary of his professional career—all pretty dry, routine stuff. A feature article, however, could give the new president a human dimension. It would focus on his or her philosophy of management, college experiences, hobbies and interests and vision of the future. Such an article might run 2,000 words instead of two paragraphs.

Indeed, feature stories can add interest to a "ho hum" product, service or event if it gives readers a behind-the-scenes view of how a new product was developed or what kind of testing goes on before a new drug is released on the market.

Features are considered "soft news" instead of "hard news." In journalistic terms, this means features are not as time sensitive as the "hard" news of quarterly earnings, mergers and acquisitions, contracts, expansions and layoffs. They entertain as well as provide information, and they often show up in the specialty sections of the daily newspaper—entertainment, food, business, real estate, automotive, technology and so on.

A lot of products are not particularly newsworthy and would never get coverage in a newspaper if not for the imagination of a feature writer. Take the lowly potato, for example. It would seem that no self-respecting editor would even be interested in a news release from the National Association of Potato Growers. However, a feature directed to the food editor can generate coverage and also increase sales of potatoes. Some possible features: (1) potatoes as a source of vitamins, (2) potatoes as a low-cost addition to daily nutritional needs and (3) creative recipes using potatoes as an ingredient. Another possibility is a short history of the potato, its origins and its economic impact.

Feature stories come in all sizes and shapes, but all of them have the potential to (1) provide more information to the consumer, (2) give background and context about organizations, (3) provide behind-the-scenes perspective, (4) give a human dimension to situations and events and (5) generate publicity for standard products and services.

An important point to remember is that a feature is a "soft sell." The focus is on providing information that helps the reader. The name of the organization may only appear once or twice in the body of the feature. See the examples provided in this chapter.

PLANNING A FEATURE

Coming up with a feature idea takes some creative thinking. There are three things to keep in mind.

First, you have to conceptualize how something lends itself to feature treatment. Second, you have to determine if the information would be interesting to and useful for a particular audience. Third, you must be sure that the feature helps achieve organizational objectives. Does it position the organization in a favorable light? Does it encourage the use of a particular product or service?

Good feature writers ask a lot of questions. They need a natural curiosity about how things work and how things are related to each other. If the company has just produced a new video game, for example, you would find out exactly how the game was developed. By asking questions, you might find out that a 19-year-old computer "nerd" invented the game, or that a new technology was used to create 3-D effects. In each case, you have a potential feature. A story about the inventor would make interesting reading, but so would a story about how the new computer technology could be applied in other fields.

News events and issues can also trigger ideas for feature stories. If Congress passes a law, how does that affect your organization or industry? If there is media attention being given to sweatshops in Asia that are producing goods for the American market, perhaps you can develop a feature on how your company assures that its goods are produced in assembly plants that meet minimum pay and working standards. The possibilities are limited only by your own imagination and creativity.

Ways to Proceed

Once you have a feature idea, there are three ways that you can proceed. One way is to write a general feature and distribute it to a variety of publications in much the same way as news releases are sent. Another mass distribution method is to have a feature service distribute it for you. The story in Chapter 4 on the 10-year-old boy putting Parrott, Virginia, on the map is an example of a feature being written and widely distributed.

The second approach is to write an exclusive feature for a specific publication. In this case, you need to target a publication that reaches your selected audience, be they engineers, architects, educators or purchasing agents. You also need to review several issues of the publication to determine the topics it has covered and the style used in similar articles.

Once you are familiar with the publication, phone the editor, outline the subject in about 60 seconds and ask if he or she would be interested. You can also send a brief letter. Carol Haddix, food editor of the *Chicago Tribune,* says the ideal PR person "just sends a note explaining his or her idea in a way that is phrased to interest me."

The reason for the short phone call or a note (called a query) is to determine if there is enough interest to justify writing the feature. Perhaps the editor has recently run several features much like the one you have in mind. Or the editor might suggest another story angle that would appeal to more readers.

Many editors, simply on the basis of a phone call or a brief note, will give you the green light to submit an article for consideration. This does not mean that they are obligated to use it.

Other editors, particularly those for popular magazines, will ask you to submit a proposal that completely outlines the article and explains why the magazine should publish it. A proposal should include the following points:

- Tentative title of article.
- Subject and theme.
- Significance. Why is the topic important? Why should readers know about it?
- Major points.
- Description of photos and graphics available.

The third approach is not to write the feature at all, but to interest a reporter or free-lance writer in the idea. You can do this by telephoning the person or by sending what is known as a "pitch letter." You give the idea, provide much of the factual information, provide graphics or even set up interviews for the publication's reporter who then writes the story. See Figure 6.1 and 6.2 for a good example of a pitch letter and the resulting story. Pitch letters are further discussed in Chapter 9.

The advantage of this approach is that the publication's staff actually writes the story. Thus, the publication has invested time and money in the story and is more likely to publish it. The disadvantage is that you can't always control how the story will be developed and whether it will advance organizational objectives.

Placement opportunities for features are discussed later in this chapter.

TYPES OF FEATURES

There is no formal classification of feature stories and no practical limit to the variety of stories that can be written. Whenever you find something that can be made interesting to some segment of the public, it may be the beginning of a feature. Some ideas are obvious, but many more can be developed if you hunt for them. Among the most frequently seen features are case studies, research studies, backgrounders, personality profiles, historical pieces and application stories. Although these do not represent the entire range of possibilities, some familiarity with the more common types will help you come up with ideas.

Case Study

The case study is frequently used in product publicity. The story of how some product solved a problem or how a unique service enabled some organization to save money or improve its own service can be important and interesting.

Andy Marken, a public relations counselor, writing in the *Public Relations Journal* (September 1991), says that case studies offer excellent exposure because they quickly inform the market of new and different solutions, demonstrate products and services in use, illustrate a company's innovative technology, show acceptance and experience in the marketplace and encourage readers to relate solutions to their own needs.

A good example of a case study is one distributed by the Hewlett-Packard Company that told how Nissan used HP computer equipment to monitor prototype

DOBISKY ASSOCIATES

Media Relations for Higher Education

181 Washington St. • Keene, NH 03431 • 603-352-8181
FAX 603-352-8529

April 14

Mr. Kim McDonald
The Chronicle of Higher Education
1255 23rd Street, NW - Ste 700
Washington, DC 20037

Dear Kim:

Mark Twain once called the fly God's worst creation. So why does Ron Woodruff have the world's biggest collection of these insects?

Ron's bugs—*not* any ordinary housefly—are genus *drosophila*: fruit flies. Woodruff, a geneticist at Bowling Green University, rides herd on 4,000 different genetic varieties of drosophila melanogaster, the type highly favored by scientist trying to save human lives.

As head of the Mid-America Drosophila Stock Center, Woodruff ships his flies to genetic labs worldwide. He ships fast because, although they're energetic breeders, the little devils live only 10 days. In lab research, a short life-span is a plus, along with the fact that having sex cells and four pairs of unusually big chromosomes that are similar to those in humans makes the fruit fly easy to study.

Raising them is no small-potatoes operation either, since the federal government annually underwrites research to the tune of about $70 million—research that calls for fruit flies from Bowling Green.

One of three such centers, the Mid-America Drosophila Stock Center is the world's largest in terms of varieties and sheer numbers. Periodically, Woodruff visits places like Africa in search of new varieties for his collection.

Woodruff, head of biological sciences at Bowling Green, may be the best man around to dispel Sam Clemens' notion that he never met a fly he liked, especially one that was useful to mankind.

You can reach him at 419/372-2332 (Office). For help catching him, give me a call at 603/352-8181.

Cordially,

John McLain

Figure 6.1 Personalized "pitch" letters can effectively sell reporters on doing a feature about your client or employer. Notice how this writer makes even a bug collection a news-worthy and interesting topic. (*Courtesy of John McLain, Dobisky Associates, Keene, NH.*)

THE CHRONICLE
of Higher Education®

Scholarship

PHOTOGRAPH BY GLENN TRIEST FOR THE CHRONICLE

Ronny C. Woodruff in the Mid-America Stock Center: "The questions that you ask and answer with Drosophila *have direct implications to our genetics."*

Fruit-Fly Capital of the World
Bowling Green State supplies researchers around the globe

By Kim A. McDonald

BOWLING GREEN, OHIO
Mark Twain once dubbed the fly God's worst creation. So why does Bowling Green State University have the world's largest and most diverse collection of fruit flies?

The reason is evident to the thousands of biologists who, each each year, receive shipments of the gnat-like insects from two centers here, both of which are supported by the National Science Foundation to serve as repositories of living fruit flies for scientists around the world.

A VARIETY OF GENETIC ANOMOLIES

Tucked away behind several office doors in the university's biology building, the two centers collectively house more than 6,000 of the most valuable strains and species of flies from the genus *Drosophila.*

The larger of the two facilities, the Mid-America Stock Center, keeps 5,000 mutant strains of *Drosophila melanogaster,* the species on which genetic, molecular, and developmental researchers have based much of their work for the past century.

The other facility, the National Drosophila Species Resource Center, maintains more than 1,200 strains from 265 different species of *Drosophila,* some of which became extinct long ago in the wild. These flies are typically used in ecological and evolutionary-biology research.

The difference between the two centers may seem trivial to most visitors, who see in both racks of cotton-plugged vials what appear to be the same flies as those that swarm around rotten bananas on summer days. But to geneticists, the contents of the two facilities are as different as night and day.

Continued on Page A13

Figure 6.2 The resulting story. The letter shown in Figure 6.1 resulted in a two-page story with several pictures in the *Chronicle of Higher Education,* a weekly newspaper serving the academic community.

HOW TO WRITE A CASE STUDY FEATURE

A satisfied customer is the key to writing a case history that shows how a company's product or service was successfully used. Here is a list of questions that a public relations writer should keep in mind.

- What can be told about the company, its place in the industry, its size, and other details?
- Why did the company first need the products or services in question?
- Who was involved in the application?
- What did the products or services do for those people? What can they do now, as a result of the products or services, that they couldn't do before?
- How does the solution save time and money and add quality?
- Could the company get the same results with a competitive solution? If not, how does this solution provide savings that couldn't otherwise be achieved?
- What is the customer contact protocol? Who should clear and approve the article?

Source: Adapted from G.A. "Andy" Marken, "Getting Your Written Message Heard: Case Studies Spread Story," *Public Relations Journal*, September 1991, pp. 35–35.

---

electronic engine-control systems in its racing cars. The story quotes a Nissan executive saying, "Our jobs are simplified knowing that the engine computer will perform up to specifications under severe race conditions. With HP's help, we can get down to the business of winning races."

Research Study

Surveys and polls, as well as scientific studies, can provide opportunities for features. This is particularly true if the research is about some aspect of contemporary lifestyles or a common situation in the workplace. Domino's Pizza Meter index, discussed in Chapter 4, is a good example.

Residence Inn, a chain owned by the Marriott Corporation, got extensive coverage with a research study about the effects of long business trips on female managers and executives. The feature concentrated on the research finding that women feel more productive and stimulated by extended business trips than men, who report feeling more lonely and bored.

The feature went on to quote psychologists, female executives and Residence Inn managers about the findings of the study. According to Marriott, women now comprise 31 percent of all business travel "roomnights."

Backgrounder

There are several kinds of backgrounders. One focuses on a problem and how it was solved—by an organization or a product. Often there is considerable historical material and an opportunity for injecting human interest into the story. One example is a story on the reclamation of strip-mined land and how a coal company restored an area to productive use for farming.

Another kind of backgrounder explains where a product comes from or how it is made. A manufacturer of woolens might release a feature on sheep farming and the differing characteristics of wool from the various breeds, finally leading up to the excellent products made from that wool.

Personality Profile

People like to read about people. Within any organization, there are people about whom interesting stories can be written and published. A good example is a feature story that Pacific Bell produced about the new manager of the company's Vietnamese Service Center. It was distributed in English but, more important, it was also translated to Vietnamese for publications serving the Vietnamese community in the San Francisco Bay Area. The article is reprinted below. See Figure 6.3 also.

**Escaping War-torn Vietnam or Helping Pacific Bell Customers
Vu Ho's Goal in Life Is to Serve
(New Vietnamese Service Center Manager)**

"Even when we were fleeing Vietnam, I remember wanting to help people. I held the other families' little babies so the mothers could climb on board the fishing boat," said Xuan-Nhi (Vu) Ho, the newest manager in Pacific Bell's rapidly expanding Vietnamese

Figure 6.3 Photos often accompany a feature story. This photo was sent with the feature about the new manager of Pacific Bell's Vietnamese Service Center. (*Courtesy of Pacific Telesis, San Francisco.*)

Residential Service Center. The Center was established in 1988 to provide communications service in the customer's native language.

Vu Ho was only 15 on the final day of his government's collapse in 1975 when he, his mother and two brothers fled the airbase where they lived. "The base was being bombed," Ho explained. "Many of us who lived there were able to fly out to a safe island, but my father had to stay behind."

The refugee families found terror on the island. As their nation disintegrated, guards at a major prison on the island had abandoned their posts. The convicts were escaping and heading toward the beach. "Families with fathers were allowed to fly off the island, but hundreds of us had no fathers, and we were left on the beach knowing the prisoners were coming our way," Ho said.

A fishing vessel pausing off shore saved the mothers and children, who waded and swam to the boat. For two days the refugees huddled together until a U.S. battleship picked them up and took them to the Philippines and then to Guam. In Guam, Ho's father rejoined his family.

Today, Ho's desire to serve is met through his work at Pacific Bell and as assistant pastor of the Vietnamese Christian Church in Santa Ana. He says he sees connections between his two jobs. "The work we do at the Service Center is very personal. Just like at church, we need to understand those we serve. We need to have real affection for them. We need to know their needs and try to meet them," Ho said. "Our customers are pleased to be able to use their own language when talking with us. Our job is to answer their questions so they can make informed choices."

The Vietnamese Service Center growth has been dramatic. In 1990, Pacific Bell had 12 Vietnamese customer representatives responding to about 2,500 calls a month. Today there are 26 representatives handling 19,000 calls a month.

Ho, who studied electrical engineering at Long Beach State University and earned his theology degree from Southern California Theological Seminary, said the number of customers continues to increase.

Krystal Bichhuyen Vu, Another Dedicated Manager

Krystal Bichhuyen Vu also fled Vietnam in 1975, when she was 6. With two relatives as her guardians, she was able to fly out of the country where her mother was buried and her father missing. "When I came to the states it was a tough time for me," she said. "I struggled to learn the language and adapt to a new culture. In Vietnam, having a phone was rare—it was a real luxury," she continued. "One of my tasks at the center is to help our customers learn about available technology and resources such as Call Waiting, Call Return, or Message Center, the residential voice mail product. I like the challenge of meeting the customer's needs and staying competitive. We can also help customers understand about our discount plans for toll call competition."

"I feel that at the Service Center we help keep our culture and language alive. I'm very proud to be a part of that. And at the same time, we're offering excellent service. We're a good business," Vu continued. "I love every minute of my job."

Vu's dedication to Vietnamese Americans doesn't stop with her Pacific Bell job. She is active with the Asians for Corporate and Community Action, Orange County Community Service and the Vietnamese Council for Colleges and Universities in Orange County. "I help raise scholarship funds for Vietnamese students," she said.

Vu works with Ho as a manager at the Pacific Bell Vietnamese Center.

For information about telecommunication services and to reach the Pacific Bell Vietnamese Service Center for residential customers, call 1–800–300–5315. The number for business customers is 1–800–799–2828. The Centers are open Monday through Friday 8 a.m. to 5:30 p.m. The residence center is also open on Saturday, 8:30 a.m. to 5 p.m.

Pacific Bell is a subsidiary of Pacific Telesis Group, a San Francisco based diversified telecommunications corporation.

Historical Feature

Anniversaries, major changes, centennials and many other events lend themselves to historical features. Whenever a significant milestone is passed, there may be an opportunity to report on the history of the organization, its facilities or some of its people. Stressing the history of an organization lends it an air of stability and permanence. The public can logically deduce that if an organization has lasted "that long," it must have merit (see Figure 6.4 on page 151).

Historical features are also a staple of publicity about tourism. The Alaska Division of Tourism developed features about the history of the state to encourage visitors. One article was titled, "Following 19th-Century Russians Across Alaska." The lead paragraph was:

> Visitors to Alaska who have forgotten their American history are quickly reminded that the 49th state was once a Russian colony. One reminder is the large number of Russian names sprinkled across the map. . . .

Application Story

The application story tells how to use a new product or how to use a familiar product in a new way. Much food publicity consists of application stories—new recipes or new variations on familiar ones. The food pages of newspapers carry many such features. Some are published exactly as received; others are rewritten or combined in a longer feature.

A feature on home maintenance could provide a basis for publicity on a new kind of paintbrush or paint. Wherever there is a product or service that serves some useful purpose, there may be an audience for information about it.

A variation on the application feature is the technical article. It may describe the technology behind a new product, or it may simply explain how a product can be used in specialized settings. The major outlet for technical articles is the trade press that covers specific industries.

Reprinted below is a technical feature distributed by Pacific Bell about the new technology of ISDN data transmission lines.

LA Creates Another Rush Hour as the Demand for Data Services Grows 25 Percent a Month

The House of Blues sends live concerts to the Internet. Realtors from the San Fernando Valley escort homebuyers through electronic open houses. Caltech seismologists retrieve earthquake data seconds after a tremblor starts. Physicians interview Alzheimer's patients and evaluate detailed brain images over videoconferencing systems.

It's not science fiction. It's rush hour on the communications superhighway.

In greater Los Angeles last year, the public and private sectors started a love affair with data. In 1994, data transmission lines were installed at a rate five times greater than the telephone lines that carry voices. Trend watchers at Pacific Bell—which saw its customer log a 25 percent *monthly* increase in the use of new high-speed data transmission services—say it's demand created by the growing popularity of the Internet, the nearly ubiquitous PC, the need to link computer networks, and the constant imperative to find new customers and provide faster service.

"In the Information Age, customers expect faster service," said Gene Sherman, Pacific Bell vice president. "That's why microwave popcorn is one of America's favorite snacks and the reason television networks scrapped commercial breaks and theme music between sitcoms. Today's buying public wants immediate gratification, and if consumers can't get it from one source, they often move on to another."

In such a volatile marketplace, data communications can help business develop a reputation for speed and error-free service. Businesses seeking just such a competitive advantage have made ISDN the fastest-growing data service in Los Angeles.

ISDN is a copper telephone line that's been "digitized" to speak the language of computers. It offers virtually error-free data transmission at speeds five times greater than the rates of today's fastest modems. ISDN also can divide itself into three channels for simultaneous voice, video and data communication.

In Los Angeles, ISDN was distinguished as the transmission medium chosen by city's hipper-than-hip House of Blues to inaugurate its series of live concerts on the Internet.

The technology made news again when the San Fernando Valley Association of Realtors announced that ISDN would provide high-speed access to a new database of 32,000 residential listings. Through ISDN, realtors can download up to 10 color photographs of each house listed in the database. Realtors can also use the service to create a shopping list of properties tailored to a homebuyer's specifications. A list of 100 properties with 11 lines of text each can be retrieved, sorted and downloaded in under 10 seconds.

In the past 24 months, Pacific Bell introduced three new data communications services—Frame Relay, Switched Multimegabit Data Service (SMDS) and Asynchronous Transfer Mode (ATM). Speed is the primary difference in the three services. Using John Grisham's 566-page bestseller "The Client" and a one-second time frame as yardsticks, Frame Relay can transport one quarter of the book; SMDS can handle seven copies of the novel; and ATM can carry 90 copies.

Last year, scientists selected Frame Relay as the transmission medium in a test of new digital seismometers dotted around Southern California. Scientists believe that with Frame Relay, they could cut as many as 30 minutes off the time required to collect, calculate and broadcast vital data for major earthquakes.

As for SMDS, it's the service chosen by the California State Automobile Association to replace a cumbersome web of expensive private lines to link nearly 100 claims offices. The County of Los Angeles Department of Health uses SMDS to connect 55 clinics and five hospitals with the agency's main computer.

Meanwhile, physicians at UC Irvine are using ATM technology to enhance the diagnosis and research of Alzheimer's Disease. By connecting ATM's huge capacity and speed to videoconference systems, physicians will be able to interview patients who live in distant locations while simultaneously retrieving their individual brain images electronically. ATM will be the on-line link to research libraries and brain image archives of all nine Alzheimer's Disease Diagnosis and Treatment Centers in California.

For hundreds of businesses in the Southland, the communications superhighway already exists, and within a few years, it will become part of everyday life for many residential customers when Pacific Bell finishes building a new telecommunications network.

The new network will offer consumers an alternative to their existing cable franchise. Customers also will be able to order movies delivered directly to their television sets, replay television programs they missed the night before, play video games with people in other locations, and browse merchandise catalogs, music collections and the world's libraries electronically.

Health NEWS&NOTES

HMOs—How It All Began

(NAPS)—Fifty years ago, Kaiser Permanente opened its unique health plan to the public.

Today, the world's largest and oldest health maintenance organization (HMO) provides care to 6.6 million Americans in 16 states and the District of Columbia.

During the past five decades, Kaiser's idea of providing quality, comprehensive healthcare for a set monthly fee—originally a dime a day—has endured and the HMO movement has flourished.

Nationwide this year, HMOs will provide comprehensive care to more than 50 million people. And, President Clinton and Congress are looking to these managed care plans to help the government control Medicare costs.

The idea of a health plan, hospitals and doctors working as a team to emphasize prevention, coordinate care and control costs has spread across the American landscape. But more importantly, this idea that worked for Henry J. Kaiser's 200,000 workers in California and the Northwest during the 1930's and 1940's is now producing a new standard of quality care for the 1990's.

"The best measure of quality is whether you produced a good result for the patient," explains David M. Lawrence, MD, Kaiser Permanente Chairman and CEO. Two examples:

• The Kaiser Permanente Pediatric Vaccine Study Center in the Northern California Region sponsored clinical trials that led to the 1990 development of a vac-

Oregon Govenor Charles Sprague, Henry J. Kaiser and Edgar Kaiser accompany President Roosevelt during a visit to Kaiser Shipyards in Portland in 1942. Three years later, Henry Kaiser launched Kaiser Permanente.

cine to prevent infant meningitis.

• The Kaiser Permanente Breast Screening Program in Colorado helps detect breast cancer at an early stage—an extremely important factor in beating this potentially fatal disease. Program specifics include protective screenings, which automatically enter into the program database all female members age 40-75; a personal profile detailing family history and other potential risk factors; and a computerized tracking system that monitors surgical referrals and sends out screening reminders.

Clearly all the data show that the benefits of Kaiser Permanente's efforts to continually improve care have paid off, according to Dr. Lawrence.

Figure 6.4 A feature with a historical angle. Kaiser Permanente used the timely topic of HMOs to distribute a short feature via a camera-ready distribution firm. Camera-ready means that editors merely clip the article and place it in the newspaper's layout. (*Courtesy of North American Precis Syndicate, New York.*)

PARTS OF A FEATURE

The formatting of a feature is similar to that of a news release. You should use the organization's letterhead, and give the standard information such as contacts, headlines and datelines. Lines should be double-spaced, and sentences or paragraphs should not break between pages.

The Lead

News releases usually have a summary lead that tells the basic facts in a nutshell. The name of the organization is in the lead, and readers would get the key information if the summary was all they read.

In contrast, the purpose of a lead feature story is to attract attention and get the reader interested enough to read the entire article. A good lead requires creativity on the writer's part because it must intrigue people and appeal to their curiosity. A lead is a promise; it tells people that they will learn something that is beneficial to them.

The human interest angle often makes a good lead. Here is the lead that Ketchum Public Relations of Chicago used on the feature story for Rand McNally, makers of maps and atlases, featured in Chapter 4:

> PARROTT, Va.—The town of Parrott, Va., a sleepy hamlet of 800 residents nestled among the Appalachian Mountains in western Virginia, couldn't be found by most of the outside world—until now. That's because Chris Muncy, a 10-year-old boy from Mishawaka, Ind., helped put Parrott "on the map."

As you may recall, the story goes on to relate that the boy had written to Rand McNally, asking the mapmaker to put his grandparents' town in the next edition of the company's road atlas.

Excellent examples of the human interest or personalized lead are found on the front page of the *Wall Street Journal*. Here are some examples:

> Gregory Miller is kneeling to repair a fence when, without warning, a 35-pound baboon hurtles through the air and lands on his shoulders. Mr. Miller doesn't flinch, but quietly reaches for his pliers to continue his work. (Story about the establishment of a refuge for exotic animals.)

> Seated around a hotel conference room are two dozen men involved in a nearby construction project. The men are here because they hate each other's guts. (Story about construction companies using group therapy facilitators to reduce infighting and legal disputes among contractors.)

> In Arthur Bushkin's view of the future, he will never rent a second-choice video. He will never queue up at an airline counter. And he will never wait in a bank line behind a customer signing traveler's checks for a world tour. (Story about the new president of Bell Atlantic Corporation, who envisions the television company offering a host of innovative new services in the next several years.)

A good lead may focus on the most unusual part of the feature. Thus a lead introducing the machine that builds curbs without forms could start with these words: "The formless curber lays concrete curbs without the use of expensive forms." This statement is factual and true, but the feature would be much more interesting if it started like this: "It's just like squeezing toothpaste out of a tube. In fact, it works on the same principle. By squeezing the concrete through a die shaped like the final curbing, it is possible to lay concrete curbs without the labor and materials needed for forms." This lead should appeal to the contractor who is a prospective buyer of the machine. It is unusual, it is interesting, and it promises the reward of savings.

Body of the Feature

Chapter 5 pointed out that news releases use the inverted pyramid, presenting the most important facts first and elaborating on them in the succeeding paragraphs. It also pointed out that news releases should be relatively short.

The feature story, in contrast, has none of these constraints. It doesn't need to follow Ryan's four basic paragraphs, and it can be 2,000 or 3,000 words long (six to eight pages).

The practical guide to length is to use enough words to tell the story thoroughly but to stop writing when it is told. Since most features are planned for specific publications, you should look at the average length of features in the chosen medium. Food sections in the newspaper, for example, tend to want features that are 500 to 750 words long.

Feature stories emphasize the following:

- Quotes from people.
- Concrete examples and illustrations.
- Descriptive words that paint mental pictures.
- Information presented in an entertaining way.

Keep in mind the use of parallels. A strange subject will be more understandable if it is explained in familiar terms—as in the curbs-as-toothpaste example. In the amplification of that story, the writer would undoubtedly explain how the concrete is squeezed out of the die using a screw like that in a meat grinder, which extrudes the concrete mix and at the same time pushes the machine away from the newly cast curb.

If a feature runs to several pages, insert subheads. The subheads, often bold-faced or underlined, indicate the major sections of the story. Subheads, however, should also provide information. Instead of saying something vague such as "Adaptability," it is better to write "Adaptability at Local Offices."

The body of the story essentially delivers the reward promised in the lead.

Summary

In many cases the summary is the most important part of the feature. It is often quite brief, but it must be complete and clear. Essentially, it is the core of the idea that the writer wants to leave with the reader. The summary of a toxic waste feature could stress that the company's program makes the area's groundwater safer.

Photos and Graphics

A feature story is often accompanied by photos and graphics to give it more appeal. Pacific Bell, for example, sent a photo of the Vietnamese manager with its release (refer back to Figure 6.3). Ketchum Public Relations enclosed the photo shown in Figure 6.5 with stories sent to food editors. Product features often include photos of the product.

Increasingly, publications are using "infographics," computer generated artwork that attractively displays simple tables and charts. *USA Today* pioneered the use of infographics, and newspapers around the nation now use them with great frequency. A feature story about a survey, for example, might include colored pie and bar charts graphically showing the results of the survey. See Chapter 7 for more information on infographics.

Try to come up with some ideas about photos and artwork that will give your feature story extra appeal. Chapter 7 gives more information about photos and artwork.

Figure 6.5 Food recipes and features are made more attractive with photographs. This photo accompanied a feature story from the California Prune Board that highlighted prunes as an ingredient in a pancake recipe. (*Courtesy of Ketchum Public Relations, San Francisco.*)

PLACEMENT OPPORTUNITIES

The possibilities for feature story placement are endless. Media Distribution Services, a company that sends news releases and feature stories, says there are more than 50,000 print and broadcast media in the United States, and more than 165,000 editors, broadcasters, free-lance writers and syndicated columnists are on its database.

Your challenge is to figure out what kind of publication would be most interested in your feature story. It may be only one particular trade publication, or it may be all weekly newspapers in the country. See Chapter 10 for a discussion of press directories that can help you make that decision.

In general, placement opportunities for the print media include newspapers, general circulation magazines, specialty/trade magazines and internal publications. Placement opportunities for broadcast media are discussed in Chapter 8.

Newspapers

The primary use of features generated by public relations personnel is in the special sections of daily newspapers. The food section is a popular place for manufacturers and producers of food products, and the automotive section gets its fair share of features from Ford, General Motors and Chrysler.

Weekly newspapers aren't as specialized, but editors are always on the lookout for features that affect the average citizen. The Internal Revenue Service, the Social Security Administration and even producers of grass seed often get space because they give tips to the public about how to save on taxes, file for social security or grow a great lawn.

General Magazines

Although it can be argued that there is no longer any such thing as a "general" magazine, we use the term to mean "popular" magazines such as *Better Homes and Gardens, Redbook, Popular Mechanics* and *People.*

These magazines usually have their own staffs and regular free-lancers who write features, but they do rely on public relations sources for ideas and information. Thus *Seventeen* magazine might carry an article about the difference between suntan lotions and sunscreens. Most of the information would probably have originated with a sunscreen manufacturer that hired a public relations firm to create publicity and increase sales to female teenagers.

Specialty/Trade Magazines

There are two kinds of magazines in this category. The first is magazines that serve particular interest and hobby groups. There are magazines for golfers, surfers, car buffs, stamp collectors, scuba divers, joggers, gardeners, and even soap opera fans. The list of hobbies and interests is endless.

Dear Editor,

NewView, Inc. has the ultimate solution to managing kids' online access to the wonders -- and sometimes unacceptable content -- of the Internet and World Wide Web without alienating the kids or infringing on the freedom of speech rights of content creators.

This new software is an innovative solution to the ongoing controversy regarding indecency on the internet. These kinds of solutions are a positive alternative to government censorship on the net. Please go to the site and check it out, then call me with any questions.

Developed by father-of-five and former Charles Schwab CIO Woody Hobbs who traded the comfort of corporate life to pioneer Internet access management solutions, NewView's *iscreen!*™ service is the most advanced, easy-to-use online management tool for concerned parents and schools:

- Most current and reliable range of site ratings
- Wider range of rating categories extend past usual pornography, obscenity and violence to include religious, politcal and lifestyle content, games, money transactions, bulletin boards, email, etc,
- Customers can create personalized profiles with specified degrees of Internet access for each individual child or select easy-to-use age-based defaults
- Inclusive approach only allows access to *safe-sites*™, so unrated sites cannot slip through
- Client server based system eliminates need for customers to download/update files
- *iscreen!* software can be downloaded for free from the Internet and customers only pay one low annual subscription fee.
- Fun *iball!*™ kids page is starting point for online adventures

I would be glad to provide more detailed information on NewView and *iscreen!* Here is the url: http://www.newview.com. The initial pricing has been set at $39.95 per year. I'll call you soon to see if you need additional information.

    Contact: *Rebecca Garcia*
          Neal-May & Partners
          415/328-5555 ext. 117

Figure 6.6 A generic "pitch" letter to trade editors encouraging them to write a feature about a new technology. Notice the use of bullets to highlight key information. A news release for the same product is shown in Chapter 5. (*Courtesy of Neale-May & Partners, Palo Alto, CA.*)

Whenever your organization has something bearing on a special field of interest, there may be a theme for a feature—and it is possible to write more than one feature on the same subject. With a new line of golf clubs, one story might tell how the line was developed under the guidance of a well-known player; another might deal with unusual materials and manufacturing techniques; and a third could describe the experience of several golfers with the new clubs. Each of these stories might be placed with a different golf magazine.

The second category is publications that serve a particular industry. There are, for example, about 2,600 publications covering the computer industry. The advent of the Internet has spawned a whole new set of publications.

Another thing to remember in preparing features for business or trade publications is that a given subject might be of interest in several fields. The remodeling of a hotel could lead to features for a number of unrelated publications. Engineering magazines could be interested in structural problems and solutions, architectural magazines might use stories about design and decoration, travel publications might use stories about the renaissance of an obsolescent favorite and hotel supply magazines might use stories about new carpeting, furniture, kitchen facilities and so on.

Internal Publications

Many internal publications use material from outside sources. The most likely prospects are those where there is a built-in interest. A feature telling how something produced by your organization is helping another organization has an innate interest. For example, you might have a feature describing exactly how your company makes the special insulating material that the XYZ company is using to produce cold-weather footwear. The XYZ company newsletter or magazine might welcome such a piece.

SUMMARY

1. Feature writing requires right brain thinking—intuition, image-making and conceptualization.

2. A feature story can generate publicity for "ho hum" products and services. It also can give background, context and the human dimension to events and situations.

3. Feature writing uses the "soft sell" approach. The name of the organization, the product or the service may only appear once or twice.

4. A good feature writer is curious and asks a lot of questions. He or she can conceptualize and see possibilities for the development of a feature article.

5. There are three approaches to feature writing: (1) distribute a general feature to a variety of publications; (2) write an exclusive article for a publication and (3) interest a free-lancer or reporter in writing a story.

6. There are several types of features: (1) case study, (2) research study, (3) backgrounder, (4) personality profile, (5) historical feature and (6) application story.

7. Feature stories are formatted much like news releases in terms of using letterheads, contacts, headlines and datelines.

8. A feature should use quotes, concrete examples, highly descriptive words and information presented in an entertaining way.

9. Photos and graphics are an integral part of a feature story package.

10. There are numerous placement opportunities for feature articles in specialty newspaper sections (food, real estate, etc.), general circulation magazines, special interest magazines, business and trade magazines and internal publications.

EXERCISES

1. Feature leads are different in form and tone than straight news leads. Write a feature lead for each of the following story subjects:
   a. The Florida Grapefruit Growers Association has announced that this year's crop is larger than last year's, and greater availability will mean lower prices for the consumer.
   b. IBM has announced a major breakthrough in the technology of computer design, which will enable the company to sell its new generation of personal computers at half the current price.
   c. A Los Angeles company, Map Guide, has introduced a dashboard computer for cars that will show local maps on a screen and let drivers know exactly where they are at any given time.
   d. Because of the weak Australian dollar, wines from that nation are now good bargains in the United States.
   e. The Denver Livestock Show and Rodeo, a tradition for 75 years, will begin on January 5 and run through January 12.
   f. An Arizona insurance company has cut its utilities bill in half by converting its trash into electrical energy at its headquarters building.

2. The personality profile often appears in the business section of the daily newspaper. It usually outlines how a businessperson became successful or overcame major difficulties to make his or her company profitable again. Select a business executive in your community, and write a personality profile about him or her. The feature should be six to eight pages long, typed and double-spaced.

3. A number of university professors are engaged in research projects that increase our understanding of a subject. Select a professor on your campus, and write an in-depth feature explaining his or her research and why it is important.

4. The food section of a daily newspaper often carries background features on the origin and contemporary uses of various food products. Do some library research about the introduction of oranges into this country and the current status of the orange-growing industry. Since this feature is for the food section of a

daily newspaper, include information that would be helpful to consumers. The objective of the feature story, of course, is to increase the sale of oranges.

5. The historical feature is often written when an organization or even a building reaches a major milestone such as its fiftieth or hundredth anniversary. Write a historical feature about a building or an academic department on your campus. Or write a historical feature about something in the community.

6. Contact a local manufacturing company to find out if its product is being used in any new and innovative ways. On the basis of information provided by the company or consumers of the product, write an application feature. Write the feature article for possible use in a trade publication covering a particular industry.

7. Nike, Inc., has just introduced a new running shoe that collects energy released by each step and returns some of it to the wearer. These "high-tech" shoes, made with polyurethane and having compressed air sandwiched in the sole, represent a new "biomechanical design." This new product could lead to a number of feature stories in various general, business, and trade publications. Compile a list of possible publications, and name the feature angle that could be used for each one.

7 *Photos and Graphics*

*P*hotographs and graphics are an important component of news releases and feature stories. They add interest and variety, and they often explain things better than words alone. According to Media Relations Insider, *a California-based newsletter,* "Today, more than ever, editors and reporters are starving for 'good art' to supplement text and fill pages. . . ."

You should continually think of ways to use photos and graphics to supplement your words. Good quality artwork can increase the chances of media placement and can do a more effective job of communicating your story in today's highly visual culture. This chapter explores the elements that make a good publicity photo or graphic and explains how to prepare the material for media consideration.

ELEMENTS OF A GOOD PUBLICITY PHOTO

The adage says a picture is worth a thousand words. A picture in a newspaper or magazine often takes the same space as a thousand words, but it has much more impact.

Studies have shown that more people "read" photographs than read articles. The Advertising Research Foundation found that three to four times as many people notice the average one-column photograph as read the average news story. Another researcher, Wayne Wanta, found that articles accompanied by photographs are perceived as significantly more important than articles without photographs. This also applies to graphics, which will be discussed later in the chapter.

Publicity photos, however, don't get published if they are not high quality or do not appeal to media gatekeepers. Although professional photographers are hired to take the photos, the public relations writer often supervises their work and selects the "best" photos to distribute. Therefore, you need to know what makes a good publicity photo.

This section discusses such factors as (1) quality, (2) subject matter, (3) composition, (4) action, (5) scale, (6) camera angles, (7) lighting and (8) color.

Quality

The visual quality of a photo is very important. The key elements are good contrast and sharp detail so that it will reproduce well on any paper, including newsprint. You must also consider that photos are often reduced in size or, on occasion, enlarged when they are published. If they have good contrast and detail to begin with, they will hold their quality.

The industry standard is to submit photos printed on glossy paper in an 8- by 10-inch or 5- by 7-inch format. Simple mug shots (head and shoulders) can be submitted in a 4- by 5-inch format. Matte photos, which have a dull finish, do not work well for printing, but they can be used for television. Today, many photos are transmitted in digital form directly to an editor's computer. This and other details will be discussed in the section on placement and distribution.

Subject Matter

There is a wide variety of subjects for a publicity photo. On one level, there are somewhat static photos of a new product or a newly promoted executive. On another level, photos are used to document events such as a groundbreaking or a ribbon cutting ceremony.

Major publications, however, no longer use many of the "grip and grin," "giant check passing," or "ribbon cutting" shots that have been a traditional staple of publicity photos in the past. These kind of photos have become tired clichés, and editors want more unusual or artistic material.

Group pictures nearly always present a problem; with them, it is relatively easy to violate the concepts of newsworthiness, action and central focus. There is often the danger of showing too many people, and most public relations professionals have adopted the rule that no more than three or four people should be in any one photo. Such a rule provides for more action, keeps the picture simple and makes every face easily identifiable.

A common mistake is to please everyone by having people pose for a group photo. This might mean the entire board of directors, 60 real estate salespeople, 125 college graduates or even all 250 members of a club. A group photo may be legitimate when you want to give a souvenir of a particular meeting or conference or provide documentation for a specialized publication such as a fraternal or alumni magazine. However, pictures of this kind should never be sent to the mass media.

One way to handle large groups is to take a series of small group pictures of individuals from the same town or company. These then let you multiply the coverage by localizing the event for hometown newspapers or employee publications.

In organizing these photo shoots, you should make sure there is activity in the picture; have people talking to each other, looking at a display, or shaking hands with a notable person in an informal pose. They should not be lined up looking at the camera. A common composition is to show three people all talking or listening to a fourth person who is at the left of the picture. This fourth person may be a keynote speaker, the president of an organization or someone who has just received an award. Such a composition can provide a focus.

In a group situation, it is extremely important that you take down the names and titles of people as they are photographed. This will make your job much easier later on, when you have to write the caption. Don't rely on memory—yours or anyone else's.

Composition

We have already discussed ways to compose photographs of groups. Inherent in all this is the concept of keeping the photo simple and uncluttered.

A look at the family album will illustrate the point. We have Aunt Minnie and Uncle Oswald looking like pygmies because the family photographer also wanted to include the entire skyline of New York City in the background. Consequently, Aunt Minnie and Uncle Oswald are standing about 35 feet from the camera.

In most cases, the photographer should move into, not away from, the central focus of the picture. If the purpose is to show a busy executive at his or her desk, the picture should be taken close up so that the subject fills most of it. Sufficient background should be included to provide context, but it is really not necessary to show the entire surface of the desk—including the disarray of papers, picture of spouse and kids and paperweight from a recent convention. All this tends to conflict with what the reader is supposed to look at.

Another reason for moving in on the subject and minimizing the background or foreground is to achieve good composition. That picture of Aunt Minnie and Uncle Oswald also shows the Empire State Building growing out of Uncle Oswald's head.

Experts have made the following suggestions about composition and clutter:

- Take tight shots with minimal background. Concentrate on what you want the reader to get from the picture.

- Emphasize detail, not whole scenes.
- Don't use a cluttered background. Pick up stray things that intrude on the picture.
- Try to frame the picture.
- Avoid wasted space. There should not be a large gap between an object, such as an award, and the person's face. In the case of a group picture, have people stand close to each other.
- Have anyone in a group picture wearing sunglasses remove them.

All this advice is logical, but there may be times when the background plays an important role. If the picture is to show a group at the opening of some structure, such as a building or a dam, it will be necessary to include it in the background. In doing this, the photographer should place the group in such a way that the background or a portion of it is visible but contrasts with the group.

You may also think of ways to get the client's product or name into the background. A standard procedure is to get the executives of a company in the foreground with the name of the company on a building or a sign directly behind them.

Action

Action is important because it projects movement and the idea that something is happening right before the reader's eyes. A picture of someone doing something—talking, gesturing, laughing, running, operating a machine—is more interesting than a picture of a person standing still and looking at the camera.

America's amateur photographers have filled the nation's family albums with pictures of Aunt Minnie and Uncle Oswald in rigid, formal poses, staring blankly, but a quick look through your daily newspaper will not turn up this kind of shot. Prize-winning news photographs bear out that action is the key element in successful photography. A football quarterback throwing a ball makes a better picture than the same player standing on the field during a time-out.

With some thinking, an action photo can be taken of almost any situation. Good examples of this will be found in the pictures released by the White House. Instead of a rigidly posed group staring at the camera, the pictures usually show the president and other people in animated discussion or greeting each other. This conveys action and spontaneity and creates interest.

An announcement in an employee publication of a new hire or a promotion can be made into an action picture. Instead of merely showing a head-and-shoulders shot of the employee, show the employee in the working environment—talking on a phone, operating a machine, talking to another new employee or an immediate superior.

There are times when a straight head-and-shoulders portrait is exactly what's needed. For example, a press release announcing a promotion or the new president of a club or organization is often accompanied by just a mug shot.

You can add interest to a picture of a machine by showing someone examining or operating it. You can generate more reader interest by focusing on just one part of the machine that has an unusual design or looks interesting. For example, show

Figure 7.1 Photo composition is important. This publicity photo is tightly focused, shows activity and uses an interesting camera angle. (*Courtesy of California Culinary Academy, San Francisco.*)

the part of the machine where the bottles are being capped or the labels are being applied.

Although buildings cannot show action, you can add interest by placing people in the foreground, either walking by the building or talking together. If you are taking a picture for a restaurant or a supermarket, remember that people and activity in the picture convey more than just the picture of the building on a Sunday morning surrounded by an empty parking lot. A publicity photo does not have to show the entire building. In many cases, it is better to focus on an unusual aspect or an area that offers human interest.

You should not conclude, however, that all good pictures must suggest overt action. Some of the greatest photos have been character studies of people whose faces reflected their happiness at having won an award, their intense concentration on a critical issue or their sorrow at having lost an election.

Scale

With inanimate objects, it is important to consider the scale. The picture should contain some element of known size so that the viewer can understand how big or small the object is. With large machines, it is common and effective to place a person in the picture. This helps the viewer estimate the approximate size of the picture's subject.

When smaller things are photographed, the scale guide is even more important. This also offers an opportunity to provide drama and adds the news value of novelty. For example, a transistor has been photographed inside a walnut shell, a miniature radio beside a quarter and a computer in a wallet.

Camera Angles

Interest can also be achieved through the use of unusual camera angles. Shooting upward at a tall structure makes it look even taller. An aerial shot often gives the viewer a chance to see something that might otherwise be unnoticeable. Telephoto shots can bring an unreachable object close enough to show details that are not visible from a distance. A fish-eye lens can capture a 180-degree image.

Lighting and Timing

If you want a picture of the company's executives in front of the new headquarters and the photo has to be taken in a westward direction, you should schedule the shooting in the morning. Otherwise the glare of the afternoon sun may have a detrimental effect. In general, outdoor pictures taken in the morning or late afternoon are better for contrast than pictures taken at midday. Of course, the photographer can use a flash to lighten dark areas.

Another tip is to take your picture before a planned event like a banquet. Before the keynote speaker and the officials go to the head table, take pictures in an anteroom. This is easier than trying to corral everyone after the banquet.

Selecting the location or setting of a picture is important if you want good, sharp results. For example, if you know that the people involved will be wearing

Figure 7.2 Scale increases impact. The photo shows a technician using a magnifying glass to examine a strand of hair to determine its properties for best coloring and conditioning results. (*Courtesy of L'Oreal Worldwide, Paris.*)

light colors, you should not use a white background. Conversely, don't select a dark background if your photo subjects will be wearing dark clothing.

Color

The vast majority of publicity photographs are still produced in black and white because they are economical, versatile and acceptable to most publications. However, color photographs are increasingly being used by all kinds of publications as print-

HOW TO TAKE PRODUCT PHOTOS THAT GET PUBLISHED

1. Show the product in a scene where it would logically be used. If it's used in an office, show it in an office. Don't fake it.
2. Clean up the area where the picture is to be taken. Remove any litter or extraneous items. Repaint if necessary.
3. If people are in the picture, be sure that they are dressed for the situation. They should wear the kind of clothing that they would wear while using the product.
4. Get perspective into the photo so that viewers will know how big the item is. Show a hand, a person, a pencil.
5. If you need black-and-white pictures, don't rely on making prints from color negatives. They won't be as good.
6. Don't accept anything but the best in photographs. They have a potential shelf life of five years; many may be used by others to illustrate books or brochures. Give them quality.
7. Take at least two photos—vertical and horizontal—of each new product. This makes them adaptable to a variety of situations. When possible, show the product in use. Application stories need illustrations.
8. If there are other products in the picture, be sure that the new one is in the dominant position. The setting should be realistic, with everything hooked up and ready to go.
9. Every picture must have an identifying caption.
10. Be sure that the background contrasts with the product. Make the product stand out.
11. Check your models. Look at complexions. Is there anything that would ultimately require retouching? Are neckties straight? Is hair combed?

Source: Adapted from an internal memo for the product publicity department of the Hewlett-Packard Company.

ing technology becomes more sophisticated and less expensive to use. Color can be used in at least three types of publications: in leaflets or brochures, in magazines that publish color photos and in special sections of daily and weekly newspapers. Color is now commonly used in the food, business, sports, entertainment and travel sections of newspapers.

Everything that has been said about composition and quality should be underlined in relation to color pictures. To be used, they must be outstanding in both interest and technical quality. They must be produced by professionals.

Color film offers two options: color negative film or color transparency film. The latter involves a one-step process because the film is developed directly into transparencies that can be reproduced by publications or used for slide presentations. According to public relations counselor Benjamin Chapnick (*Public Relations Quarterly*, Fall 1990), this process costs only one-fourth what it costs to make prints from color negative film. Printing reproduction is done from a four-color separation made from the transparency.

Figure 7.3 Product photos use lighting and dark backgrounds to focus attention on the product. (*Courtesy of Hewlett-Packard Company, Palo Alto, CA.*)

Color negative film, by contrast, involves a three-step process. The film is developed into negatives from which contact sheets are made. You then select the pictures you want, and they are made into color prints. The extra steps add costs, and the negatives, unlike transparencies, have no practical use on their own.

The preferences of various publications vary; the best procedure is to ask editors whether they want to receive transparencies or negative film. This can be done by telephone or in a letter that accompanies press materials. Some press directories indicate the photo preferences of publications.

WORKING WITH PHOTOGRAPHERS

It is important to use a skilled photographer with professional experience. Too many organizations try to cut corners by asking some amateur in or associated with the organization to take pictures. More often than not, the results are disappointing and unacceptable.

It will cost more money to hire a professional photographer, but at least you won't end up with pictures that are unusable. Another reason is that it is better business practice to use a professional. You can give direction to a photographer who is being paid, whereas it may be awkward to criticize the boss's nephew or a colleague.

Finding Photographers

You should have a file of photographers, noting their fees and particular expertise. If you have no such file built up, you might consult colleagues to find out if they can make any recommendations. If you are unfamiliar with a photographer's work, ask to see his or her portfolio. This is important because photographers are skilled at different things.

A good portrait photographer, for example, may be bad at photographing special events. A news photographer, by contrast, may be an expert at special events but unable to take good product photographs. In sum, you should find the special photographer you need for each kind of job.

Photographers' fees vary widely, so it pays to compare prices. If you are on a tight budget, you might also consider using college students who are majoring in photojournalism. They are not quite professional yet, but they have learned most of the basics and may be good enough.

Contracts

Any agreement with a photographer, as Chapter 2 pointed out, should be in writing. A written document helps you to avoid misunderstandings about fees, cost of prints and ownership of the negatives.

A letter of agreement with a photographer should cover the following matters:

- The photographer's basic fee for taking pictures and a statement of exactly what this includes (developing the film, making prints and so on).
- Costs of prints or transparencies. (Most photographers charge for each item ordered.)
- Who will supervise the photographer. (Will you or someone else in the organization help the photographer set up shots?)
- Who pays expenses—mileage, food, lodging—while the photographer is on assignment.
- Who will retain the negatives. (Photographers generally want to retain all negatives in their files. This gives them the opportunity to sell you more prints at a later date.)
- Nature of use. (Does the organization have unrestricted use of the photograph, or does it have to get permission from the photographer each time it wants to use the shot?)
- Photographer's use of negatives. (Can the photographer sell prints to outside parties, either individuals or other organizations?)

The last point can be a bone of contention and create poor public relations for an organization. It is not uncommon for a photographer to expand the revenues from a photo session by contacting people in the pictures individually and asking if they want to purchase prints.

Before you hire the photographer, you should clearly establish whether it is all right for the photographer to make additional money selling prints to individuals.

In many cases, the organization wants exclusive rights to all photographs and their distribution for purposes of its own public relations outreach.

The Photo Session

You will save time and money if you plan ahead.

1. Make a list of the pictures you want. For pictures of people, arrange for a variety of poses.
2. Know who you need, where and when you need them and what props will be required.
3. Notify people whose pictures are to be taken. Get releases if needed (see Chapter 2).
4. Be sure that the location for the photo session is available, clean, orderly and so on.
5. Consider lighting. Will the photographer have everything needed, or should you make preparations?
6. Have everyone and everything at the right place at the right time.
7. Tell the photographer what you want, not how to do the job.

Cropping and Retouching

A photographer usually produces a series of contact sheets or proofs that show all the pictures on a roll of film, in regular negative size. This gives you an opportunity to review everything available and decide which pictures you want.

You can further improve the quality of the picture through the techniques of cropping and retouching. Cropping is editing the picture by slicing portions off. Eliminating parts of the picture permits a tighter focus on the key elements. For example, if a group picture includes the distracting element of a waiter at one side, clearing a table, you can crop the photo to eliminate the waiter.

The second technique, retouching, is usually done to alter the content of the picture. A retoucher's airbrush can also eliminate unwanted portions of the picture. Let's assume that the group picture just mentioned was taken in such a way that a basket of flowers on the stage behind the company president looks like it is planted on top of her head. The flowers can be airbrushed away and the void filled in.

Computer Altering of Photos

Cropping and retouching are common and uncontroversial practices in photography, but there are increasing ethical and legal concerns about the computer manipulation of photographic images.

Computer software and graphics programs are now so sophisticated that photographic images can be easily altered. An original photograph or drawing, for example, can be scanned by a laser beam and converted into digital signals that are fed into a computer. An editor can then call up the image on a computer screen and make alterations—for example, more stars can be added to the night sky or a per-

Figures 7.4 and 7.5 Edit photos by taking out surrounding clutter and getting a tighter composition. The first photo shows too much uninteresting background. The second picture has better composition; the men now dominate the photo and provide a focal point. (*Courtesy of Chevron Corporation, San Francisco.*)

son's dark suit can be changed to a light tan. The editor can airbrush out distracting background or merge the photo with another one stored in the computer's memory. An "output" device generates the new image for use on a printed page.

Advertising and public relations people often use computer alteration to enhance the quality of publicity photos. Thus the directors are shown with the company's production line behind them even though the original photo was taken in a studio. Or a new product is enhanced by blacking out the background and putting more light on the actual product.

The examples cited so far are relatively harmless, but news editors worry about additional liberties that may be taken. For example, *National Geographic* provoked a major outcry when it used a computer to move two of the pyramids of Giza closer together so that they would fit on the magazine's cover.

Sensational tabloid newspapers have also come under fire for computer merging of photos to show celebrities who have never met talking to each other at an intimate dinner party.

Photographers also worry about the new computer technology because their photos can be altered and used without permission or the payment of royalties. One photographer's picture of a racing yacht was used on a poster after the art director changed the numbers on the sail and made the water a deeper blue. This raises the issue of who owns such a new "original" picture.

Computer alteration of a photo is a judgment call that you, as a public relations specialist, will have to make. You have a professional responsibility to honor the original photographer's work and present accurate information; if an altered photo misleads and deceives the public in a significant way, do not use it.

WRITING PHOTO CAPTIONS

Photos, sent with a news release or by themselves, need what is called a "caption." This is the brief text under the photo that tells the reader what is going on.

This doesn't mean describing a photo. Some novice caption writers make the mistake of writing, "Pictured above . . ." or "This is a picture of . . . ." Don't write the obvious; write to provide context and additional information that are not readily apparent by looking at the picture.

Most captions are two to four lines long. In fact, one study by Gallup Applied Science showed that two-line captions are the most effective. The *New York Times*, for example, consistently uses two-line captions.

Use the active, present tense. Don't write "The park gates were opened by Mayor Jones"; instead say "Mayor Jones opens the park gates." You should use active, present tense when describing activity in the picture, but you can shift to past tense when you begin to give the context or situation. For example:

- John Iwata, president of IBM, speaks to employees at the company's plant in Dayton. He was in town as part of a multi-city tour to promote total quality management (TQM).

- Northern Telecom's Donald Jones explains the Norstar system to Gussie Brown, chairperson of the Urban League. In the past year, the company has donated 100 systems to community agencies.

Sometimes the photo shows no activity but is just an informal portrait of someone who is the subject of the news release or feature article. Here are examples of captions carried by the *New York Times:*

- Michael Edwards started Exodus Productions, which markets Christian-themed apparel, by selling T-shirts at a church in Texas where his wife was a youth minister.
- Steeler's Pro Bowl cornerback Carnell Lake will go head-to-head with the Cowboy's Pro Bowl receiver Michael Irvin in the Super Bowl.
- Fran Tarkenton, who works out of an Atlanta office, now hopes to teach small business people how to profit from the Internet.

On the other hand, a caption for a head-and-shoulders picture of a person (the mug shot) can be even shorter. The caption may contain just the person's name.

Captions for publicity photos of new products should include a key selling point. For example:

The new HP OmniGo 100 handheld organizer is for the busy professional who wants the dual-functionality of pen and keyboard.

There is some argument about stating "from left to right" in a photo caption. To many people this seems redundant because people read copy—and probably scan photographs—from left to right anyway. If there are two or three people in the picture, it is assumed that you are identifying them from left to right. You can also indicate identity by the action taking place in the picture—for example, "John Baroni presents Nancy Southwick with a $5,000 scholarship at the annual awards banquet."

In general, the most important person in the photograph should be the first person at the left side of the picture. This ensures that this person is mentioned first in the photo caption. The most important person may alternatively be in the center of the picture, surrounded by admirers. In this case, you can write, "Sharon Lewis, the singer, is surrounded by adoring fans after her concert in Denver." Any reader should be able to figure out which person in the picture is Sharon Lewis.

Here are two captions for the same picture, the first poor, the second better:

From left to right, Hazel Oatley and Les Steinberg are shown standing amid sandbags at a Parker, Arizona, resort on the banks of the swollen Colorado River. They are part of a Red Cross team working all night to keep the river from flooding the resort and surrounding residential areas. The water was 5 feet deep and covered the boat dock behind them.

Hazel Oatley and Les Steinberg stand amid sandbags at a Parker, Arizona, resort on the banks of the swollen Colorado River. They were part of a Red Cross team working all night to keep the river from flooding. Five feet of water covers the boat dock behind them.

Notice that the second version uses the active present tense and eliminates words that slow the reader down.

Format of a Caption

A caption has a format similar to a news release in terms of identifying information. Here are some tips:

- Start copy about halfway down a 8 1/2- by 11-inch sheet of paper. This leaves enough blank space for attaching it to the photo (see next section).
- Give identifying information such as name of organization, date, contact and telephone numbers.
- You may wish to use a headline—a short phrase that indicates the nature of the caption.
- Do not indent. All the lines of a caption should be flush left.
- Keep the caption clear, concise and in the present tense.

Attaching the Caption

There are two methods of attaching the caption to the photograph.

The traditional way is to affix the back of the photo (8- by 10-inch or 5- by 7-inch is the preferred size) to the upper half of the page, which is blank. Remember that you started your copy about halfway down the page. Rubber cement is the best adhesive, but you can also use tape; just be sure that it can be peeled off without harming the photo. Never use paper clips or staples because they damage the photo.

You then fold the caption up over the photo. This will give the photo extra protection from scratches or marring. When the publication receives the photo and caption, the reporter or editor simply unfolds the caption and can look at the photo while reading the caption.

The second method, which is used in extensive mailing of the same photo to multiple media outlets, is to simply incorporate the caption into the bottom of the photo. An example of this method from the Minnesota Zoo is shown in Figures 7.6 and 7.7. Photo and graphic production companies can make you 100 or 1,000 copies of a publicity photo using this technique.

The two methods outlined above work fine for printed photos, but what about color slides and transparencies? It doesn't make much sense to attach an 8 1/2- by 11-inch sheet of paper to a slide.

Summertime visitors to the Minnesota Zoo will be treated to the wondrous colors of this tiger swallowtail. Zoo-goers will be able to view many different types of butterflies and moths in varying stages of their life cycles. BUGS! will feature thousands of butterflies, insects and spiders, and runs May 28 through Labor Day. (*Photo by David Reconnu, Charleroi, PA.*)

Creeping and crawling this summer at the Minnesota Zoo, this spider will be one of many on exhibit at BUGS! Visitors will be able to view the spiders and other creepy crawlies up close (but not too close!). BUGS! will feature thousands of butterflies, insects and spiders, and runs May 28 through Labor Day. (*Photo by Minnesota Zoo.*)

Figures 7.6 and 7.7 Captions can be printed right on a picture. This makes for more efficient mailing of photos to multiple media outlets. These photos were part of a press kit on a new zoo exhibit. (*Courtesy of Minnesota Zoo, Apple Valley, MN.*)

The proper approach, in this instance, is to prepare captions on a separate sheet of paper. Each slide will carry the company name or logo and a number. This number is keyed to the caption on the sheet of paper. For example:

SLIDE NO: 00793–96

CAPTION: HP's Pavilion line of personal computers includes full multimedia capabilities, a friendly interface for a range of user sets, 16-bit sound cards and stereo speakers.

This color slide, from Hewlett-Packard Company, is reproduced in black and white in Figure 7.3 as an example of product publicity.

PACKAGING AND DISTRIBUTION

Photos, particularly color slides or negatives, add considerable expense to the distribution process.

Publications still receive numerous black and white photos, which are the least expensive, but you should still do some homework before shotgunning photos all over the country. Metropolitan dailies, for example, don't use as many photos from public relations sources as smalltown weeklies. And some newspapers, such as the *Wall Street Journal*, don't use any photos.

Because of expense, color slides and negatives are not usually distributed with news releases, feature stories or press kits. Instead, the editors are told what is available and how to request what they want via fax, E-mail or telephone. For example, a food editor on a large daily may receive several features from a public relations firm along with a note describing what artwork is available. The editor will make one or more selections and then phone the listed contact who, in turn, will send the artwork.

The new technology makes photos and graphics even easier to receive. One approach is to scan the photos into the computer and E-mail them to the editor. Another way is to place publicity photos in the company's home page on the World Wide Web and let the editor download what he or she likes. Using the Internet as a distributor of publicity materials is covered more fully in Chapter 10.

Publicity photos, as well as news releases, can also be distributed via commercial services, such as Business Wire, that electronically transmit them into a newspaper's computer.

All this high technology is quite impressive, but remember that not everyone is cruising down the information highway. A small weekly publication in Montrose, Colorado, may still need the photo sent the old-fashioned way. That means a photo and accompanying material placed in a first class envelope, delivered by the U.S. Postal Service. If you are sending photos that way, make sure you provide a sheet of heavy paper to protect the photos and mark the envelope—Photos: Do Not Bend.

COMING NEAR YOU: THE ILLUSTRATED NEWS RELEASE

Visibility Public Relations in New York City is now using what is termed the illustrated news release.

The firm uses a scanner to incorporate photo stills into the news release itself. For example, in promoting Elton John's latest music video, Visibility made three stills from the video as part of the news release. The release gave editors a quick take on the story line and artwork available. They could then order a color slide or videotape. According to the firm, the process cuts duping costs and they don't have to send art to everyone on their mailing list.

Source: (PRSA) *Tactics,* August 1995, p. 3.

In sum, the distribution of photos and other graphics should be highly selective and based on the requirements of the publication.

As a cost-conscious public relations writer, it is your responsibility to ask editors and use media directories to find out the publication's policies. The day of mass distribution is over.

GRAPHICS

Photographs are not the only art form that you can use for publicity purposes. Charts, diagrams, renderings and models, maps, line drawings and clip art are widely used.

Many of these visuals can be formatted on your own computer using various software applications, but you should also consider using graphic artists and commercial illustrators. This is particularly true if you are preparing material for distribution to the media. As with photographers, ask to see illustrators' portfolios before you commission a particular assignment.

Charts

The primary reason for using charts is to make figures understandable. There are three basic charts for this purpose, and each seems to work best for certain kinds of information.

- *Pie Chart.* Ideal for showing what part of a total is used for each of several purposes. An organization may use such a chart to show how a budget is divided.

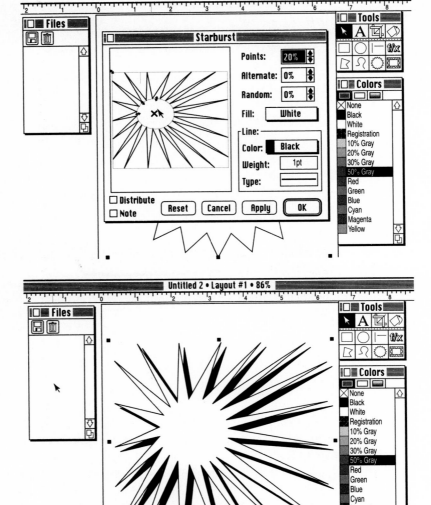

Figure 7.8 Computer graphics allow you to manipulate and shape a final product. You can add shading, reshape a design, place copy in the middle of it, and decide on a color combination. A number of desktop publishing programs have such capabilities.

- *Bar Chart.* Ideal for showing comparisons between years in such things as income, population, sales and prices.
- *Graph.* Somewhat like a bar chart, but better suited for showing changes over a long period of time. A simple graph may track sales and profits in relationship to each other.

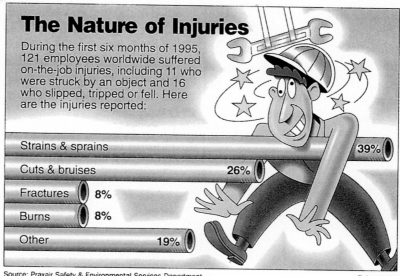

Did You Know?
Statistics About Praxair and Its People

The Nature of Injuries

During the first six months of 1995, 121 employees worldwide suffered on-the-job injuries, including 11 who were struck by an object and 16 who slipped, tripped or fell. Here are the injuries reported:

Strains & sprains	39%
Cuts & bruises	26%
Fractures	8%
Burns	8%
Other	19%

Source: Praxair Safety & Environmental Services Department   Robert Laird

Figure 7.9 Infographics liven up information and statistics. This graphic was prepared for an employee newsletter. (*Courtesy of Praxair, Inc., Danbury, CT.*)

Today, with computer graphics, charts are being dressed up to be more appealing and decipherable. Reading a copy of *USA Today* makes the point. Instead of showing a simple bar chart or graph, an attempt is made to incorporate representations of the subject into the chart.

A logging company, for example, might produce an "infographic" that uses trees instead of bars to show the number of trees planted annually. A chocolate company may use chocolate bars to show growth of sales over a five-year period. A good example of an infographic is Figure 7.9 from Praxair, Inc.

Infographics are popular with editors because they liven up an otherwise dull page. Editors want material that is appealing and relatively simple. Too much detail doesn't reproduce well and tends to turn readers off. Make sure the material is relevant and newsworthy. If the graphic is too commercial and promotional, it won't be used. Surveys also indicate that editors want one- or two-column graphics.

Infographics can be prepared on paper or sent to editors on a diskette. As with color photos, ask editors if they want the material before sending it. Another method, used by Porter/Novelli public relations, is to post infographics about their clients on a computer bulletin board. Editors can tap into the toll-free bulletin board with just a modem and a PC.

Large dailies usually have their own graphics departments and make their own infographics. However, many smaller dailies and thousands of weeklies have no such capability so they are less adverse to using material from outside sources.

Diagrams

Diagrams are most valuable in showing how something works. The functioning of an engine, the attachment of some accessory, the use of some product—all can be made clearer with a diagram.

In planning diagrams, you should not only check with the engineers but also pretest the final diagram on potential readers for comprehension and understanding. The key to effective artwork, particularly diagrams, is simplicity.

Renderings and Models

A rendering is an architect's drawing that shows how a finished structure will look. Increasingly, such artwork is being produced by computer drawing programs or the alteration of photos.

Photos of scale models are also used to give readers a thorough understanding of what is being built or renovated. Both renderings and scale models are widely used in news and feature stories about construction projects. The availability of such artwork often makes the difference between a major news story and a brief mention.

Maps

Maps can show where a road is to be built, how to get to a meeting, how traffic is to be routed or which streets will be closed or opened. They can explain the site of a proposed housing development, the location of a dam or the borders of a new lake created by a dam.

For your purposes, maps should, as far as possible, show the details necessary to understand the situation but avoid clutter and irrelevant information. Too much detail makes a map difficult to read. Remember, maps sent to the media are often reduced, so small type or thin lines may not reproduce.

Line Drawings and Clip Art

Cartoons are a form of line art, but most people think of line art as drawings of symbols, designs, and objects. These drawings are still made by artists using paper and ink, but the process is now available to almost anybody with a personal computer.

Barnaby Feder, a *New York Times* reporter, summarizes the state of the art as follows:

> Today's PC graphics programs typically come with hundreds or even thousands of stored images, called clip art, that users can put into their graphics as building blocks. Photographs, shots from video clips and animation can be pasted in as well. Users can also chose from virtually infinite varieties of color and quickly change perspectives, shading, overlapping images and other features.

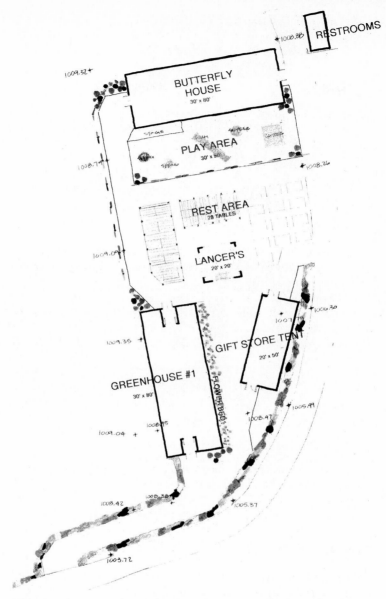

Figure 7.10 Maps can help readers easily understand where something is located. The Minnesota Zoo distributed this layout along with its information on a new exhibit that was opening. (*Courtesy of Minnesota Zoo, Apple Valley, MN.*)

Some popular art software programs are *QuarkXPress, Aldus PageMaker,* and *Adobe Illustrator.* On a commercial level, many newspapers and magazines use *Multi-Ad Creator.*

Figure 7.11   Clip art can be provided to media outlets so they can use graphics to illustrate a story. Note the different sizes of clip art that the Minnesota Zoo sent to publicize its new bug exhibit. (*Courtesy of Minnesota Zoo, Apple Valley, MN.*)

Clip art can be ordered on floppy disk or CD from a number of specialty companies. CD-ROM (read-only memory) technology has increased the variety of type fonts and line drawings considerably. Multi-Ad Services sells one compact disk set with over 3,000 graphics, symbols, and logos. Customers can also order a CD with over 1,500 Adobe and Monotype PostScript type fonts.

All of this puts a heavy demand on computer memory, display, and processing technology, which means that you need a high-powered personal computer to handle it. You also need a CD-ROM player and changer connected to your personal computer if you're importing programs and databases. However, if you don't have this capability, there are smaller clip art files embedded in the latest versions of *Microsoft Word*, *WordPerfect*, and *AppleWrite*. In addition, you can still use the traditional method of ordering binders of clip art that you can cut out and paste down

Figure 7.12 Line drawings and cartoons can be used to provide a graphic element in a story. Line drawings can be commissioned or simply taken from a commercial clip art catalog or CD-ROM. (*Courtesy of North American Precis Syndicate, New York.*)

on layouts. The advantage of computer clip art is that you can edit and alter the symbols to create new formats and designs.

A number of companies produce CDs and clip books on a monthly basis devoted to upcoming seasons and events such as Easter, Labor Day, the Fourth of July, Halloween, and Thanksgiving. For names of clip art vendors, consult a local printer or advertising firm. In addition, trade journals in art and design and public relations often contain advertisements for such firms.

Line drawings and clip art are used primarily for organizational advertisements, leaflets, brochures, and newsletters. They can also be used to illustrate press kits, position papers, and backgrounders sent to the media.

PHOTO AND ART FILE

A properly indexed and rigidly controlled illustration file is a necessity. Without this, negatives or artwork will be lost or the last print will be used and no one will know how to order replacements. Historically important pictures will lose their identity and be useless because everyone who knew what they meant is dead or gone from the organization.

You will probably have two kinds of pictures to deal with: those used in releases to the media and those used in printing internal materials. (Sometimes a picture will be used for both purposes.)

You may wish to file the news releases—including the captions—separately and maintain a different file for other pictures. In either case, the important thing is to be able to find pictures, know what they mean and order replacements. A further value of such a file is that it provides a permanent record of which pictures were used for which purpose. It also documents your activity.

Photos (you may have several prints of each subject, together with their negatives or original artwork) should be placed in file folders with readily identifiable headings. These may be names such as "J. Gladwyn Jones, Chairman" or topical areas such as "1995 Employee Recognition Banquet," "Grand Opening of Lansing Store" or "Scale Model of Springfield Office Bldg." If you do not have the negative, mark one print "File Copy" and attach the name and address of the photographer together with his or her identifying number so that you can reorder.

It is important to place in the file folder all pertinent data such as date picture was taken, location, photo releases from people portrayed, complete names and titles of people shown, name and address of photographer and restrictions on use of the picture.

SUMMARY

1. Photographs and graphics add appeal and increase media usage of news releases or features.

2. A public relations writer should be familiar with the elements of a good publicity photo: quality, subject matter, composition, action, scale, camera angle, lighting and color.

3. Publicity photos should be sharp, clear and high contrast.

4. Photos should be creative. Traditional pictures of "ribbon cuttings" no longer work.

5. A publicity photo should have no more than three or four people in it. Save the large group shot for the photo album.

6. Photos with action and informality are more interesting than rigid, posed shots.

7. Use professional photographers to produce photos for publication.

8. Crop photographs to remove clutter and get a tighter focus on the main subject.

9. Photo captions are short, use present tense to describe the action and provide context.

10. Photos and graphics can be distributed by regular mail, E-mail and the Internet.

11. Photos, particularly color slides, are expensive to distribute. Always check with an editor before sending them.

12. Charts, diagrams, maps, etc. should be simple and uncluttered.

13. Through computer technology, charts can be made more visually attractive. They are often called "infographics."

14. Line drawings and clip art can be commissioned or purchased. Many compilations are now on CD-ROM.

15. It is important to keep a well-organized photo and graphics file for reference purposes.

EXERCISES

1. Illustrative material can include photographs, line drawings, diagrams, models, charts and graphs. Find at least two examples of each from sources such as company newsletters, trade magazines, and newspapers. Mount each example on a single sheet of paper, and indicate the context in which it was used.

2. News releases and features, when accompanied by illustrative materials, often stand a better chance of being used. What types of illustrative materials would you recommend for the following news releases? Use your imagination and try to think of as many kinds as possible. Describe in what way each would be applicable.
a. The appointment of a new company president.
b. An announcement that a new 15-story hotel will be built.
c. An announcement of a new digital compact disk recorder manufactured by Sony.
d. A news story about the shortage of nurses in local hospitals.
e. A how-to feature about planting rosebushes.
f. A feature story about the rising popularity and sales of a sports car.
g. A feature story about the growth and success of a pizza chain since its beginning five years ago.
h. A chamber of commerce story about the ethnic diversity of a city.

3. A civic organization will be honoring five outstanding citizens at its annual banquet. Describe how you would organize and compose publicity photos of this event that would be acceptable to the photo editor of the local newspaper.

4. A local bank is having a grand opening for its new facilities, including the traditional ribbon cutting by city officials and an open house for the community. Describe what kinds of publicity photos could be taken of this event to ensure media acceptance.

5. Product publicity photos pose a major challenge, since it takes creativity to make a product look interesting and unusual. What kinds of publicity photos would you recommend for the following products?
a. An electric frying pan.
b. A new tamper-resistant bottle of aspirin.
c. A personal computer.
d. A golf cart.
e. Nonfat potato chips.
f. A toy.

6. Using the guidelines in this chapter, write a photo caption for the following situation: The picture shows two people and two collie dogs. One person is Dr. Ronald F. Jackson, former president of the American Heartworm Society. The other is Carolyn Matlack, owner of Teddy and Rose, the two collies. She is giving one dog a newly developed pill recently approved by the FDA to prevent heartworm disease in dogs. This medication, marketed by Merck & Co., is taken once a month. Prior to its development, the standard prescription was a daily pill. Dr. Jackson is petting one of the dogs.

7. The use of computer graphics and clip art is now common. Use a classroom computer or your own personal computer to create some symbols and designs that could be used in the newsletter of an organization. The objective of this exercise is to experiment with what can be done on a computer.

8. Charts and graphs can be more attractive if some creativity is used. A bottled water company wants to show how much water a person needs per day based on weight and activity level (light activity, moderate activity and strenuous activity). Create a rough draft, either freehand or on a computer, of an "infographic" that would attractively show this data (see Figure 7.9 for some ideas).

8 | *Radio and Television*

*R*adio and television, including cable, offer many opportunities for the *public relations writer who wants to effectively reach both mass and specialized audiences.*

Broadcasting and its various forms are important because they serve as the primary source of information for most of the population. More than 80 percent listen to the radio daily, and people spend more time watching television than doing anything else other than working or sleeping.

Writing for electronic media, however, requires a special perspective. This chapter explains how to think in terms of how writing sounds to the ear, how sound bites can be integrated into copy, and how visual elements can be used to tell a story.

RADIO

Radio, lacking the glamour of television and the gee-whiz technology of space satellites, is not always the first medium that public relations people think of when planning an information campaign.

Yet on a local level, radio is a cost-effective way to reach large numbers of people in various age, ethnic and income groups. Radio benefits by its ability to be heard almost anywhere. It is the only medium, for example, that can reach millions of Americans as they commute to and from work in their cars. In addition, the miracle of the transistor brings radio to mail carriers on their routes, carpenters on construction sites, homeowners pulling weeds in their gardens and exercise enthusiasts working out at a gym or jogging.

Approximately 10,000 radio stations are on the air in the United States, ranging from low-powered outlets operated by volunteers to large metropolitan stations audible for hundreds of miles. Although radio is a mass medium, each station has its own defined audience.

The station's format often determines the nature of the audience. There are hard rock stations for young people, all-news stations for commuters, classical stations that appeal to an older and better-educated group, and stations playing 1960s music for aging baby boomers.

A public relations practitioner should study each station's format and submit material suitable to it. There is little sense in sending information about senior citizen recreational programs to the news director of a hard rock FM station with an audience primarily of teenagers.

You can determine the demographics of a station by consulting radio and television directories or contacting the station's advertising and marketing department. One common source of advertising rates and demographic data is published by Standard Rate and Data Services.

Radio News Releases

Because so many radio stations completely rewrite all the news releases they receive, some public relations people just send newspaper-type releases to radio stations. However, numerous radio stations accept real radio releases and definite rules apply to these. Radio is based on sound, and every radio release must be written so that it can be easily read by an announcer and clearly understood by a listener.

Format   There are several major differences between a radio release and a news release prepared for print media. Although the basic identifying information is the same (letterhead, contact, subject), you also need to give the length of the radio release. For example, "RADIO ANNOUNCEMENT: 30" or "RADIO ANNOUNCEMENT: 60." This indicates that the announcement will take 30 or 60 seconds to read.

The timing is vital because broadcasters must fit their messages into a rigid time frame that is measured down to the second. Most announcers read at a speed of

150 to 160 words per minute. Because word lengths vary, it is not feasible to set exact word counts for any length of message. Instead, the general practice is to use a line count. With a word processor set for 60 spaces per line, you will get the following times:

- five lines = 20 seconds.
- eight lines = 30 seconds.
- 16 lines = 60 seconds.

Another difference is style. A print news release uses standard English and punctuation. Sentences can be quite long at times. In a radio release, a more conversational style is used and the shorter the sentence, the better. This allows the announcer to draw a breath between thoughts and the listener to easily follow what is being said. An average sentence length of 10 words is a good goal.

It's also possible to use incomplete sentences in a radio news release. Here is an example of a 30-second announcement:

It's been called the best investment a woman can make for herself . . . For her own health—and for her family. It's a mammogram for the early detection of breast cancer. October is National Breast Cancer Awareness Month . . . and all month long you can get discounted mammograms by calling the American Cancer Society at 1–800-ACS–2345. That's 1–800–227–2345. Get a mammogram—it can save your life.

Notice that the telephone number is repeated twice. This is always a good idea because listeners don't always get the number on the first mention.

TIPS FOR WRITING THE RADIO NEWS RELEASE

- Time is money in radio. Stories should be no longer than 60 seconds. Stories without actualities (sound bites) should be 30 seconds or less.
- The only way to time your story is to read it out loud, slowly.
- A long or overly commercial story is death. Rather than editing it, a busy radio newsperson will discard it.
- Convey your message with the smallest possible number of words and facts.
- A radio news release is not an advertisement; it is not a sales promotion piece. A radio news release is journalism—spoken.
- Announcers punctuate with their voices; not all sentences need verbs or subjects.
- Releases should be conversational. Use simple words and avoid legal-speak.
- After writing a radio news release, try to shorten every sentence.
- Listeners have short attention spans. Have something to say and say it right away.
- Never start a story with a name. While listeners are trying to figure out who the person is, they forget to listen to the sentences that follow.

Source: News Broadcast Network, 600 First Avenue, Suite 316, Seattle, WA 98104.

Audiotape News Releases

Audiotape sent to a radio station can take two forms: the straight message, recorded by an unidentified announcer, and the "actuality," which uses the voice of an identified spokesperson. When an actuality is used, it is customary to have an introduction and a close that identify the person speaking.

Actualities are better than straight announcements because the message comes from a "real person" rather than a nameless announcer. They are also more acceptable to stations, possibly for the same reason.

Here is an example of an actuality:

For: **Marshal Hale Memorial Hospital**
     Radio News Actuality
     "Eating Disorders Program"

LEAD: Today, a new local clinic is being dedicated that exclusively treats the eating disorders anorexia and bulimia. Here's Dr. Erica Goode, medical director of the eating disorders program at Marshal Hale Memorial Hospital.

DR. GOODE: We've seen a higher incidence of anorexia and bulimia partially because body conformation has become an important priority in our society. In other words, many people, especially women, feel pressured to keep their bodies thin. Here at Marshal Hale, we have a treatment process that emphasizes psychotherapy, body image therapy, and a food and eating group. I'm excited about our program because we're able to separate anorexics and bulimics from psychiatric patients and provide them with a relaxing atmosphere where more help can be given to them.

CLOSE: The goal of the eating disorders program is to normalize the patients' eating and bring back their emotional well-being.

Format   The preferred length for an audiotape is one minute; however, shorter tapes can be used. It is advisable to accompany any sound tape with a complete script of the tape. This enables the news director to judge the value of the tape without having to run it.

Not all sound tapes are limited to one announcement. It is a common practice to record several public service announcements (PSAs) on one tape. They may be of varying length, but they should be accompanied by cue sheets and scripts. The format and structure of PSAs will be discussed shortly.

Production   Every audiotape starts with a carefully written and accurately timed script. The next step is to record the words. In doing this, it is imperative to control the quality of the sound. A few large organizations have complete facilities for this; some get help from moonlighting station employees; but most people use a professional recording service.

The recording services have first-class equipment and skilled personnel. They can take a script, edit it, eliminate words or phrases that will not be understandable, record at the proper sound levels, and produce a finished tape suitable for broadcasting. They can find an announcer of whatever type is best suited to the kind of message to be delivered, and they can produce many copies of a tape.

Radio news stories and PSAs can be produced on cassette or reel-to-reel tapes. The most common method, and the most economical, is cassettes. If you're doing a national distribution, the CD format is also suitable. You can find a recording service by asking your colleagues for recommendations or by looking under "Recording Services" in the Yellow Pages.

Delivery   Audiotapes can be mailed to stations, and this is often done if the topic doesn't have a crucial time element. The radio news feature in Figure 8.1 is an example. In the trade, such features are called "evergreens" because they are in season year-round.

However, most late-breaking news material is now transmitted by telephone. When a forest fire threatened California's Napa Valley, a large winery featured its president in a topical actuality. He reported that the fire had not endangered the grape crop and went on to forecast an excellent harvest. When the tape was offered by telephone to 50 or so radio stations, almost 40 accepted it for use.

Use   Producing audiotapes can be costly. When Sears distributed a radio news release responding to charges of overcharging customers at auto repair centers in California, the cost of preparing and distributing a national release was $3,900. Ford racked up a $3,500 bill for a news release on battery recycling as part of Earth Day festivities.

The basic point is that you should be selective about distribution to stations that have an interest in using such material. Radio releases, like news releases, should not be shotgunned to every radio station.

You also need to monitor usage. Many organizations send a return postcard on which the station can report use. However, News Broadcast Network estimates that usage cards only generate a 5 to 7 percent response rate. Other organizations simply call the station and ask how many times a particular story or announcement aired. By using Arbitron ratings, which give estimated audience figures, public relations people can then calculate how many listeners were exposed to the message. Evaluation procedures are discussed in Chapter 20.

The use of audiotapes is popular among radio stations and is expected to increase as stations search for ways to cope with reduced news staffs. One survey, by Coleman Research, found that 45 percent of the radio news directors surveyed nationally planned to increase the use of sound bites in their news shows.

Public Service Announcements *Review*

A public service announcement (PSA) is defined by the Federal Communications Commission (FCC) as an unpaid announcement that promotes the programs of government or voluntary agencies or that serves the public interest. In general, as part of their responsibility to serve the public interest, radio and TV stations provide free time to charitable and civic organizations. Thus a PSA may be a message

ℝADIO ℝOUNDUP
a collection of features, oddities, and helpful tips

NORTH AMERICAN PRECIS SYNDICATE
201 east 42nd street
new york, n.y. 10017

150 WORDS, 60 SECONDS

NEWS OF YOUTH

IF A TEEN SAYS YOU'RE "WACK," IS THAT A COMPLIMENT—OR ARE YOU GETTING "DISSED" (PUT DOWN)? IS WAZDA 4-1-1 A NEW PHONE EXTENSION? IF A GUY SAYS A GIRL IS "MOBILE," DOES THAT MEAN SHE HAS A REALLY NICE CAR? IF YOU FEEL LIKE A "BARNEY"—A NEWCOMER OR NOVICE—TO THE WORLD OF TEEN SLANG, YOU'RE CERTAINLY NOT ALONE. READY TO CLEAR UP THE CONFUSION ARE RESEARCHERS AT LEO BURNETT, THE CHICAGO-BASED ADVERTISING AGENCY THAT CONDUCTS A SEMI-ANNUAL STUDY OF YOUNGSTERS NATIONWIDE ON SUCH TOPICS AS TELEVISION, FASHION AND MUSIC. WAZDA 4-1-1 MEANS "WHAT'S UP?" MOBILE MEANS ATTRACTIVE. WACK IS COOL AND BONK IS UNCOOL. SOMEONE WHO'S WIGGIN' IS STRANGE OR WEIRD. AND A COUCH COMMANDER IS A TV REMOTE CONTROL! DATA FROM THIS STUDY ON WHAT'S HOT AND WHAT'S NOT WITH TODAY'S TEENS IS USED BY MANY OF THE NATION'S TOP COMPANIES.

Figure 8.1 Ever wonder where disc jockeys get their material? One source is the topical news feature. In this case, the source is Leo Burnett, a Chicago advertising agency. Notice, however, that the focus is on information—and the agency is mentioned only once. (*Courtesy of North American Precis Syndicate, New York.*)

from the American Heart Association about the necessity of regular exercise or an appeal from a civic club for teacher volunteers in a literacy project.

Profit-making organizations rarely receive free broadcast time despite the "public service" nature of their messages, but sometimes an informational campaign by a trade group qualifies. For example, the Aluminum Association did get free airtime on a number of stations by producing a PSA about how to recycle aluminum cans. Before the announcement was released, the association received an average of 453 calls a month. Five months after the PSA began appearing, the association had received 9,500 calls at its toll-free number. The PSA was used in 46 states, and 244 stations reported 16,464 broadcasts of the announcement.

OFFER PSAS IN VARYING LENGTHS

It is important to furnish a radio station with public service announcements of varying lengths. This gives the station the opportunity to vary the message and use the appropriate one for the time available. Keep in mind that you should use active voice and simple sentences. Never use a clause between a subject and a verb. Here are some sample PSAs from the American Red Cross:

20 Seconds

Ever give a gift that didn't go over real big?

One that ended up in the closet the second you left the room?

There is a gift that's guaranteed to be well received.

Because it will save someone's life.

The gift is blood, and it's desperately needed.

Please give blood. There's a life to be saved right now.

Call the American Red Cross at 1–800-GIVE LIFE.

30 Seconds

Ever give a gift that didn't go over real big?

One that ended up in the closet the second you left the room?

There is a gift that's guaranteed to be well received.

Because it will save someone's life.

The gift is blood, and the need for it is desperate.

Over 20,000 people must choose to give this gift every day.

We need your help.

Please give blood. There's a life to be saved right now.

Call the American Red Cross at 1–800-GIVE LIFE.

This public service message brought to you by the Advertising Council and the American Red Cross.

60 Seconds

We want you to give a gift to somebody, but it's not a gift you buy.

We want you to give a gift, but not necessarily to someone you know.

Some of you will be happy to do it. Some of you might be hesitant.

But the person who *receives* your gift will consider it so precious, they'll carry it with them for the rest of their life.

(continued)

This gift is blood / and every day in America, thousands of people desperately need it.

Every day, we wonder if there will be enough for them.

Some days, we barely make it.

To those of you who give blood regularly, the American Red Cross and the many people whose lives you've saved would like to thank you.

Those of you who haven't given recently, please help us again.

There's a life to be saved right now.

To find out how convenient it is to give blood,

call The American Red Cross today at 1–800-GIVE LIFE.
  That's 1–800-GIVE LIFE.

Tag

This public service message has been brought to you by this station, The Advertising Council and The American Red Cross.

This example shows the potential effectiveness of PSAs. Remember, however, that others are aware of the potential; therefore, many PSAs are available to the stations. Only those that are timely and of high recording quality stand a chance of being used.

Here are a few more points to remember about PSAs:

1. Only nonprofit, civic, and voluntary organizations are eligible to use PSAs. Announcements by profit-making organizations are considered advertisements, and stations charge regular advertising rates for carrying them.
2. Since deregulation of the broadcasting industry in the 1980s, stations feel less pressure to provide a community service by running PSAs for nonprofit groups. Although a station's renewal of its license is still based to a certain extent on serving the community and the public interest, there is no minimum standard for broadcasting PSAs.
3. PSAs, which are broadcast free of charge, are rarely used during periods of peak listening, when a station can run revenue-producing advertisements. Consequently, the PSA about a community health fair may only be heard at 5 a.m. or late Sunday night, when there are fewer ads. Because of this, even non-profit groups, wishing to reach the largest possible audience, often pay regular advertising rates to get their PSAs on the air.

TELEVISION

The fundamental factor that separates television from the other media and gives it such pervasive impact is the visual element. The combination of color, movement, sound, and sight on a screen in your own living room is hard to resist. No wonder the medium is the primary source of news, information and entertainment for most people.

PLACEMENT TIP: SEND A PHOTO STORYBOARD

Your television PSA has to compete with dozens of others for the attention of the station's public service director. One approach is to send a cover letter and a photo storyboard of the PSA. This way, the public service director can evaluate your spot with a minimum of effort and make a quick decision.

Below is a video storyboard about drunk driving that Holden Lewin Communications, Sacramento, used on behalf of the California Office of Public Safety:

"DON'T DRINK—DRIVE STRAIGHT"
30 second Public Service Announcement (English Version)
Sponsors: CA Office of Traffic Safety and CA Highway Patrol

Concept: The virtues of driving 'straight' are presented in a lively, hip, music video format by a teenage rap artist

(Beer can being passed)

Rapper:
You can fool some of the people
Some of the time
But if you plan on it
Keep this on your mind...

(Rapper with dancers)

There's only one way
to cross that thin line...

(CHP pulls over car)

Caught under 21 with alcohol
and you'll find...

(Rapper with dancers)

You're walking with your friends
'Cause you paid the price when...

(Close-up: CHP writing report)

You had to straight just give up your
license...

(Rapper)

For the next year,
plus you might do the time...

Network television and cable offer a variety of public relations opportunities. To find and use these opportunities, you need to know how a television station is organized and who is in charge of various programs. The titles may vary somewhat, but the following positions are common at both radio and television stations:

- *General manager.* This person, comparable to the publisher of a newspaper, determines general policy and manages all the departments.
- *Program director.* This person decides which programs to produce and broadcast—including news, public affair and entertainment programs.
- *Directors and producers.* These people moderate the various interview and talk shows that are the staple of many stations. They are comparable to the section editors of daily newspapers.

- *News director.* This person, comparable to the managing editor of a newspaper, manages the entire operation of gathering and producing newscasts.
- *Assignment editor.* This person, comparable to the city editor of a newspaper, assigns reporters and camera crews to cover news stories.
- *Reporters.* These are the people who write and report the news, as well as the sound and camera technicians who accompany them on assignments.
- *Public affairs or public service director.* This person is the station's public relations representative. Duties may include working with community organizations to broadcast public service announcements and organizing public affairs programming.
- *Promotion director.* This person promotes the station by sponsoring contests and events, often in partnership with other community groups.

You may have reason to contact all of these people at one time or another. Specific placement opportunities for talk shows, call-in programs, product placement, community calendars and other messages are discussed later in the chapter. Here, we focus on working with television news directors, assignment editors and reporters to generate news coverage of your organization or client.

Every station gathers local news with its own facilities. To get your news story on local television, there are three possible procedures: You can phone the news department, ask for the assignment desk (or assignment editor) and give the highlights of your story; you can send a news release; or you can send a videotape.

For a station in your own town, the first method is by far the best. For out-of-town stations, the news release with accompanying slides, film or videotape is the only possibility. Some people have had success with this: When a local station covers a news story, the public relations person arranges for extra videotapes of the item. These are then rushed to the nearby stations in time for their next news programs. For example, a station in Harrisburg might not be able to cover a story in Philadelphia but might use the story if the tape were provided.

The major networks also have news-gathering departments that cover stories throughout the world. The networks maintain bureaus in major cities, both domestic and foreign. In addition, a network may pick up a story from an affiliated station or use material from another network, with permission. Also, the networks get news from the wire services.

To get onto a network, news must be of great interest. It must be of national importance or have such a strong human interest that it will appeal to practically everyone.

If you are convinced that you have a story worth national exposure, you should telephone the nearest office of each of the networks and ask for the news department. Give the highlights of the story and ask if the network is interested. If so, you must set up a place and time for the news team to cover the story.

Remember that it takes some hours to cover a story, get it to a studio, and edit it for broadcast. If it is hot news, it should get to the networks in the morning so as to have a chance of making the evening broadcast. Morning news may use material from the afternoon of the preceding day.

Television News Releases

As with radio, the written release is not as satisfactory as a recording. Nevertheless, all television announcements start with a written message that is then turned into an audiovisual presentation.

Format   There is one basic difference between a television release and a radio release. With television, it is necessary to supply not only the words but also the illustrative material. Accordingly, the script will describe the illustrative material (graphics) on the left side of the page and present the words (audio) on the right. This script is accompanied by the visual material.

The graphics may be in the form of 35-mm slides, art cards or videotape. They must be in color. As with all audiovisual materials, it is vital to coordinate what is seen with what is heard. The words should describe the visuals, and the illustrative material must show what is being talked about.

A good example of how visuals and copy are coordinated is the following television PSA for local stations by the American Red Cross. Notice that both videotape and slides are used.

Dr. Snyderman in lab coat walking down hospital corridor—tracking shot	Infectious diseases used to cause the greatest concern about the health of children, but today, accidents are responsible for most childhood injuries and death.
Art card	You can learn how to cope with accidents and injuries by attending a *free* 90-minute training session in your community on Saturday, March 13, cosponsored by the American Red Cross and KPIX.
Snyderman at nurse station with clipboard	"Survival Saturday" is absolutely free, and sessions are held throughout the day at 28 locations in the Bay Area.
Zoom to CU	Because accidents happen, you need to know how to respond. Make a commitment to learn "Skills for Life" on March 13.

Video News Releases

The best way to get your news used by a television station or cable system is to provide a videotaped news release (VNR).

Large organizations seeking enhanced recognition for their names, products, services and causes are the primary clients for VNRs. The production of VNRs can

NORTH AMERICAN PRECIS SYNDICATE, INC.
201 East 42nd Street • New York, NY 10017 • (212) 867-9000

LAND OF FIRE AND ICE

ALL ONE HUNDRED THIRTY TWO OF THE ISLANDS THAT MAKE UP THE HAWAIIAN ISLANDS WERE FORMED BY ANCIENT VOLCANOES, ALTHOUGH ONLY KILAUEA (KILL-A-WAY-AH) VOLCANO ON THE "BIG ISLAND" OF HAWAII IS STILL ACTIVE. TWO, NOW-DORMANT VOLCANOES THAT HELPED FORM HAWAII—MAUNA LOA (MAWNA-LOW-AH) AND MAUNA KEA (MAWNA-KAY-AH)—ARE THE TALLEST MOUNTAINS IN THE WORLD MEASURED FROM THEIR UNDERSEA BASES.

MAUNA KEA (MAWNA-KAY-AH), WHICH MEANS "WHITE MOUNTAIN" ACTUALLY HAS SNOWFALL DURING THE WINTER, ALLOWING SKIERS TO SCHUSS (SHOOS) DOWN THE SLOPES. THE SNOWY PEAK PROVIDES AN ICY BACKDROP FOR THE SWIMMERS, SNORKELERS, SUNBATHERS, AND SURFERS BELOW WHO BASK IN THE WARM, TROPICAL SUNSHINE.

KILAUEA (KILL-A-WAY-AH) VOLCANO, WHICH GENERATES LAVA FLOWS WITH TEMPERATURE TWELVE TIMES HOTTER THAN BOILING WATER, IS CONTINUOUSLY ADDING TO THE SIZE OF THE ISLAND. KILAUEA (KILL-A-WAY-AH) AND MAUNA LOA (MAWNA-LOW-AH) ARE BOTH PART OF VOLCANOES NATIONAL PARK, THE THIRD MOST POPULAR ATTRACTION IN THE STATE OF HAWAII. IT IS ONE OF MORE THAN EIGHT HUNDRED TOURS, ATTRACTIONS, AND EVENTS AVAILABLE IN THE ISLANDS, SAY THE EXPERTS AT PLEASANT HAWAIIAN HOLIDAYS, THE LARGEST TRAVEL COMPANY TO HAWAII.

FOR FREE INFORMATION ABOUT VISITING HAWAII, THE LAND OF FIRE AND ICE, OR THE OTHER HAWAIIAN ISLANDS, CONTACT YOUR TRAVEL AGENT OR CALL 800-2-HAWAII.

Figure 8.2 This television feature was prepared for a travel agency specializing in Hawaii. In this case, slides were used for the visual element. Notice that complex names are phonetically spelled out to help the announcer reading the script. (*Courtesy of North American Precis Syndicate, New York.*)

more easily be justified if there is potential for national distribution and multiple pickups by television stations and cable systems.

A typical 90-second VNR, says one producer, costs $20,000 to $25,000 to produce. Costs for production and distribution vary, however, depending on the num-

VNRS REACH MILLIONS OF PEOPLE

Here's a sampling of video news releases that, according to Nielsen Media Research, were widely used by television stations:

- Michael Jackson's new CD, *Scream,* by Sony Music (161 million viewers).
- The Beatles: Live at the BBC, by Capitol Records (130 million viewers).
- Chrysler's new minivan door latch (91 million viewers).
- American Medical Association (AMA) findings on tobacco addiction (90 million viewers).
- Disneyland's 40th anniversary celebration (85 million viewers).
- Feature about Doritos/Super Bowl commercials (77 million viewers).
- Reebok's Shaq vs. Shaq (66 million viewers).
- McDonald's *Batman Forever* (62 million viewers).
- Wrestlemania XI news conference (56 million viewers).
- Bean Bag Chair recall by the Consumer Product Safety Commission (44 million viewers).

ber of location shots, special effects, and staff required to produce a high-quality tape up to network standards. A sampling of brochures from various producers gives a range of $4,000 to $50,000 for VNRs. In addition, distribution costs (via satellite or mail) can run $4,000 to $12,000.

Because of the cost, you must carefully analyze the newsworthiness of your information and consider whether the topic lends itself to a fast-paced, action-oriented visual presentation. If you have nothing to show except talking heads or graphs and charts, you should think twice about producing a VNR.

You should also consider whether the information will be current and newsworthy by the time a VNR is produced. On the average, it takes 4 to 6 weeks to script, produce and distribute a high-quality VNR. In a crisis situation or for a fast-breaking news event, however, VNRs can be produced in a matter of hours or days.

A good example of rapid response is Pepsi. Within a week of news reports that syringes and other sharp objects had been found in cans of Diet Pepsi, the soft-drink company produced and distributed a VNR showing that the insertion of foreign objects into cans on their high-speed bottling lines was virtually impossible.

This VNR reached an estimated 186 million television viewers and helped avoid a massive sales decline of Pepsi. Subsequently, Pepsi commissioned three more VNRs on such subjects as a message to consumers from Pepsi's president, a surveillance camera catching an alleged tamperer, and a "thank you" to consumers for their support. According to Medialink, the producer and distributor, the VNRs were seen by an aggregate of 500 million viewers on 3,170 news programs.

Format Essentially, a VNR is a television release converted to a finished tape that can be broadcast. The standard length is 90 seconds, which is preferred by the overwhelming majority of TV news directors. Some features, however, can run up to two minutes.

AMERICAN EXPRESS
NEW TRACK FOR FREQUENT FLYERS
VIDEO NEWS RELEASE

VIDEO	AUDIO
	LOCAL ANCHOR LEAD-IN: THEY'VE BECOME THE CURRENCY OF THE NINETIES: FREQUENT FLYER MILES. YOU CAN EARN THEM BY EATING IN RESTAURANTS, RENTING CARS, OR EVEN ORDERING FLOWERS. TODAY, XXX TELLS US THE BEST WAY TO GET THE MOST MILEAGE OUT OF YOUR POINTS.
Frequent flyer signage; Domestic and Foreign airlines; someone checking in with FF card (Use either Delta/ USAir/Continental, Southwest, Aeromexico and Mexicana.)	THERE ARE NOW MORE THAN 70 DIFFER-ENT FREQUENT FLYER PROGRAMS IN PLACE. ALMOST EVERY MAJOR AIRLINE HAS ONE. IT'S NO WONDER THAT MEMBERSHIP IN FREQUENT FLYER PROGRAMS IS CLIMBING ABOUT 12 PERCENT A YEAR.
Man on street	Casey: "The frequent flyer cards are with me always. I carry them with me every single day." (22:53-23:58)
Hotel checking in scene	BUT KEEPING TRACK OF ALL THESE PROGRAMS CAN BE CONFUSING.
Randy Peterson, Editor Frequent Flyer Magazine	"People belong to an average of seven programs. A lot of different mail. A lot of different offers. Mail coming at you 31 days a month."
Visuals of airport/hotel scenes; REWARDS PLUS GOLD CARD flies in over visuals; ticketing; vacation scenes	TO HELP SOLVE SOME OF THAT CONFUSION, AMERICAN EXPRESS HAS JUST INTRODUCED ITS REWARDS PLUS GOLD CARD, WHICH CAN PROVIDE MEMBERS WITH A MONTHLY STATEMENT THAT SHOWS POINTS IN ALL OF THEIR FREQUENT FLYER AND FREQUENT STAYER PROGRAMS, AND EVEN TELLS THEM WHEN THEIR POINTS EXPIRE.
Frank Skillern, American Express Travel Related Services	SOT: It's the only card with the ability to keep track of airline frequent flyer and hotel frequent stayer programs on a monthly consolidated statement." (1:06:15–1:06:30)
Generic travel scenes	REWARDS PLUS MEMBERS ALSO GET AUTO-MATIC FREE ENROLLMENT IN THE MEMBERSHIP MILES PROGRAM.
Person at airport	Kimm: I've travelled to London on vacation. I've been to Hawaii once. I'm going to Hawaii again.
Airport scenes, etc.	THE NEW CARD ALSO GIVES MEMBERS DOUBLE MILES IN THE MEMBERSHIP MILES PROGRAM THE FIRST YEAR—FOR ALL CHARGES WITH PROGRAM AIRLINE AND HOTEL PARTNERS. THIS IS XXX REPORTING.

Figure 8.3   A draft of a television VNR. The left column describes the video elements in relationship to the script and sound bites in the right column. (*Courtesy of PCS Broadcast Services, Ridgewood, NJ.*)

Your VNR package should also include two or three minutes of B-roll, or background pictures, for use by the TV news producer in repackaging the story. Typical B-roll includes additional interviews, sound bites and file footage. A Nielsen Media

Research survey of 130 TV news directors, for example, found that almost 70 percent wanted a VNR with a B-roll attached.

An advisory will accompany the VNR package or will be sent to news directors before the actual satellite transmission of the video to the station. The advisory, in printed form, should contain the basics: the key elements of the story, background and descriptions of the visuals, editorial and technical contacts, satellite coordinates and date and time of the satellite transmission.

Production   Although public relations writers can easily handle the job of writing radio news releases and doing basic announcements for local TV stations, the production of a video news release is another matter. The entire process is highly technical, requiring trained professionals and sophisticated equipment. Consequently, the public relations writer primarily serves as an idea creator and a facilitator.

He or she may come up with the idea, write a rough storyboard (outlining the visual and audio elements) and make arrangements for a video production and distribution service to produce the video. Such firms are listed in the Yellow Pages under "Video" and "Television." The advertisements in public relations magazines (see Chapter 1) are also a good source.

It is important to keep in mind that the video producer follows the basic storyboard (outline of who and what should be included) to achieve the organizational objective, but will usually videotape many minutes of footage and use the editing room to make the finished 90-second product.

THE JARGON OF WRITING FOR VIDEO

Do you know where your SOT is? Do you need a CU or a V/O for your script? The video industry has its own vocabulary and you should be familiar with it when writing storyboards and scripts. Here are a few of the most common terms:

- **A-Roll** Video that contains the audio portion. This may be an announcer speaking or a quote from someone being interviewed.
- **B-Roll** Only the video portion without sound.
- **CU** Close up shot of a person or object. An MCU is a medium close up.
- **Dub** A duplicate of an audio- or videotape.
- **On Cam** Person or object is on camera—part of what is being videotaped.
- **Pan** Moving the camera (while shooting) from side to side.
- **SOT** Sound on tape. Usually refers to an interview.
- **Super** Printed material, usually words, to show name of a person, a telephone number, or a location.
- **V/O** Voice-over. A story where someone off camera, usually an announcer, reads a portion of the video story. Sometimes listed as ANNCR:V/O.
- **Zoom** Changing the camera angle by going from a wide shot to a close shot, or vice versa.

Consequently, it is not necessary to write a prepared script for everyone who appears on video. It is better, and more natural, to have them talk informally in front of the camera and then use the best "sound bite."

Medialink, a major producer and distributor of VNRs, gives some tips about the production of VNRs that best meet the needs of TV news directors.

- Give TV news directors maximum flexibility in editing the tape using their own anchors or announcers. This can be done by producing the VNR on split audio (the announcer track on one audio channel and the natural sound of the VNR on another). In this way, the producer has the option of "stripping" the announcer's voice.
- Produce the VNR with news footage in mind. Keep sound bites short and to the point. Avoid commercial-like shots with sophisticated effects.
- Never superimpose your own written information on the actual videotape. TV news departments usually generate their own written notes in their own typeface and style.
- Never use a stand-up reporter. Stations do not want a reporter who is not on their staff appearing in their newscast.
- Provide TV stations with a local angle. This can be done by sending supplemental facts and figures that reflect the local situation. These can be added to the VNR when it is edited for broadcast.
- Good graphics, including animation, are a plus. Stations are attracted to artwork that shows things in a clear, concise manner.

Pintak Communications, of Washington, D.C., adds to the Medialink list of suggestions. The firm says that VNR disasters can be prevented if you do the following:

- Use outside experts to give credibility. A VNR with only corporate spokespeople is not a good idea. In addition, don't clutter up the VNR with an excessive number of corporate logos.
- Avoid commercialism and hype. The VNR is a news story, not a corporate advertisement.
- Avoid overproduction. Slick dissolves and flashy effects are great for music videos, but news producers equate it with advertising.

Delivery Satellite distribution is the most cost-effective way of distributing VNRs. In addition, it is the preferred method of most news directors. Virtually every television station in the country now has at least one satellite receiving dish.

The mechanics of satellite distribution, including media tours, are discussed in Chapter 9. In brief, the master VNR cassette is delivered to a studio where the signal is transmitted via microwave or fiber-optic cable to a satellite "uplink" facility.

According to the *Video News Release Handbook*, distributed by Medialink, the transmission is then beamed from the uplink to one of several communications satellites used for news transmission. The satellite receives the transmission and beams it back to earth on any of its leased "transponders" or "channels," which project the signal ("footprint") across wide areas of the country, TV stations,

PCS Broadcast Services
1 Robinson Lane   Ridgewood NJ 07450
Voice 201-445-1711 Fax 201-445-8352

Diabetes PSA's:
DON'T CONTROL :30

OPEN ON A CAPE COD HOUSE WITH LOTS OF YARD, ZOOMING IN TO A TIGHT SHOT OF ITS WOODEN SHINGLES.	
CUT TO BLACK AND WHITE FOOTAGE OF TERMITES INSIDE WOOD EATING AWAY AT IT (THIS AND SUBSEQUENT B&W FOOTAGE HAVE EXAGGERATED SOUND EFFECTS, GROWING LOUDER).	Think of your body as a home where you plan to live into your golden years ...
CUT TO SERIES OF OTHER B&W SHOTS OF WEATHER AND WEAR CAUSING DAMAGE TO A HOUSE AND YARD, GETTING PROGRESSIVELY WORSE.	if there were something eating at its structure, you'd want to know ...
CUT TO SERIES LIKE ABOVE, BUT RAIN IS SUBSIDING, TERMITES ARE FEWER, ETC. (AND SOUND EFFECTS GET QUIETER).	Yet many people who have *diabetes* let it break down the body's own tissues, destroying blood vessels in the heart, eyes kidneys, limbs ... leading to heart attack, stroke, blindness, kidney failure, amputation.
CUT TO COLOR SHOT: A PAINT BRUSH ... PULLING BACK TO SHOW PAINTING OF SHINGLES ON THE CAPE COD ... BY AN OLDER WOMAN. SHE STOPS PAINTING, REMOVES GLOVES, SITS IN PORCH SWING (DRINKS ICED TEA?) AND CHECKS BLOOD SUGAR WITH ONE TOUCH II.	Long-term effects can be prevented ... by using regular blood sugar monitoring to balance diet, exercise and medication. Properly maintained, any home can last as long as you need it!

SUPER TITLE:

People with diabetes can get help
learning to ontrol it:
 1-800-TEAM-UP-4
American Association of Diabetes
Educators

Figure 8.4 This draft of a 30-second television PSA describes both the audio and the video. Television stations would receive two versions: an A-Roll with both the video and sound bites combined, and a B-Roll with just the video portion so the station announcer could read the script. The term "super title" at the end designates printed material that appears on the video. In this case, it is the name of the organization and a telephone number. (*Courtesy of PCS Broadcast Services, Ridgeway, NJ.*)

alerted to the transmission via a wire service advisory or a telephone call, orient their receiving antennae to the correct position. The signal is then "downlinked" for recording in a studio or for live on-the-air transmission.

VNRs can also be distributed by mail, but this is time-consuming and expensive. Multiple cassettes must be produced and mailed. The preferred format is 3/4-inch VHS cassette, but stations also accept 1-inch VHS tapes and Beta tapes.

On occasion, however, VNRs that are not time-sensitive can be mailed to selected stations. As previously noted, these are known as *evergreens* because they are always in season. A VNR on general research into AIDS could be held by a producer for use in an eventual series, or a VNR from the U.S. Forest Service on how to prevent fires could be held in reserve until summer, when the danger is highest.

Mail distribution is also used for what is known as *stock footage*—standard video shots of a company's production line, headquarters or activities that the station can store until the company is in the news. Then, as the anchor gives the news, the viewer sees the stock footage on the screen. A news story about an electric power plant, for example, may use stock footage from the utility company showing interior scenes of the facility.

Broadcast Use of VNRs

VNRs are widely used by television stations and cable systems. A survey by Nielsen Media Research, for example, found that every one of the 92 television stations surveyed regularly used VNRs.

As early as 1990, *Broadcasting* magazine editorialized that video news releases had become a staple of local TV broadcasts. This is particularly true among stations in small markets that don't have the staff and facilities to generate their own coverage. But larger news operations in metropolitan areas are also using VNRs as stations cut costs and reduce news staffs.

The television networks and CNN also use VNRs. For example, a VNR by the Aetna Insurance Company featuring dogs trained to investigate fires was aired nationally on *CBS This Morning*. And Toys 'R' Us got national network coverage with its VNR announcing that it would no longer buy look-alike toy guns, including those that could be altered to look like real guns.

Remember, however, that VNRs go through the same gatekeeping process as news releases and features submitted to newspapers and magazines. Emil Gallina, senior vice president of Hill & Knowlton's Electronic Media Services, makes the comparison by writing in *Communication World* (October 1991):

> Video releases look like TV news in the same way that press releases read like newspaper articles. And the moving pictures we distribute for television are the equivalent of the 8 × 10 glossies we send to newspapers and magazines. Their purpose is the same: to encourage coverage and to provide materials the reporter might not otherwise obtain. . . . They are merely one source of raw material from which news reports can be created.

In other words, television news directors ultimately decide what they want to use, and they may edit a VNR substantially before it is aired. This is comparable to the newspaper practice of rewriting news releases.

Despite their almost universal use, VNRs are not without controversy. In a 1992 cover article, *TV Guide* blasted the use of VNRs by television stations. Calling them "fake news," the article chided TV stations for using VNRs prepared by public relations sources to "plug a product, polish an image, or ensure that a particular political spin is spun" and passing it off to viewers as legitimate news.

The article went on to say that TV news directors have a responsibility to identify VNRs on-screen as supplied by "nonnews outfits." It contended that the integrity of the news would "continue to erode" if newscasters "pretend out of pride that what they broadcast is real news, instead of labeling it for what it is."

Although VNR producers and distributors strongly objected to the idea that their releases were "fake news," most of them did agree that TV news directors should do a better job of acknowledging the source of VNR materials that they use on the air. Indeed, a number of VNR distributors and producers subscribe to an informal code that includes the following rules:

- VNR producers and distributors should clearly identify the sponsor or client in any materials sent to broadcasters.
- Television news organizations should identify the source of the VNR material used on the air.
- Blatant commercialism should be avoided.
- VNRs should be authentic footage and materials, and the context should not be manipulated.

While broadcasters worry about source credibility and slick VNRs masquerading as news, many public relations people continue to express doubts about the expense of VNRs and whether the audiences reached are worth the costs. Related to this issue is the problem of monitoring the use of VNRs by broadcasters. One technological innovation that is now widely used is to give each VNR a code that can be read electronically by various monitoring services, such as Nielsen's SIGMA system. This is discussed in Chapter 20.

Client expectations are another concern. Well-publicized success stories, such as Pepsi's VNR responding to tampering claims, have caused clients to think their story will be on every TV set in America. In reality, a well-done VNR will usually get 40 to 50 station airings with an audience of 2.5 to 3 million viewers.

It is important that you understand the value, purpose and limitations of VNRs. Before you commit $20,000 to $25,000 to have a quality VNR produced and distributed, you should first assess (1) the news value of the topic, (2) whether the topic lends itself to a visual treatment and (3) whether reaching various broadcast audiences can contribute significantly to organizational objectives.

Another approach to getting broadcast coverage is the satellite media tour, which can be more cost-effective than a VNR. Such tours are discussed in Chapter 9.

The Rise of Infomercials

Video news releases are now an established part of television and cable news programs. As noted, they are "news releases" that are distributed to news departments as news; they are not considered paid advertising.

TURNING PITCHES INTO PLACEMENTS

Radio and television news directors, as well as the producers of various talk and interview programs, receive numerous letters offering subject ideas and spokespersons. A good, persuasive query or "pitch" often results in multiple placements.

Unfortunately, too few pitches are well conceived and tailored to the media gatekeeper's needs. Here are some tips on writing good pitch letters.

1. *Keep the pitch to one page.* If a news anchor can highlight the essence of a major news story in a few sentences, you can write about a client's product in the same amount of words.
2. *Localize your pitch.* If you're pitching nutrition to a certain segment of the population, write about that segment of the market. For instance, "The 450,000 women in Boston . . ." or "We estimate that one out of four children in Tampa. . . ."
3. *Think trend.* How does your product or program fit into the trends, take a lead in trends, or even buck the trends that have already been noted by the media?
4. *Keep pitch letters informative and lively.* Makes them interesting to the reader. Stiff prose won't make a story shine and come alive.
5. *Research your pitch.* Imagine being a news director or talk show producer and then ask the type of questions these people would want answered. Target marketing, not a shotgun approach, is the name of the game.
6. *Consider alternative dates.* Negotiate with news directors and program producers. If they can't use the idea or your representative this month, how about next month? If they can't interview a person at the studio, how about a phone interview?
7. *Reach beyond the client and your immediate program.* Offer to help a reporter on stories that may be only indirectly connected to your product or event. You'll make an editorial friend for life.
8. *Take no for an answer.* But get a sense of why the story has been rejected. It may offer you an opportunity to repackage and get a yes on your next pitch.

Source: Adapted from Ketchum Public Relations, New York.

In the advertising arena, however, infomercials seem to be gaining popularity. Many top companies find program-length formats to be an effective advertising medium for demonstrating uses of a product or explaining a complex issue.

Advertisers, according to one study by an association of electronic dealers, spend about $290,000 to produce a 30-minute program and $3 million in paid time to air it. In contrast, a 30-second commercial on a prime time program may cost double that amount.

Political candidates also use "politimercials" to get in-depth messages to the voting public. Ross Perot, in 1992, first used such programs to promote his views. The advantage of infomercials is that the advertiser or political candidate can present information without the filtering mechanism of regular news reporting.

However, the Advertising Council has also begun to do public service announcements as 30-minute programs on behalf of charitable organizations. Its first effort, a program to promote volunteering to help children, was aired on the majority of ABC's 225 affiliated stations.

Although the air time is usually paid for by corporations or donated to nonprofit groups, many of the same rules apply to infomercials as video news releases. They can't be too commercial, and they must present information in a journalistic, objective format. As one producer says, "It is a documentary in the truest sense of the word."

PLACEMENT OPPORTUNITIES

Radio and television stations, as well as cable systems, increasingly operate on round-the-clock schedules. They require a vast amount of programming to fill all the time available.

So far in this chapter we have concentrated on how to prepare and generate timely material for newscasts. Here we will present an overview of other placement opportunities in broadcasting, from getting people booked on talk shows to having a popular sitcom use your employer or client's product on the show.

In these cases, your contact is no longer the news department but the directors and producers of various specialty features and shows. Your most valuable communication tools are the telephone and the persuasive pitch letter.

Before using either tool, however, it is necessary to do your homework. You must be familiar with a show's format and content, as well as the type of audience that it reaches. You can obtain this information in several ways.

One method is to study the station and descriptions of its shows in a broadcast directory. Directory listings can tell you program format, types of material used and the name of the director or producer.

A second approach is to watch the program or feature and study the format. In the case of a talk or interview show, what is the style of the moderator or host? What kinds of topics are discussed? How important is the personality or prominence of the guest? How long is the show or a segment? Does the show lend itself to demonstrations and visual aids? The answers to such questions will help you tailor your phone calls and pitch letters to achieve maximum results.

Talk Shows

Radio and television talk shows have been a staple of broadcasting for many years. KABC in Los Angeles started the trend in 1960 when it became the first radio station in the country to convert to an all-news-and-talk format. Today, more than 1,110 radio stations (out of about 10,000 total) have adopted the format. Thousands of other stations, of course, have talk shows as part of their programming.

The same growth rate applies to television. Seven years after KABC started the talk format, Phil Donahue began his TV show. Today, there are more than 20 nationally syndicated talk shows and a countless number of locally produced shows. For the past decade, the No. 1 daytime talk show has been *Oprah Winfrey,* attract-

WJJD-AM, 1160 **(312) 977-1800**
180 N. Michigan Ave. FAX: (312) 855-1043
Chicago, IL 60601-7474 News Phone: (312) 977-0981
Owner: Infinity Broadcasting E-Mail: wjjd@ aol.com
Network: **AP, Westwood One**
Profile: Talk; T.A.–35-64; W–50,000; News–7 B'casts, 30% Staff Prod.; Talk–100% Staff Prod.; Guests–Live, Phone
General Management/News Executives:
General Manager .... Harvey A. Pearlman
Operations Manager .... Rick Patton
Program Director .... Michelle Dirks
News Director .... Christopher Michael
Sales Director .... Dave Murphy
Promotion Director .... Michelle Dirks
AM Drive-Time Host .... Ed Vrdolyak
AM Drive-Time Host .... Ty Wansley
Programs:
Chicago Law (Sun, 11:00 AM-1:00 PM)
Profile: General Interest, Government/Law; **Format:** Talk, Listener Phone-In
Host .... Greg Adamski
Host .... Karen Conti
Producer .... Greg Adamski
Producer .... Karen Conti

Chicago Viewpoint (Sun, 9:00-9:30 PM)
Profile: Public Affairs; **Format:** Interviews
Host .... Richard Cantu
Guest Contact .... Richard Cantu

Ed Vrdolyak & Ty Wansley Show (Mon-Fri, 5:30-10:00 AM)
(312) 977-1160
Profile: General Interest; **Format:** Talk, Interviews, Listener Phone-In
Host .... Ed Vrdolyak
Host .... Ty Wansley
Executive Producer .... Barack Echols
Guest Contact .... Mercedes Escobar
News Anchor .... Christopher Michael

Sounds of Chicago (Sun, 9:30-10:00 PM)
Profile: Public Affairs; **Format:** Interviews
Host .... Christopher Michael
Guest Contact .... Christopher Michael

Your Computer Connection (Sunday, 2:00-3:00 PM)
Profile: Computers/Hi Tech; **Format:** Talk, Interviews
Host .... Jason Prost

Your Health Matters (Sun, 9:00-11:00 AM) **(312) 977-1160**
Profile: Medical/Health; **Format:** Interviews
Host .... Michele Lowrance
Executive Producer .... Michelle Koferon
Producer .... Michele Lowrance

Your Money (Sun, 1:00-2:00 PM)
Profile: Business/Finance, Consumerism; **Format:** Talk, Listener Phone-In
Host .... Steve Ruxton
Producer .... Steve Ruxton

WKQX-FM, 101.1 **(312) 527-8348**
Merchandise Mart Plaza, #1700 FAX: (312) 245-0073
Chicago, IL 60654
Owner: Emmis Broadcasting
Profile: Rock Alternative; T.A.–18-49; W–6,000; News–7 B'casts, 10% Staff Prod.; Talk–5% Staff Prod.; Guests–Live, Phone; Releases/Scripts
General Management/News Executives:
Vice President .... Chuck Hillier
General Manager .... Chuck Hillier
Program Director .... Bill Gamble
Assistant Program Director .... Mary Shuminas
Music Director .... Mary Shuminas
Public Affairs Director .... Francine Fields
Sales Manager .... Val Maki
Marketing Director .... Rey Mena
AM Drive-Time Disc Jockey .... Lance Tawzer
AM Drive-Time Disc Jockey .... Doug Stoll
PM Drive-Time Disc Jockey .... Brian Paruch
Late Night Disc Jockey .... Jeff Gibson
Programs:
Sound Opinions (Sun, 10:00 AM-12:00 PM)
Profile: Music; **Format:** Interviews
Host .... Bill Wyman
Host .... Jim DeRogatis
Executive Producer .... James Van Osdol

WLIT-FM, 93.9 **(312) 329-9002**
150 N. Michigan, #1135
Chicago, IL 60601-7524
Owner: Viacom
Profile: Adult Contemporary; T.A.–25-54; W–9,900; News–10 B'casts, 100% Staff Prod.; Talk–100% Staff Prod.; Guests–Live, Phone, Taped
General Management/News Executives:
General Manager .... Philip L. Redo
Program Director .... Mark Edwards
News Director .... Mary Ann Meyers
Public Affairs Director .... Eva Rhodes
Sales Manager .... Kathleen Cahill
AM Drive-Time Disc Jockey .... Bob Brynteson
Mid-Day Disc Jockey .... Meagan Reed
PM Drive-Time Disc Jockey .... Margo Johnson
Programs:
Consumer Network (Sun, 6:30-7:30 AM)
Profile: Consumerism
Guest Contact .... Anne Henghold

Portraits (Sun, 7:00-7:30 AM)
Profile: General Interest; **Format:** Interviews
Guest Contact .... Mary Ann Meyers

The Race Question (Sun, 7:00-7:30 AM)
Profile: Minority Affairs; **Format:** Talk, Commentary
Host .... Lowell Thompson
Host .... Derek Simons

Figure 8.5 Media directories give valuable information about the programming of a broadcast station and who to reach if you want to get on a talk show. Complete addresses and phone numbers also facilitate the distribution of news releases and PSAs. (*Courtesy of Bacon's Information, Inc., Chicago.*)

ing about 8 million viewers on a daily basis. *Jenny Jones,* the nearest competitor, gets about 4.6 million viewers. *Live with Regis and Kathie Lee* is third in the ratings with about 4.3 million viewers.

The talk show gained new prominence during the 1992 presidential elections when all of the candidates suddenly discovered the concept of "access media." Ross

GETTING ON A TV TALK SHOW

Publicists constantly work to get their clients on a television talk show. Here's some advice from the producers of some shows:

- "It's important to know the host you're pitching and the show you're pitching. If you haven't seen the show, how do you know that you have a client who'd be great?" (David Armour, the *Ricki Lake* show)
- "If you think a client has an idea that will play on a national scale or has a solution to a problem that is nagging society, let me know." (Lucy Spiegel, *The Today Show* on NBC)
- Send a picture and biography in advance. "I can't book old people." (Andrew Scher, the *Montel Williams Show*)
- Give verbal, upbeat pitches. "If you're excited, we will be too." (Glenda Shaw, the *Rolonda* show)
- "Call us, don't bother writing." (Paul Faulhaber, the *Gordon Elliott* show)
- "Guests should be interesting for at least 20 minutes." (Katie Thomson, the *Larry King Live* show)

Source: *O'Dwyer's PR Services Report,* March 1995, p. 46.

Perot announced his candidacy on *Larry King Live,* CNN's highest rated program, and Bill Clinton headed for the *Arsenio Hall Show* to play his saxophone and talk. George Bush took the more conservative route and appeared on *CBS This Morning.* The advantage of talk shows, as the candidates realized, was the opportunity to tell their views directly to the American public without the filter of journalists and editors interpreting and deciding what was newsworthy. Another advantage was the opportunity to be on the air for longer than the traditional 30-second sound bite in a news program.

You may never work for a presidential candidate or have the opportunity to book a guest on the *Oprah Winfrey Show,* but you should be aware of such shows and their ability to reach large audiences. Talk shows on local radio and television stations, as well as a proliferation of cable channels, provide excellent placement opportunities for organizational spokespersons talking on any number of topics.

Here are some questions you might ask when thinking about placement on a talk show:

- Is the topic newsworthy? Do you have a new angle on something in the news?
- Is the topic timely? Can you tie the idea to some lifestyle or cultural trend?
- Is the information useful to the viewers? How-to ideas may be welcomed.
- Does your spokesperson have viewer appeal? A celebrity may be acceptable, but there must be a logical tie-in to your organization and to the topic to be discussed. A professional athlete might be plausible talking about running shoes but out of place in a discussion about the economy.
- Can the spokesperson stay on track? It is easy for celebrities to get involved in discussions of their personal affairs.

Figure 8.6   Talk shows give guests direct access to the audience. One popular show is *Larry King Live* on CNN. Here, King interviews Brian "Kato" Kaelin, whose claim to fame is being the house guest of O.J. Simpson on the night that Nicole Simpson and Ron Goldman were murdered. (*Photo by James M. Kelly/Globe Photo, Inc.*)

- Can you keep the speaker from stressing the commercial angle? Most talk show hosts will allow a brief mention of a brand name or sponsor identification. If your speaker gets too commercial, the entire interview may be deleted—and your organization may land on the list of those who can't come back.

When you know the answers to these questions, you will be ready to look for a booking—or several. Here are some tips that should help:

- Be sure that your speaker fits the program. If he or she isn't a fast thinker, avoid shows full of rapid exchanges and loaded questions.
- Be sure that you know the requirements of the program and the abilities of your spokesperson.
- Plan to use visuals if possible. Charts, diagrams, samples and videotapes may help the producer decide.
- Deal with only one person on the program. But you may certainly approach producers of other programs on the same station.
- Be careful about exclusivity. Some stations will refuse to book a guest who appears on a competing station. Find out before you commit. By committing to one station, you may miss an opportunity to get on others.
- Plan variations so that you can offer the same person to different shows or different stations without giving the same thing to each.
- Prepare your speaker (see Chapter 16).

After you've done your homework on the format of a radio or television talk show, you will contact the show's producer or associate producer. If it is a network or nationally syndicated show, the contact person may have the title of talent coordinator or talent executive. Whatever the title, these people are known in the broadcasting industry as *bookers* because they are responsible for booking a constant supply of timely guests for a show.

You can place a phone call briefly outlining the qualifications of your proposed speaker and why the person would be a timely guest, or you can write a one-page pitch letter that convinces the producer to book the guest. As mentioned previously, the more you know about the format and the audience of the show, the better you can tailor a persuasive pitch.

In general, talk shows book guests three to four weeks ahead of time. Unless a topic or a person is extremely timely or controversial, it is rare for a person to be booked on one or two days' notice. Keep this in mind as you plan talk show appearances as part of an overall public relations plan.

The booker may request additional information, video clips of your spokesperson's performance on other programs or a personal interview to assess the candidate's personality. Remember that talk shows are looking for entertainment value, not necessarily news value.

The proliferation of talk shows in the 1990s has intensified the competition for fresh feature ideas, and producers rely more and more heavily on ideas pitched by individual publicists, corporate public relations departments and public relations firms.

There also are firms that specialize in booking talk show guests. One such firm is Media Relations of Bloomington, Minnesota, which handles everyone from Elvis channelers and sex-book authors to corporate executives. The firm packages concepts, including a guest, a proposed segment topic and a question list for the interviewer.

Public Service Programs

In addition to interview or talk shows, many stations regularly produce features devoted to special interests of the community. Among the subjects covered are education; gardening; home repair; problems of the elderly, children, or minorities; foreign-language or ethnic topics; human interest stories; religion, political forums; documentaries; homemaking; recreation; and entertainment.

You book a guest on one of these programs the same way as for a talk show or an interview program. A review of the local weekly television schedule and broadcast directories will show what might be available.

Magazine Shows

Magazine shows are excellent outlets for topical feature stories. Depending on the program, they can be human interest features or in-depth investigative stories on some contemporary issue such as the high cost of medical care or the plight of the homeless in major cities.

Network magazine shows such as *60 Minutes, 20/20, PrimeTime Live* and *Dateline NBC* tend to concentrate on investigative reporting. *Dateline NBC*, for example, had to apologize to General Motors for rigging a video sequence showing gasoline tanks on GM trucks exploding after an impact.

On the local level, there are more human interest magazine shows. A sampling of magazine shows in one large city featured such subjects as a 1-pound baby who survived, a treatment for anorexia nervosa, a couple who started a successful cookie company, remedies for back pain, tips on dog training, a black-belt karate expert, blue-collar job stress and the work habits of a successful author.

Most, if not all, of these features came about as the result of someone making a pitch to the show's producers. The objective of the segment, at least from the perspective of the people featured, is exposure and the generation of new business. The tips on dog training, for example, featured a local breeder who also operated a dog obedience school. The karate expert ran a martial arts academy.

Entertainment Programs

A national organization concerned with a social or health issue can propose an episode involving that issue in a dramatic or comedy series. You can assist the program producer by supplying technical information. Such programs do not make overt sales pitches, but the message is inherent in the story line.

In a popular soap opera, for example, a leading female character has to deal with breast cancer. This enables millions of women to get the American Cancer Society's information even though they don't take the time to read the society's brochure. Other popular network series have dealt with such issues as battered wives, alcohol abuse, AIDS, racism, depression, suicide and a host of other social ills.

Community Calendars

Civic clubs and other community groups can publicize upcoming events by sending short announcements to local broadcast outlets. Radio stations, in particular, operate community calendars as a service to their listeners.

To be used, however, the event must be open to the public and of general interest. A meeting of the local automobile dealers' association doesn't qualify, but a forum on the global economy sponsored by the local chapter of the World Affairs Council would be acceptable.

Radio stations serving specialized audiences have variations on the community calendar. For example, a classical radio station might have an "arts calendar" that would list upcoming plays, musicals and art shows. By the same token, a rock music station might have a "concert calendar" to list all the upcoming rock concerts.

You write a calendar announcement in much the same way as you write a radio news release. The announcement should be to the point. It should give the name of the event, the sponsoring organization, the date and time, location, cost and a telephone number listeners can call for more information.

Here's an example of a typical announcement for a community calendar:

- *10 seconds*: The Amadeus (ah-ma-day-us) Quartet will perform at Mills College on Sunday, May 11. Phone area code 510, 793–7043.

- *20 seconds:* The Amadeus (ah-ma-day-us) Quartet will perform at the Mills College auditorium on Sunday, May 11, at 3:30 p.m. The program for this Chamber Music Concert will include compositions by Mozart, Britten and Beethoven (bay-toe-ven). For information, phone area code 510, 793–7043.
- *30 seconds:* The Amadeus (ah-ma-day-us) Quartet will perform at the Mills College auditorium on Sunday, May 11, at 3:30 p.m. In it thirty-fourth year with the same personnel, the Amadeus Quartet offers the widest active repertory among the world's string quartets. Their program for this Coleman Chamber Music Concert will include compositions by Mozart, Britten and Beethoven (bay-toe-ven). For information, phone area code 510, 793–7043.

Community calendar items should be sent to the station via mail or fax at least three weeks in advance.

Editorials

Many radio and television stations regularly broadcast editorials on topics of public interest. They are usually delivered by a representative of the station's management and aired as part of the news program. The editorial is clearly identified as a statement of opinion.

Statements of support, from either newspapers or broadcast stations, can be a valuable aid to your organization if the objective is to influence public opinion and generate community support. For example, you might propose an editorial against a new state tax on the grounds that it will discourage business development.

On a less controversial level, many stations are routinely asked to air editorials supporting the programs of community organizations. Thus the station encourages everyone to participate in the United Way campaign or give donations to the local food bank.

If you are seeking editorial endorsement from a station, write a persuasive letter to the general manager, outlining the reasons for your point of view and explaining why the station should do an editorial. A personal interview with the station manager, if possible, may also be beneficial.

By contrast, if the station airs an editorial that your organization disagrees with, it is appropriate to let the station know that you have a rebuttal. The station may offers you free-speech time or may include your comments in a future editorial.

Free-speech Messages

Free-speech messages are guest editorials. They are expressions of opinion presented by an individual or a group on a topic of general public interest. The topic must be timely and relate to a contemporary issue. For example, an individual or a group may wish to record a free-speech message about the city council's lack of support for public libraries or make a statement about the necessity of passing legislation to provide universal health insurance.

There is no automatic right to deliver a free-speech message. The radio or television station reserves the right to review the message for libel or slander, as well as the choice of words. The station also decides when to air the message and how many times.

If you want to record a free-speech message, you usually contact the station's public service director. One approach is to write a letter outlining the topic and its importance to the station's audience. If your proposal is accepted, the next step is to record the message at the station. Free-speech messages are usually short, ranging from 30 to 90 seconds.

Radio Promotions

Public relations representatives for nonprofit organizations, record companies, concert promoters and community events committees often generate publicity and exposure through radio promotions.

Promotions are beneficial to both the station and the outside organization. For example, a concert promoter may arrange with a radio station's disc jockey to award tickets to every tenth listener who calls the station and correctly answers a trivia question on the air. Prize giveaways tend to increase the number of listeners, and the concert promoter gets publicity.

A nonprofit group sponsoring a fund-raising festival may make arrangements for a radio station (or a television station) to cosponsor the event as part of the station's own promotional activities. This means that the station will actively promote the festival on the air through public service announcements and disc jockey chatter between songs.

The arrangements may also call for a popular disc jockey to broadcast live from the festival and give away T-shirts with the station's logo on it. This too is good promotion for the station and often attracts people to the fund-raising event because the disc jockey is a well-known personality. It is a win–win situation for both the station and the nonprofit group.

If you are handling an event or a cause that is suitable for this type of promotion, you contact the director of promotions for the radio or television station. If the station is interested, you negotiate the terms of the sponsorship. For example, the station may promise to air a specified number of announcements for the event in return for being listed in the organization's news releases, programs and print advertising as a sponsor of the event. Such terms are spelled out in a standard contract, often supplied by the radio or television station.

Stations will not necessarily promote or cosponsor your event just because it is worthy. They must be convinced that their involvement will benefit the station in terms of greater public exposure, increased audience and improved market position.

Creative Publicity

Organizations that have a creative idea can often get publicity by providing newscasters and disc jockeys with something unusual to talk about.

A public relations firm for Burger King, for example, came up with the idea of introducing the fast-food chain's new Breakfast Buddy sandwich by delivering the sandwiches to morning radio DJs live on the air.

The announcers were asked to sample them and ask listeners to call in and win a free phone call to their "best buddy" anywhere in the United States. One delivery resulted in a ten-minute interview on one major New York show; in all, the promotion secured time on 150 stations and more than 391 minutes of announcer endorsements.

The California Strawberry Advisory Board also garnered a great deal of broadcast publicity by sending television weather reporters a crate of strawberries on the first day of spring. Weather reporters like unusual situations to begin or end a weather report, and the strawberries were a good tie-in to the first day of spring.

Feature Films and Videos

Television stations and especially cable systems require a vast amount of programming to fill their schedules. Short features of two or three minutes and full-length productions that run 20 minutes or more are often used to fill gaps in the programming day.

Many of these *fillers* are produced and distributed by businesses, nonprofit organizations, trade associations and professional groups. For maximum acceptability, they must be relatively free of commercial hype and must concentrate on informing or educating the viewing audience.

Some typical features available for use by television stations and cable systems are:

- *Waltzing Matilda*, a 32-minute travelogue on Australia, sponsored by the Australian Tourist Commission.
- *Rethinking Tomorrow*, a 28-minute report on energy conservation, sponsored by the U.S. Department of Energy.
- *Oil over the Andes*, a 27-minute account of the building of an oil pipeline, sponsored by the Occidental Petroleum Company.
- *Noah Was an Amateur*, a 27-minute history of boat building, sponsored by the National Association of Engine and Boat Manufacturers.

Getting such films and videos distributed requires some method of informing the broadcast stations of their availability. You can handle this yourself by writing to media outlets and having them fill out an order card, but it is more efficient to use a distribution service. These organizations can distribute your materials by mail or satellite, depending on the preferences of the TV stations or cable systems that order them. In addition, these distribution services have an established program that can place your films and videos with schools, clubs, special interest groups and civic groups.

Product Placement

Television dramatic and comedy series are good vehicles for promoting a company's products and services. It is not a coincidence that all the cars used in a detective show will be of one make or that a transition shot will show a United Airlines jet taking off.

Such product placements, or *plugs*, as some people call them, are often negotiated by product publicists and the television production company. Rogers & Cowan, a major entertainment public relations firm, is one such company that specializes in placing its clients' products in movies and television shows.

One client, Giorgio Armani, launched a line of fashion eyewear through product placement. Rogers & Cowan arranged for the character Miles Silverberg, the station manager on *Murphy Brown*, played by Grant Shaud, to wear the glasses.

Hotels and resorts also get high visibility by doing trade-offs with a television series. Hyatt Regency, for example, provided lodging for the cast and crew of *The Cosby Show* while they were filming an episode in Atlanta. The deal saved the show about $50,000 in hotel expenses, and the Hyatt got considerable visibility as the location for the episode. If the hotel chain had placed a 30-second ad on *The Cosby Show,* it would have cost $380,000.

You should always be alert to opportunities for publicity on television and cable programs. If the company's product or service lends itself to a particular program, contact the show's producer directly or through an agent who specializes in matching company products with the show's needs.

SUMMARY

1. The broadcast media are important channels of communication, but using them requires thinking in terms of sound and visual elements.

2. Radio releases are similar to press releases, but they require more concise writing and different wording.

3. Audiotapes are more effective than written releases because they contain material that is ready to use with little or no cost.

4. Public service announcements (PSAs) are short broadcast announcements used by nonprofit groups and public agencies.

5. Television is an excellent medium of communication because it combines the elements of sight, sound, motion and color.

6. Television news releases must contain both sound and visual elements such as graphics, slides or videotape. A TV release can consist of a written script plus the accompanying graphics, but it will be more acceptable if it is on videotape.

7. Video news releases (VNRs) are now the standard in the industry and are widely used by TV stations and cable systems.

8. VNRs require professional preparation and high technical quality. To be used, they must be newsworthy and timely. Satellite distribution is the most cost-effective method.

9. A good, persuasive query or pitch letter is used to get placements on news programs and talk shows.

10. Talk shows offer numerous opportunities for reaching mass and specialized audiences.

11. Organizations and groups can get exposure by making use of community calendars, free-speech messages, radio promotions and creative publicity ideas.

EXERCISES

1. Lysol has a new antibacterial kitchen cleanser on the market. This is not exactly earthshaking news. Your assignment is to suggest a VNR that would be newsworthy enough to get on the evening news. Come up with a news angle and

then develop a rough storyboard outlining the visual and audio elements. Use the two-column format: the visual description on the left and the audio portion on the right.

2. The United States Forest Service wants to alert summer campers to the dangers of forest fires and how to take care of campfires. Write a 20-, 30- and 60-second PSA for radio use. In addition, write a 30-second PSA for television using the correct format and suggesting visual material.

3. Your client is a book publisher who has just published a book about Japan's economic strength and how the country is pulling ahead of the United States in global economic influence. The book's author is Clyde V. Prestowitz, a professor of economics in the School of Business at Stanford University. The book's title is *Trading Places: How We Allowed Japan to Take the Lead*. Write a persuasive pitch letter to the producer of ABC's *Good Morning America*, suggesting that the author should be featured on this talk and interview show.

4. A company has just introduced a new line of exercise equipment that is compact and can be used in the home. The primary market is middle-aged men and women who want to get more exercise but are so busy that they can't make it to a health club.

   Using various media directories, try to identify television interview or talk shows in Minneapolis, Milwaukee and Chicago that might be interested in having a spokesperson from the company talk about the value of exercise and demonstrate the equipment. For each show, indicate what type of show it is and why you selected it. Then suggest a good spokesperson. The company doesn't have a big budget, so hiring a Hollywood celebrity or a famous professional athlete is not possible. Finally, draft a pitch letter that could be sent to the producers of the TV shows you've selected.

5. Write a critique of three television talk shows. At least one should be produced by the local station; the other two can be nationally syndicated or produced by a television network. The report should include the format of the show, the length of the segments, the type of topics covered and typical guests. You should also try to ascertain the primary audience for the show.

6. The local YMCA is engaged in a campaign to raise funds for sending inner-city children to summer camp. Write a 20-, 30- and 60-second PSA for use on the local radio station urging the public to make contributions.

7. Your public relations firm handles Perrier, the bottled water from France. What television entertainment programs might be good outlets for product placements in the show? Name some popular shows, and suggest how Perrier could be portrayed.

8. The local fire department is sponsoring a chili cook-off to raise funds for a new fire engine. Various community groups, including firefighters, will have booths serving various kinds of chili. There will also be a contest to declare the best chili recipe of the day. This is a community event, and you would like to have the local rock radio station cosponsor it. Write a persuasive pitch letter to the station's director of promotions.

9. Creative publicity gimmicks can generate exposure on drive-time radio shows that feature popular DJs. Can you think of a product or a service that would lend itself to a publicity gimmick in such a way that DJs would mention it on the air?

10. Interview a professor on campus with expertise in some social issue or recent news event. Now write a radio news release using this professor as an "actuality." See the sample on page 190.

9 | *Pitch Letters, Advisories, News Conferences and Op-Ed*

*P*ublic relations people work with the media in many ways. This chapter explores the various tools and techniques that are used to encourage and facilitate media coverage.

The first part discusses how to write effective pitch letters, organize a media advisory, compile a fact sheet, write a position paper and a backgrounder and prepare a press kit. The second part concentrates on preparing for the media interview, organizing a news conference and on how satellite media tours can expand your potential media audience. The third part explains how to get on the editorial page, including meeting with editorial boards, writing op-eds and sending letters to the editor.

TIPS AND BACKGROUND MATERIALS

To do their job, reporters and editors need a continual supply of news tips and background materials. Your role in public relations is to come up with ideas and sell them. On another level, you are responsible for providing background information so that reporters understand a subject well enough to write intelligently about it.

This section discusses selling ideas and packaging background materials, including pitch letters, media advisories, fact sheets, position papers, backgrounders and press kits. Through these vehicles, you are what Frederick Andrews of the *New York Times* describes as "facilitators who put reporters and sources together."

Pitch Letters

Pitch letters have been mentioned previously in the context of convincing an editor to cover an event or persuading a talk show producer to book your spokesperson.

Publicists write a lot of pitch letters, most of which are not particularly creative. The vast majority, in fact, are rather dull and uninspired. Editors and reporters are busy people who receive stacks of mail every day, so it is important to write letters that will get their attention.

First, a pitch letter is at most one or two single-spaced pages. Many publicists draw the line at one page, using the "one-foot rule": You should be able to pitch your story standing on one foot; if your second foot comes down, your pitch is too long.

Second, a pitch letter should have an enticing lead. Melvin Helitzer, author of *The Dream Job: Sports Publicity,* cites these examples:

- John Driscoll, 32, a security trader for the First Boston Corporation, leads a double life.
- Today, Robin Yount may reach another milestone. If he gets one hit in his game at Yankee Stadium, he will have 2,500 hits and become the youngest player to reach this mark.

Third, a pitch letter should get to the point as soon as possible. Here is a letter written by Michael Klepper, owner of a New York public relations firm, that netted eight minutes on NBC's *Today* show.

Plastics!
  How can we get rid of them? Some environmentalists say we can't. Ralph Harding says we can. He is executive vice president of the Society of Plastics Industry. He has just returned from Europe where they easily dispose of plastics in modern incinerators.
  I'll call you in a week to see if the *Today* show would be interested in talking to him.

Klepper, who has written hundreds of pitch letters in his career, adds, "The pitch letter should be newsy, not groveling. It shouldn't read 'respectfully submitted' or 'I need this one' or 'my client is breathing heavy.' You are never asking for a favor;

you are submitting good, topical, newsworthy material that is directed to a decision maker."

Helitzer says a pitch or query letter should have the following six elements:

1. Enough facts to support a full story.
2. An angle of interest to the readers of that specific publication.
3. The possibility of alternative angles.
4. An offer to supply or help secure all needed statistics, quotes, interviews with credible resources, arrangements for photos and so on.
5. An indication of authority or credibility.
6. An offer to call the editor soon to get a decision.

Inherent in all this advice is doing your homework. To write a good pitch letter, you must be familiar with the medium, the subjects it features, and how they are covered.

Roger Ryerson, senior vice president for Gibbs & Soell, Chicago, says, "The more you understand the news angle and the publication you are pitching it to, the easier it is to approach the editor. Otherwise, it's a fishing expedition, and that's frustrating for an editor as well as for a publicist."

Media Advisories

These are also called *media alerts* because they tell reporters and editors about upcoming events and story opportunities in a brief listing of journalism's five Ws and H—who, what, when, where, why and how.

The format uses short, bulleted items instead of long paragraphs. A typical one-page advisory might contain the following elements: a one-line headline, a brief paragraph outlining the story idea, the five Ws and H, and a short paragraph with additional background information.

It's also important to indicate how the reporter or editor can get more information or make arrangements to cover the event. A contact and telephone number should be part of the letterhead.

Fact Sheets

A fact sheet summarizes the basic facts about an event, an organization, a product or a service. It is a resource document to help reporters check basic facts and convey accurate information.

Organizational fact sheets should explain the organization—its nature and objectives, main business activity, size, revenues, products and key executives.

Event fact sheets may include basic information about an upcoming event in terms of time, place and special guests. A fact sheet on a community festival may mention the purpose of the event, participating organizations and sponsors, estimated size of the event, location, time of day and when the event was first held.

Fact sheets are often included in press kits, which will be discussed shortly.

DOBISKY ASSOCIATES

Media Relations for Higher Education

181 Washington St. • Keene, NH 03431 • 603-352-8181
FAX 603-352-8529

July 27, 1995

Mr. Robert Chadbourne
Freelance
69 Lee Street
East Longmeadow, MA 01028

Dear Bob:

Most students have taken tests that are real killers, but those taking the final in Ronald Holmes' class *know* it's murder -- right down to the partly nude bound-and-gagged "body."

For his class titled "Profiling Homicides," Holmes decided for the first time this year to structure the final examination for his 120 University of Louisville students along the lines of a crime scene.

Holmes, a professor of justice administration and noted academic sleuth who leads unsolved-murder seminars for police departments nationwide, armed his students with "official homicide investigator handbooks" and turned them loose to determine who dunnit.

The victim, a mannequin trussed up with coat-hanger wire and gagged with clothing items, wasn't talking. But Ron Holmes, who actually serves as a deputy coroner, was on hand in the role of deputy coroner to answer specific questions the student investigators might have.

"This is so exciting," said Robyn Bennett, a senior majoring in criminal justice. "This is our final grade and I've been looking forward to it."

Holmes, who has consulted on more than 425 murder and rape cases with about 100 police departments, says his course isn't limited to students in criminal justice or justice administration, but includes a

Figure 9.1 A pitch letter that takes the feature approach. The writer immediately engages the reader's interest. Pitching ideas to successful freelance writers is a good strategy because they are regular contributors to several publications. See Figures 4.2 and 6.1 for other examples of pitch letters by the same writer. (*Courtesy of John McLain, Dobisky Associates, Keene, NH.*)

PAGE TWO
Mr. Robert Chadbourne
July 27, 1995

range of undergraduate majors. The bogus crime scene is from a real case.

"This is a re-creation of an actual crime scene I worked on out West," Holmes says. "In that case, there was an arrest and conviction."

Of the hands-on course, criminal justice senior Rebecca Bailey says, "It's practical work that you can apply later on in your field."

Holmes, author of the books, *Serial Murders*, *Profiling Violent Crimes*, and *Sex Crimes*, imparts to his students a wide variety of investigative techniques that make use of psychological and sociological aspects of the suspect, as well as careful attention to minute details.

As a police consultant and working deputy coroner for Jefferson County, Holmes commands a credibility that criminal justice students would be hard-pressed to find elsewhere.

And finding out who murdered the dummy, in order to ace the final exam, is no snap -- just 35 percent of the class solved this year's case.

Give me a call at 603/352-8181 if you'd like me to put you in touch with Ron Holmes.

Cordially,

John McLain

JM/mc

Figure 9.1   *(continued)*

Position Papers

A position paper is a statement of the organization's stand on some public issue. An example might be the position of a public utility on nuclear power. Such a paper is an official document and is often prepared at the request of top management. However, an alert public relations person who is aware of public issues will suggest the preparation of a position paper when the need first arises. In either case, the paper must be approved by the head of the organization.

The first item in a position paper is an explanation of the issue. This must be presented clearly and honestly. It should be supported with enough background to

(text continues on page 227)

LAW and ORDER

Vol. 43, No. 11
November 1995

THE MAGAZINE FOR POLICE MANAGEMENT

POLICE EDUCATION TAKES NEW COURSE

by Robert D. Chadbourne

"They tend not to come from police family backgrounds, and they tend to be pretty idealistic, altruistic really, seeking 'do-for-others' type careers." That's the profile of today's criminal justice college majors from Dr. Ronald Holmes, a tenured professor of justice administration at the University of Louisville in Kentucky. Along with teaching classes on Sex Crimes, Sociology of Murder and Profiling Violent Crimes, Holmes is a frequent consultant on unsolved capital crimes. His approach to law-enforcement education has a new twist: no more written exams.

Beginning with the `95 spring semester final in his Profiling Violent Crimes class, Dr. Holmes' 120 students got their final grade from attempting to solve one of the 425 murders their professor has been called in on as a consultant. The scene: a mock reenactment of the crime scene.

"Galt House, a Louisville hotel, loaned us a room. A department store donated a mannequin, and I added some small items," Dr. Holmes said, explaining the scene of a partially nude woman who had been raped, then strangled, and bludgeoned to death.

The male killer and the woman had met for the first time at the hotel bar, and had a drink together. However, the woman did not intend for the association to go further. When the man appeared at her hotel door he forced his way in. A computerized telephone check showed the killer had been in the room a total of seven hours before leaving.

CJ Students in Louisville Face Crime Scenes, Not Finals

Figure 9.2   The published result. The pitch letter in Figure 9.1 led to this article in a professional magazine. (*Courtesy of* Law & Order.)

April 18, 1994

Dear Media Representative:

Thousands of live bugs will be creeping and crawling at the Minnesota Zoo when BUGS! opens May 28. The special summer exhibit continues through Labor Day and will feature thousands of insects and other arthropods including colorful North American butterflies and moths; a working colony of leaf-cutter ants, giant millipedes; centipedes; land crabs; arachnids, such as the world's biggest spider, tarantulas and scorpions; and zebra cockroaches.

The visitors' initial "yuk" factor may be high for this exhibit, but the entertaining and educational experience will soon supplant any repulsion. Visitors will become immersed in the exhibit's greenhouse full of these creatures and impressed by the impact they have on us all. Zoo-goers will be unable to resist the beauty and colors of the butterfly garden where up to 600 free-flying North American butterflies and moths will be feeding, resting and emerging into adult butterflies.

The BUGS! exhibit will occupy a wooded area on the Northern Trail, west of the Weesner Family Amphitheater and will include a picnic and playground area in addition to the BUGS! greenhouse and butterfly garden.

Come out and see BUGS! for yourself. If you need color slides or more information, please call Julie Lee at (612) 431-9322 or the communications office at (612) 431-9217 or 431-9253.

Thank you.

Figure 9.3 A generic pitch letter. This letter accompanied a press kit about the opening of a bug exhibit at the Minnesota Zoo. (*Courtesy of Julie Lee, Minnesota Zoo.*)

Nancy Malitz
Detroit News
615 W. Lafayette Blvd.
Detroit, MI 48226

Dear Nancy,

Thanks for your interest in the 3Com Impact ISDN modem. Enclosed is a press kit, the photo will be coming directly from 3Com.

They call it 'netsurfing. But the experience of "browsing" the World Wide Web--the universal information service of the Internet--can feel more like paddling a canoe up a river!

*   Want to see the first 20 minutes of The Rolling Stones' concert at the Cotton Bowl? You'll need 55 minutes just to download it in monaural.

*   Want to see a color picture of that Maui hotel you're thinking of trying? Plan on a half minute watching it come through line by line.

But now, there's a new product that will break the "netsurfing speed limit." Now shipping from 3Com Corporation, the Impact ISDN External Digital Modem enables corporate, small business and home users to access the Internet, on-line services and office networks *four times faster* than the latest analog modems and *twice as fast* as existing ISDN installations.

Proof of Impact's speed and user-friendliness are in evidence at an unusual testing site -- San Francisco's Candlestick Park (known as 3Com Park by virtue of a corporate sponsorship.) 3Com has set up several web browsing stations at the park, where 49er fans can surf hot web sites -- and gather information about the 49ers and other teams -- all in less time than it takes to stand in line for the bathroom!

I look forward to speaking with you soon. B-roll is available of the kiosks, and a side-by-side demonstration of the speed of ISDN. If you have any questions, do not hesitate to call me at 415-904-7070 ext. 274.

Regards,

Kathy Tom Engle

Figure 9.4 A follow-up pitch letter. The writer first contacted the reporter by telephone to determine interest in the product. This letter lets the reporter know what the product does and offers a video demonstration. (*Courtesy of Access Public Relations, San Francisco.*)

MEDIA ADVISORY

SIDE-LINED SAN FRANCISCO 49ER WILLIAM FLOYD TO TACKLE QUESTIONS ON CAREER, INJURY AND VIDEO GAMES

WHO:	Injured San Francisco 49er William "Bar None" Floyd San Francisco video game maker U.S. Gold, Inc.
WHAT:	William Floyd answers questions regarding career and involvement in new U.S. Gold video game SHELLSHOCK
WHEN:	Tuesday, November 14
TIME:	5:00 PM
WHERE:	U.S. Gold Building 303 Sacramento Street 2nd Floor Financial District, across from One Embarcadero Plaza San Francisco
RE:	San Francisco 49er fullback William Floyd will answer media questions for the first time following his season ending injury, discussing his future in the sport and his new career in the development of next-generation 32-bit video games. Floyd will also unveil his new, much-anticipated U.S. Gold game, SHELLSHOCK. The football star's work on the soundtrack was key in creating the mood for this futuristic battle tank game.
VISUALS:	Beta tapes available at event featuring William Floyd's original music work on SHELLSHOCK and footage of the game itself Official launch of SHELLSHOCK with Floyd at event
NOTE:	No lighting or audio equipment will be provided for electronic media
CONTACTS:	Garth Bradley/Dave Karraker Frank Alizaga Access Communications U.S. Gold (415) 904-7070 (415) 693-0297 x127

Figure 9.5 Media advisories give reporters a quick review of the five Ws and H. (*Courtesy of Access Public Relations, San Francisco.*)

---

let the reader understand exactly what is at issue. The organization's position statement is next. It must be brief but complete, clearly written and backed up with facts. In many cases it is advisable to present and refute the position of the opposing side. Also, it may be a good idea to discuss alternative solutions and the reasons why they are not acceptable or workable.

The Company:	Palladium Interactive is a publisher and development manager for interactive multimedia products. The company forms partnerships with some of the industry's most accomplished development organizations and collaborates with various teams to create high-quality original titles and superior product lines.
Location:	3 Harbor Drive Suite 301, Sausalito, California 94965 (415) 289-4000 telephone (415) 289-4090 fax
Founded:	1994
Management:	Ed Bernstein, President and CEO Steven Horowitz, VP Research and Development Ed Roffman, VP Finance and Operations Susan Sinclair, VP Sales
Investors:	U.S. Venture Partners and Canaan Partners
Initial Products:	Four CD-ROM compilations featuring a variety of popular and award-winning edutainment and entertainment multimedia titles schedule to be available October 1995. Titles of the compilations are: • *Kid's Fun & Learning Pack* (PC-compatible, $29.95) • *Kid's Creativity Pack* (PC-compatible, $29.95) • *Kid's Mac Pack* (Macintosh systems, $39.95) • *Best Sellers Pack* (PC-compatible, $29.95) All PC products run under Windows 3.1 and are Windows '95 compatible. Original titles from Palladium Interactive are scheduled for release beginning in Q2 of 1996.
Company Focus:	To produce original titles that enrich, inform and entertain, with a focus on children's entertainment, edutainment, reference and productivity/creativity.
Markets:	IBM-compatible PC and Macintosh
Unique Characteristics:	Palladium *Collaborative Publishing Program,* a true collaboration that shares risk and reward more equitably with developers and content providers. Palladium *Multiple Channel Distribution Program,* where Palladium products are designed early on to appeal to multiple channels including retail, OEM, international, direct, education and catalog distribution.
Contact:	Dave Karraker, Access Communications (415) 904-7070 x265

Figure 9.6 Fact sheets give reporters a quick overview of an organization. Such basic facts are good reference points when reporters write and broadcast stories. See Figure 5.6 for a fact sheet from the Minnesota Zoo. (*Courtesy of Palladium Interactive, Sausalito, CA.*)

Position papers may be distributed in response to media requests, they may be included in press kits or they may be sent to all media that might want to know the organization's position.

Backgrounders

[handwritten: summary of company who what stand for .]

In contrast to the position paper, which states an organization's stand on a particular subject, the backgrounder is only a recap of information and doesn't necessarily lead to any conclusion.

It is a summary of pertinent facts about some subject. It must be accurate, complete and objective. A good example is a backgrounder from Sun Microsystems that outlined the history of the company and how it became a *Fortune* 500 company within ten years of its founding.

Backgrounders don't have to be dull. Sun Microsystems took the approach of an in-depth feature article and used desktop publishing to create an attractive three-column format complete with computer-generated graphics. The backgrounder also highlighted various quotes about the company from competing companies and outside experts. In the early days of the company, for example, "Apollo's leaders dismissed Sun with comments like, 'Everything that's loose rolls to the West Coast.'"

Press Kits

[handwritten: can have graphics]

A press kit is a packet of materials that may include news releases, photographs, graphics, feature stories, fact sheets, position papers, backgrounders and brief biographical sketches of organizational executives. In short, it is a collection of press materials assembled in a large envelope or folder. Press kits are typically prepared for major events and new product launches.

Compiling and producing a press kit is time-consuming and expensive. It is not uncommon for press kits to cost $5 to $7 each by the time all the materials are produced and the folder cover is prepared. Consequently, press kits should be distributed selectively and only to reporters who regularly cover your employer or client.

Press kits are a valuable opportunity to get publicity placements, but several surveys of editors indicate that such kits often miss the mark. They are too large, contain too many sales brochures, include poor-quality photos and have poorly written news and feature stories.

Apple Computer, for example, once won a "dubious achievement" award from a group of journalists for regularly distributing press kits the size of phone books. Other companies get roundly criticized for emphasizing packaging and ignoring the content.

You should keep press kits slim and cost-effective. Provide reporters and editors with information that is simple, factual and relevant to their audiences. Give them story ideas, local angles, interesting infographics and information based on solid research.

Press kits can be electronic. EPKs, as they are called, can be placed on an organization's home page (on the Internet's World Wide Web) and downloaded with a click of a mouse. They can also be placed on CD-ROM or beamed by satellite to

The McKinley Group, Inc.

Internet Publishers

Contact: Zoë Arden <zarden@accesspr.com>
Nicol Davis <ndavis@accesspr.com>
Access Public Relations
(415) 904-7070, ext. 287 or 281

Christine Maxwell <publisher@mckinley.com>
The McKinley Group

EUROPE ONLINE SA AND THE MCKINLEY GROUP, INC. TO LAUNCH EUROPEAN INTERNET DIRECTORY (EID)

SAUSALITO, Calif. and Luxembourg, (December 14, 1995) — The McKinley Group, publisher of the *Magellan* Internet directory, and Europe Online, the Luxembourg-based online service provider, announced today that they have signed a letter of agreement to jointly launch a European directory for the Internet.

Europe Online has chosen McKinley's *Magellan* as its directory of choice. Additionally, McKinley will create for Europe Online a specialized European Internet Directory (EID) which will serve as an online guide to European resources on the Internet. The EID will be initially launched on Europe Online on December 15, 1995. Additionally, the two companies will cooperate in the joint development of new products for print, CD-ROM and vertical market applications.

"We are delighted to be working in partnership with Europe Online," says David Hayden, President and CEO of The McKinley Group. "Our goal is to make the EID the standard guide that Europeans use to explore the vast global resources of the Internet."

- more -

85 Liberty Ship Way, Suite 201 Sausalito, CA 94965-1768 • Tel: 415-331-1884 Fax: 415-331-8609
E-mail: mckinley@mckinley.com • Site: http://www.mckinley.com

Figure 9.7 News releases are an integral part of press kits, which also include a variety of other background materials. (*Courtesy of Access Public Relations, San Francisco.*)

The McKinley Group, Inc.
Internet Publishers

Contact: Zoë Arden <zarden@accesspr.com>
           Nicol Davis <ndavis@accesspr.com>
           Access Public Relations
           (415) 904-7070, ext. 287 or 281

           Helene Atkin <hfa@mckinley.com>
           The McKinley Group, Inc.
           (415) 331-1884

Corporate Backgrounder:
The McKinley Group, Inc.

The McKinley Group was founded in 1993 by a team of international publishers, technologists and information specialists, committed to delivering the best navigational and informational directory for the Internet.

Magellan (http://www.mckinley.com), the company's innovative on-line Internet directory, contains listings for more than one million sites, many of which are fully described, reviewed and rated (with one to four stars). The McKinley Group's editorial process is monitored by an in-house team of high-level subject matter specialists, in coordination with The McKinley Editorial Advisory Board, a panel of international experts.

The cyberspace equivalent to a deluxe motoring guide, *Magellan* enables Internet users, novices and pros alike, to navigate the vast resources of the Internet and to have the unique facility to preview rated resources and valuable descriptions about the sites before having to review them.

Magellan is currently available at no cost via the Internet. Due to overwhelming demand from users to keep the service free, McKinley has begun to accept advertising within its *Magellan* database providing targeted placement of ads that match user queries. It is also available through licensed Internet access providers, such as NETCOM, IBM, AT&T and NYNEX.

- more -

85 Liberty Ship Way, Suite 201 Sausalito, CA 94965-1768 • Tel: 415-331-1884 Fax: 415-331-8609
E-mail: mckinley@mckinley.com • Site: http://www.mckinley.com

Figure 9.8 Corporate backgrounders are like fact sheets, but are written in paragraph style. This is an example from a press kit distributed by the McKinley Group. (*Courtesy of Access Public Relations, San Francisco.*)

The McKinley Group, Inc.
Internet Publishers

Contact: Zoë Arden <zarden@accesspr.com>   Helene Atkin<hfa@mckinley.com
            Nicol Davis <ndavis@accesspr.com>   The McKinley Group, Inc.
            Access Public Relations   (415) 331-1884
            (415) 904-7070, ext. 287 or 281

EXECUTIVE PROFILES

DAVID HAYDEN
President & CEO

David Hayden oversees day to day operations of The McKinley Group, as well as the
overall design and structure of *Magellan's* database. His responsibilities also include
business development and strategic alliances both nationally and internationally. He has
formerly served as director of Spectrum Holobyte Inc., an entertainment software
company, as well as co-chairman and CFO of S.R.H. Inc., a building and development
firm in Northern California. Mr. Hayden has over 20 years of experience in successfully
managing and leading companies that conceive, design, and produce products to bring to
market. Mr. Hayden holds a B.A. degree from Stanford University.

CHRISTINE MAXWELL
Publisher

As publisher of The McKinley Group, Ms. Maxwell has day to day responsibilities for
content acquisition and quality of *Magellan's* Database. She is also responsible for
developing publishing products in vertical markets nationally and internationally.
Additionally, Ms. Maxwell serves as president and CEO of Research On Demand Inc., an
international information broker company. With 25 years in the publishing and information
business, she has held senior marketing, strategic business and development positions with
Pergamon Press Publishers, Science Research Associates (SRA) and Macmillan Publishing
Company. Ms. Maxwell is on the board of the Santa Fe Institute and is the co-author of
the *McKinely Internet Yellow Pages* published by Macmillan Computer Publishing. Ms.
Maxwell has a B.A. from Pitzer College.

DAVID H. BRANDIN
Senior Vice President, International Operations

Mr. Brandin directs the international operations of The McKinley Group, including
activities in Europe and Japan. He brings over 30 years experience in the information
technology marketplace to the company. He has served as senior vice president of
international operations and founding director of Interop, vice president and director of the
Computer Science and Technology Division of SRI International, and as president of the
Association for Computing Machinery. He co-authored *The Technology War*, and he is a
pioneer member of the Internet Society. He chaired the US Department of Commerce
Japanese Technology evaluation program on computer science and he was the ACM
nominee to the Public Cryptography Study Group. He holds a B.S. in Mathematics from
Illinois Institute of Technology, and he attended the Stanford GSB Executive Program.

---

85 Liberty Ship Way, Suite 201 Sausalito, CA 94965-1768 • Tel: 415-331-1884 Fax: 415-331-8609
E-mail: mckinley@mckinley.com • Site: http://www.mckinley.com

Figure 9.9 Biographies of key executives are often included in press
kits. This is from a press kit distributed by the McKinley Group. (*Courtesy of Access Public Relations, San Francisco.*)

broadcast and cable outlets. Movie studios, in particular, are using satellite to promote new films by sending out EPKs that include film clips, a featurette and interviews with the stars, directors and producers. Recording companies are doing the same thing with music videos.

MEETING THE PRESS

Press interviews, news conferences, media tours and other kinds of gatherings provide excellent opportunities to communicate your message to a variety of audiences. They are more personal than just sending written materials and allow reporters to get direct answers from news sources.

Company executives who are prone to stage fright may view direct one-to-one contact with the media as a nightmare. They fear that they will say something stupid, be misquoted or be "ambushed" by an aggressive reporter who will slant the interview to imply that the organization is guilty of some wrong doing.

Nevertheless, media interviews help the organization accomplish the objectives of increasing visibility, consumer awareness and sales of services or products. They key is preparation. As book author Dick Martin points out, "In dealing with the press, as in any other business dealing, preparation is compulsory." The following discussion will provide tips and techniques to make sure that you or your organization's executives are prepared to meet the press.

Individual Interviews

An old public relations joke goes, "You know you're going to have a bad day when your secretary tells you that Mike Wallace of *60 Minutes* is in the lobby."

A local newspaper or television reporter can cause the same sort of discomfort, particularly if he or she shows up unannounced. However, most press interviews are set up in advance. They can be initiated by you as the public relations representative, or they can be requested by a reporter who is looking for credible experts to fill out a story.

Chapter 16 provides tips on how to answer questions in such an interview, but some additional points are worth noting here. First, if a reporter calls to request an interview, you should interview the reporter first. Some common questions are, "What's the nature of your story?" "Why did you call me?" "What are you looking for from me?"

By asking such questions, you can decide if you are qualified to answer the reporter's questions or whether someone else in the organization would be a better source. You may also decide that the context of the story is not appropriate for your organization and decline to be interviewed. For example, the reporter may ask you to comment on some topic that has nothing to do with your organization.

One danger in a telephone interview is that you're caught off guard and don't have time to formulate your thoughts. But before you know it, you and the reporter are chatting away like old friends about a number of topics. This is fine, but do re-

Figure 9.10 Radio and television reporters often conduct spot news interviews on location. Here, they talk with Republican House Speaker Newt Gingrich after a meeting with President Clinton. (*Courtesy of Reuters/Bettmann.*)

member that your name and a quote will probably appear in the article or as a sound bite on a newscast. It may be used accurately, or it may be completely out of context.

A better approach for a major interview, whether initiated by you or the reporter, is to schedule it in advance. If you know the purpose of the story, you can better prepare yourself or other spokespersons for the session.

Sandra Miller of Impact Communication Techniques gives some tips on how to handle being interviewed:

- Anticipate questions and plan answers. Memorize facts, figures, details that will help you sound credible.
- Know your audience and frame your answer from its point of view, using language it will understand.
- Develop a message—one or two key points you want to get across.
- Answer questions, but link them to your message whenever possible.
- Be quotable. Say it briefly, clearly and directly in 30 seconds or less.
- State your conclusions first and then back them up with facts. Your answer will probably be edited.
- Speak conversationally and use personal anecdotes when appropriate.
- Don't let reporters put words in your mouth. Rephrase their words, avoiding negative ones.
- Don't lie if you don't know the answer. Ask for clarification or tell the reporter you will find out and get back to him or her.

- Don't ever say "no comment." It makes you sound guilty. Try to give a reason if you can't comment and offer alternative information if appropriate.
- There is no such thing as "off the record."
- Don't answer hypothetical questions.
- Don't speak badly about anyone else.
- Practice your answers out loud.
- Dress and act appropriately. Don't distract your listeners with defensive nonverbal language such as crossing your arms.
- Always answer positively. It's the answer that counts, not the question.

Other media training experts have added to and elaborated on Miller's list. One common suggestion is to provide reporters with company background materials in advance. This will help them get facts and names correct. Body language is important. Be confident and relaxed, always look a reporter in the eye, keep your hands open, smile and lean forward when you're talking.

News Conferences

A news conference is a setting where many reporters ask questions. It is called by an organization when there is important and significant news to announce, news that would attract major media and public interest.

Bulldog Reporter, a public relations newsletter, gives the following list of instances that are appropriate for news conferences:

ATTRIBUTION IN INTERVIEWS

A person being interviewed by a reporter should be familiar with the four levels of attribution. Guy L. Smith, head of his own public relations firm in New York, gives this explanation:

- *On the record.* Everything you say can be attributed to you, either with quotes or paraphrased. ("We are not raising prices," says Betsy Knoop . . . .)
- *Background.* You can be quoted directly, but your name is not used. ("We are not raising prices," a Widget executive said.)
- *Deep background.* No quotes can be used. (A Widget executive said no price rise was being considered.)
- *Off the record.* There can be no direct or indirect quote of the information provided, nor can any of the information provided be attributed in any way to you, either directly or indirectly. (An industry source said . . . .)

Smith also advises that you take the time to make sure both you and the reporter have the same understanding of these terms before you proceed with any interview. It avoids unpleasant arguments later.

Other media relations experts take a cautious approach: they say it's better to assume that anything you say will be reported. It's risky to assume that a reporter will remember exactly what was "on the record" and "what was "background" or "off the record."

Source: *O'Dwyer's PR Services Report,* February, 1995, p. 52.

- An announcement of considerable importance to a large number of people in the community is to be made.
- A matter of public concern needs to be explained.
- Reporters have requested access to a key individual, and it is important to give all media equal access to the person.
- A new product or an invention in the public interest is to be unveiled, demonstrated and explained to the media.
- A person of importance is coming to town, and there are many media requests for interviews.
- A complex issue or situation is to be announced, and the media need access to someone who can answer their questions.

The two major reasons for having a news conference are to give all media an opportunity to hear the announcement at the same time and to provide a setting where reporters can ask follow-up questions. Many announcements, particularly ones involving research breakthroughs, major corporate decisions and crises, raise numerous questions as reporters seek information on all aspects of an issue or event.

Your role as a public relations professional is to determine when and if a news conference is needed. All too often, executives in an organization want to call a news conference to stir up publicity and make routine announcements that can just as easily be handled with a news release. Not only is this an expensive proposition, but it also alienates the media, who have better things to do than attend news conferences where there is no news.

Figure 9.11 News conferences require detailed planning. Time of day, location, room setup and presentation of information are important components. This news conference, held at UCLA, was about new developments on the Information Highway. (*Courtesy of PhotoEdit.*)

Scheduling a News Conference The conference should be scheduled at a time that is convenient for the reporters—that is, with an eye on the deadlines of the media represented. In general, Tuesday, Wednesday or Thursday mornings are best for dailies and broadcast media. This allows sufficient time for reporters to get stories in the next morning's daily or on the 6 p.m. news. If the primary audience is the trade press—reporters representing publications in a particular industry—late afternoon news conferences may be more convenient.

Avoid Saturdays and Sundays, as well as major holidays. Most media operate with skeleton staffs on these days and hence don't have the personnel to cover news conferences. Also, avoid news conferences after 5 p.m. Major newspapers and broadcast outlets are unionized, and they prefer not to pay reporters overtime.

Another consideration, which often can't be planned for, is to schedule the news conference on a day when there aren't a lot of conflicting news events. It's wise to avoid election days, for example.

Selecting a Location A location for a news conference must meet several criteria. First, it must be convenient for the media invited and relatively close to their places of work. Second, the room selected must have the necessary facilities to accommodate both print and broadcast media.

Organizations often use hotels and conference centers for news conferences, as well as the corporate headquarters. It is important for the room to have plenty of electrical outlets, particularly for radio and television crews. Television people may prefer a room on a ground floor near an entrance so that they can park a mobile communications center outside the room. In some cases, they will want to run cables from the truck to the room for live broadcast.

Live radio can involve microwave, cellular phone or land line transmission. Radio reporters will want a room with phone jacks or a bank of phones nearby.

You should make the room available one or two hours in advance so that radio and television crews can set up. Have a general seating plan to make sure that the equipment doesn't obstruct the view or hinder the work of the print reporters. An elevated platform for TV cameras in the back of the room is helpful.

Another consideration is to have several smaller rooms reserved nearby for exclusive interviews with a company representative after the general news conference.

Invitations The invitation list should include all reporters who might be interested. It is better to invite too many than to omit some who may feel slighted.

Invitations take various forms, depending on the event and the creativity of the public relations person. The standard approach is a letter that can be delivered by first class mail, by E-mail, by fax or even by hand. A second approach is a more formal invitation (see Figure 9.12) that incorporates some graphic elements. This approach is often used for new product announcements, acquisitions and mergers.

A third approach is the stunt. When Swatch invited reporters to a news conference announcing a new line of diver's watches, it had people in scuba gear deliver aquariums, containing invitations.

If the news conference will also be broadcast live via satellite to reporters in various cities, a satellite distribution firm will send a media advisory. Silicon Graphics, for example, held such a news conference when it announced a joint business venture with movie producer Steven Spielberg.

Figure 9.12 Invitation to a news conference and product demonstration. This invitation was a 3.5 x 5 inch self-mailer and had four panels. (*Courtesy of Access Public Relations, San Francisco.*)

Use the telephone if the conference is being scheduled on short notice. In any case, the invitation should state the time and place, the subject to be discussed and the names of the principal spokespeople who will attend.

NEWS CONFERENCES BY SATELLITE

The news conference of the 1990s is increasingly being done via satellite.

Johnson & Johnson set the standard in 1982 by calling a 30-city video news conference that attracted 500 journalists. The purpose was to announce the return of Tylenol with new tamperproof packaging after an unknown killer had put cyanide in eight of the old-style bottles.

A satellite news conference was also set up by General Motors to refute a story on *Dateline NBC* about the rigging of a demonstration that showed the gasoline tanks of certain GM trucks exploding during impact. The GM satellite feed was sent to newspapers and broadcast outlets across the country, including the press room of the National Automobile Dealers Association's annual meeting in New Orleans. There, about 60 auto reporters took part in a telephone question-and-answer session with GM officials.

Satellite news conferences are set up in much the same way that video news releases are sent to stations via satellite, as explained in Chapter 8. Essentially, spokespeople give a news conference in a television studio, and the picture is uplinked to a satellite that distributes the signal to dish antennae at newspapers and broadcast stations. Reporters can speak to the spokespeople via telephone.

Print invitations should be sent 10 to 14 days in advance, and should be marked "RSVP" so you can make appropriate decisions regarding the size of the meeting room, the number of press kits needed and what special equipment will be required. Reporters are notorious for not responding to RSVPs, so it is usually necessary to phone them several days before the event and to get a tentative answer.

Handling the Conference   It is important that a news conference be well organized, short and punctual. It is not a symposium or a seminar. A news conference should run no more than an hour, and statements by spokespeople should be relatively brief, allowing reporters time to ask questions.

You should brief your employers or clients on what they are going to say, how they are going to say it and what visual aids will be used to illustrate their announcement. Reporters should receive copies of the text for each speech and other key materials such as slides, overheads, charts and background materials. These are often given to reporters in the form of a press kit. Short bios with the accurate names and titles of the participants can be added to the press kit, as can general news releases.

Coffee, fruit juice and rolls can be served prior to the opening of a morning news conference. Avoid trying to serve a luncheon or cocktails to reporters attending a news conference. They have deadlines and other assignments, and don't have time to socialize.

After the Conference   At the conclusion of the news conference, the spokespeople should remain in the room and be available for any reporters who need one-on-one interviews. This can be done in a quiet corner or in a room adjacent to the site.

As the public relations person, you should be readily accessible during the remainder of the day in case reporters need more information or think of other questions as they prepare their stories. You should know where the spokespeople are during the day and how they can be reached, just in case a reporter needs to check a quote or get another.

Another duty is to contact reporters who expressed interest but were ultimately unable to attend. You can offer to send them the printed materials from the news conference and, if you have recorded the news conference, offer excerpts of videotape or sound bites. Another possibility is to arrange a one-on-one interview with one of the spokespeople. In media relations, as previously stated, service is the name of the game.

Teleconferences

A variation of the news conference is the teleconference. The technology is simple: a speakerphone hookup and a conference call linking reporters throughout the country.

A teleconference can be effective for several reasons. First, it's a cost-effective way to interact with reporters on a one-to-one basis. Second, it's convenient for the media. Rather than taking time to travel to and from a news conference, reporters can participate from their desks. Third, conference calls can be scheduled much more easily than a meeting.

Here are some guidelines for holding a teleconference:

- Invite reporters to participate in advance.
- The teleconference should last no more than 45 to 60 minutes.
- Remember time zones when scheduling a teleconference.

Media Tours

An alternative to the news conference, which is held in one location, is the media tour. This involves multiple sites and a number of media throughout the region or the nation. There are three kinds of media tours, ranging from interviews on talk shows to visiting editors at their offices.

Local Talk Shows and Newspapers

Getting people on talk or interview shows was discussed in Chapter 8. In many cases, the spokesperson for an organization goes on a media tour and is booked on local shows in a number of cities. The publicist will try to book local print media interviews in these cities, too.

A good example of how this works is a marketing communications program conducted on behalf of Step Reebok, an adjustable device for step training. The objective was to promote the product and physical fitness in general.

Rich Boggs, founder of Sports Step and creator of the adjustable step, was an ideal spokesperson. He was once an overweight, three-pack-a-day smoker who completely changed his lifestyle and now has a strong commitment to health and fitness.

Boggs went on a 14-city media tour to promote step training and his product. Because physical fitness was topical and trendy, he was able to get on 24 different TV news and talk shows, four of which were national. He also gave 21 radio interviews and was the subject of more than 20 newspaper feature articles.

The media tour, a key element in an overall marketing communications program, led to a 45 percent increase in sales of Step Reebok. A comparable advertising campaign would have cost almost $750,000.

Business and Trade Press

The second kind of tour has a longer range in terms of results. An organization's officials make calls on publications that reach important audiences that can invest in the company or purchase the product or service. In this case, the news conference comes to the publication.

It would be difficult to get representatives from national business and trade publications to visit the offices of a small company. Yet by taking the president, the director of public relations and perhaps the chief financial officer to the publication, it is possible to arrange for a one-on-one news conference with the publication's principal editors.

Dataspeed, Inc., wanted to be known as a telecommunications company with innovative products such as a portable stock market quotation device. The solution was a media tour. Regis McKenna, Inc., a public relations counseling firm, not only prepared Dataspeed's chief executive for media interviews but also arranged appointments with key journalists and financial security analysts on the East Coast.

In a five-day swing, an account executive from Regis McKenna and the president of Dataspeed visited 22 journalists and analysts in New York, Boston and Washington. They were able to see editors at *Fortune, Business Week, Time, Newsweek* and a number of trade publications serving the high-technology indus-

The McKinley Group, Inc. West Coast Media Tour
Isabel Hayden, Alex Cohen

	Thursday, January 25	Friday, January 26
9am	8:30 PC COMPUTING, Rich Schwerin, Foster City	INVESTOR'S BUSINESS DAILY, Steve Higgins, San Francisco (Access)
10am	BUSINESSWEEK, Rob Hof, SF	10:30, WIRED MAGAZINE, Rod Simpson
11am	11:30 SAN FRANCISO CHRONICLE, David Einstein, SF	
12pm	travel/lunch time-SF to Portola Valley	12:30, RED HERRING, Gin Pelletier, San Francisco
1pm	INTERACTIVE WEEK, Tim Clark, Portola Valley	(previous meeting time allotment-12:30-1:30) travel time 1:30-2:00
2pm	travel time-Portola Valley to San Francisco	FINANCIAL TIMES OF LONDON, Louise Kehoe, San Mateo
3pm	3:30, PC WORLD, Rick Overton, San Francisco	HOME PC, John Eckhouse, San Mateo (1/2 hour only)
4pm		

Figure 9.13 A media tour schedule for spokespeople from the McKinley Group. Attention to logistics and timing are important. Such a schedule is usually part of a briefing book for clients on media tours. (*Courtesy of Access Public Relations, San Francisco.*)

try. In addition, they visited a number of key security analysts specializing in the high-tech field.

These visits accomplished several things for the company. First, they introduced Dataspeed and its innovative products to editors and security analysts who had never heard of the company. Second, they helped build a personal relationship between the company's president and key editors and analysts. Third, the demonstration of an innovative product resulted in major stories about the technology and established Dataspeed as a well-managed and innovative company. This coverage boosted both sales and the value of the company's stock.

Regular background briefings of the business and trade press may not result in immediate publicity, but they can build relationships that will pay dividends in the future.

Satellite Media Tours

A media tour doesn't have to involve long plane trips, countless nights in hotel rooms and rented cars in unfamiliar cities. In fact, you needn't leave home at all.

The alternative is the satellite media tour (SMT). In a world of global communication and events being shown in real time, the SMT is becoming the standard

SAN FRANCISCO CHRONICLE

Thursday, January 25   11:30 a.m.

David Einstein
901 Mission Street
San Francisco, CA 94103
(415) 555-2600
Fax: (415) 555-2603

Audience:	General public of San Francisco, Silicon Valley, and surrounding areas.
Description:	The San Francisco Chronicle is Northern California's largest newspaper. It is a regional daily newspaper whose coverage stretches from the Oregon border to Santa Barbara and includes Silicon Valley. Though advertisers rightly think of the newspaper as the morning complement to the San Francisco Examiner, the news and editorial departments run independent—and competitive—operations.
Frequency:	Daily
Circulation:	556,715 (weekly)/708,542 (Sunday)
Notes:	On the August tour, McKinley met with features writer. David is a business writer and is the main contact for Business Coverage and the Technology column. He is fairly familiar with The McKinley Group and *Magellan*—he wrote about McKinley on 11/29 and 1/4.
	This editor is very interested in the Internet Directory wars and he believes that the industry will undergo a shakeout in the near future. Given this, he needs to understand how *Magellan* is going to survive this consolidation. For this meeting, focus on *Magellan's* superiority in terms of technology and process, as well as how *Magellan's* advertising structure stands to generate revenue for the company.

Figure 9.14 A page from a media tour briefing book that gives the client some background on the publication and reporter who will be interviewing them. Such information is valuable in preparing spokespersons for what to expect. (*Courtesy of Access Public Relations, San Francisco.*)

rather than the exception. Nielsen Media Research, for example, once surveyed 96 television stations and found that 85 percent of them regularly use interviews and video footage from SMTs.

An SMT operates electronically in much the same way as the traditional media tour. Instead of spending a week or more on the road, however, a spokesperson can spend two hours in a studio being interviewed one-on-one by reporters located around the globe. Each reporter is booked in advance to have a 5- to 10-minute window for their own interview in much the same way that a spokesperson would be scheduled to visit four or five media outlets in a day.

A SATELLITE TRANSMISSION GLOSSARY

Satellites are now commonly used for everything from the transmission of video news releases to the conduct of media tours and teleconferences. The following is a partial list of terms used in the field.

air check an off-air recording of a television program showing how your satellite interview or video news release was used on a particular newscast at a local station.

bird slang for a communications satellite.

booking the process of pitching and scheduling local news stations to interview your client.

B-roll the prerecorded raw videotape accompanying satellite media tours or video news releases. This portion gives news producers action shots, scenery or graphics associated with your spokesperson's message.

dish a satellite receiving antenna.

downlink the reception of a television signal from a satellite by an earth station or antenna.

earth station a complete satellite receiving system.

footprint the coverage area of a satellite TV signal.

pad the time built into a satellite tour for transition from station to station.

remote locations locations outside a studio. Live satellite media tours and press conferences can originate from remote locations such as Yellowstone National Park using special equipment.

satellite press conference a press conference that is uplinked and distributed nationwide so that television news departments can view and tape the session. Sophisticated versions allow two-way interaction.

talent person or persons being interviewed.

uplink the transmission of video and audio signals from a broadcast facility to a communications satellite.

window the time allotted to individual stations for the talent to be interviewed by news reporters or anchors at local stations. A typical media tour will contain 15 to 20 windows of approximately 10 minutes each.

Source: *Satellite Media Tour Handbook,* Medialink Video Broadcasting Corporation, 1991, p. 16.

While the spokesperson's image and voice are transmitted to the TV station via satellite, the local reporter's questions are received through phone lines at the studio and fed through audio lines into the spokesperson's earpiece. The effect, on a TV screen, is that the reporter and the source are talking to each other in the same room. This technique is used extensively on ABC's *The NewsHour with Jim Lehrer.*

DON'T FORGET RADIO TOURS

Satellite media tours are not just for television stations and cable systems. If you don't have a big budget and visuals are secondary, the radio media tour is also effective.

Novelist Salman Rushdie, for example, used a radio media tour to promote his new book, *The Moor's Last Sigh*. He spent two hours at a studio in New York answering questions from hosts of news and talk radio shows in Detroit, Minneapolis, St. Louis, Miami, Houston, San Diego, Dallas and Seattle.

You can get additional mileage from an SMT if you also provide B-roll footage, discussed in Chapter 8. This provides background material so stations can produce a locally packaged story, or illustrates aspects of the interview that takes place. Here are some examples of satellite media tours:

- Pizza Hut opened its 10,000th restaurant in Sao Paulo, Brazil. For the grand opening, the company used soccer star Pelé as its spokesperson; he gave interviews via satellite to reporters around the world.
- Two medical experts answered questions about AIDS on an SMT sponsored by Burroughs Wellcome.
- Del Monte used an expert to explain new nutritional labeling required by the FDA. An interview conducted by NBC News was transmitted on a News One feed to its affiliates, resulting in broadcasts by hundreds of stations.

An SMT is usually planned in advance, but one can also be held on short notice if there is a crisis or late-breaking news. Companies often make executives available via SMTs to announce a product recall or, like Pepsi, to quell concerns about product tampering. Florida tourism officials also used SMTs to reassure European journalists that Florida was still safe despite the murder of several German tourists.

Conventions and trade shows also lend themselves to SMTs. They attract experts and celebrities as speakers, and extra publicity is gained by making it possible for reporters across the country to interview them without actually attending the meeting. An SMT was set up for Bill Gates, chairman of Microsoft, when he visited the world's largest technology exposition in Hannover, Germany.

An SMT is relatively cost-effective, especially if you are trying to reach journalists on a national or international level. A studio-originated two-hour production costs about $12,000 and an "on location" one costs somewhat more, depending on the location and event. According to *Public Relations Journal*, "Satellite media tours from the scene of an event have special appeal to local stations, adding 'live from the scene' excitement to their newscasts and shows."

GETTING ON THE EDITORIAL PAGE

If you are trying to reach opinion leaders and citizens who are actively interested in public affairs, a good technique is to get on the editorial pages of major daily newspapers.

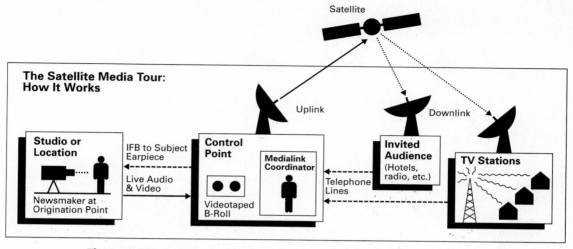

Figure 9.15 Satellite media tours are efficient and save traveling time. This illustration shows the mechanics of a satellite media tour. The process is interactive because the spokesperson and the interviewer can talk as if they were in the same room. (*Copyright Medialink, used with permission.*)

The indirect approach is to meet with the editorial boards of the newspapers and ask them to write an editorial supporting your idea, project or cause. Another approach is to submit short essays that are called *op-ed articles*, intended to appear opposite the editorial page. When all else fails, there is always the standard letter to the editor.

Editorial Boards

IMP

The key editors of a newspaper meet on a regular basis to determine editorial policy. they would be interested in talking to you if your employer or client is involved in a current controversy or in emerging issues. They do not want to meet with you if your purpose is just to get publicity.

In general, you contact the editorial page editor and request a meeting with the newspaper's editorial board. Most editors want a tightly written one- or two-page letter outlining whom you represent, what issues you would like to cover, and why your people are the best qualified to discuss the issue. Don't weigh down your first letter with a press kit or other background information.

Once you have an appointment with the editorial board, you should develop a message that focuses on three or four key points. You should also decide in advance what you want to accomplish in the meeting. Do you simply want to let editors know about your side of the issue, or do you want them to write an editorial supporting you?

The best approach is to have a well-informed senior person in the organization give the presentation. This may be the company president, but it can be an expert in a particular field such as law, accounting or environmental standards, depending on the issue. In general, your role as the public relations person is not to give the presentation but rather to make arrangements for the meeting and help your spokespersons prepare for it.

If you represent a community organization, you should think about meeting with the editorial board to arrange for an editorial supporting your particular goal—the current Girl Scout cookie sale or a downtown festival that raises money for teenage drug prevention programs. Newspapers are community boosters and they do write editorials supporting worthy causes.

Op-ed Articles

The term "op-ed" literally means opposite the editorial page. The concept originated at the *New York Times* some years ago and has now spread to many major newspapers and magazines across the country. The purpose of the op-ed article is to present a variety of views on news events, governmental policies and social issues.

From a public relations standpoint, the op-ed provides an excellent opportunity for individuals and organizations to reach an audience of readers who also tend to be opinion leaders. Indeed, if an organizational executive wants to become a spokesperson for a particular industry or cause, public relations counsel often recommends writing one or more op-ed pieces.

Universities and think tanks such as the Brookings Institution also make considerable use of op-ed pieces to gain visibility and position the organization as a leader. The public relations department of Washington University in St. Louis, for example, got 426 placements in one year by sending op-ed articles written by 62 faculty members.

The op-ed pages of the *New York Times*, the *Wall Street Journal*, and the *Washington Post* are the best-known and the most prestigious in terms of placement. They regularly carry op-eds written by ambassadors, former presidents, CEOs of major corporations, senators and a host of other prominent or influential people. The competition is steep; the *Wall Street Journal* receives about 500 to 700 op-ed articles a month and only has space for a few of them.

Your employer or client may not be a former ambassador or a general, but that should not discourage you from submitting op-ed pieces to these three newspapers and to other U.S. dailies. Editorial page directors are always looking for fresh insights from those who have expertise or experience on a particular topic.

In addition, you should not overlook the trade press. Publications that serve a particular industry or profession also use commentaries and short opinion articles. A company's head of research, or the vice president of human resources, might have something to say that would be interesting to the readers of these publications.

Public relations writers often do the initial work of drafting an op-ed for a client or employer. Another way to approach it is to ask a person for notes from a recent speech. Speeches to organizations are often recycled as op-eds to newspapers.

Letters to the Editor

The next best thing to an op-ed article is a published letter. Letters are generally shorter than op-ed pieces. They focus primarily on rebutting an editorial, clarifying information mentioned in a news story or column or adding information that might not have been included in the original story.

GUIDELINES FOR WRITING AN OP-ED ARTICLE

- Daily newspapers prefer articles of about 750 to 800 words, which is a bit more than three double-spaced pages.
- Concentrate on presenting one main idea or a single theme in your op-ed.
- Have a clear editorial viewpoint. Get to your point in the first paragraph, and proceed to back up your opinion.
- Use facts and statistics to add credibility to what you say. Double-check your facts before using them.
- Don't ramble or deviate from your principal points. An op-ed is not an essay that slowly builds to its point.
- Use short declarative sentences. Long, complex sentences and paragraphs cause readers to tune out.
- Be timely. The article should be about a current social issue, situation or news event.
- Give a short biography of the writer in the cover letter to the publication. This helps editors determine the person's qualifications.
- Don't do a mass mailing of an op-ed piece. A standard practice is to offer the piece to one publication at a time.

A good example is a letter that appeared in the *Wall Street Journal* from the president of a company that makes AstroTurf. He was reacting to a recent investigative story in the paper that reported a trend toward the use of natural grass in stadiums because of concern about injuries related to playing on AstroTurf. The president politely rebutted this line of thinking by writing, "There is a perception that AstroTurf is being removed in favor of grass because a few high-profile teams have switched surfaces. Actually, for every synthetic field that was removed in 1995, four new synthetic fields were installed."

There is limited space for letters, so you should closely follow any guidelines that the publication has established. Many of the op-ed guidelines apply, but here are some that directly relate to letters:

- Keep it short. About 250 words or less is recommended.
- Be temperate and factual. Don't call the editor names or question the integrity of the publication.
- Identify the subject in the opening paragraph. If your letter is in response to a specific article, briefly refer to the article and the date it appeared.
- State the theme of your letter in the second paragraph. Do you agree, disagree or want to clarify something.
- The next several paragraphs should give your viewpoint, supported by convincing facts, examples or statistics.
- Close. At the end of your letter, give your name, title, organization and telephone number. Publications often call to confirm that you wrote the letter.

SUMMARY

1. Pitch letters to editors must be brief, raise interest and immediately come to the point.
2. Media advisories should include the 5 Ws and H in outline form.
3. Fact sheets summarize the basic facts about an event, a product or an organization.
4. Position papers give the organization's perspective and viewpoint on a subject or topic.
5. Backgrounders are a compilation of basic facts. They give the history of an organization, its major products and services, the number of employees and profiles of its major executives.
6. Press kits are packets of material that may include news releases, photographs, feature stories, fact sheets, position papers, backgrounders and brief biographical sketches.
7. Interviews with the press require advance preparation and the ability to get across two or three main points in statements of 30 seconds or less.
8. News conferences are held for special announcements and require extensive planning.
9. The teleconference is a variation of the news conference. It enables reporters to ask questions without leaving their offices.
10. Media tours can be used to generate publicity in a number of cities, or they can be background briefings for reporters at their place of business.
11. Satellite media tours cut travel costs and save time.
12. Organizations can receive support by requesting that editorial boards write an editorial or cover a particular topic.
13. Op-ed articles are a good way for individuals to gain visibility and position themselves as leaders of an industry.
14. A letter to the editor is an effective way of refuting or elaborating on previous news coverage and opinion columns.

EXERCISES

1. The first step in getting someone booked on a broadcast talk show or becoming the subject of a newspaper interview is to write a pitch letter. Using the subject of Rich Boggs and his Step Reebok, cited in the section on media tours, write two pitch letters. One should be to the producer of a local TV talk show, and the second should be to the lifestyle editor of the local daily. Before writing your letters, review the chapter material on pitch letters.
2. A national business magazine has decided to do a profile of your company because of its dynamic executive leadership and innovative manufacturing

technologies. A reporter and a photographer will be visiting the company next week. How would you, as director of public relations, plan for their visit?

3. The Arts Council of Northwest Florida is sponsoring the Great Gulf Coast Arts Festival October 31 through November 2 in Pensacola. About 2,000 artists will exhibit their works, and there will be a series of jazz concerts. Write a fact sheet for the media about this event.

4. A company wants to hold a news conference announcing the acquisition of another large national company. Outline and describe the materials that should be placed in a press kit about this acquisition.

5. You are hired to organize a news conference for a company based in Norfolk, Virginia, that is announcing a major expansion of its department stores into the Florida and Georgia markets. Previously, the company had stores only in Virginia, Tennessee, and South Carolina. Outline and describe the steps for organizing this news conference. The resulting plan should be a blueprint of the entire event, including selection of site, use of visual aids and list of invitees.

6. Magic Johnson, the basketball star, will be attending a state-wide conference in your city about AIDS prevention and treatment. Using the five Ws and H, write a media advisory that informs the press that he is coming and will be available for a news conference.

7. The National Organization for Women (NOW) has declared June to be a month for concentrating on the problems of spousal abuse in our society. One strategy is to organize a satellite media tour to kick off the month. Who would be a good spokesperson for a satellite media tour?

8. The Foster Company, owner of a national chain of retail clothing stores, has had some tough years. However, a new president was brought in a year ago and has been able to rescue the company from bankruptcy. The stores have a new marketing strategy and sales are strong again. It's time to let the financial and trade press know about the turnaround. What kind of media tour would you organize for the company? Organize a tentative tour and give the names of publications and organizations that the president would visit.

9. Select an organization or major event in the community and compile a press kit for it.

10. The owner of a local radio station has written an op-ed article for the weekly business tabloid about journalism as a major in college. He says that journalism courses are a waste of time and that aspiring journalists or public relations personnel should get a broad-based education in the liberal arts. He says that today's journalism majors can't write and would benefit from majoring in English or history. As a journalism or public relations major, draft a letter to the editor rebutting his ideas.

11. The president of your company feels strongly that business has an obligation to provide childcare facilities for its employees. You are asked to write a 750-word op-ed article for the president that expresses his view on the subject. Use the library to gather facts and data that can be used for the article.

10 Media Lists, Mailings and the Internet

*P*erhaps the most important part of any publicity effort is the distribution of information to the appropriate media and audiences.

This chapter concentrates on how to find information about the media, compile accurate mailing lists and send materials in a variety of ways.

There are many distribution channels available to you, including mail, fax, electronic wire services, feature placement firms, diskettes and even CD-ROM. The most exciting technology is the Internet, which garners reams of publicity in its own right.

The chapter details distribution opportunities on the Net, profiling such aspects as E-mail, the World Wide Web and the thousands of discussion groups. Despite the glamour of the Internet, the public relations writer must realize that it has limitations, and that traditional media still reach a much wider audience.

FINDING THE MEDIA

Previous chapters emphasized that an essential part of public relations writing is making sure that the right media—and the right audience—receive your material.

Indeed, a common complaint of editors is that they receive reams of news releases that are not relevant to their publication or their audience. A second major complaint is that news releases are often sent to the wrong person. Compounding this problem is the estimate that nearly one-third of all journalists change their jobs or beats every 90 days.

So how do you find the right medium and the correct, current contact person? How do you reach every daily newspaper real estate editor in the nation? How do you contact every Spanish-speaking radio station in Texas? What if your release should go to every columnist who specializes in new computer products?

Finding media, their addresses and the names of editors would be nearly impossible if not for the existence of media directories in print and electronic form.

Media Directories

Directories vary in format and scope. However, a common denominator is that they usually give such essential information as (1) names of publications and broadcast stations, (2) mailing addresses, (3) telephone and fax numbers, (4) E-mail addresses and (5) names of key editors and reporters. Some directories even give a profile of the media in terms of audience, deadlines and placement opportunities.

Some directories focus on a specialty such as medical publications or periodicals that serve senior citizens. Others are compiled for a particular city or metropolitan area. Still others focus on specific regions or states, such as *California Publicity Outlets*. You can also get directories for various ethnic publications and broadcast outlets, such as the *Hispanic Media and Markets Directory*. For media outlets abroad there is *Benn's Media Directory* and *Ulrich's International Directory*.

Depending on your needs, you may use one or more of the above directories. Or you may find everything you need in a set of five comprehensive directories published by Bacon's International, Inc. These volumes, priced at about $250 each, include *Newspaper/Magazine Directory*, *Radio/TV/Cable Directory*, *Media Calendar Directory*, *Business Media Directory*, and *International Media Directory* (mostly Western Europe). The directories list a total of more than 200,000 contacts at more than 40,000 addresses.

Although printed directories are still used extensively, the new technologies of CD-ROM, software programs and on-line databases are rapidly replacing the dog-eared print directory of the past.

Bacon's, for example, now offers all its directories on CD-ROM. The new technology not only takes up less space in an office, but it's also more versatile. A special software program, used in conjunction with the CD-ROM database, allows you to rapidly compile a tailored media list for your messages.

For example, if you need a list of business editors in four markets at dailies with a circulation above 50,000, you can compile it with a few key strokes on your computer. With a few more key strokes, you can print out the entire list on address labels or even send the news release to Bacon's by modem for faxing or mailing to the selected media. Bacon's software also allows you to select media by location or even by kind of publication or broadcast station. The *Editor & Publisher Year Book*, also available on CD-ROM, has similar capabilities.

Other software programs on the market include *SpinWARE*, *Media Map* and *Press Access*. All these programs allow the user to track media lists; distribute news releases by mail, fax or electronic wire services; and even obtain information on deadlines and the background of various journalists. Some even offer updated databases on a quarterly basis or tell you the preferences of editors for receiving information.

Media directories and databases are also available on-line. Media Distribution Services (MDS), for example, has a program called *Targeter*. It contains a database of more than 150,000 editors and reporters at more than 40,000 print and broadcast media in the United States and Canada. The advantage of an on-line service is that MDS updates the database daily. As many as a 1,000 separate changes are sent to your computer electronically via modem. The software cost about $1,500, and there is a nominal charge for address labels and printed reports.

Maintaining up-to-date media lists has always been a mundane and tedious job, but the computer has considerably improved the process. Many organizations use the commercial databases described above, but a number also maintain their own media lists.

There are a number of software programs designed for storing and retrieving mailing lists. Popular database programs are *Professional File* for IBM and, for the Apple Macintosh, *dBase Mac* or *File Maker*.

There is also preconfigured database software designed for managing media lists. *NewsTrack*, by the Right Brain, is one. The media section of *NewsTrack* consists of preformatted records ready for you and your staff to expand. It allows you to assign special interest and distribution codes to each record, such as media type and editorial interest. From this list you can print mailing labels or even localize news releases by merging key items into them.

The concept of distribution codes, or various media lists, is important. An organization, for example, may set up several mailing lists. List One may include only local media in the organization's headquarters city. List Two might include local media in cities where the organization has manufacturing plants. List Three might include statewide media. List Four might include regional and national media. List Five might include trade and business media covering your industry.

After writing a news release, a public relations writer would fill out a distribution form that would indicate which media should receive the news release. If the story has only local significance, you would check "List One" so the mail room will know what mailing labels to use. In small organizations, you might even print off the address labels on your own computer.

A final note of caution. Once compiled, media lists must be constantly updated. If you're using a standard media directory of CD-ROM version, remember that last year's edition is out of date. That's why organizations buy new editions every year.

Television Stations   **California – continued**

KCBS-TV, Channel 2   **(213) 460-3000**
6121 Sunset Blvd.   Fax: (213) 460-3294
Los Angeles, CA 90028-6493   News Phone: (213) 460-3437
                                            News Fax: (213) 460-3733
                             Homepage: http://www.kcbs2.com
                                          Network: **CBS,O&O**

Owner: Westinghouse/CBS
General Management/News Executives:
Operations Director................................... John Kruer
Program Director...................................... Jay Strong
News Director.. Larry Perret
Assistant News Director............................... Steve Blue
News Assignment Manager...................... Maryhelen Campa
News Assignment (Night) Manager................... Rod Foster
News Assignment (Weekends) Editor................. Robert Yanez
Public Affairs Director............................. Joseph Dyer
Public Service Coordinator.......................... Rolando Lira
Sales Manager....................................... John McKay
Promotion Director.............................. Michael Benson
Business News Reporter......................... David Horowitz
Consumer Interest Reporter...................... David Horowitz
Consumer Interest Reporter......................... Jed McIlvain
Political Editor............................... Linda Breakstone
Sports Director.. Jim Hill
Meteorologist................................... Maclovio Perez
Programs:
  2 The Point (Sat, 6:00 AM)
    Profile: Public Affairs; **Format:** Interviews; **Description:** Local public
    affairs talk show on community issues.
    Guest Contact.................................. Judy Huern

  Action News at 4:00 PM (Mon-Fri, 4:00-4:30 PM)
    Profile: News/Weather/Sports
    Anchor... Tritia Toyota
    Anchor... Michael Tuck
    Executive Producer......................... Wendy MacNeill
    Guest Contact.............................. Nicole Bluett

  Action News at 4:30 PM (Mon-Fri, 4:30-5:00 PM)
    Profile: News/Weather/Sports
    Anchor.. Beverly Burke
    Anchor... Bob Jimenez
    Executive Producer......................... Wendy MacNeill
    Guest Contact.............................. Nicole Bluett

  Action News at 5:00 PM (Mon-Fri, 5:00 PM)
    Profile: News/Weather/Sports
    Anchor.. Jerry Dunphy
    Anchor... Ann Martin
    Executive Producer......................... Wendy MacNeill
    Guest Contact.............................. Nicole Bluett

  Bob Navarro's Journal (Sun, 9:30 AM)
    Profile: News Features; **Format:** Interviews; **Description:** Covers im-
    portant news features of the day.
    Host.. Bob Navarro
    Executive Producer........................... Bob Navarro
    Producer....................................... Linda Burns

  Channel 2 News at 11:00 PM (Mon-Sun, 11:00-11:30 PM)
    Profile: News/Weather/Sports
    Anchor... Ann Martin
    Anchor... Michael Tuck
    Executive Producer......................... Wendy MacNeil
    Guest Contact.............................. Nicole Bluett

  Channel 2 News at Noon (Mon-Fri, 12:00 PM)
    Profile: News/Weather/Sports
    Anchor.. Linda Alvarez
    Anchor.. Tritia Toyota
    Executive Producer......................... Wendy MacNeill
    Guest Contact.............................. Nicole Bluett

  Channel 2 Weekend Evening News (Sat, 5-6 PM & Sun, 6-7 PM)
    Profile: News/Weather/Sports
    Anchor.. Larry Carroll
    Anchor.. Linda Alvarez
    Executive Producer......................... Wendy MacNeil
    Guest Contact.............................. Nicole Bluett

Figure 10.1 Press directories are indispensable for finding media gatekeepers. They help channel publicity to the right media outlet and the right person. This illustration is from *Bacon's Radio/Television Directory*. (*Courtesy of Bacon's International, Inc., Chicago.*)

If you have compiled your own media list, you must constantly and regularly update its accuracy. Whenever and however you learn of a change, correct your mailing list immediately. Nothing annoys an editor or reporter more than a useless news release, but a close second is a release sent to someone who hasn't been around for months—or years.

Some public relations people try to keep lists current by addressing envelopes to titles instead of people. For example, a news release will be sent to the "news editor" or the "features editor" of a publication. Although this seems a logical approach, recipients react much as they do to junk mail addressed to "occupant."

Professional public relations people make it a point to keep media lists up to date. They also make it a point of pride that any address label contains the name of the person who holds the position. When the competition is great for attention and news space, anything less is unacceptable.

Editorial Calendars

Not only do media directories help you find the names and addresses of media gate-keepers, but several of them also tell you when to approach publications with specific kinds of stories.

Trade publications and business periodicals, in particular, tend to operate on what is known as an *editorial calendar*. That means that certain issues will have a special editorial focus. Special issues are used to attract advertising, but news stories and features on the subject are also needed.

For example, a high-technology magazine may have a special issue on laptop computers planned for April. Companies who manufacture laptop computers will no doubt want to advertise in that issue. If you're in the public relations or marketing communications department of the company, this special issue should also alert you that the publication would welcome news and feature stories about laptop computers.

Indeed, one of your major duties for a client or an employer is to review the editorial calendars of various publications to determine stories and features that might be submitted to coincide with the theme or editorial focus of a particular issue. It also pays to check your local daily to get a list of special supplements planned for the year. Doing this sort of homework will dramatically increase your story placements.

Periodicals often set their editorial calendars a year in advance, and many keep the same special issue calendars from one year to the next. Several media directories provide the editorial calendars of publications, including *Bacon's*, *Media Map* and *Standard Rate and Data Services*.

Tip Sheets

Another good way to find media gatekeepers seeking information and stories about your subject is to use *media tip sheets*. These are regular newsletters that report on what is needed by various columnists, writers and editors.

Public relations newsletters such as *Jack O'Dwyer's Newsletter* and *Public Relations News* provide regular tips as part of their content, but the *PartyLine* weekly newsletter is devoted entirely to providing media placement tips. Here are some sample items from *PartyLine*:

> **Michael Conlon Goes Away on Business,** the weekly column from Reuters that is available to newspapers in North America and some overseas newspapers as well. He seeks information of interest to the business traveler in North America, everything from hotels, gadgets, technology, cultural training for overseas visits, frequent flier programs, safety and security. The column also appears online. He also covers spot news, both national and international, for the middle of the country as well. He prefers mail or fax contact at Reuters, 311 S. Wacker Dr., Ste. 1170, Chicago, IL 60606, (312)408–8730; Fax: (312)922–6657; E-mail: mike.conlon@reuters. com.
>
> **The Darrell Ankarlo Show** is a new show on SuccessRadio, the newest in a series of radio networks owned by Sony. The Ankarlo show is a magazine format, lifestyles program, covering finances, health, fitness, psychological, consumer, relationship, education, leisure, parenting, and business. The thrust of SuccessRadio is to build shows to help their listeners be more successful in every part of their lives. Guest suggestions should go to Lisa Ferrari, Success Radio, 1370 Ave. of the Americas, New York, NY 10019, (212)833–8589; Fax: (212)833–5438; E-mail: Ferrari@SWNETWORKS.COM.
>
> **Tania Grossinger** is looking for information on all-inclusive resorts in Mexico, especially those catering to families, for an article in *Ladies Home Journal*. Send material to her at 1 Christopher St., Ste. 7E, New York, NY 10014, (212)243–5063; Fax: (212)741–7488.

PRODUCTION OF MATERIALS

With a properly specialized mailing list, the total number of items going out to the media will be much smaller than if you conduct a mass mailing. The rate of use will be higher, and your costs will be lower.

However, certain aspects of production are involved whether you are sending a few releases or many.

Mailing Labels

A number of software programs allow you to format media names and addresses on labels. In addition, you can purchase equipment that takes commands from the computer to print addresses on individual envelopes automatically. Printing directly on the envelope makes a cleaner, more professional impression than a label.

An address must be complete. It should include honorific (Mr., Ms.) and full name, job title, name of media, street address, city, two-letter state abbreviation and zip code. The U.S. Postal Service now uses nine-digit postal codes to expedite mail delivery. Most businesses use the nine-digit code; make sure your database has it.

1A-Advertising

1A-180 ADVERTISING AGE, 220 E. 42nd Street, New York, NY 10017-5846; (212) 210-0100, Fax: (212) 210-0200; Fred Danzig, Editor; Valerie Mackie, Managing Editor; Weekly, Mon., 90,000.
LEAD TIMES: News and Adv. - 2 weeks prior. Special Reports - 3 weeks prior.
EDITORIAL PROFILE: Designated as the international publication of the marketing industry. Content is geared towards members of the communications field, ranging from the advertising world to public relations. Highlights include updates of current events, developments in the print and broadcast segments of the media and analyses of communications trends. **Ad Rate:** $11,410

ISSUE	EDITORIAL FOCUS/SPECIAL ISSUES
JANUARY 6	Feature on the Advertising Fact Book.
JANUARY 13	A Look at Data Base Marketing.
JANUARY 20	Profile on TV Syndication.
JANUARY 27	Market Profile on Palm Springs.
FEBRUARY 3	Outlook on the Hispanic market.
FEBRUARY 10	Supplement on Marketing to Kids.
FEBRUARY 17	Round-Up on Sales Promotion.
FEBRUARY 24	Cable TV Guide Supplement.
MARCH 9	Analysis of the Magazine Market.
MARCH 16	What's New in High-Tech and Business Marketing.
MARCH 23	Report on Entertainment Marketing.
MARCH 30	Developments in Automotive Marketing.
APRIL 6	Coverage of the Cable Industry.
APRIL 13	Showcase on Agency Issues.
APRIL 20	A Look at the Premium and Incentive Guide Directory.
APRIL 27	Showcase on Food Marketing.
MAY 4	Evaluation of Sales Promotions.
MAY 11	New trends in TV Buying and Planning.
MAY 18	Round-Table on Advertising in Politics.
MAY 25	Innovations in Licensing.
JUNE 8	Suggestions on Marketing the Health Industry.
JUNE 15	Examination of the Magazine 300 List.
JUNE 22	Review of Research Techniques.
JUNE 29	Meetings and Conventions Supplement.

1A-200 ADVERTISING COMMUNICATIONS TIMES, 121 Chestnut Street, Philadelphia, PA 19106-3017; (215) 629-1666, Fax: (215) 923-8358; Carol Morganti, Editor; Libby Barland, Advertising Director; Monthly, 1st Week, 40,000.
LEAD TIMES: Features, News and Adv. - 1 month prior.
EDITORIAL PROFILE: Edited for the Eastern United States section of advertisers. Focuses on regional developments in the communications and advertising areas, and reports on changes in marketing and planning strategies through the advent of new technology and management innovations. **Ad Rate:** $4,480

1A-280 ADWEEK/EASTERN EDITION, 49 East 21st Street, New York, NY 10010-6213; (212) 529-5500, Fax: (212) 529-7845; Greg Farrell, Editor; Weekly, Mon., 90,000.
LEAD TIMES: Features - 2 months prior, News - 6 weeks prior, Adv. - 2 weeks prior.
EDITORIAL PROFILE: Focuses on current business transactions within the East Coast advertising community. Geared toward advertisers who want up-to-date information on account changes, regional industry trends and current events that affect the advertising world. **Ad Rate:** $4,250

ISSUE	EDITORIAL FOCUS/SPECIAL ISSUES
JANUARY	Spotlight on the BADvertising Awards for '91.
FEBRUARY	Annual New Trends in Creativity Report.
MARCH	Focus on America's Favorite Advertising Campaigns.
APRIL	Annual Newspaper Report - Review of Audio and Video Media for '92.
MAY	Update on Developments in Business Marketing and the Press - Annual Salary Survey.
JUNE	Examination of Global Advertising Trends - Annual Report on TV Broadcasting.
JULY	Spotlight on Women and Advertising.
AUGUST	Report Card for Marketers.
SEPTEMBER	Annual Fall Preview - Exclusive Guide to Special Event Marketing.
OCTOBER	Overview of Commercial Production.
NOVEMBER	Review of New Trends Used in Advertising in '92.
DECEMBER	Perspective on New Ideas in Research and Marketing Theories.

1A-440 AMERICAN DEMOGRAPHICS, P.O. Box 68, Ithaca, NY 14851; (607) 273-6343, Fax: (607) 273-3196; Caroline Arthur, Managing Editor; Michelle DeChant, Advertising Director; Monthly, 35,000.

Figure 10.2 Advance information about special issues enables publicists to prepare material that will be timed to fit the needs of the editor. Trade publications, in particular, have editorial calendars that focus on major topics around the year. This excerpt is from *Bacon's Media Calendar Directory. (Courtesy of Bacon's International, Inc., Chicago.)*

Don't forget that media outlets and bureaus can be located in multistory build-ings. Make sure you include the room or suite number in your street address. If you don't, the mail may be delayed or not delivered at all.

Copies

In Chapter 5 we emphasized that news releases should be clean, professionally for-matted, and printed in a highly readable typeface. A good type size is 10 or 12 points. You can also use boldfacing, underlining, and other techniques—spar-ingly—to improve readability.

A small number of news releases can be run on a laser printer connected to your personal computer. For large numbers of releases, however, you will use a high-speed commercial photocopying machine that is capable of producing high-quality reproductions. Every copy should look exactly like the original.

Illustrations

Chapter 7 gave considerable guidance on what makes a good photo or illustration. If you need only a few photos, you can have the photographer print them up for you. This ensures high quality and good reproduction in a newspaper or magazine.

In many cases, however, you will need multiple prints. A photography lab has equipment to machine-produce quantities of the same picture, but you will have to provide the original negative. If you do not own the negative, make arrangements with the photographer. The terms for this should be spelled out in the contract signed when the picture was taken.

Photos and artwork distributed for publicity purposes often have the caption printed directly on the photo print. The other approach is to have captions pro-duced on separate sheets of paper and attached to the photo.

Make sure that photos and artwork are not damaged in the mail. A cardboard stiffener in the envelope protects the photo from being bent. Rubber-stamp the en-velope "Photo—Do Not Bend."

Specializing for Exclusives

Another thing you'll have to do is make sure that the same item is not sent to com-peting publications. If it is only a brief announcement—as of a change in person-nel—the same release could go to all media concerned. If your material is detailed, you will have to give different versions to different publications. For example, if there are two food editors in the same market, you'll give each of them a different recipe release. To reassure the editor, mark your release "Exclusive to you in your market." Then he or she will know that there is no chance that the recipe will ap-pear in the competing paper.

To make the exclusive release really mean something, it may be necessary to have several variations, not just two. Suburban newspapers often reach subscribers who also read a metropolitan daily. These, too, should be given their own releases. A reader in Arlington, Virginia, may read a Washington paper and a local evening paper but probably not a paper published in Silver Spring, Maryland.

DISTRIBUTION OF MATERIALS

The vast majority of media materials are distributed in four major ways: (1) by mail, (2) by fax, (3) by electronic wire services and (4) by feature placement firms. This section also discusses the increasing use of diskettes and CD-ROMs.

SELECTING A DISTRIBUTION CHANNEL

This chapter gives a number of channels for the distribution of media materials. That still leaves the question, "What channel should I use for my material?" The answer is not simple. It depends on the purpose and objectives of your message—and who you want to reach with it. Here are some general tips:

- **Mail** The best, and most cost-effective, method for distribution of routine materials to local and regional media. Mailing houses are effective for mailing press kits on a regional or national basis.
- **Fax** Good for sending media advisories and alerts, late-breaking important news. Not recommended for mass distribution of news releases.
- **Electronic Wire Services** Best for distribution of financial news to large newspapers and major broadcast outlets on a national or international basis where immediate disclosure is needed. National announcements of major new products can also be sent via electronic news wires.
- **Feature Placement Firms** Good for reaching suburban newspapers and small weeklies. Best for feature-type material, when you want to create awareness and visibility for a product or organization.
- **Diskettes and CD-ROMs** Best used for background material. Not generally accepted yet for distribution of news releases.
- **E-Mail** Good for suggesting story ideas to journalists and editors, answering media questions and queries and sending news releases—but only if the journalist prefers or requests it.
- **Web Sites** A place to post news releases and background material for possible reference by reporters and the public.
- **Usenet** A good place to post messages and engage in dialogue with the public and media personnel. Not recommended for posting news releases or other press materials.

You should use several channels of distribution whenever you do a publicity program. However, each channel has particular characteristics and advantages that you must take into account when preparing material.

Mail

A popular and widely used method is the mail, either delivered by the post office or by private companies such as Federal Express, Airborne Express and DHL Worldwide.

In fact, more than one survey has indicated that editors and journalists still prefer information sent to them on paper. One survey of 1,100 journalists by a Dayton, Ohio, public relations firm, for example, found that 74 percent of the respondents wanted materials mailed to them.

Another survey by a Kansas City public relations firm found that journalists preferred to receive news releases by mail by a margin of 18 to 1 over E-mail or other new technologies. And yet another survey of Florida journalists found that 55 percent prefer to get information by mail.

The U.S. Postal Service is particularly good, and cost-effective, for sending local news releases, press kits, fact sheets, position papers and other background materials. It is important, however, to send materials by first class or express mail. It is never acceptable to send material by second or third class mail.

Many organizations use services such as Federal Express on a routine basis to mail everything from letters to packages. Overnight delivery is usually guaranteed, and these services are particularly good for sending materials on a regional, national or even international level. Another advantage is sophisticated tracking so you know exactly when a package was delivered.

Some publicists think that delivery by overnight service increases an editor's perception of the material's importance and newsworthiness, but the widespread use of these services has pretty much eliminated any feeling that the material is special or urgent. In fact, most editors say they treat such envelopes just like any other mail that is delivered to their desks by the mail room.

Mailing can be done by the organization. All you need is a good address list, properly prepared labels and envelopes, a postage meter and a way of getting to the post office before the last pickup of the day. If you are able to mail in the morning, chances are good that media in the area will receive the material the next working day. Letters sent nationally are received in two or three days. However, if you're mailing materials to international media, you're better off using another channel of distribution such as fax, electronic wire services or E-mail. These will be discussed shortly.

Another approach to mailing is to use a distribution firm, also called a mailing house. A number of firms serve the public relations industry, including Media Distribution Services (MDS), which was discussed in the last section. The company has centers in 10 U.S. cities and offers full-service printing, production and mailing of everything from news releases to press kits, newsletters and brochures.

All you need to do is specify the mailing list and provide one copy of the news release. MDS will then print the number of copies or photographs needed, insert the materials into envelopes, address them, stamp them and deliver everything to the post office. Figure 10.3 is an excerpt from the MDS mailing list. Mailing services, many of which are found at the local level, can also assemble press materials and mail them for you.

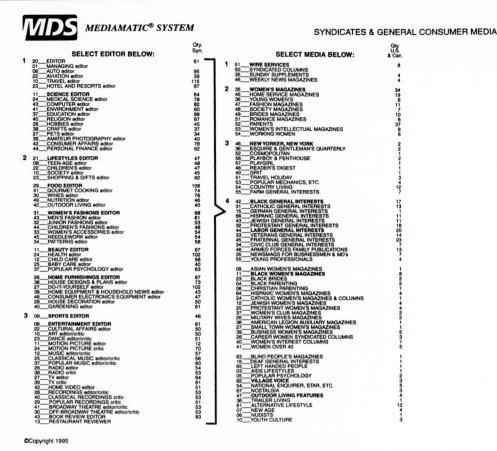

Figure 10.3 This is an excerpt from a catalog of a news release distribution service. All you have to do is send a copy of the news release and check off the list of publications and editors to receive it. The numbers in the right column indicate the number of publications in each category. (*Courtesy of Media Distribution Services, New York.*)

Fax

Sending timely news releases and media advisories by facsimile transmission is now quite common. A fax is as quick as a telephone call and has the advantage of providing information in written and graphic form.

Ideally, the fax is used only if there is a late-breaking news development or the editor has given you permission to contact him or her by fax. The reality is that the modern technology has made it possible to send faxes to every media outlet in the country within minutes. One fax distribution service, for example, claims that it can transmit information over as many as 1,000 phone lines simultaneously.

This is called *broadcast fax* or *bulk fax*. Presidential candidates in the 1996 election, for example, extensively used bulk fax to let media editors know their latest statements on the economy, health care and a host of other public issues. They also used bulk fax to give media alerts about upcoming speeches, rallies and public appearances.

Sending bulk faxes, despite the gee-whiz technology, is less than popular with editors. In fact, many newspapers actively discourage faxes of routine news releases and even change their fax numbers on a regular basis to avoid reams of "junk" faxes—which are like "junk" mail. Another approach tried by more than one daily is to have 900 numbers so the publicists are charged for sending unsolicited faxes.

But the problem still remains. George Condon, Washington bureau chief for Copley News Service, told *Jack O'Dwyer's PR Services Report* that "Junk faxes are one of our biggest problems. There is nothing more annoying to me than having those faxes clog up our machines."

The opposite of sending bulk faxes is fax on demand (FOD). In this situation, a reporter can call an 800 number and, through a series of custom-designed prompts, ask for various organizational materials to be sent by fax. This service helps reporters on deadline if they can't reach an organizational spokesperson.

Kmart Corporation is a good example. It provides a toll-free access number to reporters who regularly cover the organization. By dialing certain extensions, reporters can automatically have the material immediately sent to the newsroom by fax. Also available are executive biographies, information about earnings, fact sheets and position papers. Such materials can also be downloaded from a web site, which will be discussed shortly.

Fax material only if the medium specifically requests it or gives permission in advance. Check with your regular media contacts to find out how they feel about faxes and whether they want material sent by this method.

Electronic Distribution Services

Although mail and fax distribution will be with us for the foreseeable future, many organizations have already moved to electronic news release distribution. This is particularly true for distribution of corporate and financial news under the Securities and Exchange Commission (SEC) regulations that require immediate disclosure.

The two major national distributors are Business Wire and PR Newswire. These services deliver a combined total of about 900 news releases daily right into the main computer at many newspapers and broadcast stations. There is no paper involved. Your news automatically enters the appropriate computer queues in computerized newsrooms at about 8,400 words per minute and can be accessed with a single keystroke.

Using their PCs, editors and reporters can call up your news release for review. They can edit it on the screen, write a headline for it and then push another key to have it printed in the right typeface and column width. Of course, they can also push the delete key and send the whole release to the electronic trash can.

The advantage of electronic distribution services is timely and immediate delivery of your material in a format that can be easily used. Mailed releases, by contrast, must be processed manually. They can be scanned electronically and placed in a computer file, but most of the time they are simply used as background material as reporters write stories on their PCs.

Like other services, electronic distributors can customize the distribution of your news release or photos and graphics to specific media. They can send your news release to every daily newspaper in Ohio, or you can send it to a select list of financial publications in North America, Europe and Asia. They can also distribute full-text news releases to TV newsrooms throughout the nation, to hundreds of trade publications and even to on-line retrieval services.

The cost varies according to distribution. A 400-word release distributed nationally costs about $450, but one sent only to the Rocky Mountain States would only cost $95. See Figure 10.4 for a sample news release. Business Wire also sends photos electronically. A color photo sent to the 200 largest dailies in the United States costs about $800 but would only cost about $500 for California newspapers. Black and white photos are somewhat less expensive.

In other words, using an electronic distribution service costs about the same as using first class mail. As a result, electronic distribution has been touted as the wave of the future.

For the present, however, you should be aware that electronic distribution of news releases is most effective if you want to reach major media. There are thousands of smaller publications and broadcast stations that don't use the services of electronic distribution firms such as Business Wire and PR Newswire. Consequently, you still have to supplement electronic distribution with other channels such as mail, fax and camera-ready feature placement firms.

Feature Placement Firms

A number of distribution services specialize in preparing columns and features that are camera-ready—sent out as entire layouts complete with headlines, photos and graphics.

The material is called "camera-ready" because a camera makes a negative of the entire page as part of the process of getting pages ready for offset printing. A newspaper editor simply cuts the article out from a glossy sheet of paper (called a *repro proof*) and pastes it down in the layout. No headline writing, picture sizing or editing is necessary.

Even cutting and pasting is becoming obsolete. News USA and others, for example, now package camera-ready stories for its clients on floppy disks or CD-ROMs that editors can pop into their PCs. Editors receive a new disk every month.

The newest way of delivering camera-ready materials is to put them on an Internet web site. Editors then download articles and high-resolution photos and graphics that they want to use. However, in a survey conducted by Steven Ross and Don Middleberg at Columbia University, 65 percent of the 6,000 editors and journalists surveyed are still using camera-ready art distributed in the traditional way—on paper.

Camera-ready stories are commonly used by suburban newspapers to fill news space inside the newspaper. According to the distribution services, the demand for camera-ready stories is booming as a result of rising newsprint and postage costs.

PROFILE OF A NEWS RELEASE

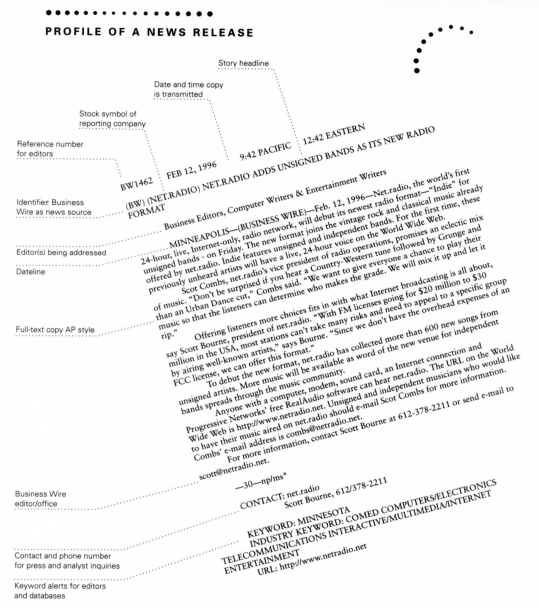

Story headline

Date and time copy
is transmitted

Stock symbol of
reporting company

Reference number
for editors

Identifies Business
Wire as news source

Editor(s) being addressed

Dateline

Full-text copy AP style

Business Wire
editor/office

Contact and phone number
for press and analyst inquiries

Keyword alerts for editors
and databases

9:42 PACIFIC   12:42 EASTERN

BW1462   FEB 12, 1996

(BW) (NET.RADIO) NET.RADIO ADDS UNSIGNED BANDS AS ITS NEW RADIO FORMAT

Business Editors, Computer Writers & Entertainment Writers

MINNEAPOLIS—(BUSINESS WIRE)—Feb. 12, 1996—Net.radio, the world's first 24-hour, live, Internet-only, radio network, will debut its newest radio format—"Indie" for unsigned bands - on Friday. The new format joins the vintage rock and classical music already offered by net.radio. Indie features unsigned and independent bands. For the first time, these previously unheard artists will have a live, 24-hour voice on the World Wide Web.

Scot Combs, net.radio's vice president of radio operations, promises an eclectic mix of music. "Don't be surprised if you hear a Country-Western tune followed by Grunge and than an Urban Dance cut," Combs said. "We want to give everyone a chance to play their music so that the listeners can determine who makes the grade. We will mix it up and let it rip."

Offering listeners more choices fits in with what Internet broadcasting is all about, say Scott Bourne, president of net.radio. "With FM licenses going for $20 million to $30 million in the USA, most stations can't take many risks and need to appeal to a specific group by airing well-known artists," says Bourne. "Since we don't have the overhead expenses of an FCC license, we can offer this format."

To debut the new format, net.radio has collected more than 600 new songs from unsigned artists. More music will be available as word of the new venue for independent bands spreads through the music community.

Anyone with a computer, modem, sound card, an Internet connection and Progressive Networks' free RealAudio software can hear net.radio. The URL on the World Wide Web is http://www.netradio.net. Unsigned and independent musicians who would like to have their music aired on net.radio should e-mail Scott Combs for more information. Combs' e-mail address is combs@netradio.net.

For more information, contact Scott Bourne at 612-378-2211 or send e-mail to scott@netradio.net.

—30—np/ms*

CONTACT: net.radio
Scott Bourne, 612/378-2211

KEYWORD: MINNESOTA
INDUSTRY KEYWORD: COMED COMPUTERS/ELECTRONICS
TELECOMMUNICATIONS INTERACTIVE/MULTIMEDIA/INTERNET
ENTERTAINMENT
URL: http://www.netradio.net

Figure 10.4 Several services distribute electronic news releases directly to a publication's computer. This illustration shows the elements of such a news release. (*Courtesy of Business Wire, San Francisco.*)

Thousands of suburban papers, which receive the stories free, find that using such materials reduces their operating costs.

The primary use of a feature placement firm is to distribute features and other information that is relevant over a period of several months. In the business, these stories are often called "evergreens." Popular camera-ready items are about food, travel, health, education, special events and consumerism. Here are some headlines of typical feature stories prepared for various clients:

- "What to Do About Childhood Cancer" (National Childhood Cancer Foundation).
- "Experts Warn: Itching Can Signal Serious Illness" (GenDerm Corporation).
- "How to Protect Your House When You Go on Vacation" (Schlage Lock Company).

Trade groups, national charitable organizations, national membership organizations, state tourism departments and various businesses use camera-ready releases to create awareness and visibility. The most successful ones emphasize information and keep commercialism to a minimum. In fact, most camera-ready features only mention the organization once or twice in the entire article. See Figure 10.5 for an example of a camera-ready feature.

Camera-ready features are relatively short. A one-column feature is about 225 words, and a two-column story is about 350 words. To attract editor and reader interest, most also include a photo or a graphic of some kind.

The cost for national distribution is about $3,000 for a one-column story and $3,750 for a two-column story. This includes writing, production, distribution, clippings of story usage and summary reports of how many publications used the feature. North American Precis Syndicate (NAPS), one of the largest distribution firms, will also put your camera-ready release on the Internet at no additional cost.

Radio and television stations also receive materials from feature distribution firms. If you want to reach these mediums, a radio and four-slide TV script are prepared. See Figures 8.1 and 8.2 for examples of such scripts.

In addition to regular mailings, distribution services send out camera-ready stories on a central theme. Metro Publicity Services handles themed mailings on everything from Mother's Day to health and fitness to spring and summer car care. Many of these articles show up in themed advertising supplements of daily newspapers. For example, a back-to-school supplement might use a camera-ready story from IBM about how to select a computer for writing term papers.

Diskettes

Diskettes have been around since the dawn of the computer age, but they haven't been used extensively as a method of sending news releases to the media. They are primarily used for sending camera-ready feature material, as mentioned in the previous section, or by firms distributing clip art.

The electronic age, however, has prompted some additional interest in this form of distribution. For example, the complete text of President Clinton's proposed health plan was sent to the media via diskette.

In another situation, the Federal Aviation Agency (FAA) placed all its rules and regulations on floppy disk for distribution to interested reporters. The material included narrative text and charts, showing when each of various regulations would take effect. The same information was also made available on the FAA's Internet web site.

A Home Alone

How To Protect Your House When You Go On Vacation

(NAPS)-When you go on vacation, your home is left alone with no one to protect it and the valuables it contains. In the rush to pack, to remember everything (and everyone) to take, to book flights, and get traveler's checks, people often forget very simple home security precautions.

To maximize the security of your home and your own peace of mind, so that you can enjoy your vacation, Schlage Lock Company has compiled a Home Security Checklist for Vacationers that should serve as a pre-departure security reminder.

• Keep a "lived in" look to your home. If gone for an extended period of time, be sure to maintain the appearances of normal maintenance. For example, be sure the lawn is mowed and watered, the mail and newspapers picked up, etc.

• Leave a car in the driveway or ask a neighbor to use your driveway while you are away. If the house is being watched, the appearance of "traffic" might discourage a break-in.

• Install adequate outdoor lighting. Floodlights positioned at each corner of the house can prevent would-be intruders from creeping through the darkness when no one is home. Use the outdoor lights every night—not just when on vacation.

• Purchase and use automatic light timers. Timers are simple to use and effective. Hook up to lamps, as well as to a television or radio and outdoor lighting.

• Remove any spare keys hidden under a doormat or in planters outside the house. Instead, leave a spare key with a trusted neighbor.

• Lock all doors and windows. Sounds simple. But 42 percent of home burglaries do not involve forcible entry—simply unlocked entrances. Also, do not overlook pet doors which can provide access to clever criminals.

• Hook up an answering machine to your phone. Thieves use the phone to determine whether or not a house is vacant.

"THANKS.. I'LL BE O.K BECAUSE OF THE HOME SECURITY CHECKLIST."

• Install deadbolt locks on all doors.

• Secure double-hung windows by drilling an angled hole through the top frame of the lower window and bottom frame of the upper window. Then insert a nail or eyebolt.

• Replace doors in poor condition with solid core wood doors at least 13/4-inch thick. A burglar can put his fist or foot through a hollow or fragile door.

• Mark all valuables with permanent identification numbers. Use your driver's license number so you can be easily located when items are found.

• List the serial numbers, purchase dates and prices of your expensive items and keep the information in a safe place out of the home. In case of burglary, these numbers will assist in recovery.

• Make one final check before you leave. Think like a burglar and ask yourself how you would break into your house.

For more information, call Schlage Lock Company Customer Service at 415-467-1100 or write to Schlage Lock Company, 2401 Bayshore Blvd., San Francisco, CA 94134.

Figure 10.5 Camera-ready features are widely accepted by the media. Distribution companies provide material on paper, diskettes and even the Internet. Notice that the emphasis is on giving useful information. The organization is listed only once at the end of the story. (*Courtesy of North American Precis Syndicate, New York.*)

At one time, editors avoided diskettes because they were afraid of introducing computer viruses into their computer systems. The survey by Ross and Middleberg, however, shows that 65 percent of the editors aren't particularly worried about this issue anymore.

The survey also found that only about one in four journalists have actually used diskettes sent by public relations sources. There is some indication, however, that the use of diskettes for press kits and so on will probably increase in the future. One factor is the increasing number of reporters who have terminals at their desks and can use diskettes.

CD-ROM

The technology of using digital compact disks (CD) and read-only memory (ROM) is well advanced in the reference field. As mentioned at the beginning of this chapter, most media directories now come on CD-ROM, as well as many standard encyclopedias, games and even software programs.

The use of CD-ROM for the distribution of publicity materials, however, is still in its infancy. A major limiting factor, up to now, has been that most editors and reporters don't have CD-ROM drives on their desktop PCs. In fact, Ross and Middleberg's 1995 survey of 6,000 journalists and editors found that only 4 percent of the reporters and 11 percent of the editors could handle material sent on CD-ROM.

On the other hand, 32 percent of the art departments at major newspapers and broadcast stations had CD-ROM capability. However, the art department is usually located in another part of the building, so editors and reporters don't actually see the material.

The entertainment industry has made some use of CD-ROM for press kits. ABC, for example, used CDs to publicize its 1995–96 network schedule, the three-part anthology of the Beatles and a new daytime series titled "The City."

The disks, which were mailed to editors and reviewers at thousands of publications, contained high-resolution photographs, bios and press releases. Also included were digital video clips of the shows, the stars and the producers. Media personnel could access the information and then select only the items they wanted.

ABC found this distribution less costly and more effective than using paper press kits. Cal Vornberger, president of Tumble Interactive Media in New York, told *Jack O'Dwyer's Newsletter*, "Instead of assuming the cost, the time and the logistics to reproduce thousands of photographs and press releases and collate them together in a mailer, the information is programmed once on high resolution digital images and printable versions of the press releases. . . ."

As media outlets upgrade their computers to include CD-ROM drives, the expectation is that this medium of distribution will increase. "CD-ROM will increase in prominence," says Brian Croft, a consultant with the Toronto office of Towers, Perrin.

One idea is that organizations will use CD technology to store and distribute background material about the organization to interested editors and reporters. A CD library would eventually replace the old method of simply storing press kits and other material in file cabinets.

THE INTERNET: NEW KID ON THE BLOCK

Many people say they have seen the future of communications, and it is summarized in one word: the Internet.

The Internet, originally started by the U.S. Defense Department as a way for academics and government scientists to communicate with each other, burst onto the public consciousness in the early 1990s when computer geeks and on-line information services such as CompuServe and America Online (AOL) discovered that the Internet could also be used by almost anybody for sending E-mail, participating in discussion groups and retrieving information.

Nobody owns the Internet. The Internet actually consists of more than a million computers on an estimated 48,000 networks that encircle the globe. The Internet has doubled in size every year since 1988 and continues to grow at an estimated rate of 10 to 15 percent per month. Consequently, any Internet figures in this text will be out of date even before the book is published.

The number of people actually using the Internet is subject to considerable guessing and debate. As *Time* magazine reported in 1995, estimates vary from 3 million to 60 million worldwide. The highly respected Nielsen Company (which also tabulates TV audiences) did a survey in late 1995 and reported that 37 million people in the United States and Canada have access to the Internet—either through a friend, a colleague or a commercial on-line service such as CompuServe, Prodigy, or America Online.

It further reported that 24 million people in the United States and Canada actually accessed the Internet during a three-month period. This means that about 11 percent of the North American population over age 16 are already on the "Net." This finding, however, was disputed even by proponents of the Internet who said the figures were inflated.

Whether the Nielsen figures are right or somewhat exaggerated, everyone agrees that the Internet has changed the geography of communications forever. It has now reached mass-market proportions, and there is virtually a stampede of individuals and organizations enthusiastically endorsing the Internet as the wave of the future.

On-line services that provide access to the net, such as CompuServe and America Online, were signing up subscribers at the rate of 60,000 to 75,000 a week in late 1995, and companies inventing the software to directly access the Internet, such as *Netscape*, suddenly became worth $5 billion in market value—more than Delta Airlines, General Dynamics or Bethlehem Steel. Not bad for a company that didn't even exist in 1993.

The advertising and public relations industries have joined the stampede to the Internet. Basically, they see the Internet as a marvelous vehicle for the distribution of information to a highly educated, affluent audience. A survey by SRI International, for example, indicated that "Net" users were mostly male, had median annual incomes of $40,000, and had attended college.

From a public relations standpoint, the Internet has also been touted as the wave of the future for the distribution of materials to the media. The feeling is bolstered by one survey in which the majority of editors and reporters (56 percent) said they expect that all news releases and other publicity "submissions" will be distributed on-line by the year 2001. Electronic wire services such as Business Wire already do this, as previously discussed.

Another strength of the Internet, from a distribution standpoint, is that interested users can directly access news releases, press kits, corporate backgrounders and so forth without the filtering mechanism of the mass media. In a newspaper or broadcast station, space and time are limited. In cyberspace, the "news hole" has neither of these restrictions. Some of the downsides to this will be discussed later in the chapter.

At present, public relations professionals are using the Internet to distribute information in at least four areas: (1) E-mail, (2) web sites, (3) discussion groups (Usenet) and (4) Listserv.

E-mail

Electronic mail or E-mail is the oldest feature of the Internet. It was first developed in the 1970s to send messages on closed networks, and even today many organizations maintain their own E-mail systems for internal communications.

System networks, however, can also be linked with other networks on the Internet, thus creating the opportunity to communicate with anyone in the world in real time. Indeed, the most popular feature of the Internet is the ability to send individual messages to anyone in the world if you have their E-mail address. The major asset of E-mailing people is the cost. Calling a friend in Australia costs a lot of money in terms of a long-distance phone call, but sending E-mail costs the same as a local phone call.

Indeed, having an E-mail address seems to be the "in" thing. People put it on their business cards, organizations publicize their E-mail addresses and media personnel increasingly rely on E-mail to get news releases, media advisories and other communications.

As previously mentioned, surveys indicate that many editors and reporters (particularly in the general press) still prefer information on paper. On the other hand, publications in the computer industry not only prefer to receive news releases by E-mail, they demand it.

Various surveys provide conflicting information about the percentage of journalists who want to receive press materials via E-mail. In general, the figure is between 25 and 50 percent. That means that you must keep separate lists of reporters who want mailed news releases, those who want faxes, and those who want E-mail.

You must also keep in mind that the same news release format won't work for all situations. If you are sending a news release via E-mail, you need to give a one paragraph summary before starting the actual news release. This summary paragraph appears on the screen first, and helps the editor quickly determine whether to review the entire news release. As with print releases, a headline of five words is also helpful.

There are several advantages to E-mail. Ron Solberg, one of the pioneers in using new technologies for public relations purposes, wrote in *Public Relations Tactics*:

Reporters receiving news releases by E-mail don't have to re-key your words. They can easily save or discard the document. And if a reporter wants to keep the release for future reference, it's more convenient to store it on their computer's hard drive than in an overstuffed file drawer. In addition, any copy you key in and send directly to a reporter by E-mail will appear on his or her computer screen exactly as you sent it. There is less opportunity for re-keying error if the reporter uses a quote from your electronic news release in a story.

Advocates of E-mail also say that it is less intrusive than a phone call. If a reporter or editor receives the message at deadline, he or she can leave it in his or her "in box" until a more convenient time. Others say E-mail is much more efficient and less annoying to editors than faxes.

Another advantage of E-mail is the elimination of telephone tag. Reporters and public relations personnel can easily engage in an E-mail dialogue, posting messages on each other's computer—instead of trying to reach each other by telephone, which is often frustrating.

See the box for more tips on how to distribute press materials via E-mail.

The World Wide Web

The fastest growing part of the Internet is the World Wide Web. In April of 1994, there were 1,000 sites. By October of 1995, there were 110,000 sites. Indeed, the number of sites on the "Web" continues to increase in geometric proportions.

TIPS ON SENDING NEWS RELEASES VIA E-MAIL

Distributing news releases and other publicity materials by E-mail requires sensitivity and a knowledge of basic procedures. Here are some tips:

- Don't automatically mass distribute news releases to every address you have. Make sure media addresses accept news releases via E-mail, and reporters have told you that they will accept your releases.
- Send the release in two parts. The first should contain only the essential information (a summary) and should fit on a single screen. That way, the reporter can immediately tell if he or she is interested.
- Don't automatically add a reporter to a general distribution list. Instead, ask the reporter first if they would like to be on such a list.
- Don't send news releases by E-mail if they have already been distributed by mail, fax or other services such as PR Newswire or Business Wire.
- Be selective. As with print releases, only E-mail reporters and editors who would be interested in the information.
- Send releases individually; don't send a mass mailing with all the E-mail addresses at the top. This immediately tells reporters they are part of a mass mailing.
- Don't E-mail a reporter or editor and ask "Did you get my news release?" This is annoying, and the reporter may use a "bozo filter" to instruct the E-mail program to reject or delete any further E-mail from you.
- Make sure your news release is factually correct and free of any spelling, grammar or punctuation errors.

Source: *Interactive Public Relations* newsletter, May 15, 1995, p. 6.

Essentially, the World Wide Web (WWW) is a collection of computerized documents that individuals, nonprofit agencies, government agencies and businesses want to make available to Internet users. Each collection is called a "web site" or a "home page."

A web site, from a public relations standpoint, can be a distribution system in cyberspace. Organizations, for example, use their web sites to post news releases, corporate backgrounders, product information, position papers and even photos of key executives or plant locations. Individuals, as well as media personnel, can access the information and download selected materials into their computers. They can even get a hard copy through their laser or inkjet printers.

Various organizations use their web sites in different ways. Here's a sampling:

- Federal Express uses its web site for investor relations. Stock prices, analyses of company performance, the annual report and other financial information are available.
- Presidential candidates Clinton and Dole used web sites to distribute campaign speeches, position papers and campaign news.
- Rutherford Hill Winery in California used a web site to give a video tour of the winery.
- The Federal Emergency Management Association (FEMA) used its web site to give the public and the press updates on the Oklahoma City federal building bombing.
- L. L. Bean has a web site that gives a history of the company, how it hand sews its shoes and a list of attractions at 900 state and national parks.
- Silicon Graphics, Inc. posts a variety of messages on its web site. Users can get a company profile, recent news releases, sales brochures, a list of special interest groups, the company's annual report, financial performance and the addresses of various sales offices.

In many cases, an organization's web site is hyperlinked to other web pages and information sources. A user can immediately jump to a related web site by clicking the mouse on various icons. Business Wire's web site, for example, is hyperlinked to the home pages of various organizations that use Business Wire services.

In theory, reporters and editors can access web sites to retrieve current news releases and other materials. In reality, most experts think E-mail is more efficient because it is sent directly to the medium. With a web site, reporters must first be told the address and then take the time to access the home page. Since more than 50,000 companies in North America alone have web sites, it is unlikely that a reporter will make this effort unless there is a major news event involving the company.

Web sites, however, have their advantages. Here are the major ones:

- A great amount of material can be posted. There is no space or time limitation.
- You can reach niche markets and audiences on a direct basis without going through mass media.
- Low cost for worldwide distribution.

Caught up in the Web

As a company with roots that go back nearly 130 years, Mobil is justifiably proud of its heritage. But we're even more excited about the future. Thanks to developments in communications technology—namely, the evolution of the Internet and the World Wide Web—people and companies are changing the way they work and how they relate to each other.

As a relative newcomer to cyberspace, our experience suggests that the communications and business potential of this new universe shouldn't be ignored. With the creation of a home page on the World Wide Web, our ability to communicate with employees, customers, shareholders and business partners has been transformed. Communication is no longer one-way; it's interactive and responsive. Not only can people from all parts of the globe learn about us and our industry, they also can decide precisely what interests them.

Barely two years old, the Web is now the communications homesite for hundreds of thousands of individuals and companies. Millions of people from around the world "surf," "browse" and "chat" on the Web. And its use is growing by 40 percent to 60 percent a year.

For 25 years, we've used the traditional medium of print to communicate who we are. Readers of Mobil ads, for example, know we have strong opinions on issues like the need for a balanced budget, free trade and regulatory reform. People also know Mobil sponsors programming on PBS, underwrites art and cultural events and supports a variety of educational endeavors.

Now, with the creation of a home page on the Web, visitors can learn a whole lot more about us. They can, for example, apply for a credit card, consult a locator map for a list of nearby Mobil service stations, check out our shareholder service center and even purchase caps and jackets that sport our Mobil 1 racing logo. Of course, the latest Mobil op-ed ads are there, along with a box to click if you agree with us or not. And for those who want to give Congress a piece of their mind or a pat on the back, we offer a Congressional E-mail service that can zip your letter to elected officials within seconds.

As a company with strong opinions, a powerful brand name and extensive global operations, we expect our ads and our behavior to elicit opinions. Bouquets and brickbats—we get both. We want to hear from you—readers, customers, shareholders and partners. Web browsers can reach us on our home page. For those without a computer linkup, put pen to paper and fax or mail us your thoughts. Regardless of which medium you use, let's keep talking.

Mobil®

Visit us on the Internet:
http://www.mobil.com.
©1995 Mobil Corporation

3225 Gallows Rd.
Fairfax, VA 22037
Fax: 703-846-1044

Figure 10.6 Thousands of organizations now have a web site on the Internet. To attract users, however, extensive advertising in the print media is needed. This ad, by Mobil, tells about its web site. (*Copyright 1995. Reprinted with permission of Mobil Oil Corporation.*)

HOW TO TALK INTERNET

Public relations writers should be familiar with the vocabulary of cyberspace. Here are a few key terms:

- **BBS** Bulletin Board System. An electronic version on which people can leave messages.
- **Browser** Software designed to view documents created for the Internet's World Wide Web.
- **Cyberspace** The unreal world in which information passes between computers.
- **E-mail** Short for electronic mail. A message passed from one person to one or more other people via computer.
- **FAQ** Frequent Asked Questions. A list of questions and answers about a particular Usenet group.
- **FTP** File Transfer Protocol. A principal means of retrieving files from the Internet.
- **Home Page** Information on the World Wide Web is organized like a book. The home page for an organization is the table of contents. By clicking on certain icons, you can read different pages from the "book."
- **Internet** A vast network of interconnected computer networks that allows computers to instantly access other computers anywhere in the world.
- **URL** Uniform Resource Locator. This is an address where material on the Internet is located.
- **Usenet** An international meeting place where people can meet friends and discuss issues.
- **Web Site** A place on the World Wide Web where an organization has its home page.
- **World Wide Web** A section of the Internet. In addition to text, the Web format accommodates graphics, photographs, sound and video.

- You can update information quickly without having to reprint brochures and other materials.
- The media and other users can access details about your organization 24 hours a day from anywhere in the world.

Competition to attract users, or "hits," to a web site is intense, and the public relations writer must think in visual terms. It is not enough to just post the company's annual report or corporate profile on the home page in its original printed form. Instead, the material must be reduced to highly graphic displays and the writing must take the form of sound bites.

Anyone browsing the World Wide Web will testify that the majority of home pages are visually boring and not worth a second look. In order to avoid the pitfalls of having such a home page, experts offer this advice:

- Define the objective of the site.
- Design it with the audience in mind.
- Don't just place existing materials on it; redesign the material with strong graphic components.
- Update the site constantly. This is the real cost of a home page.

- Don't overdo the graphics. Complex graphics take a long time to download.
- Make the site interactive; give the user buttons to click on for exploring various topics.
- Use feedback (an E-mail address or computer bulletin board) to evolve the site.

Although you can design your own web site and even uplink it to the World Wide Web, experts recommend that you hire professionals who are experienced in the field of graphics and interactive media.

A good site on the Web will cost between $20,000 and $50,000 to set up. Then you must maintain the site and replace materials on a periodic basis. In fact, experts say that the only way you can get users to revisit the site is by constantly changing the information. General Electric, fully realizing this, spends $10,000 a month to maintain its web site.

Usenet and Listserv

No one knows for sure, but experts estimate there are more than 10,000 discussion groups (also called "newsgroups" or "bulletin boards") on the Usenet portion of the Internet. Basically, Usenet is an international meeting place where people gather (but not in real time) to discuss events and topics in specialized areas.

PUBLIC RELATIONS IN CYBERSPACE

Many organizations, including public relations firms, use Internet web sites to post publicity materials that can be accessed by the media and the public. Here are a few examples and how to reach them.

- Reebok uses its web site to reinforce its image as a good corporate citizen. It publicizes its relationship with Amnesty International, its long-standing involvement in human rights and how to mobilize political support for human rights issues. **http://planetreebok.com**

- Edelman Worldwide, a public relations firm, uses its web site to promote itself and distribute client information in such areas as business-to-business, technology, health and medicine. Users can "subscribe" to topics and get information sent directly to their E-mail address. http://www.edelman.com

- Ketchum Public Relations Worldwide has a Ketchum Kitchen on its web site. It serves up food tips, recipes and advice for on-line users in an interactive format. In addition, there's a section of the web site where users can ask questions via E-mail and get a reply. The service features information from Ketchum's food and beverage clients. **http://www.recipe.com**

- The U.S. Defense Department set up a web site giving information about American troops stationed in Bosnia. Called Bosnia Link, the web site gives information and maps on conditions, features on the troops and routine news releases. **http://www.dtic.dla.mil/bosnia**

Figure 10.7 The web site of Snapple Corporation on the World Wide Web. The "home page" uses strong graphics (full color) and enables users to access various topics such as the "mailroom" or the "archives" by clicking on the name.

Chapter 1 outlined some Usenet groups that specialize in public relations topics. Other groups may focus on topics such as the environment, television shows, college classes, even O.J. Simpson. There are also numerous discussion groups about sex and pornography that have become a political issue, with some people lobbying Congress to pass legislation to forbid "indecent" material.

From a public relations standpoint, Usenet is a good way to distribute information to users who are interested in your organization. In fact, many organizations create their own bulletin boards, often within their own web sites, for the purpose of posting messages and getting feedback from users. Organizations can also post messages on more generalized bulletin boards.

A good example of how this works is Slocan Forest Products, a Canadian company, which was threatened by a hostile takeover bid. In order to drum up support to remain independent, the president of Slocan posted messages on various computer bulletin boards that reached stockholders, the business community, the press, environmental groups and government regulatory agencies. He also posted his own personal E-mail address so people could directly comment on the takeover bid. The hostile bid was beaten back.

Organizations also use the Usenet to monitor issues and what people are saying, electronically sampling public opinion to determine how people feel about various issues that affect the organization.

Listserv is similar to Usenet, but instead of messages being posted to a bulletin board, items are sent directly to users via E-mail. Edelman Worldwide, as previously noted, has a Listserv on its web site so you can automatically get various kinds of information in your interest area.

Listserv is generally more appropriate for distributing news releases and other press materials because individuals (such as reporters and editors) can automatically get materials on their E-mail every time you post something on a Listserv bulletin board. However, they have to be "subscribers" to receive the information.

Commercial On-line Services

CompuServe and America Online (AOL) are on-line services that offer access to the Internet. In addition, they also generate their own material for on-line users. AOL, for example, has channels devoted to health and fitness, fashions and lifestyles and food.

These programs provide another vehicle for the distribution of publicity materials and the placement of advertising.

THE INTERNET'S LIMITATIONS

There is no doubt that the advent of the Internet has radically changed the way public relations professionals distribute information, now and in the future. It offers new vistas of publicity opportunities, but the Internet is not a total solution.

You should realize, for example, that the Internet is a supplemental form of message dissemination and doesn't replace traditional media.

Carole Howard, long-term vice president of public relations for *Reader's Digest*, told *PR Reporter*:

It's easy to get drawn into the hype. Yet it's important to remember that the Net is just another tool in your arsenal. It may be the latest—but it's not necessarily the greatest distribution vehicle for every publicity opportunity.

One problem with the Internet is its current reach and audience. Although millions now have access to the Net, and it is estimated that 24 million users in the United States and Canada regularly use the Internet, it is still important to remember some of the following figures:

- 35 million families in the United States still get a daily newspaper.
- The combined circulation of dailies and weeklies in the United States is about 138 million.
- 10 million families are heavy readers of magazines.
- Families still watch more than seven hours of television daily.
- Radio reaches over 150 million Americans daily.

In other words, traditional media still have more reach and breadth than the Internet. You must also remember that the Internet is still not particularly user friendly in terms of finding information. In fact, it is more like a giant library with 2,500 branches and no Dewey Decimal System.

Patrick Jackson, editor of *PR Reporter* (August 14, 1995), also wonders if people will bother to look for your information on the Internet. He says people are basically lazy when it comes to information retrieval—and are bored easily. He notes, "If 98 percent don't respond to a direct mail piece placed directly in their hands, what percentage is going to drop out of cyberspace with all the chit-chat and irrelevance?"

Although the Internet has no time or space constraints, this is a double-edged sword. On one hand, publicists are thrilled that the public can now access the full text of news releases—instead of shortened versions (or no mention) in the news media. However, the flip side is that 10 million documents are added daily to the Internet and no one has the time or ability to cope with absorbing this mountain of information.

The traditional media perform the valuable function of distilling and synthesizing information so people can easily access it at home, on a bus or even on a Stairmaster in a health club.

W. Russell Neumann, writing in *The Future of the Mass Audience* (Cambridge University Press, 1991) adds:

> People will continue to rely on the editorial judgment of established news media to relay what are deemed to be the significant headlines of the world and the nation. Packaging, formatting, filtering and interpreting complex flows of information represent the valued-added components of public communications. In a more competitive, complex and intense communication environment, that value-added component will be equally important to the individual citizen, if not more so.

There's also the matter of credibility. Publicity materials in the mass media have increased credibility because media gatekeepers, a third party, have already decided that the information is newsworthy. Two media researchers, Robert Merton and Robert Lazarsfeld, termed this the status conferral role of the press. Other researchers say media coverage of your organization represents an implied third-party endorsement by the press. No such status conferral occurs when you can post anything and everything on the Internet.

In sum, the Internet has been added to your tool box as another way to distribute information to the traditional mass media and the public. It is not, however, a tool that replaces all existing tools. The Internet, like a specialty tool, does some things better, but it doesn't do all things well. You don't use a power saw to fix the toilet.

Kirk Hallahan, a public relations professor at Colorado State University, echoes this theme when he writes in *Public Relations Quarterly* (Summer 1994):

> In the future, public relations professionals certainly will spend more time developing messages for increasingly specialized audiences—and will tap many of the new technologies in creative ways. However, we will continue to need public media that enable us to reach the broad spectrum of society. . . .

SUMMARY

1. Media directories, in print or on CD-ROM, are needed to find the names and addresses of the media.

2. Media lists must be constantly updated and revised; journalists move around a lot.

3. Publicists use editorial calendars to find out what special editions or sections a publication is planning for the year.

4. Tip sheets let publicists know what kind of material a publication or broadcast station is seeking for a particular purpose.

5. Mailing labels must be accurate; they should be addressed to a specific editor by name and include such details as the floor or suite in an office building.

6. The vast majority of news releases and other press materials are still mailed, either through the post office or commercial vendors such as Federal Express.

7. Mailing houses can assemble press materials and mail them for you.

8. The fax machine is a good way to send media advisories and late-breaking news releases. However, don't mass distribute routine news releases by fax.

9. New technology allows firms such as Business Wire to send your news releases electronically to the computers of the mass media.

10. Feature materials can be distributed "camera-ready" on paper, diskettes or online.

11. Press materials distributed by diskette or CD-ROM are still not widely used.

12. The Internet is the newest technology for distribution of publicity materials.

13. E-mail is now a popular way of communicating with reporters and editors. Certain guidelines, however, should be followed.

14. The World Wide Web allows an organization to establish its own "home page" to post a variety of materials, which can be accessed by the press and the public.

15. A good web site is highly visual and interactive, with short blocks of text.

16. Publicists can use Internet discussion groups to post information and receive feedback.

17. The Internet is a supplemental tool for distributing information; it doesn't replace traditional mass media.

EXERCISES

1. A manufacturer of golf carts has developed a new, smaller cart for one person that requires fewer batteries to operate. Using media directories, compile a list of trade and specialized publications that would be interested in this new product announcement.

2. The Wisconsin Cheese Board has prepared a packet of recipes and photos showing the use of cheese in various dishes. These packets will be sent to every

newspaper food editor in Wisconsin. Using press directories, compile the names and addresses of food editors who would receive the packet.

3. A manufacturer of sunscreen has developed a feature article about the need for protection to avoid the dangers of overexposure and skin cancer. The target audience for this kind of information is women from 18 to 35. Using press directories, compile a list of general circulation magazines that reach this specific audience.

4. Using the library, compare the contents of two or three press directories. What are the advantages and disadvantages of each?

5. Camera-ready releases are used extensively by suburban newspapers and special supplements of daily newspapers. Review the contents of several local publications. Can you find five samples of camera-ready stories that were published?

6. The *Wall Street Journal* has announced its editorial calendar for the year. The newspaper will devote a special supplement in June to the theme "Work and the Family," a topic that many experts predict will dominate the corporate agenda in the coming years. As the public relations director for a computer software company, can you think of any story ideas that would get your company mentioned in this special issue?

7. Camera-ready features sent out by distribution firms usually contain about 350 words for a two-column article. Select a product or event and write a feature in this style. A typical format is shown in Figure 10.5. Remember that a feature must be newsworthy and noncommercial.

8. News releases that are sent via E-mail should have a summary paragraph that an editor sees on the screen before the actual news release appears. Take a previous news release that you've written and modify it for E-mail.

9. Do some browsing on the World Wide Web. Select several web sites (home pages) for organizations and write a critique of them. Are they visually attractive? Can the user easily access various kinds of information? Do they offer news releases? What other features do they have?

10. Find some discussion groups (Usenet) on the Internet. Some suggestions can be found in Chapter 1. Write a report on what you find in terms of topics, format of discussion and the quality of the messages.

11. Editors and reporters like to receive news releases in different ways. Do a mini-survey of local media outlets in your city. What distribution method seems to be the most popular—mail, fax, E-mail, electronic wire services or some other means?

11 | *The Basics of Media Relations*

*P*ublicists and journalists have long had a love–hate relationship. There are flashpoints of friction and distrust, but there is also the realization that both are mutually dependent on each other to do their jobs.

This chapter explores the symbiotic relationship between publicists and journalists from several perspectives. First, we discuss how each depends on the other. Second, we examine some areas of friction such as name-calling, excessive hype, advertising influences, sloppy reporting and tabloid journalism.

We then give some guidelines for effective media relations on a daily basis, as well as how to handle crisis situations. By keeping these guidelines in mind, you should be able to build a trusting and productive relationship with journalists.

MEDIA DEPENDENCE ON PUBLIC RELATIONS

The reality of mass communications today is that reporters and editors spend most of their time processing information, not gathering it. And, although many reporters deny it, most of the information that appears in the mass media comes from public relations sources that provide a constant stream of news releases, features, planned events and tips to the media.

Gary Putka, the Boston bureau chief of the *Wall Street Journal*, admits that "a good 50 percent" of the stories in the newspaper come from news releases. His assessment is backed up by several research studies.

One such study goes back to 1973 when L. V. Sigal wrote *Reporters and Officials: The Organization and Politics of Newsmaking*. He studied 1,200 *New York Times* and *Washington Post* front pages and found that 58.2 percent of the stories came through routine bureaucratic channels, official proceedings, news releases and conferences, and other planned events. Just 25.2 percent were the products of investigative journalism, and most of these were produced by interviews, the result of routine access to spokespersons. Sigal explained, "The reporter cannot depend on legwork alone to satisfy his paper's insatiable demand for news. He looks to official channels to provide him with newsworthy material day after day."

More recent studies have the same basic finding. Professors Masel Walters and Timothy Walters looked at press acceptance of news releases from a state government agency. Writing in the Spring 1992 issue of *Public Relations Review*, they reported that 86 percent of the news releases were used by newspapers with a combined circulation of nearly 135 million readers.

In another study, Jericho Promotions (New York) sent questionnaires to 5,500 journalists worldwide and got 2,432 to respond. Of that number, 38 percent said they got at least half of their story ideas from public relations people. The percentage was even higher among editors of lifestyle, entertainment and health sections of newspapers, according to an article in the September 1991 issue of *O'Dwyer's PR Services Report*.

All this amounts to what O. H. Gandy calls "information subsidies" to the press. In his book, *Beyond Agenda Setting: Information Subsidies and Public Policy*, he explains that material such as news releases constitute a "subsidy" because the source "causes it to be made available at something less than the cost a user would face in the absence of a subsidy."

In other words, public relations materials save media the time, money and effort of gathering their own news. Indeed, no medium—including the *New York Times*—has enough reporters to cover all the available news. As one editor of the *San Jose* (CA) *News* once said, publicists are the newspaper's "unpaid reporters."

PUBLIC RELATIONS DEPENDENCE ON THE MEDIA

The purpose of public relations, as discussed in the early chapters of this book, is to inform, shape opinions and attitudes and motivate. This can be accomplished only if people receive messages constantly and consistently.

The media, in all their variety, are cost-effective channels of communication in an information society. They are the multipliers that enable millions of people to receive a message at the same time. Through the miracle of satellite communications, the world is a global village of shared information.

On a more specialized level, the media are no longer just mass communication. Thousands of publications and hundreds of radio, television, and cable outlets enable the public relations communicator to reach very specific target audiences with tailored messages designed just for them. Demographic segmentation and psychographics are now a way of life in advertising, marketing and public relations.

The media's power and influence in a democratic society reside in their independence from government control. Reporters and editors make independent judgments about what is newsworthy and what will be disseminated. They serve as filters of information, and even though not everyone is happy with what they decide, the fact remains that media gatekeepers are generally perceived as more objective than public relations people, who represent a particular client or organization.

This is important to you because the media, by inference, serve as third-party endorsers of your information. Media gatekeepers give your information credibility and importance by deciding that it is newsworthy. The information is no longer from your organization but from the *New York Times*, the *Wall Street Journal*, or CNN.

AREAS OF FRICTION

The relationship between public relations and the media is based on mutual cooperation, trust and respect.

Unfortunately, certain actions compromise the relationship. On the public relations side, these actions involve excessive hype and promotion. On the journalistic side, these actions include name-calling, sloppy/biased reporting and tabloid sensationalism. Both groups face the issue of improper advertising influence, which tends to undermine the credibility of the news coverage.

Hype and Promotion

As noted in Chapter 5, journalists receive hundreds of news releases every month. Far too many of them contain hype words such as "unique," "revolutionary," "state-of-the-art" and "sophisticated." Journalists, dulled by the constant flow of news releases that sound like commercials, generally conclude that the majority of publicists are incompetent.

Journalists also resent the gimmicks that often accompany news releases and press kits. A press kit for Diet Rite Cola once included a pair of binoculars, a playback recorder and a self-destruct tape because the theme of the campaign was a "salt assault" promotion.

Conner Peripherals also took the gimmick route. It sent 40 computer writers a two-foot long scale model of an 18-wheeler truck to promote a bigger, faster disk drive. On the side of the truck, Conner wrote, "Big Rig Capacity: Sports Car

Speed." Inside was a toy Ferrari, and included in the shipping box was a pair of driving gloves.

Although many publicists think sending such gimmicks helps separate their press kits and releases from the pack, most journalists think they are a waste of time. In a survey of Florida journalists, for example, 70 percent didn't like receiving them.

Matt Lake, a senior editor at C-Net, an on-line publication in San Francisco, was even more blunt. He told the *Wall Street Journal*, "These things are really stupid."

As a general rule, the value of such gimmicks and giveaways is kept under $25 to avoid conflicting with ethics guidelines that limit the value of gifts that can be accepted. Some newspapers even return such minor things as key chains, T-shirts and coffee mugs.

The best approach is to avoid the hype and promotion; it only irritates journalists and lowers the credibility of your message. If you insist on using a gimmick with a news release or press kit, carefully assess the recipient's potential reaction. There's a thin line between humorous and tacky.

Name-calling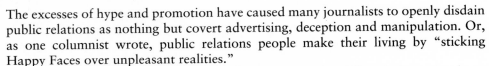

The excesses of hype and promotion have caused many journalists to openly disdain public relations as nothing but covert advertising, deception and manipulation. Or, as one columnist wrote, public relations people make their living by "sticking Happy Faces over unpleasant realities."

As a consequence, journalists tend to stereotype public relations people as "flacks," a derogatory term for press agents. It is somewhat like calling all lawyers "ambulance chasers" or all reporters "hacks."

While some reporters still use the term "flack" to describe anyone in public relations, concentrated efforts by the public relations community has made the practice less common. The *Wall Street Journal*, for example, finally adopted a policy that forbids the use of the word "flack" by reporters in their stories. Unfortunately, reporters at other publications haven't gotten the word or have decided to update the word "flack" with the term "spin doctor." Such name-calling by reporters impedes mutual respect and cooperation.

Sloppy/Biased Reporting

The quality of reporting doesn't seem to inspire much confidence among public relations people and organizational executives.

One survey, for example, found that 82 percent of executives think news coverage today reflects the reporter's personal opinions and biases. Another survey of *Fortune* 500 communications executives found that 43 percent of them would give reporters a "B" grade, and another 38 percent would give reporters a "C" grade on covering their companies.

The biggest complaint of the *Fortune* 500 communication executives is that journalists are perceived as having no background in the subject they cover or are considered biased. These findings echo a survey some years ago by the American

Management Association. It found that the majority of the public relations directors who participated thought that sloppiness on the part of reporters was the major reason for inaccurate stories. Reporters were also faulted for not doing their homework before writing a story, having a tendency to sensationalize, and making simplistic generalizations.

On the other hand, business executives often don't have a clear idea of how the media operate and what they need to write a fair, objective story. Many times, for example, they give vague answers and stonewall reporters—and then complain that the story is not totally accurate. Executives also don't seem to realize that news stories go through various levels—writing, editing, headline writing and placement—that are done by several people. This, of course, increases the chance of distortion.

You can reduce the percentage of sloppy reporting by doing three things:

- Educate executives about how the media operate and how reporters strive for objectivity. That means other viewpoints, sometimes unfavorable, will be in a story.
- Train executives to give 30-second answers to questions. This reduces the possibility of answers being garbled and distorted.
- Provide extensive briefing and background material to reporters who are not familiar with the topic or the organization.

Tabloid Journalism

Newspapers and broadcast shows are not all alike, and the level of commitment to journalistic standards ranges from wholehearted to nonexistent. For example, the *Wall Street Journal* is highly praised for its objective and fair reporting, whereas the *National Enquirer* and *Star* are famous for manipulated photos and headline stories based on hearsay.

The same situation exists in television. Shows such as *Morton Downey, Geraldo, A Current Affair* and *Hard Copy* are known as "tabloid television" and "trash TV" because they concentrate on the sensational and have used the facade of traditional journalism on what is pure entertainment. This has been called "journaltainment."

The proliferation of tabloid television and its gloves-off approach means that you have to be very careful. Professor Fran Matera of Arizona State University, writing in the May 1990 *Public Relations Journal*, puts it succinctly:

> Tabloid journalists, no matter how pleasant, are not your friends. They are often there to trick or trap your client. They are looking for the one killer shot where they catch you or your client stammering and fumbling. That's what sells, and earns the reporter accolades.

Organizations are even becoming more wary of traditional shows such as *60 Minutes, 20/20* and *Dateline NBC*. In the race for ratings, these shows have started to offer more sensationalism and the manipulation of events for greater effect. As mentioned earlier, NBC was sued by General Motors and had to make an on-air apology for rigging a sequence that showed gas tanks on GM trucks exploding. The people responsible were all fired.

Such lapses of journalistic standards are a major concern for the media because the antics of an isolated few affect the credibility of all journalists.

Your challenge is to make sure you don't paint all media with the same brush. You should continue to give service to responsible journalists and provide information. However, if a reporter has a reputation for sensationalism, you are probably better off if you simply refuse to be interviewed or provide information.

If you do decide to work with a tabloid television reporter, Professor Matera provides some points that can help you keep control of the situation:

- Never do an adversarial interview alone. One option is to have a media-savvy lawyer sit in on the interview.
- Research the interviewer's record before facing the camera. Know his or her method of questioning.
- Don't accept any document on camera. Surprise documents can be used to trip up subjects and make them look foolish.
- Get a commitment that you will be able to respond to accusations made by others as part of the story.
- If cornered, counterattack. Take the offensive and accuse the reporter of unprofessional conduct, incompetence or a lack of understanding of the subject.

Advertising Influence

It's a fact of economic life that most media are dependent on advertising revenues for survival. Increased competition, coupled with a soft economy in the early 1990s, has created an environment where some advertisers also get favorable news stories and features in a publication.

Although mainstream news periodicals and daily newspapers generally keep a high wall between the news and advertising department, this isn't always the case in the trade press and among specialized magazines. Beauty and fashion magazines, for example, are well known for running stories and fashion layouts that tend to feature their advertisers. Escada, for example, increased its advertising budget from $3.7 to $5.2 million over a two-year period. In that same period of time, according to *Time* magazine, the number of Escada's appearances in the fashion pages of national publications and *Women's Wear Daily* tripled from about 30 to 90.

Conflicts of interest are another problem. *Family PC* magazine, for example, gave a rave review to a CD-ROM produced by Walt Disney Co. What the review didn't say was that the magazine is a joint venture of Walt Disney Co. and Ziff-Davis, a publisher of many trade magazines. On another level, many editors write books for Microsoft Press, a division of Microsoft Corp., as well as articles about the company's products.

Editors commonly serve as consultants on product development. The editors of *PC Magazine*, for example, are often involved in products that have later gone on to win the magazine's highly sought "Editor's Choice" award. In the car industry, automotive editors also serve as paid consultants to major auto companies.

Related to advertising influence is the wining and dining of journalists, including giving expensive gifts. When Tse Cashmere opened a Madison Avenue boutique, some 250 members of the fashion press attended. When they left, most of them carried a small memento from Tse: a $160 cashmere sweater.

All this, of course, raises troubling questions about journalistic ethics and integrity. The editors and reporters on specialty publications loudly proclaim that advertising contracts, gifts and consulting assignments don't affect their editorial judgment, but their protestations seem a bit hollow and hypocritical.

The situation also affects public relations personnel. If the public increasingly takes a skeptical view of what they read and hear, the value of the media as an objective, independent source of information is compromised. Thus, messages from organizations won't have the same impact and believability that the media now bestow on such messages.

Advertising influence also presents practical problems for the public relations practitioner. How do you sort out the publications that are "for sale" and those that maintain high ethical standards? How do you convince management that a fat advertising contract probably won't influence the tone and level of coverage in the local daily newspaper? Should you build an advertising budget into your plans to pave the way for product reviews in some specialty publications?

If a publication connects advertising with news coverage, should you go along with it? The PRSA Code of Ethics (Chapter 2) states that you should not engage in any activities that would "corrupt" the channels of communication. Is buying a full-page ad in a publication or paying an editor a consultant fee a violation of professional ethics? Or is it just good business? Remember that media demands for advertising dollars and gifts also test the integrity of the public relations professional.

EFFECTIVE MEDIA RELATIONS

There will always be areas of friction and disagreement between public relations people and journalists, but that doesn't mean there can't be a solid working relationship based on mutual respect for each other's work.

A good working relationship with the media is vital for a public relations writer. Indeed, one definition of public relations is the building of relationships between the organization and its various publics, including journalists.

Dealing with the Media

Many checklists and guidelines for dealing effectively with the media have been compiled. Most of them are well tested and proven, but you must always remember that there are no ironclad rules. Media people are also individuals to whom a particular approach may or may not be applicable. Here's a list of general guidelines, many of which will sound familiar to you from reading previous chapters.

1. *Know your media.* Be familiar with the publications and broadcast media that are regularly used. Know their deadlines, news format, audiences and needs. Do your homework on other publications and broadcast shows before sending a pitch letter or news material.

2. *Limit your mailings.* Multiple news releases are inefficient and costly, and they alienate media gatekeepers. Send releases only to publications and broadcast outlets that would have an interest in the information. You are not running a mass-mailing house.

3. *Localize.* Countless surveys show that the most effective materials have a local angle. Take the time to develop that angle before sending materials to specific publications.

4. *Send newsworthy information.* Don't bother sending materials that are not newsworthy. Avoid excessive hype and promotion.

5. *Practice good writing.* News materials should be well written and concise. Avoid technical jargon in materials sent to nontechnical publications.

6. *Avoid gimmicks.* Don't send T-shirts, teddy bears, balloon bouquets, or other frivolous items to get the attention of media gatekeepers.

7. *Be environmentally correct.* Avoid giant press kits and reams of background materials. Save trees.

8. *Be available.* You are the spokesperson for an organization. It is your responsibility to be accessible at all times, even in the middle of the night. Key reporters should have your office and home telephone numbers.

9. *Get back to reporters.* One press joke asks, "How many public relations people does it take to screw in a light bulb?" The answer is, "I don't know, but I'll get back to you." Make it a priority to respect your promises and call reporters back in a timely manner. They have deadlines to meet.

10. *Answer your own phone.* Use voice mail systems as a tool of service, not as a screening device. Reporters (like other people) hate getting bogged down in the electronic swamp of endless button pushing.

11. *Be truthful.* Give accurate and complete information even if it is not flattering to your organization. Your facts and figures must be clear and dependable.

12. *Answer questions.* There are only three acceptable answers: "Here it is," "I don't know but I'll get back to you within the hour," and "I know but I can't tell you now because . . . ." "No comment" is *not* one of the three alternatives.

13. *Protect exclusives.* If a reporter has found a story, don't give it to anyone else.

14. *Be fair.* Competing media deserve equal opportunity to receive information in a timely manner.

15. *Help photographers.* Facilitate their work by getting people together in a central location, providing necessary props, and supplying subjects' full names and titles.

Q:

Plastics?

A:

American Plastics Council.

For answers to your questions about plastics and the environment, call Jimmy Hendricks, media relations manager.

202/371-5319

American
Plastics
Council

1275 K Street NW   Suite 400
Washington, DC 20005

Figure 11.1   An important part of media relations is making sure reporters know where to get information. Many companies and trade groups place advertisements in journalism publications to encourage reporters to call if they have questions. Other approaches include sending printed Rolodex cards and publicizing the company's home page on the Internet. (*Courtesy of American Plastics Council, Washington, DC.*)

16. *Explain.* Give reporters background briefings and materials so that they understand your organization. Tell them how decisions were reached and why.

17. *Remember deadlines.* The reporter must have enough time to write a story. One good rule is to provide information days or weeks in advance. In addition, don't call a reporter to make a pitch at deadline time.

18. *Praise good work.* If a reporter has written or produced a good story, send a complimentary note. A copy to the editor is also appreciated.

19. *Correct errors politely.* Ignore minor errors such as misspellings, inaccurate ages, and wrong titles. If there is a major factual error that skews the accuracy of the entire story, talk to the reporter who wrote the story. If that doesn't work, talk to the editor or news director.

Media Etiquette

In addition to the foregoing guidelines, there are several matters of media etiquette that should be observed. Failure to do so often leads to poor media relations.

Irritating Phone Calls   Don't call a reporter or an editor and say, "Did you get my news release?" Simply assume that it was received if you used a regular channel of distribution such as first-class mail, a courier service, fax or E-mail.

Unfortunately, the practice of phoning reporters with such an inane question is widely used as a pretext for calling attention to the news release or making a pitch for its use. Although the approach seems logical, it's better to call a reporter to offer some new piece of information or a story angle that may not be explicit in the news

---

YOU HAVE THE RIGHT TO REMAIN SILENT . . .

Most media guidelines emphasize that public relations personnel should always be helpful to and cooperative with the media. However, there are times when the best course of action is to remain silent.

Ron Levy, president of North American Precis Syndicate and a lawyer, says public relations people should remain silent when:

- You don't know the answer.
- Management prefers that the answer come from someone who is an expert on the subject.
- You think the reporter will twist or distort your answer.
- Management says any answer to a particular question should be checked with legal counsel.
- The question deals with proprietary information that would benefit competitors.
- The inquiry is about the personal lives of employees.

Source: *Jack O'Dwyer's Newsletter,* January 24, 1996.

release. The telephone call then becomes an information call instead of a plea to read the release and use it.

If you do call a journalist, the best time is usually in the morning. Never call after 4 p.m., and never call when a publication is close to deadline.

Inappropriate Requests   Don't call reporters to ask them when a story will be used. Most reporters don't know when the story will be used, or even *if* it will be used. Editors make that decision based on the space and time available.

In addition, don't ask the publication or broadcast station to send you a news clipping or broadcast segment. If you want such materials, make arrangements with a clipping service or broadcast monitoring firm.

Finally, don't ask to see a story before it's published or broadcast. The media, citing policy and the First Amendment, usually refuse. It is permissible to ask a reporter, however, if you can check any quotes attributed to you. In many cases, you'll still get a frosty no.

Lunch Dates   Don't take a reporter to lunch unless the purpose is to discuss a possible story or to give a background briefing on some upcoming event. In other words, a lunch should have a business reason. You need to be well informed about the product or idea and be organized. Reporters don't like to waste time in idle chitchat, nor are they impressed by being taken to the most expensive restaurant in town.

If you do have lunch, give the reporter the opportunity to select the restaurant and pay for his or her portion of the meal. Many publications have strict rules forbidding reporters to accept free lunches. Others, of course, have no such restrictions. In your case, it's always acceptable to ask and then do whatever feels comfortable for the reporter.

Previews and Parties

Press previews are often scheduled for events to which the general public is invited. Usually a preview is held a day or two ahead of the event so that reporters can write stories that appear on the day that the event actually occurs. Press previews are almost routine for events such as the opening of new facilities—corporate headquarters, a hospital's new wing, a shopping mall, a department store, a restaurant, even a new toxic waste dump. In most cases, the press gets a background briefing and a tour of the new facilities.

Demonstrations of new products also lend themselves to press previews. This is particularly true in the area of high technology, where sophisticated products can be put through their paces by the engineers who developed them. Many companies have a press preview of their products just before a major trade show. The advantage is that reporters from all over the country are already gathered in one place

Planning a press preview is like planning any other event (see Chapter 18). Great attention must be paid to detail and logistics to ensure that the guests have a positive experience.

But even the best plans sometimes go awry. The staff of Daniel Edelman Public Relations was red-faced when a USAir 757 flight crew did not show up to fly a plane for a demonstration of In-Flight Phone's new air-to-ground communication system. On board waiting for the demonstration were more than 100 newspeople who were brought to Washington, D.C., to cover it.

Previews may also include such things as a cocktail party or a dinner. One national company combined a press preview of its new headquarters building with a party that included cocktails and dinner. This kind of event is in the category of relationship building and networking. It allows company executives to mingle and socialize with reporters in a casual atmosphere. Ultimately, this helps executives feel more relaxed when a reporter they already know wants to interview them for a story. Unlike news conferences, press previews are often held after "working hours" when reporters are not on deadline.

Gift Giving

Many organizations like to give reporters a souvenir for attending a preview or party. Gifts can be appropriate if they have nominal value, such as a coffee mug, a T-shirt, or even a CD. However, it's not wise to give expensive gifts because it raises questions of "influence buying." In any case, the gift should be available at the door, and reporters should be given the option of taking the gift or bypassing it.

Junkets

A variation on the press party is the junket. Although the use of junkets has declined in recent years, they are still part of the travel and entertainment industry. Junkets usually involve invitations to reporters for an expense-paid trip to witness an event or see a facility.

An example of a large-scale junket: Disney World in Florida invited 10,000 writers, publishers and broadcasters to a three-day celebration of the park's fifteenth anniversary. Although large numbers of media representatives took advantage of what columnist Mike Royko said was the largest "freebie" in U.S. journalistic history, a number of prominent newspapers blasted the event. The *New York Times* editorialized that the press was debasing itself by accepting Disney's hospitality and questioned whether reporters could be objective about Disney operations after accepting an all-expense-paid trip.

Junkets, particularly when there is little newsworthy information, raise considerable controversy among journalists and public relations professionals. As a consequence, companies must carefully consider all aspects of sponsoring a junket and its possible negative effect on media relations.

To be effective and garner media attendance, press parties or junkets must be handled discreetly. It is against the code of ethics of the Society of Professional Journalists (SPJ) and the Public Relations Society of America (PRSA) to have lavish banquets and expensive souvenirs simply for the sake of impressing the press. Journalists, although they may attend, generally "bad-mouth" the affair if they think there is an overt attempt to "buy" favorable coverage.

SETTING THE RECORD STRAIGHT

News coverage isn't always objective, factual or accurate. Mistakes happen, and it is likely that you or your employer will have complaints about inaccurate and unfair news coverage. Here are several steps you can take.

Ascertain the facts. Analyze the offending article or broadcast news segment. What exactly is inaccurate, incomplete or unfair about it? If it's simply a matter of not liking the tone of the story, there probably isn't much you can do about it. Oftentimes, organizational executives think any article that doesn't praise the organization is unfair and biased. If it's a matter of inaccurate information or something taken out of context that distorts the true picture, you should document the correct facts to make a convincing argument.

Talk to the reporter. Call the reporter and politely point out the inaccuracies. The reporter may correct the information in subsequent articles or broadcasts. Many newspapers also print corrections under the rubric of a clarification.

Talk to the editor. If you don't get satisfaction from the reporter, and the complaint is a major one, you may wish to write a letter to the editor and request publication. Another approach is to request a meeting with the editor and the reporter.

Go public. An old adage holds that you should never pick a fight with anyone who buys ink by the barrel; nevertheless, many companies take the offensive and make every effort to inform key publics about their side of the story. Letters can be sent to community opinion leaders, employees or even stockholders depending on the story. Another approach is to purchase advertising to rebut the allegations.

File a lawsuit. The last resort is to file a lawsuit if legal counsel believes that the newspaper or broadcast outlet has intentionally distorted the truth. A threatened libel suit often encourages the media outlet to print a correction or an apology. A lawsuit also gets media coverage, which gives the organization a platform to inform the public about inaccuracies in the original story.

CRISIS COMMUNICATION

A good working relationship with the media is severely tested in times of crisis. All the rules and guidelines previously stated about working effectively with the press are magnified and intensified when something out of the ordinary occurs and thus becomes extremely newsworthy.

There are many dimensions of what constitutes a crisis for a company or an organization. Pacific Telesis, the parent company of Pacific Bell, defines a crisis as "an extraordinary event or series of events that adversely affect the integrity of a product; the reputation or financial stability of an organization; or the health of well-being of employees, the community, or the public-at-large."

Here is a sampling of major crises that have hit various organizations:

- The safety of Dow-Corning's silicone gel breast implants comes under fire from both the medical community and thousands of women who claim that they were harmed by the product.
- Sears is charged by consumer agencies in several states for defrauding customers and making unnecessary repairs at its auto centers.
- An outbreak of food poisoning, leading to the death of a 2-year-old, is traced to contaminated beef served by Jack-In-The-Box restaurants in Washington State.
- An activist environmental group claims that the pesticide Alar used on apples is a health hazard to children. The claim is featured on *60 Minutes*, causing a major drop in apple sales, affecting thousands of apple growers.
- A Florida man claims that his wife's fatal brain tumor was caused by her frequent use of a cellular phone. He files a lawsuit and gets national exposure with an appearance on *Larry King Live*.

These situations, no matter what the circumstances are, constitute major crises because the reputation of the company, industry or product is in jeopardy. Economic survival is at stake, and a company can lose millions of dollars overnight if the public perceives that a problem exists.

Johnson & Johnson, owner of the maker of Tylenol, saw the brand's market share shrink from 37 percent to barely 6 percent in a matter of days after capsules laced with cyanide killed seven people in Chicago. By the time it was established that someone had tampered with the product after it had reached store shelves, the ordeal had cost the company more than $50 million to recall the product and test all its manufacturing processes.

During such times of crisis, the media can be adversaries or allies. It all depends on how you and your organization manage the crisis and understand the media's point of view. Keep in mind the following guidelines developed by *PR Newswire*:

- "No comment" fuels hostility. Even a simple "Can I get back to you?" can be misconstrued as evasive.
- Always try to be helpful. Too many executives are so guarded in conversations with reporters that they miss opportunities to get their own case across.
- Be familiar with print and broadcast deadlines. Calling a news conference on or after a deadline may hurt your organization's chance to get fair or full treatment.
- Get to know the journalists in your area before a crisis hits. That way, they will already know something about you and your company, and you'll have an idea of how they work.

The key to successful dealings with the media during a crisis is to become a credible source of information. *PR Newswire* suggests the following:

- Appoint a spokesperson whom the media can trust and who has authority to speak for the company. It also is a good idea to designate one central spokesperson so that the organization speaks with one voice.

- Set up a central media information center where reporters can obtain updated information and work on stories. You should provide telephone lines, modular jacks so that reporters using computers can reach their offices and facsimile machines. Provide food and transportation if necessary.
- Provide a constant flow of information, even if the situation is unchanged or negative. A company builds credibility by addressing bad news quickly; when information is withheld, the coverup becomes the story.
- Be accessible by providing after-hours phone numbers or carrying a cellular phone with you at all times.
- Keep a log of media calls, and return calls as promptly as possible. A log can help you track issues being raised by reporters and give you a record of which media showed the most interest in your story.
- Be honest. Don't exaggerate, and don't obscure facts. If you're not sure of something or don't have the answer to a question, say so. If you are not at liberty to provide information, explain why.

These guidelines reflect plain common sense, but when a crisis hits, it is surprising how many organizations go into a defensive mode and try to stonewall the media. Dow-Corning, for example, got considerable negative coverage by treating the media as an enemy.

Corporate spokespeople accused the media of reporting only the "sensationalistic, anecdotal side of the breast implant story, which has unnecessarily frightened women across the country." At a news conference, the head of Dow's health care business continued the attack by telling the assembled reporters that they took "memos out of context and distorted reality." It would be an understatement to say that this is a poor way to get the press on your side.

Jack-In-The-Box also violated the tenets of crisis communications in the first days of the reported food poisonings. The company initially said "no comment" and then waited three days to hold a news conference, at which the company president tried to shift the blame to the meatpacking company.

David Vogel, a business professor at the University of California in Berkeley, says, "There are two principles: accept responsibility and take action." Even if you are no directly at fault, the organization should take responsibility for its product and the public safety.

Johnson & Johnson did this with Tylenol, but Dow-Corning chose to defend its product even after evidence had mounted that the company knew the product had a history of causing medical problems. Experts also say that Jack-In-The-Box fumbled early on by not showing concern for the poisoned customers. The company would have won more public goodwill and favorable press coverage by more quickly offering to pay all medical bills, which it eventually did.

Pacific Telesis, perhaps learning from the mistakes of others, emphasizes two considerations in its crisis management plan:

- Demonstrate our commitment to good corporate citizenship by taking prompt and decisive actions to control problems in our operations.
- Communicate swiftly, constantly and consistently to all appropriate audiences in clear, straightforward, nontechnical language.

SUMMARY

1. Journalists are dependent on public relations sources for receiving most of their information; public relations people are dependent on the media for widespread distribution of information.

2. A major friction point with journalists is that so much public relations material contains excessive hype and promotion.

3. Gimmicks, appropriate in marketing campaigns, are not well received by reporters and editors.

4. "Flack" is a disparaging term for a press agent or publicist.

5. The major complaint about journalists is that they are sloppy and often don't take the time to do their homework.

6. Journalists for publications and broadcast programs that engage in sensational journalism require special handling and precautions.

7. Media credibility is undercut when publications link advertising contracts with the amount of coverage that an organization receives.

8. Public relations personnel are concerned about media integrity; if the public is skeptical of what they read and hear, it reduces the credibility of all information.

9. There are many guidelines for how to conduct effective media relations. The bottom line is to be accurate, truthful and helpful.

10. Don't irritate reporters by placing unnecessary phone calls, asking when a story will run or requesting an advance copy of the story.

11. Previews and parties are acceptable ways of giving organizational staff and reporters a chance to know each other better. Gifts are not necessary.

12. Avoid junkets unless there is a legitimate news story that requires coverage.

13. If you need to set the record straight, first begin with the reporter who wrote the story.

14. Crisis communications is a test of excellent media relations. You need to work closely with the media to assure that the public is fully informed.

EXERCISES

1. Do a content analysis of your local daily newspaper. What percentage of the articles probably originated from a news release, an advisory or other public relations sources? Count news conferences (such as presidential ones), government reports, announcements of community events and so on. In other words, look for information that probably wasn't gathered directly by a reporter.

2. You send a new product release to a trade publication. You then get a call from the publisher asking if you would be willing to buy a full-page ad in the publication. He explains that the extra advertising revenue would help the publica-

tion have enough space to run your news announcement. What would you do? Explain your answer.

3. The editor of *Glamour* magazine once said, "All things being equal, if we are looking at two items that are equally available nationally, if one of them is an advertiser we'd use it." Would you agree? Why or why not? What other criteria might be used?

4. The vice president of marketing, which oversees public relations, thinks it's a great idea to get press attention by sending a press kit in a box that also includes a big teddy bear. The idea, he explains, is that the new product is "user friendly." What do you think of the idea?

5. You're the public relations director of a repertory theatre. The city editor of the local daily calls you and asks if you could send him about 10 complimentary tickets. He explains that his wife's family is in town for the weekend. What would you do? Explain your answer.

6. You're new at a job in public relations. You've been taught to keep news releases factual and skip the hype. However, management wants you to "jazz up" the news release and say the new product is, among other things, "revolutionary." What would you do? Explain your answer.

7. Effective media relations are particularly important during a crisis or an emergency. Do some library research on a crisis situation for an organization or a company. You can choose a crisis such as Exxon's *Valdez* oil spill in Alaska, Dow-Corning's breast implant product, the food poisoning problem at Jack-In-The-Box or any other crisis in the news. Using the guidelines in this chapter, analyze how well the organization handled its media relations.

8. The local newspaper has published a series of articles that criticize the quality of health care in the community. Your hospital, St. Vincent's, was the subject of an article in which a number of facts were misstated. For example, the article said that the hospital had the highest rate of patient deaths in the region. This is literally true, but the article didn't place this "fact" in perspective by saying that St. Vincent's operates the only hospice in the area—a facility where terminally ill patients are cared for until they die. What steps would you take to inform the newspaper of this and get it to print a correction?

PART 3

Writing for Other Media

Many media can be used to convey ideas and information, including those produced and paid for by the organization. Such media are often called *controlled communication* or *sponsored communication* because the organization "controls" the content and pays for the distribution of the message. There are no independent or outside gatekeepers, as in the mass media, to make judgments about the newsworthiness of the information or to determine whether it will be used.

Part 3 devotes six chapters to exploring the other media that require the skills of public relations writers. Your job is to know the needs of the audience and the media that can most effectively convey the message.

□ *Chapter 12, "Newsletters and Magazines,"* examines the editor's dual role, content, mission statements, design, desktop publishing, headline writing, distribution, E-mail and costs.

□ *Chapter 13, "Leaflets and Brochures,"* discusses planning, writing, production, printing processes, paper selection, type families, inks and preparing copy for the graphic designer.

□ *Chapter 14, "Public Relations Advertising,"* covers the concept of public relations advertising, the advantages and disadvantages of using advertising, the five types of public relations advertising, the basics of a print ad, using an advertising agency, billboards, posters and T-shirts.

□ *Chapter 15, "Letters, Direct Mail and Reports,"* explains how to write a business letter, E-mail, direct mail, memos, voice mail, proposals, special reports and annual reports.

□ *Chapter 16, "Speakers and Speeches,"* explores speaker training and placement, speaker bureaus, the basics of a speech, media interviews, speechwriting and publicity opportunities.

□ *Chapter 17, "Audiovisual Aids,"* describes the importance of audiovisual aids, computer including graphics, charts, transparencies, slides, CD-ROM, video and film.

12 | *Newsletters and Magazines*

*T*he *newsletter, newspaper or magazine that an organization publishes for the purpose of communicating directly to internal and external publics is a major communication tool.*

Sponsored periodicals are designed for a specific audience, such as employees, or for a variety of groups that may include stockholders, community opinion leaders, government officials, suppliers or customers. They serve as effective channels of continuous information about the organization. They also have the advantage of reaching their audiences without the filtering process of mass media reporters and editors who, as noted in Part I, control the distribution of the message and its content.

This chapter gives a brief overview of sponsored periodicals, particularly those intended for employees. We will examine the editor's role and the content, design, production and distribution of these publications.

THE EDITOR'S DUAL ROLE

Editing a sponsored publication has been described as something of a highwire act. You must produce a periodical that advances and promotes management's organizational objectives. After all, management is the publisher of the periodical and is paying all the bills. Indeed, a weekly newsletter or a monthly magazine is the most expensive component of a communications budget for most organizations.

In addition, you have a responsibility to serve the interests of the employees or other constituents. Some public relations texts consider public relations personnel, including periodical editors, as "boundary spanners" who must continually make sure that the views of various publics are heard in the management suite.

There's also the matter of editorial freedom. Many editors, particularly former newspaper reporters, think that they have the right to decide what stories will be covered and in what context. They resent management trying to use the publication as a propaganda tool and resist anything that smacks of editorial interference, including story ideas that support organizational objectives.

The dilemma many editors face is how to balance the needs of management, the interests of readers and their own editorial independence. Some never do solve the dilemma and stick to folksy stories that please many and offend none. Actually, the balancing act can be done if the editor is able to understand that the needs of all three are interrelated.

Take company strategies and goals. These are usually based on broad concepts such as human resources, corporate image, business expansion, competitiveness, productivity, marketing and economic development. Communication goals should be based on corporate goals, so the editor may decide to support the goal of increased competitiveness by publishing at least six stories during the year about the organization's market share and what factors are involved in making the organization more competitive.

These stories, if done well, should also interest employees because they are concerned about job security and making sure that the company remains competitive. If the company is successful, it could also mean bonuses and higher pay scales.

Even if management has set broad or specific goals for the year, it is usually the editor who decides how the periodical can support each goal. In this case, the editor can choose any number of journalistic treatments, including the angle of what's in it for employees. The stories about competitiveness don't have to be propaganda. They can be written with the same degree of objectivity as any article in an independent publication.

It is to management's advantage if the story is objective. Liz MacKay, editor of an employee newsletter for a firm in Australia, says, "The paper's power to influence staff [members] is in direct proportion to their confidence that it is keeping them honestly informed, rather than operating as an organ of management."

Gary Kemper makes a similar point in the September 1991 issue of *Communication World:*

> The task faced by those responsible for communication within an organization is very demanding. To produce a relevant, interesting employee publication, they must first con-

vince management that it is in their best interest to permit open, candid communication. Then they must use the credibility of their program to help integrate two endeavors that often are not compatible: the accomplishment of organizational goals and the satisfaction of employee needs. Excellent publications succeed—and those who achieve this seem to enjoy the challenge and take pride in their success.

In other words, you contribute to the success of management's objectives by producing a highly credible publication that satisfies the reader's need to know what the organization is doing and where it is headed.

A good example is *Praxair News,* the employee magapaper (14- by 21-inch page format) of Praxair, Inc., of Danbury, CT (see Figure 12.1 on page 302). Mailed to 10,000 employees around the world, the periodical has several objectives:

- To inform employees about company activities and its business directions in innovative, easy-to-understand ways.
- To build the company's image as an aggressive, on-the-move organization.
- To be a useful tool for salespeople to give to customers to illustrate Praxair's products and services.
- To accomplish the above as attractively and economically as possible.

One measure of success is employee readership surveys. In one survey, 97 percent of the Praxair employees said they enjoyed reading the publication. And 80 percent rated the "look" of the newspaper "excellent."

CONTENT

The content of sponsored periodicals, in broad terms, is news and information. That is why many of these periodicals are called newsletters—they are letters from management to various publics that want news about the organization.

Civic and professional groups use newsletters to inform their members of upcoming meetings and events. Nonprofit organizations send donors and prospective contributors information about the agency's programs and needs and recognize the efforts of current volunteers. Companies keep wholesalers informed about new product developments and offer ideas on how to market existing products. The list is practically endless.

The four-color magazine of the Department of Conservation and Land Management (CALM) in Western Australia (WA) is an example of the multiaudience publication. *Landscope* is sent to key groups who can influence the operations of the Department—government, industry, community opinion leaders, educators, the media, employees and other Western Australians with an active interest in the management of the natural environment.

As such, *Landscope*'s broad editorial goals are geared to the Department's strategic plan. According to Ron Kawalilak, director of corporate relations at CALM, this is: "to increase community awareness, understanding and support for CALM's nature conservation and natural land management programs, services and

Figure 12.1 *Praxair News* is a four-color, six-page magapaper (14- by 21-inch page format) that is sent to 10,000 employees worldwide. Extensive graphics make the publication visually attractive and easy to read. (*Courtesy of Mary-Anne Ward, editor, Praxair, Inc., Danbury, CT.*)

policies, and to promote wider cooperation in the prevention and solution of conservation and land management problems in Western Australia."

To accomplish this goal, the 56-page quarterly generally follows a standard pattern:

- **Cover Story** Emphasizing CALM's activities in the area of broad public interest.
- **Six or Seven Features** Articles covering CALM activities in nature conservation and wildlife management, forest resource management and management for tourism and recreation.
- **In Perspective** A column written by CALM's chief executive, and letters to the editor.
- **Bush Telegraph** Short articles on natural history topics of interest.
- **Endangered** A one-page article on an endangered plant or animal and what CALM is doing to preserve it.
- **Urban Antics** A one-page article on a WA natural history topic aimed primarily at school children.

Meeting Audience Interests

Every sponsored periodical is unique, but there are some guidelines that can be applied. The International Association of Business Communicators (IABC) and Towers, Perrin, Forster & Crosby, a consulting firm, surveyed 40 companies and

IDEAS FOR NEWSLETTER STORIES

Periodicals carry a variety of feature articles and news stories. Here are some ideas for your newsletter:

- Feature a day in the life of an employee. Describe what the person does, and how his or her work ties into the organization's goals.
- Keep people up to date on late-breaking news affecting the organization.
- Interview long-term employees or managers. Have them discuss how things have changed, and link the changes to the organization's strategy and industry developments.
- Offer "how to" tips on writing memos, choosing a health plan or even selecting a child-care center.
- Show how the functions of each department affect the others. Follow a typical customer going through all the channels to show the importance of teamwork.
- Profile customers. Describe how a customer problem was solved. Use quotes from the customer and the employee problem solver.
- Interview 10 employees about their opinions on key issues or events. Use short quotes under pictures of the employees, along with their names and job titles.

Source: *Communication Briefings,* January 1996, p. 4.

45,000 employees to determine what topics employees were most interested in. The top five choices were (1) the organization's future plans, (2) personnel policies and procedures, (3) productivity improvement, (4) job-related information and (5) job advancement information. The last five choices on the 17-topic list were (1) personnel changes and promotions, (2) financial results, (3) advertising and promotion plans, (4) stories about other employees and (5) personal news such as birthdays and anniversaries.

It must be noted, however, that the range of high to low interest was from 95 percent to 57 percent—still more than half for the last choice. The study does indicate, however, that today's employees are more concerned about the health and direction of their companies than they are about the fact that someone in the accounting department just celebrated a wedding anniversary or won a bowling tournament.

Michael C. Brandon, director of internal communication for Northern Telecom, Nashville, puts it more bluntly. He wrote in IABC's *Communication World* (March 1995) that today's employee communications need to do more than make employees feel good. He continues:

> Communicators can no longer permit bowling leagues, birthdays and babies to dominate the pages of the company newsletter. Instead, employee communication must deliver business information critical to the organization's success. The most critical information employees need is about the organization's objectives. If employees are to maximize effectiveness, management must strive for alignment between the organization's goals and the individual objectives of the employees.

A survey of employees at one corporation by Dallas consultant Tom Geddie (*Communication World,* January-February 1995) indicates that editors should always start with the assumption that employees want answers to the "what's-in-it-for-me" questions. The number one information concern for 30 percent of employees was the internal work environment and how their work was important to the company. Another 22 percent wanted to know about the company's financial health and the prospects for continued employment. Another 17 percent each were interested in information about improving the day-to-day work process and hearing about annual priorities and goals.

Despite such surveys, many publications still fail to take into account the needs of management and employees. In another study, conducted by the consulting firm of William M. Mercer, Inc., and *Industry Week,* more than 1,200 articles from the employee publications of 65 companies nationwide were analyzed. It was found that only a small percentage of the articles addressed management and employee concerns (*Communication World,* September 1991).

Such publications are prime candidates for elimination in these tight economic times. Organizations are increasingly killing off publications that don't contribute to organizational objectives or are not cost-effective. Communications consultant Cliff McGoon, for example, found that the three most expensive magazines in a 1988 survey had been eliminated by 1994. They were *Raytheon Magazine* ($135,000 per issue), *Chevron World* ($105,000 per issue) and *AT&T Focus* ($61,000 per issue).

Figure 12.2 *Measure* is a four-color, 32-page magazine that tackles a number of work-place issues for the 95,000 employees of Hewlett-Packard Company. This cover story, about safety in the workplace, uses pulp fiction artwork to attract attention. (*Courtesy of Jay Coleman, editor, Hewlett-Packard Company, Palo Alto, CA.*)

McGoon suggests (*Communication World*, October 1994) that today's editors need to make their newsletters and magazines more cost-effective and relevant. Possible ways to do this include:

- Strive to cut down on printing costs by reducing the number of issues or number of pages of the present publication.
- Perform more desktop functions and final production preparation in-house.
- Consider selling advertising to offset costs.
- Use newspapers and magazines to supplement and complement newsletters distributed by E-mail.
- Tie your publication's costs to the organization's mission. For example, "We published six articles on team building and our reader surveys indicate 82 percent read them and improved their team-building skills."

Mission Statement and Editorial Plan

The best editors, the ones who regularly win awards, seem to understand the purpose of their publication. One technique is to develop a concise, simple mission statement of 25 words or less. The statement should cover the publication's general content, its audience and its strategic role.

Writing a mission statement is tough. *Dallasite,* an employee newsletter of Texas Instruments (TI), first started out with a somewhat broad mission statement: "The *Dallasite* will serve TI by reporting news about the corporation, its people and its goals."

The advent of "bottom-line" economics in the 1990s, however, created a need for a more precise mission statement. It now reads, "We want the *Dallasite* to be a tool that helps employees understand TI's goals and how they can help achieve those goals."

Another example of a publication's mission statement is Figure 1.1 in Chapter 1, which outlines the mission of *Weyerhaeuser Today.*

It's also a good idea to prepare an annual editorial plan. Bobby Minter of Publication Productions in New York, says you need to map out what kind of articles and other material you will prepare for the entire year.

This enables you to develop story ideas that complement the organization's objectives for the year. If team building and increased productivity has been given a high priority by top executives, feature stories in the organization's publication should elaborate on and illustrate those themes throughout the year. This doesn't mean, of course, that every article in a particular issue has to do this.

DESIGN

"The publication's design should be compatible with its overall objectives," Minter advises, adding that "content and design work together to achieve a unified communication."

Consequently, periodicals have distinct "personalities" that reflect their organizations. Reebok International has an employee tabloid (magapaper) that features

THE INSIDE STORIES

FEATURES

Page 12

4 A peek into the future
MIT's Nicholas Negroponte and HP Labs' Joel
Birnbaum discuss the future of telecommunications at Telecom '95.

7 The case of the 24-hour scientist
Renowned criminologist Dr. Henry Lee uses
HP analytical equipment to solve Connecticut's
most cunning crimes.

10 A new idea takes flight
The experts said he was full of hot air, but the
father of ticketless airline travel developed a
solution that continues to soar.

12 A whole new world
HP co-founder Dave Packard returns to China
for the first time in 12 years and finds a land of
amazing change.

Page 18

14 Heeding the call
MEASURE takes a photographic look at HP's
European Customer Support Center in Amsterdam, Netherlands.

DEPARTMENTS

18 People
An HP employee turns his life
around after quadruple heart
bypass surgery.

20 On my mind
Diversity isn't about fitting in, says
Spokane (Washington) Division
G.M. Jim Rundle. It's about valuing
our differences.

22 Web-wise
Dr. Cyberspace returns with more
tips on how to use the World Wide
Web effectively.

24 Your turn
MEASURE readers share their
views on matters of importance.

26 Letter from Lew Platt
HP's chairman, president and CEO
explains the apparent contradiction
between good financial performance
and the falling stock price.

28 Extra*MEASURE*
News from around the HP world.

Figure 12.3   The table of contents for an issue of Hewlett-Packard's *Measure* magazine. The magazine supports corporate objectives by running stories about how products are used in unusual ways, how European customer support works and the value of diversity in the workplace. (*Courtesy of Hewlett-Packard Company, Palo Alto, CA.*)

modern typefaces, cutaway photos of athletes in action, and brown as a dominant second color. Stories are set in large type, ragged right, surrounded by a lot of white space. The publication, in sum, projects ruggedness and the great outdoors.

On the other hand, *One Lime Street,* published by Lloyd's of London is a 24-page newsletter with simple headlines, pages jam-packed with small type, and mug shots. It's a rather conservative publication, again reflecting the nature of the financial and insurance business.

Praxair News, mentioned earlier, is more like *USA Today* in feel and layout. There is extensive use of four-color photos, second color to highlight pages, attractive graphs and charts and short, snappy stories. It gives the image that the company is modern, up-to-date and on the move—exactly the image the organization wants to project.

The sharp graphics and short stories also reflect that the newsletter goes to employees worldwide, and in many cases, English is their second language. The graphics and illustrations clarify the written stories so that the average person—with no technical expertise—can readily understand what is being said. (See Figures 12.1 and 12.6 for illustrations of the publication.)

You need to remember that the key to good design is keeping pages simple and uncluttered. Readers should be able to count on a standard design that makes the periodical easy to follow and read. Not only is radically changing the design every issue time-consuming, it also leaves readers somewhat bewildered as to where to find regular features and articles.

Format

The most widely used format is the two- to four-page newsletter. This is the major communication vehicle of almost every organization, from the giant multinational conglomerate to the local garden club. Also popular are newsletters containing six to 12 pages.

Newsletters are relatively easy to produce, are cost-effective and can reach any number of small, specialized audiences. World processing programs such as *Word-Perfect* and *Microsoft Word* make it possible for almost anyone to produce an attractive newsletter with mastheads, a two- or three-column format and clip art. (The use of desktop publishing software is discussed shortly.)

TIPS FOR A READABLE PUBLICATION

A newsletter, newspaper or magazine should be attractive, well organized and easy to read. Here are a few tips to keep in mind:

- *Serif* typefaces, with little appendages at the end of letters, are easier to read than *sans serif* faces. Most books, including this one, are set in *serif* type. The headlines and box text, however, are in *sans serif* type.
- Use italic type for emphasis sparingly, if at all.
- Eliminate complex screens. Shading behind a block of copy often makes the type difficult to read.
- Use uncoated (not glossy) paper. Newsletters should look more business-like and less like advertising material.
- Use black ink for stories. If you use a second color, apply it as a highlight to frame a story, a quote (set in larger type) or an entire page.
- Make photos and illustrations as large as possible. Whenever possible, use action-oriented photos.
- Avoid reverse type (white type on dark background) in body copy.
- Avoid using extensive color on low quality paper. Reproduction and clarity of images suffer.
- Maintain continuity in the publication by using a minimum number of fonts and type families. A three-ring circus of type is poor design.
- Good design is based on an understanding of composition, balance and form. A fancy desktop publishing program, in the hands of an amateur, doesn't automatically produce good design.
- Use news summaries and news briefs. These columns receive high readership.

A popular format for periodicals sent to large numbers of employees or members of an organization is the tabloid-style newspaper. This format allows a great deal of flexibility in design and can contain more news stories than a newsletter, which usually comes in an 8 1/2- by 11-inch page format. A smaller number of organizations have adopted the format of what is called a *magapaper.* It has a slightly larger format than the tabloid newspaper and lends itself to somewhat larger headlines and graphic elements.

The magazine format is used by a number of large organizations as the flagship publication. These periodicals are the most expensive to produce because they often are printed on glossy paper and include multiple displays of computer graphics and full-color photographs.

They tend to be the prestige piece of the organization and concentrate on in-depth stories about people and industry trends. Stories, unlike the shorter articles found in newsletters and newspapers, tend to be two or more pages in length.

A good example of an article, which won an IABC award in the features category, is from Hewlett-Packard's *Measure* magazine. It was a five-page article, with five color pictures, about the experience of HP employees adopting babies from Romania. The same issue of the magazine also contained a six page article about how HP is responding to competitors through innovation.

Any number of formats can be used. It all depends on the purpose of the publication, the kind of messages you want to send and the nature of the audience. An added consideration is your budget.

Layout

Layout is a plan showing the arrangement of the material in the publication—the size and location of such items as stories, regularly appearing columns, headlines, photographs and artwork.

There is no exact rule for any of these items. The most important subjects should be placed on the front page of a newsletter or newspaper, and a story can be continued on latter pages.

You can place other important stories on subsequent pages by using a large display space with headlines and illustrations. Studies show that a story with a photo or a piece of artwork draws more reader attention than just black type. A rule of thumb is to place important stories on the inside right page of a publication because this is where people look first when they turn the page.

Newsletters and newspapers usually have a standardized two- or three-column framework, or *template,* that the editor uses to guide the placement of stories and illustrations. You can vary the layout by running a large headline across two or more columns.

You can also run body type across the width of two columns in a three-column publication. It is not wise to run body type across all three columns, however, because studies show that such long lines are extremely difficult to read in a newsletter. A line of type should never be more than 5 inches long.

The basic layout of a periodical should be the same from issue to issue, but each issue will vary, depending on the length of the articles, the availability of good illustrations and the relative importance of the stories.

Figure 12.4 Newsletters typically have an 8 1/2- by 11-inch page format, but they don't have to be dull. *Dateline* is published biweekly by Nissan North America for its employees and dealer network. (*Courtesy of Richard S. Christopher, internal communications, Nissan, Gardena, CA.*)

Keep the following ideas in mind as you do the layout for a publication:

- Use white space. Don't think you have to have stories or illustrations covering every single part of the page.
- Vary paragraph length. If your copy looks like the Great Wall of China, your readers will be intimidated. Make paragraphs seven lines long or less to create even more white space.

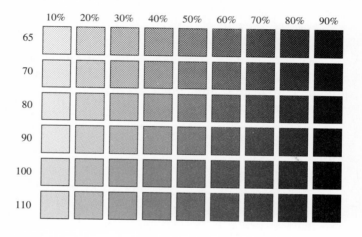

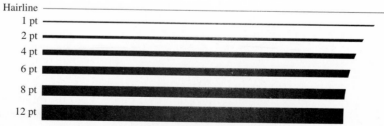

Figure 12.5 A wide variety of type and shadings are available on desktop publishing programs. If you shade a block of copy, however, keep the screen to 10 or 20 percent. *(Courtesy of LaserMaster Corporation.)*

- Break up longer stories with boldface subheads.
- Create bulleted lists. Any sentence containing a sequence of three or more items is a good list candidate. Listing also frees up more white space.
- Use only two or three typefaces to add consistency to your periodical. The variety comes in using different type sizes, not a different type family.

- Keep articles relatively short for maximum interest. If *USA Today* can summarize a world crisis in four paragraphs, you can cover the company picnic in the same amount of space.
- Inside pages should balance one another. If you use a strong graphic on one page, you should balance it with a larger headline or a graphic on the facing page.
- Use headlines that give information, not just labels such as "Company Picnic" or "New Vice President." (See the section on headline writing.)

The traditional method of layout, which hasn't changed for many people despite the computer revolution, is to work with blank dummy pages to mock up where the headlines, stories, and artwork will be placed. This requires a knowledge of copyfitting, headline writing, and photo sizing so that all your materials will fit the layout. (Copyfitting is discussed in Chapter 13.)

Once you have completed the mock-up, you take this and all your copy to a commercial printer, who will typeset the stories and headlines to your specifications. The printer will also "paste up" the finished materials according to the layout you have provided.

The other method of doing a layout is to prepare what is known as *camera-ready art*. This means that you do all the typesetting, sizing of photos and other procedures so that the printer only has to photograph your material to make a plate and put it on the offset press. This method is now known as *desktop publishing*.

Desktop Layout

The word "layout" is more accurate than "publishing" because desktop publishing software programs don't "publish" anything; what they do is allow a person to provide a commercial printer with camera-ready layouts instead of dummy pages.

Desktop publishing is discussed in Chapter 13, but it's worthwhile to mention it in the context of producing sponsored periodicals. This is particularly true since surveys of organizational editors show that almost 90 percent of them are now using desktop publishing systems to produce newsletters.

Even glossy corporate magazines are increasingly being produced with desktop systems. The Bechtel Corporation, for example, uses Quark XPress for layout and scans in photos and other artwork from a variety of sources. The result is a 24-page, award-winning magazine that makes bold use of computer graphics.

The biggest advantage of desktop publishing, according to several surveys, is keeping control over the stages of publication preparation, from the writing of copy to camera-ready output.

The computer software enables a person to draw an illustration and then crop to size, use different type fonts and sizes, vary column widths, shade or screen back graphics, add borders around copy, import graphics and photos from other sources and print out camera-ready pages for offset printing or to supply the copy on disk for laser printing in large quantities.

There is no doubt that desktop publishing has changed the old, traditional methods of producing a periodical. And thousands of novice graphic designers have been empowered to produce more attractive newsletters. At the same time, experts caution that all the fancy equipment isn't a substitute for well-trained, professional technicians and graphic designers who know what to do with the technology. Not everyone is a good designer, and one of the byproducts of desktop publishing is the "garbage dump document," put out by people who know nothing about design or good writing and think nothing of using a dozen typefaces in a single newsletter.

There's also the question of how you want to spend your time. You can write and edit the copy, take all the photos, design the periodical and prepare the camera-ready artwork—but that doesn't leave much time for other public relations duties.

Bobby Minter makes a good suggestion: "If no one on your staff is a qualified designer with desktop experience, consider hiring a designer to develop the publication's look and format and to be a consultant. You will get the benefits of the designer's skill while keeping control over production."

Illustrations

Photos and artwork were discussed extensively in Chapter 7. Many of the concepts presented there also apply to sponsored periodicals.

All publications need strong graphic elements to attract the television generation of readers. Photos must be tightly composed or cropped for impact, and a good photo should be used in as large a format as possible. A common criticism of sponsored periodicals is that they use tiny photos awash in a sea of type.

Computer-generated graphics and imported clip art are commonly used in periodicals. Clip art is available on floppy disks and CD-ROMs. In addition, if you see something in another publication or book, you can use an electronic handheld scanner to import in into your computer. (Be certain not to violate copyright laws, which were discussed in Chapter 2.) A better use of scanners is to import graphic designs commissioned by the organization.

Headlines

Writing good headlines takes practice. The headline is an important component of any story because it attracts readers. Headlines also serve as summaries for readers who want to know the basic facts but don't have time to read the story. In today's crowded information age, most of us are headline readers.

A title or a label may identify a particular feature of the publication—for example, a regular column by the president of the company could be labeled "President's Corner." For news stories, however, a sentence or capsule headline should be used. Here are a few examples from the American Express employee newspaper, *Dateline International*:

An era ends with the closing of TRS's first operations center
American Express's presence during Olympics is more than fun and games
New American dream defined by old values

The style used in these headlines is known as *downstyle* because only the first word and proper nouns are capitalized, just as in a sentence. A large number of newspapers and magazines now use this style.

A more traditional style is upper- and lowercase. In this style, all words except articles, short prepositions, and conjunctions have initial caps—for example, "New American Dream Defined by Old Values."

Both styles are acceptable; it's a matter of preference. All capital letters in a headline is not recommended because the words appear as blocks and individual letters lose their identifiable characteristics. If you want to emphasize something, it's better to use a larger type size than to use all capital letters.

Headlines should be written in active voice. It makes the news stroy more timely. Here is a headline written in passive voice: "Gift awarded to 4-H Club." Notice how much better and more timely it sounds when you write the same headline with an active verb: "Chapter awards gift to local 4-H Club."

Another way to get more information into a headline is to use what is called a *kicker*. A kicker is set in smaller type above or below the main headline. Here is an example:

Another delay
EPA hearing set for June 5

In writing headlines that require two or more lines, you should avoid splitting ideas between lines. Here is one humorous example:

Pastor Leaves for Good
Friday Services at Prison

You should also avoid ending lines with a preposition. Here is a sample of a poor headline and how it can be changed:

POOR:	Fredericks plans to take 6-month leave
BETTER:	Fredericks to take 6-month sabbatical

After writing a headline, it's always a good idea to review it for context, use of the correct word and whether it conveys the wrong impression. Here are some poor headlines found in the nation's newspapers by the *Columbia Journalism Review*:

- Auto tag fees
  to aid animals
  sitting in bank

- TV networks agree
  to police violence

- Humans have left Everglades dying of thirst

- Parking lot floods when man bursts

Praxair Development Associate Zhiyou Du (second from left), Tarrytown, N.Y., joins (left to right) Liu Ai Ping, Zhang Ning, Huang Xing Wu and Wang Ting Wu for training in Gas Technics' high-pressure cylinder fill area.

⭐ 🔄 Chinese Visitors Pick Up Technology Tips

New Techniques Attract Four from Beijing

Four supervisors and engineers from Beijing Praxair Inc. learned last month how gas packaging, product distribution and marketing are done in the USA. When they completed their three-week, whirlwind tour of Praxair distributors, labs, technical center and plants, they returned to Praxair's joint venture in Beijing to apply their new knowledge to increasing production and streamlining packaging and distribution there.

"The Beijing Praxair facility is being equipped with the most up-to-date equipment and improved technical operations and procedures," said **Jack Hercik, Praxair's Packaged and Specialty Gas technical consultant.** "This training will allow the managers and engineers to return to China and increase production and streamline packaging and distribution to supply a growing consumer base."

The four—**Wang Ting Wu, cylinder filling supervisor; Huang Xing Wu, engineering services; Liu Ai Ping, cylinder maintenance supervisor; and Zhang Ning, assistant process engineer**—spent a week at Gas Technics in North Royalton, Ohio, learning how a typical Praxair distributor conducts cylinder filling, marketing and distribution operations. The group spent the next two days at the Praxair Technology Center in Tonawanda, N.Y., where they were introduced to safety compliance management system software.

Then it was on to Praxair's facility in Harrisburg, Pa., to study cylinder and liquid container maintenance and repair. Last, they observed and had hands-on training in helium-transfill operations and instruction in proper soldering and brazing techniques at a Praxair site in Tampa, Fla.

"During our training in the States, we learned a lot of new things, especially about filling high-pressure mixed gases, filling control panels and cylinder-maintenance systems," said Wang Ting Wu. "It is really helpful to Beijing Praxair's technical innovation and development, and we will apply the techniques learned in the States to our facilities in Beijing."

The Beijing Praxair team gets some hands-on experience in Ohio.

Figure 12.6 Headlines, composition and balance make stories a single, unified unit. This story, from the pages of *Praxair News*, uses a major headline and a secondary one to convey information at a glance. Notice that the two pictures are placed diagonally across from each other to provide balance. (*Courtesy of Praxair, Inc., Danbury, CT.*)

Writing headlines requires that you know the width of the space allocated for each headline. If you have a word processing software program, you simply set the margins and type the headline in the size you want it. If it doesn't fit the space allocated to it in your mock-up or in the desktop publishing layout, you can easily enlarge or reduce it until it fits.

DISTRIBUTION

Sponsored periodicals, such as employee newsletters and newspapers, are usually distributed at the workplace. They can be placed in pickup bins through out the organization, or they can be distributed with pay envelopes.

Although this is the least expensive form of distribution, many organizations don't feel that it is very effective. Employees may not pick up the newsletter at all. Also, if it is distributed at work, productivity may suffer because people take time to read it instead of doing their work.

Many organizations feel that it is worth the expense of mailing the publication to an employee's home. A side benefit is that members of the employee's family also get a chance to read it. Corporate magazines are almost always distributed to homes, usually via second-class mail.

E-mail

Many organizations are moving to electronic newsletters. Employees receive the publication by E-mail, which is further discussed in Chapter 15. The editor, using a desktop publishing system, produces a simple newsletter that is transmitted to all employees on a computer network.

These E-mail newsletters are fast, efficient and inexpensive. However, they do have limitations. Most rely on a simple on-line format—text only, limited use of color, limited graphics, no photos or fancy design effects. This is because E-mail newsletters are received on a variety of computers, many with limited graphic capabilities.

In fact, they are simple bulletins. Headlines are one line, all caps, and the stories must be kept to one or two paragraphs. Mary Pretzer, president of Compact Training & Design in Loveland, Colorado, recommends that readers should be able to see two stories at a time on their computer screens.

Nabisco E, Nabisco's weekly electronic newsletter, uses 10 to 12 lines as the maximum story. The editor, Vic DePalo, says "You do lose readers if you put in a long, complex story." Readers don't mind scrolling between stories, but rapidly lose patience scrolling through a long story.

Since you have only about 10 lines, the writing style is more informal than in regular print publications. You can be more conversational and use less formal English than is expected in a print publication.

E-mail newsletters don't replace print publications, which still have the advantage of photos and complex artwork, but they can supplement them. Most companies use E-mail to fill the information void between the monthly or even quarterly issues of their newspapers and magazines. An organization's web site also provides an opportunity for posting E-mail newsletters.

COSTS

The cost of producing a periodical varies considerably depending on such factors as locations, use of color, number of pages, size, paper, circulation and use of outside suppliers.

Cliff McGoon, in his survey of periodicals for IABC's *Communication World* (October 1994), came up with some figures. In the category of magazines, the two-color *Arco Spark* with 20 pages cost $20,000 per issue for a press run of 50,000—or 40 cents per copy. *HP Measure,* a four-color, 32-page magazine with a press run of 95,000 cost $40,000 per issue—or 42 cents per copy. On the other hand, Beckman Instruments produced a four-color, 24-page magazine with a press run of 10,000 for $21,000 per issue—or $2.10 per copy.

In the area of magapapers, *Weyerhaeuser Today,* a two-color, 12-page publication with a press run of 60,000, costs $6,000 per issue—or 10 cents per copy. Higher up on the scale is the Shell Canada magapaper that is eight pages, four-color, with a press run of 11,000 and costs $5,000 per issue—or 45 cents per copy.

Mead Corporation publishes a two-color, 12-page newsletter with a press run of 12,500 for $4,000 per issue, or 32 cents per copy. It costs Anheuser-Busch the same amount per issue to produce a two-color, 12-page newsletter with a 10,000 copy press run.

The high cost of paper, coupled with corporate belt tightening, has forced many publications to downsize or reduce the number of issues. Many monthly publications, such as *Praxair News,* are now published 10 times a year instead of 12. Other publications have converted from a magazine format to a newsletter or magapaper format.

SUMMARY

1. Sponsored periodicals—newsletters, newspapers, magazines—are a valuable way for an organization to communicate with its key publics.
2. An editor must serve the dual role of meeting management expectations and employee needs.
3. A publication's format and content should reflect the organization's goals and objectives.
4. Today's employees want periodicals that address their concerns about the economic health of the organization and their job security.
5. Publications that merely report such information as the company teams' bowling scores and don't report business information critical to the organization's success are prime candidates for elimination.

6. Every publication should have a mission statement, about 25 words in length, that show how it helps the organization achieve success.

7. A periodical should have an editorial plan that reflects the organization's priorities for the year.

8. Periodicals differ in content and layout, according to how the organization wants to be perceived.

9. The newsletter is the most common organizational publication. Magazines, on the other hand, are often the flagship publication of the organization.

10. Desktop layout programs are now common. For best results, however, hire experienced artists and graphic designers.

11. Headlines should convey information, not just be labels.

12. Most periodicals are distributed at the workplace. A second method is by mail to the employee's home.

13. Most E-mail newsletters consist of simple on-line text. They are fast and cost-efficient, but they don't replace print periodicals.

14. E-mail newsletters require stories to be only 10 to 12 lines long; the entire story must appear on the screen at the same time.

EXERCISES

1. Collect several copies of an organization's newsletter, newspaper or magazine. Critique these publications from two perspectives. First, do content analysis. Given what you have read about what concerns employees and the organizational purpose of such publications, how does this publication measure up? Second, given the design guidelines in the chapter, how does the publication measure up? What changes would you recommend?

2. You have just been hired as editor of a new monthly employee newsletter for a chain of fast-food restaurants. Management's goals for the year are to (1) increase market share, (2) build teamwork, (3) improve customer service and (4) reduce overhead costs. Write a 25-word mission statement for the newsletter. Then prepare a 12-month editorial plan giving your ideas about the type and content of stories you would publish each month.

3. Writing headlines that are active and informative takes practice. Write a headline based on the following information. For your purposes, assume that one column is 3 inches wide and two columns are 6 inches wide. The headlines are being prepared for an employee newsletter.

   a. Lion Industries has just received a major contract from Macy's Department Stores to produce 50,000 shirts with the Macy's label in them. The $750,000 contract assures full employment at the Connecticut plant and will even necessitate the recruitment of another 50 workers.

   b. Thanks to high earnings last year, Advanced Micro Devices (AMD) has announced a 5 percent bonus for all of its 9,000 employees. According to

David Sears, president of AMD, the bonus payment will be made in the July payroll.

c. The FMC Corporation will have an awards banquet on May 15 to honor 35 workers who have made significant contributions to improving the company's productivity and reducing unnecessary costs. The workers' suggestions and ideas saved the company about $1 million in operating costs last year.

4. You are editor of a four-page newsletter for Community Hospital. The newsletter has a basic 8 1/2- by 11-inch format but measures 11 by 17 inches when opened up. The purpose of the newsletter is to inform community residents about hospital services and give tips on preventive health care. Prepare a dummy layout, showing the placement of possible stories in this newsletter. Indicate where headlines and photographs or other visual elements would be placed.

13 *Leaflets and Brochures*

Writing leaflets and brochures, like writing newsletters and magazines, requires the coordination of several elements. These include message content, selection of type, visuals, layout and design of the final piece that is distributed. It also requires working with designers and printers.

This chapter gives you a basic introduction to all these elements to familiarize you with the entire process. It won't make you an expert designer of leaflets and brochures, but it will at least make you aware of some pitfalls to avoid.

LEAFLETS

A leaflet is a single piece of printer paper. It may be a simple handbill or flier posted to a bulletin board, or it may be folded to form panels. A three-fold leaflet, for example, would have six panels with type and artwork on both sides of the page.

Because they are small and relatively low cost, leaflets are used mainly to deliver simple messages that do not involve much explanation. Among the most typical kinds of leaflets are the following:

1. *Notification*—for example, announcing an event.
2. *Information*—updating the public on new interest rates.
3. *Greeting*—welcoming visitors to an organization.
4. *Apology*—asking forbearance during construction.
5. *Activation*—requesting help.
6. *Progress*—giving periodic reports.

BROCHURES *difference between*

Brochures are often called small booklets or pamphlets. They are larger in size and content than leafles, having anywhere from eight to 48 pages or more. The pages are printed on both sides and bound together at the centerfold with staples.

Brochures are used primarily to give a thorough explanation of one specific subject. Almost anything that requires detail may be covered. Among the subjects that lend themselves to such treatment are the following:

1. *Orientiation*—for example, an explanation of the nature and composition of an organization.
2. *Rules and regulations*—restrictions and requirements that employees or constituents should know.
3. *Safety*—special warnings and procedures applicable to work and emergencies.
4. *Benefits*—health and retirement benefits available.
5. *Promotion*—opportunities and procedures.
6. *Policies*—what the organization will and will not do.
7. *Training*—study guides telling people how to do specific jobs.
8. *Obligations*—things expected of employees beyond conforming to rules (dress, conduct on the job, release of confidential information).
9. *Recreation*—organizational facilities and group activities available to employees.
10. *Recruiting*—persuading people to join the organization.
11. *Uses*—getting the most from a product. (This category includes everything from installation and operating manuals for appliances and recipe booklets to owner's manuals for automobiles and guides for home insulation.)

Whenever an organization needs to explain something to a large number of people—be they employees, constituents or customers—a brochure is the way to do it.

PLANNING

The first step in planning a leaflet or brochure is to determine its objective. Such items are always prepared to reach a specific audience and to accomplish a definite purpose, so these questions should be asked:

- Who are you trying to influence and why? Be as specific as possible in identifying the people you must reach.
- What do you want the piece to do? Be clear about the desired effect. Do you want to impress, entertain, sell, inform or educate?
- What kind of piece do you need to get your message across? Should it be a simple flier, a pocket-size brochure, a cheaply produced leaflet for widespread public distribution or a fancy four-color brochure for only key customers or opinion leaders?

Factors such as budget, number of copies needed and distribution method must be considered. In addition, you should think about the method of printing. There are various levels of printing quality that you will use depending on the answers to the above three questions. Authors Beach, Shepro and Russom refer to four levels in their book, *Getting It Printed* (Coast to Coast Books):

- **Basic** This is quick copy, such as fliers, simple business forms and one-color leaflets. Copy shops such as Kinko's and PIP are commonly used.
- **Good** This is material that requires strong colors, black and white photos and exact alignment or registration of graphic elements.
- **Premium** This requires a full-service printer, expensive paper and high-end graphic elements.
- **Showcase** Everything from design to paper and specialty inks are first class. Best for portraying an organization as well managed and successful.

WRITING

Once you have a general idea of what format you will use to communicate with your audience, you need to think about how that format shapes your writing. If you decide that a simple flier is needed, you have to be concise and to the point. Fliers, for example, contain the basic Five Ws and H—and not much more because the type must be large and the space (usually an 81/2- by 11-inch piece of paper) is limited. See Figure 13.2.

On the other hand, a simple pamphlet that has three or four panels folded to a pocket-sized format (4 inches by 9 inches) or mailed in a standard business envelope (#10) can contain more detailed information. See Figure 13.3 on page 326.

Let's face it: we'd all like a little more pay in *our* pockets each month, and a little *less* in Uncle Sam's.

But schemes to cut taxes often are risky. Complicated. *Illegal.* Or just for people whose incomes leave you wondering why they're worried about taxes anyway.

But now, it's easy to cut your taxes–no matter what your income–and even the IRS approves. With *tax-free* FlexibleFit Spending Accounts for paying health and day care expenses.

Why call them *flexible* spending accounts? Because they can s-t-r-e-t-c-h your income.

The idea behind flexible spending accounts is simple. And the way they work is convenient. You just direct PVH to set aside a portion of your income each pay period. We place it in an account–with no taxes ever withheld–and you use it to cover the cost of certain health care expenses or day care charges.

You still pay bills you would have paid anyway. But you pay them with *tax-free* money.

It's easy. It's elegant. And when April 15th arrives, you'll discover it can save you up to hundreds of dollars a year.

There are two kinds of flexible spending accounts: for health care and for day care.

You can deposit up to $2,000 a year in a Health Care Flexible Spending Account.

You can use your Health Care Flexible Spending Account to pay your annual FlexibleFit deductibles and copayments–portions of health care bills for which you're responsible. But that's not all.

Many of your medical and dental bills will be paid by FlexibleFit. But what if you've selected a dental option that doesn't include orthodontia–and now you need

Figure 13.1 Brochure copy should be conversational and concise. This page from an employee benefits brochure shows how a complex subject can be made interesting and understandable to employees. Notice that the theme is supported by the selection of artwork around the copy. The artwork goes to the edge of the page, which is called a "bleed" in printer's terms. (*Courtesy of Mike Vogel, Poudre Valley Hospital, Fort Collins, CO.*)

Whatever the format, you should keep it in mind as you write copy. The most common mistake of novice public relations writers is to write more than the proposed format can accommodate. A second major mistake is trying to cram it all in by reducing type size or margins instead of editing, thus creating a mass of dense type that nobody wants to read. Indeed, the most difficult concept to learn is that less is best. Copy should be short and should have plenty of white space around it. This means ample margins, space between major subsections, and room for appropriate graphics.

The concepts of good writing, elaborated on in previous chapters, are the same for leaflets and brochures. Short, declarative sentences are better than compound sentences. Short paragraphs are better than long ones. Major points should be placed in bullet lists or under subheads. It's always a good idea to pretest brochure copy on members of the target audience to be sure that it is understandable and that you have included all the necessary information.

Gathering Information

Gathering information for use in a leaflet or brochure may involve anything from asking a few questions to conducting a major survey. In most cases, the needed information can be found within the organization.

Keeping in mind the subject and purpose of the proposed publication, start by talking to the people in the organization who know the most about the subject. Tell them what you want to accomplish, and ask for information that will enable you to prepare a clear explanation of the subject. Often, all the needed information can be obtained from one source.

A good way to decide what to include in a leaflet or a brochure is to put yourself in the position of a member of the prospective audience. Ask every question that this person might have about the subject. The answers can constitute sections of the publication. You can even use the questions as subheads. Many successful brochures have consisted entirely of questions and answers.

Putting It Together

Publications vary so widely that no general guide is applicable. Each has a different audience, a different purpose and a different format. It is imperative to use words that your readers will understand. If you have to explain a technical topic, check with the experts once you have put the story into everyday English to be sure you've got it right. For any but the briefest publications, you will need to prepare an outline. This should cover all the main points to be included, and it should list the illustrations to be used.

As you write and plan the layout of the publication, remember to put visual variety in your pages. Illustrations, blocks of copy and headlines not only serve the direct purpose of communication but can also make the pages attractive and interesting. Some writers recommend preparing a complete layout before starting to write. Others prefer to develop the layout after the writing is finished. A practical compromise is to prepare a rough layout before writing and then to revise it as the writing progresses.

WEALTH OF HEALTH

MT. DIABLO MEDICAL CENTER

CELEBRATE HEALTH!

FREE FAMILY FUN

SATURDAY, MARCH 2
9 A.M. TO 3 P.M.

2540 East St., Concord

FREE SCREENINGS*
- Cholesterol
- Blood Pressure
- Skin Cancer
- Oral Cancer
- Foot and Ankle
- Vision and Glaucoma
- Aerobic Capacity
- Computerized Body Fat ($10)

EDUCATION
- Breast Self-Exam
- Freedom from Smoking
- Information on:
  - Arthritis
  - Cancer
  - Diabetes
  - Home Care
  - Nutrition
  - HIV/AIDS
  - Senior Health
  - Digestive Health
  - Weight Management
  - Laser Technology
  - Tattoo Removal
  - Outpatient Surgery
  - Peripheral Vascular Disease

KIDS' KORNER
- Traveler The Clown *(10 a.m.-1 p.m.)*
- Hands-on Learning
- Nutrition Tips for Parents
- Immunization Check Lists

FREE CONSULTATIONS
- Physician Consultation
- Ask-A-Cardiologist
- Ask-A-Pharmacist
- Physician Referral
- Plastic Surgery Computer Imaging

DEMONSTRATIONS/DISPLAYS
- Heart Healthy Cooking
- Mammography
- CPR and Heimlich Maneuver
- Cardiac Surgery
- Intensive Care Equipment
- New Heart Surgery Techniques
- Diagnostic Cardiology
- Emergency Vehicles
- Biofeedback, Stress & Anger Management
- Arthroscopy
- Infection Control

FREE NO-FAT, LOW-FAT FOODS

TOURS
- Regional Cancer Center
- The Family Birthplace

NO PRE-REGISTRATION IS NECESSARY. SEE YOU THERE!

MT. DIABLO MEDICAL CENTER
2540 EAST STREET, CONCORD

*Due to staffing and time limitations, screenings are done on a first come basis on this day only.

OPERATED BY MT. DIABLO HEALTH CARE DISTRICT

Figure 13.2 This flier about a health fair uses large type and bullets to convey basic information in an easy-to-read format. (*Courtesy of Teddi Grant Adel, Mt. Diablo Medical Center, Livermore, CA.*)

WELCOME!

Welcome to Knott's® Camp Snoopy,® the largest indoor themed entertainment park in America! It's seven acres of year-round excitement. And it's all yours!

Twenty-three rides and attractions. . .seven shops. . .three entertainment theaters. . . fourteen places to eat! It all adds up to a world of fun for the whole family! Welcome to endless adventure! Welcome to Knott's® Camp Snoopy®!

PEANUTS Characters: © 1950, 1952, 1958, 1965 United Feature Syndicate, Inc.

Pay-per-ride or attraction admission to Knott's® Camp Snoopy® allows guest to enter the park at no charge. Each ride and show has a point value ranging from two to five points.

GENERAL INFORMATION

Point passes may be purchased at ticket booth locations throughout the park on the first level and at the Guest Relations office on the second level. Point passes are valid for one year from the date of purchase, or until all points have been used, unless specified. Passes may also be purchased at the self-help automated ticketing systems (ATS) located throughout the park. To enter any ride or show, swipe the bar code on the point pass beneath the scanner located at each turnstile.

The Park opens at 10 a.m. Sunday through Friday and 9 a.m. on Saturdays. Closing times vary. For information call 612-883-8800.

Guest Relations, located on the second level, is available to assist with lost children, lost and found items and all general information. Please ask a friendly Knott's® Camp Snoopy® employee for assistance.

Major credit cards are honored for point passes and at all merchandise shops and restaurants in Knott's® Camp Snoopy.®

Locker rental is available for a small fee, next to the Ford Playhouse and near the Peanuts Gallery.

Restrooms are located near the Festhaus Buffet on the second level, near the Ford Playhouse on the first level and next to the Peanuts Gallery.

Group Rates are available on a pre-arranged basis for parties of 20 or more. Call 612-883-8600 for more information.

Snoopy Birthday Parties are available in the Peanuts Party Garden for groups of six or more. To reserve your date call 612-883-8600.

Special Guest Information

Special guest information is provided to accommodate physically challenged guests. Most areas of the park are accessible. To find out more about specific guidelines please request a customized print-out of all rides suitable for accommodating your special needs at the Guest Relations office. Please feel free to request additional assistance from our friendly employees at any time throughout the day.

Stroller and wheelchair rentals are located at Mall of America Guest Service areas at Mall entrances.

All hours, pricing, and information subject to change.

Figure 13.3 These two inside panels of a leaflet use line art, headlines and different type sizes to convey basic information. (*Courtesy of Knott's Camp Snoopy, Bloomington, MN.*)

Choosing the Format

Before deciding on the format of printed materials, get samples of items like those you want to produce. Note how they were done and be guided by them. As explained earlier, there are two basic formats: the leaflet, one piece of paper that may

BROCHURE AND LEAFLET PLANNING GUIDELINES

1. *Define purpose and audience.* What exactly is the purpose or objective? Are you producing a sales document? An instruction booklet? An overview of your organization's service capabilities? And what will be the target audience? It is important to define the audience in the most precise terms so that you can tailor the message to their needs.

2. *Determine usage and life span.* Size and format are determined by answering several questions. Will your publication be carried in a pocket? Mailed in an envelope? Placed in an information rack? Used as a self-mailer? Distributed widely or only to VIPs? Will the copy need frequent updating? How long will it be used?

3. *Position your subject.* No company, product, service or concept is exactly like any other. Each has its unique personality, capabilities and strong points. Determine what makes your organization's services or products different from those of the competition. In other words, your brochure should dramatize and focus on unique aspects that make your organization outstanding.

4. *Establish budget parameters.* There's no point in thinking about a fancy four-color brochure when your budget will allow only a simple one-color approach. An approximate budget should be established early. It should include the cost of planning, design, writing, finished artwork, printing and mailing.

5. *Set up a realistic schedule.* Don't decide to do a brochure one week and expect it to be printed the next week. Printed items take a lot more planning (and various skilled personnel) than a basic news release. A simple flier may be produced in a matter of days, but a complicated brochure—writing, layout, approvals, artwork, proofs, printing and mailing—can take months. For example, corporate annual reports are typically started six months in advance of publication.

6. *Research other materials.* A review of other printed materials will give you ideas about the size, look or feel that you want. This research can also give you ideas about type size, paper stock, illustrations and color. Showing these items to top managers will also give them an opportunity to envision what yours will look like when completed.

Source: Adapted from guidelines written by Robert Clay, president of Clay Publicom, Irvine, California.

be folded, and the brochure or booklet, two or more pieces of paper bound together. The binding may be *saddle stitched,* in which case the pieces of paper are folded in the middle, placed one on the other like a saddle on a horse, and then, as they lie open, stapled together on the centerfold. If the booklet is large, it may be *side stitched:* With the booklet closed, the pages are stapled about 1/2 inch from the centerfold. A side-stitched booklet will not lie flat when it is open, whereas a saddle stiched one will. If the booklet is side stitched, it will require a separate cover. Booklets can be "self-covered" or have covers made of a different paper.

With either format, you must think about the number of pages. Leaflets may be folded in many different ways, from a simple fold into four pages to elaborate arrangements with numerous panels. Remember that brochures are done in four-

---

SCHEDULING A BROCHURE'S PRODUCTION

Producing a brochure requires setting up a timetable of activities that must be done. One approach is to determine when you want to distribute the finished product and work back in time:

- What is the mailing or distribution date?
- When does printing have to be completed?
- When is the final press proof?
- When are the proofs and color keys due?
- When do camera-ready materials have to be delivered to the printer?
- When does production begin?
- When do layout and design begin?
- When are final copy and graphics due?
- When does content have to be finalized?
- When is senior management review?
- When are copy revisions due?
- When is first-draft editorial due?
- When is the editorial plan due?

Source: Publication Productions, New York.

---

page units. Your brochure should therefore be made up of eight pages or any multiple of four. For example, if you have material for 14 pages, you will either have two extra pages (which may be blank, for a total of 16), or you must cut two (for a total of 12).

Preparing a Dummy Layout

The layout is the plan for the finished piece. It may be rough or comprehensive, but it must be accurate enough for the person who assembles the parts to do exactly what you want. The first step in making a layout is to prepare a *dummy*—a blank-paper mock-up of the finished product. It should be made of the paper to be used in the printed piece and should be the same size. If the piece is to be a booklet, the dummy should be stapled just as the finished booklet will be. If it is to be a leaflet, the dummy should be folded the same way.

With the dummy at hand, you can now plan where everything is to go. For a leaflet, the layout will be complete—it will indicate what is to go on each page. For a small booklet, the layout will also be complete, but if there are many pages, you will need to design only the cover and sample pages of the body.

The layout indicates both type and illustrations. Thus a page layout might show various blocks of copy, headlines and the location of illustrations for that page. For very simple jobs, you may make the layout yourself; however, most printers are able and willing to do this for you, especially on big jobs.

PRODUCTION

With the copy written, illustrations selected, and general format decided, it is time to think about production—getting the material printed. So far this chapter has been devoted to leaflets and brochures, but we can now include newsletters, posters, placards and anything else that involves the use of typeset material and some kind of printing press. Here we give you only the highlights. For full information, see *Pocket Pal,* published by the International Paper Company.

Printing Processes

Four main processes are used: offset lithography, letterpress, gravure and screen printing.

Offset Lithography   This is the most popular form of printing. It is based on two premises. Frist, grease and water do not mix. Second, ink is offset from the plate to a rubber blanket, then from the blanket to the paper.

Offset printing has two advantages: (1) make ready or press preparation is minimal, and (2) a wide range of paper qualities can be handled.

Letterpress   This is the oldest printing method, and it was the most popular before the advent of offset printing. It uses the relief method from cast metal type or plates on which the image or printing areas are raised above the nonprinting areas. Letterpress images tend to be crisp and sharp.

Gravure (Intaglio)   This method uses a sunken or depressed surface for the image and is excellent for printing newspaper supplements and catalogs where color is used.

Screen Printing (Silk Screen)   This is simply ink, with the consistency of paint, forced through a fine silk or Dacron mesh by a squeegee. A stencil on the screen controls which areas receive ink and which do not. Screen printing is versatile and is ideal for short runs. T-shirts are printed this way.

Finding a Printer

A variety of printers and printing processes are found in every city. In even the smallest town, there is likely to be at least one printer. Some small towns may have only a photocopying service, but in most cases there will be a shop that can do offset printing.

In any case, you must find a firm that can print your material. The classified phone directory will list all of the possibilities. If there are only a few, it is possible to call on them and find out what they can do. In larger cities, the number may be

PREPARING CAMERA-READY LAYOUTS
THROUGH DESKTOP PUBLISHING

Brochures and leaflets, as well as newsletters and magazines, can now be written and designed using computer software.

The most popular software program is *Aldus PageMaker,* used by 70 percent of the respondents. Other popular programs are *Ventura Publisher* and *Quark XPress.* The most popular illustration programs used in conjunction with desktop communications are *Adobe Illustrator* and *Aldus Freehand,* but a variety of other programs are used.

Word processing programs also have some desktop publishing capability. *Microsoft Word for Windows* allows the user to set up simple two- or three-column formats and to create charts for line drawings. A simple leaflet, brochure, flyer or newsletter can adequately be prepared in such a fashion.

Electronic scanners, now handheld, can also import artwork and photos into your computer for insertion in a layout. There are also a number of clip art programs, on floppy disk or compact disc, that can be used in conjunction with a desktop publishing program.

Although desktop publishing has made it possible for individuals to do more creative layouts and to prepare materials in a more attractive manner, experts caution that you still need more than computer skills. You also need design, writing and editing skills to come up with a camera-ready layout that looks professional. As one public relations practitioner observed, "Those skills aren't necessarily found in a single person under normal circumstances," whether or not that person has a computer.

daunting. In such a situation, you can call on those nearby or talk to your colleagues and get their recommendations. In fact, word of mouth may be the best way to choose a printer.

Having located some prospects, you should meet with them or their sales representatives. Tell them what you want to do and ask what they can do. Look at samples of their work. Find out what their services cost. Some firms can and will do everything, even the writing. Others may be specialized. There are firms that do typesetting alone. Some will prepare camera-ready art from your copy and layout. Some will print only from the camera-ready art. There are also firms that do only binding.

PAPER

The weight of the paper may range from very light (such as bond) to very heavy (such as cover stock). There is also a range of weights within these classes. Usually, the heavier the paper within a class, the more it costs. Thus a 100-pound cover is more expensive than a 50-pound cover. These weights are based on the actual weight of 500 sheets of that paper in the standard sheet size. For your purposes, you need only remember that heavier paper is bulkier, stronger and more expensive.

THE JARGON OF PRODUCING A BROCHURE

When working with graphic designers and printers to produce a pamphlet or brochure, you need to know some basic terms.

- **bleed** An element that extends beyond the trimmed edge of a finished page. Most often used in the context of a photo going to the edge of the page.
- **dylux** The final proof of composed film work—made on photosensitive paper with what will print blue—used to check the position of page elements and allowances for folding and binding.
- **camera-ready** Description of artwork that is suitable for photographic reproduction on film or a printing plate.
- **mechanical** Type, photos, line art and so forth assembled on a single board to be used for reproduction by a printer.
- **plus cover** A designation that a brochure or pamphlet contains a certain number of pages not including the four pages that make up the cover. For example, "16 pages plus cover" indicates that the brochure actually contains 20 pages.
- **self-cover** A designation indicating that a printed piece such as a brochure or pamphlet uses the same paper for the inside pages as for the cover.
- **scoring** Creasing sheets of paper to make folding easier.

GETTING A COST ESTIMATE

Printers need detailed specifications before they can tell you how much your pamphlet or brochure will cost. When you contact a printer, be prepared to provide the following information:

- Size of piece
- Print quantity
- Number of colors
- Type and quantity of photos and illustrations
- Number of folds
- Whether there are "bleeds"
- Type of binding
- Quality and weight of paper
- Whether there will be die cuts or embossing
- Delivery deadlines

It's also a good idea to show printers a "dummy" or sample of what your piece will look like so they can see what you require. This preliminary "look see" will help them spot potential problems.

Source: Media Distribution Services (MDS), New York.

The intended use will guide you in selecting the weight of paper. A simple one-page leaflet might be printed on 20- or 24-pound bond. If you want it to be more substantial, you could use a 65-pound paper. Brochures are usually printed on fairly substantial paper. This makes them look more impressive and last longer. Another thing to consider is the total bulk of the item. If you choose a heavy paper for a booklet that is to be mailed, you may have to pay more for postage. Still another thing to bear in mind is folding; for example, heavy paper does not fold as readily as lighter paper.

There are seven types of paper that you are most likely to use. Their standard sheet size and characteristics are listed below.

- **Bond** (17" × 22") for lightweight directories, letters, business forms, newsletters and quick printing.
- **Text** (25" × 28") for a textured look on annual reports, announcements, books, calendars and so on.
- **Coated** (25" × 38") for a smooth, high-quality look on brochures, magazines and posters. Coated, or glossy, paper is ideal for photographs and color printing.
- **Book** (25" × 38") for an antique or smooth finish on trade and textbooks. Less expensive than text paper.
- **Cover** (20" × 26") for a stable, durable quality to complement text and coated papers for covers and booklets.
- **Tag** (24" × 26") for good bending and folding qualities. Good for pamphlets that have several folds.
- **Bristol** (22" × 28") for a softer surface than tag or index paper. Good for high-speed folding, embossing or stamping.

Paper usually represents 35 to 50 percent of the printing cost for most jobs, so you should take care in selecting the paper that is appropriate to your budget and needs. Prices on coated or textured paper, as indicated, are higher than prices on standard stocks of Bond or Bristol papers.

Another option is recycled paper. Increasingly, organizations are using such paper for letterheads, envelopes, office forms and brochures. In fact, one survey of public relations people indicated that 90 percent of them had selected recycled paper for printing documents. The main reason for selecting recycled paper was concern for the environment. A large percentage of respondents also thought that it benefited the organization's image.

TYPE

In thinking about type, you must be familiar with a few terms that apply to all type sizes and faces. "Uppercase" means capital letters, "lowercase" means small letters. "Ascender" means the part above the body of the letter, like the top of the letter "h," and "descender" means the part below the body of the letter, like the bottom of the letter "g." Capital letters do not have ascenders or descenders. A "serif" is any tiny line that projects from the main stroke of a letter, such as the strokes that form the foot on which the lowercase "r" rests. Type size is measured from the top of the ascender to the bottom of the descender.

Type Classes

There are several ways in which to classify type, but the simplest is to organize the various faces into three groups: serif, sans serif, and decorative.

Serif types, such as the oldstyle Caslon and the modern Caledonia, are the most readable because the serifs help guide the eye along the lines of type.

Sans serif types, such as Helvetica, are very popular at present. Some of the earlier types in this group were hard to read in body copy but quite satisfactory in headlines. The newer designs seem to work well for body copy also.

Decorative typefaces, such as Script and Old English, should be used with great care. They look elegant on certificates and invitations but should not be used for large blocks of text.

Type Families

Thanks to computer graphics, laser printer postscript cartridges and desktop publishing programs, any number of type fonts are available in countless variations. Among the possibilities are Times Roman, Helvetica, New Century Schoolbook, Avant Garde and Palatino. There is also a selection of decorative typefaces that have shading, stripes and ultramodern designs.

The advantage of computer type, which most commercial printers now use, is that it's scalable to any size. In desktop publishing, if a headline doesn't quite fit the layout, a few clicks on the mouse will reduce it until it fits.

Commercial printers and graphic artists have catalogs of the computer type fonts they have available on their typesetting systems.

One note of caution: People are so impressed with the variety of type styles available that they try to use too many in a given publication. Novice desktop publishing enthusiasts tend to go overboard, and the result is a mishmash of conflicting styles that almost guarantees reader confusion.

Legibility and Readability

Legibility is affected by the typeface. Any Garamond letter is more legible than any Old English letter. Readability is affected by the legibility of the type and by letter spacing, line spacing, the length of the lines, the color of paper and ink, the kind of paper and the total amount of reading matter involved. A leaflet could be effective with headings printed in 36-point Times Roman, but using such big type for body text in a 16-page booklet would waste paper and discourage reading.

The only purpose in printing anything is to get it read. Accordingly, any printed material should be planned with readability in mind. Select a legible type and, if necessary, use letter spacing to spread headlines. Use line spacing to improve the readability of lowercase body copy. Keep the length of lines short enough that each can be read as one unit. As a general rule, try to use type no smaller than 10-point for body copy. Its readability will be improved by line spacing—placing the lines farther apart. Line spacing is called *leading* and is specified in points; thus, type may be 10 or 11 points high with 2 points of leading between the lines.

Printers' Measurements

Type letters are measured in *points.* There are approximately 72 points to an inch, so a 36-point headline is about 1/2 inch high. Type lines are measured in *picas.* There are approximately 6 picas to an inch, so a 24-pica line is 4 inches wide. Picas are also used to measure the depth of a block of copy. Thus a page that is 42 picas deep will measure approximately 7 inches. Inch measurements are *not* used in typesetting. Always specify type by points and picas.

Another term used in typesetting is "em," which is a square of the size of that particular type (or roughly the space taken up by the letter "M" in that point size.) A 12-point em is about 1/6 inch high and 1/6 inch wide. The use of ems is largely

Figure 13.4   A large variety of type is available for the production of leaflets and brochures. This sample (shown at reduced size) shows some type sizes and fonts that one company makes available for use by laser printers. *(Courtesy of XLI Corporation.)*

limited to indicating paragraph indention. A very narrow indention might be one em. A wide indention could be four or five ems. The em is always related to the size of type being used in the body copy of the material being typeset.

INK

Printing ink comes in a rainbow of colors, but black is the most common in leaflets and brochures. There are two reasons for this. First, black provides the strongest and clearest contrast on white or tinted paper. Second, printers typically have presses set up for black ink so the cost is cheaper than substituting another color.

The cost of printing, of course, goes up each time you add a color. To change ink colors for multicolor production, the printer has to wash the press and change the printing plate before a new color can be applied. Although inks account for a small part of the printing budget, you pay a separate charge for each washup.

You may, however, wish to use a second or third color to make the brochure more attractive and to highlight various pieces of information. Headlines, for example, might be printed in a different color. Color can also be used as a light screen behind body text. Use the *Pantone Matching System* (PMS), a virtual catalog of colors, to help you choose an exact hue of blue or any other color. Instead of asking for a dusty light blue, you can ask for a specific number associated with a swatch on a color chart. PMS color charts are available at your local art supply store.

With any color of ink, however, you must consider the color of the paper on which it will be printed. No color will read well against a dark colored stock. Black ink on dark green paper, for example, makes the copy almost impossible to read and causes eye strain. Consequently, the best choice is white paper or something in pastel or neutral shades.

Listen to the advice of your designer and printer. They are much more knowledgeable about how inks and paper go together for maximum effectiveness and readability. A printer's input is particularly important if you plan to use full-color photography.

PREPARING COPY FOR THE GRAPHIC DESIGNER

There are two ways to prepare copy for graphic designers. One is the traditional approach, which you follow when working with designers or printers who aren't fully computerized. The other is the desktop approach, which is keyed to preparing camera-ready art and sending it via a diskette or modem to the printer. Media Distribution Services, a New York printing and distribution firm, outlines the two approaches.

Traditional Approach

- Double space your manuscript copy on 8 1/2- by 11-inch paper.
- Use one side of the paper only.
- Number the pages consecutively to coordinate the manuscript for typesetting.

COPYFITTING IN EIGHT EASY STEPS

By following these steps, you can determine how much space copy will take up when set in type. Computer typesetting can do much of this copyfitting automatically, but you should understand the process.

1. Count the characters (letters and spaces) in an average line of copy. Or measure the length, in inches, of an average line and multiply by 10 if it's pica type or by 12 if it's elite type (for example, 5 1/2 inches of elite type = 63 characters).
2. Count the number of written lines (for example, 27 lines).
3. Multiply the number of lines by the number of characters per line (63 x 27 = 1701 characters).
4. Decide how wide you want the lines of type to be (say, 24 picas).
5. From your typebook, select the type you want to use, and count the number of characters in a line of 24 picas (say, 60 characters).
6. Divide this number into the total character count (1701 ÷ 60 = 28.3 lines).
7. From your typebook, find out how many lines of the chosen type will go into an inch of depth (7 lines per inch).
8. Divide the number of lines per inch into the total number of lines (28.3 ÷ 7 = 4 1/2 inches = 26 picas).

Figure 13.5 Although aimed at different audiences, brochures often share common design elements to give a unifying theme and identity to the organization. (*Courtesy of Blossom Hill Winery, Sonoma, CA.*)

MAKE IT EASY TO READ

Leaflets and brochures should be designed to convey information in an attractive, un-cluttered way. Here are some tips.

Copy

- Less is better. Write short, punchy sentences. Keep paragraphs short.
- Use informative subheads to break up copy blocks.
- Use bullets to list key points.

Layout

- Don't cram the page with copy; allow for plenty of white space.
- Organize layout from left to right and top to bottom. Most people read in this sequence; don't confuse them with another arrangement.
- Avoid large blocks of reverse type (white on black). It's difficult to read.
- Facing pages should be composed as two-page spreads; that's how readers see them.
- Use graphics and photos to balance blocks of copy.

Type

- The best type size for text is 10 or 11 point with 2 points of leading. If the target audience is senior citizens, increase the type size to 12 or 14 point.
- Use serif type for text. It is easier to read. Headlines can be set in sans serif type.
- Use standard typefaces; fancy typography only confuses people.
- Use boldface sparingly. Use for subheads and a few key words only. Don't use for an entire paragraph.
- Avoid all caps in headlines. Caps, lowercase is more readable.

Color

- Black ink is best for body copy. Black ink on light colored paper yields a high comprehension level.
- Headlines can use color, but the ink should be on the dark side.

- Make sure copy is neat and readable.
- Mark copy with standard copyediting marks. For example, a single underline indicates *italics*. A double underline indicates SMALL CAPS. A wavy underline means **bold face**.
- Proofread your manuscript thoroughly. It saves time and costly corrections later.
- Leave sufficient space in the margins and between paragraphs to provide room for instructions to the designer.
- Mark copy blocks for type size and leading. For example, write in the margin, 10/12 Times Roman.

- Key each paragraph, as needed, for positioning in the printed piece.
- If necessary, provide a rough layout of the proposed printed piece, including position of type, illustrations and other specifications. This is often called a dummy layout.

Desktop Approach

- Prepare your manuscript in word processing software that is compatible with the designer's computer system. Another approach is to prepare the material in ASCII file format (American Standard Code for Information), which allows the designer to reformat the document in his or her computer typefaces.
- Prepare the manuscript along the same guidelines as you would for traditional copy, using whatever graphic capabilities are available to indicate type sizes, type styles (italics, etc.) and other simple design elements such as bullets and dashes.
- Send the manuscript to the designer or printer via a modem or a diskette. It's also recommended that you fax or include a dummy layout of the printed piece for general guidance. This should be a simple document; don't try to do a complete, finished design. That's the designer's job.
- Once the designer has done his or her job, request a printout so you can proofread and check everything before it is actually printed.

SUMMARY

1. Leaflets can be single-page fliers or a folded page with printing on both sides.
2. Brochures are more elaborate and contain more copy than leaflets. They are multiple-page, printed both sides, and have a binding such as saddle stitching.
3. Writing and designing a leaflet or brochure requires you to know its purpose, the target audience and the most cost-effective format.
4. Writing a leaflet or brochure requires simple sentence construction, short paragraphs and liberal use of subheads.
5. The most common mistake of a novice writer is to write too much copy for the space available. A brochure page crammed with type is a turnoff.
6. Factors such as cost, distribution and estimated life span of the leaflet or brochure help determine the format of the printed piece and the kind of writing required.
7. It pays to prepare a dummy or mock layout of the proposed leaflet or brochure before you begin writing.
8. Offset lithography is the most versatile and popular form of printing today.
9. A printer needs to know all the specifications of a planned piece before he or she can give you a cost estimate.

10. There are various grades of paper, each designed for specific kinds of jobs.
11. There are various type classes and families. Stick to standard type styles.
12. Black ink is the most popular and readable color for body copy.
13. Although you may be able to design a simple flier or leaflet, use a graphic designer for bigger jobs.
14. Desktop publishing is now widely used for preparing leaflets and brochures.

EXERCISES

1. Get several leaflets and brochures produced by various organizations—either nonprofit groups or businesses. Based on the suggestions and guidelines in the chapter, write a critique of these sample materials from the standpoint of (a) the purpose of the printed piece, (b) its intended audience, (c) writing style, (d) selection of type, (e) selection of artwork and other visual aids and (f) selection of paper stock. At the end of your critique, provide an overall evaluation of the item's effectiveness.

2. The key to writing and designing an effective brochure is planning. Select a campus or community organization for the purpose of planning a brochure. Then, in outline form, provide information under the following headings: (a) name and brief background of the organization, (b) purpose or objective of the proposed brochure, (c) intended audience, (d) major theme and key copy points, (e) budget constraints, (f) estimated number of copies needed, (g) life span of proposed brochure, (h) method of distribution and (i) schedule for writing, designing, production and distribution.

3. Write a brochure for a campus organization. You should write the copy and do a mock-up or dummy layout of the brochure showing the placement of headlines, copy blocks and any illustrations. Be sure to consider all the factors listed in exercise 2.

4. Using a word processing program or desktop publishing software, create a flyer or a leaflet for an upcoming event on campus or in the community.

5. It is often necessary to calculate how much space copy will occupy once it's printed in the size of type used in a leaflet. Using the boxed titled "Making It Easy To Read" as the original copy, convert this material to an 18-pica line using 10-point type with 2 points of leading 10/12. We know from the typebook that there are 45 characters in an 18-pica line of 10/12 type and that it takes five lines of this type to equal 1 column inch.

14 | *Public Relations Advertising*

Advertising is another communication tool that a public relations writer may use to reach target audiences.

Unlike news releases, which are sent to media editors for possible use, advertising is purchased space in a mass medium. This insures that the message is printed or broadcast exactly as you want it—in the format that you specify. It also means that you control the exact timing and context of your message.

This chapter discusses the types of advertising that can be used in a public relations campaign—image building, financial relations, public service, advocacy and announcements—and gives some tips on how to write an effective advertisement. It also reviews the use of billboards, posters, T-shirts and sponsored books as other ways to communicate public relations messages.

THE CONCEPT OF PUBLIC RELATIONS ADVERTISING

The American Marketing Association defines advertising as "any paid form of non-personal presentation of ideas, goods, or services by an identified sponsor." Melvin DeFleur and Everett Dennis, authors of *Understanding Mass Media,* go even further and state, "Advertising tries to inform consumers about a *particular* product and to persuade them to make a *particular decision*—usually the decision to buy the product."

They are describing the most common forms of advertising—national consumer advertising (the ad in *Time* magazine about a new car model) and retail advertising (the ad in the local paper telling you where to buy it).

However, advertising can serve other purposes besides just persuading people to buy a product or service. Todd Hunt and Brent Ruben, authors of *Mass Communication: Producers and Consumers,* say other purposes of advertising might be to build consumer trust in an organization *(institutional advertising),* create a favorable opinions and attitudes *(goodwill or public service advertising)* and motivate people to support a cause or a political candidate *(issue or political advertising).*

These kinds of advertising can be placed under the umbrella of public relations advertising. In fact, the American National Advertisers and Publishers Information Bureau suggests several characteristics that distinguish public relations advertising. The following list uses the word "company," but the concept is applicable to any organization, including nonprofits, trade groups and special interest groups.

1. It must educate or inform the public regarding the company's policies, functions, facilities, objectives, ideals and standards.
2. It must create a climate of favorable opinion about the company by stressing the competence of the company's management, accumulated scientific knowledge, manufacturing skills, technological progress and contribution to social advancement and public welfare.
3. It must build up the investment qualities of the company's securities or improve the financial structure of the company.
4. It must sell the company as a good place in which to work, often in a way designed to appeal to recent college graduates or people with certain skills.

In other words, public relations advertising doesn't directly sell goods or services. Instead, its purpose is to create a favorable climate of understanding and public support that allows an organization to succeed in its organizational objectives. Of course, these objectives include the selling of goods and services.

ADVANTAGES OF ADVERTISING

Advertising is paid and controlled mass communication. This means that the organization completely bypasses the newsroom gatekeepers and places its messages, exactly as written and formatted, with the medium's advertising department. Thus a

A defense against cancer can be cooked up in your kitchen.

Fruits, vegetables, and whole-grain cereals such as oatmeal, bran and wheat may help lower the risk of colorectal cancer.

Foods high in fats, salt- or nitrite-cured foods like ham, and fish and

There is evidence that diet and cancer are related. Some foods may promote cancer, while others may protect you from it.

Foods related to lowering the risk of cancer of the larynx and esophagus all have high amounts of carotene, a form of vitamin A which is in cantaloupes, peaches, broccoli, spinach, all dark green leafy vegetables, sweet potatoes, carrots, pumpkin, winter squash and tomatoes, citrus fruits and brussels sprouts.

Foods that may help reduce the risk of gastrointestinal and respiratory tract cancer are cabbage, broccoli, brussels sprouts, kohlrabi, cauliflower.

types of sausages smoked by traditional methods should be eaten in moderation.

Be moderate in consumption of alcohol also.

A good rule of thumb is cut down on fat and don't be fat.

Weight reduction may lower cancer risk. Our 12-year study of nearly a million Americans uncovered high cancer risks particularly among people 40% or more overweight.

Now, more than ever, we know you can cook up your own defense against cancer. So eat healthy and be healthy.

No one faces cancer alone.

AMERICAN CANCER SOCIETY

Figure 14.1 Public service advertisements provide information and tips that help people in their daily lives. This one discusses how to lower the risk of cancer through proper diet. (*Courtesy of the American Cancer Society.*)

primary reason for using advertising as a communications tool is that control of the message remains with the sender.

Some other advantages of advertising are its selectivity and the advertiser's control of the impact and timing.

Audience Selection

Specific audiences can be reached with advertising messages on the basis of such variables as location, age, income, and lifestyle. This is done by closely studying the audience demographics of newspapers, magazines, and broadcast shows. BMW, for example, advertises in magazines such as the *New Yorker* and the *National Geographic* that have highly educated and affluent readers. The neighborhood deli, on the other hand, may only advertise in the local weekly that serves the immediate area.

Control of the Message

Gatekeepers frequently alter or truncate the news or features they receive. Sometimes the changes do little harm, but occasionally the changes ruin an idea or eliminate an important point. Your communications plan may involve informing the public about the subject A before you say anything about subject B, but if a gatekeeper changes the order or eliminates one story, the sequence is destroyed. With advertising, however, you can be sure that your message is reproduced in the exact words you choose and in the sequence you have planned.

Control of Impact

With advertising, you can make your messages as big, frequent and powerful as you choose. The gatekeeper may think your message is worth a 4-inch space on page 9, but if you think it deserves major treatment, you can buy a whole page. And if you want the idea repeated, you can buy as many ads as the budget permits. The broadcast media present similar problems and opportunities. Your news item or feature idea may or may not be used—or, if used, may be cut to a few words—but your advertisement *will* be used without alteration.

Control of Timing

If timing is an important factor, advertising can guarantee that your message will be timely. Prompt response to a public issue, a fixed sequence of messages, continuity of communication—all can be maintained through advertising. To the gatekeeper, your message may be just as usable on Tuesday as on Wednesday; but for your purpose, Tuesday may be a day too early or Wednesday a day too late. You can't be sure about the timing unless you pay for it.

DISADVANTAGES OF ADVERTISING

Although institutional advertising can be effective in getting key messages to specific audiences, there are some disadvantages.

Cost

Paid space is expensive. Ads in multiple media, which are necessary for message penetration, can cost thousands of dollars in the trade press and millions in the consumer press. The most extreme example is the annual Super Bowl football game, during which a 30-second television commercial costs $1.3 million.

The high cost of buying space for advertising has led many companies to shift more of their marketing communications budgets to product publicity, direct mail and telemarketing.

Credibility

Public relations executives are fond of saying, "Advertising raises awareness, but publicity published as news stories creates credibility."

Because they are controlled messages, advertisements are generally less believable than publicity that appears in the news columns or on broadcast news shows. The public perceives that news reports have more credibility because journalists, who are independent of the organization, have evaluated the information on the basis of truth and accuracy.

Indeed, a major value of publicity is the concept that a third party, the medium, has endorsed the information by printing or broadcasting it. Advertisements have no such third-party endorsement because anyone with enough money can place an advertisement, provided that it meets the acceptance standards of the medium.

Timing and Context

"Let's run an ad in the newspaper" is a frequent reaction to a crisis. This approach has one major fault: It is usually too late.

This is particularly true when the crisis has already been reported by the media and the public has already developed strong opinions on the subject. For example, an organization accused of wrongdoing rarely does a good job of defending itself by spending a lot of money on advertisements denying responsibility.

After the *Valdez* oil spill in Alaska, Exxon placed several ads defending itself against charges of doing too little to contain the oil spill, but the public perceived the ads as self-serving and insincere.

Dow Corning, facing charges of unsafe breast implants, and Sears, accused by state regulatory agencies of defrauding auto repair customers, also made the mistake of thinking that a large advertising campaign would change public perceptions.

TYPES OF PUBLIC RELATIONS ADVERTISING

The largest percentage of public relations advertising is done in magazines, with television and newspapers and Sunday supplements in second and third place, respectively. The trend is increasing to closely target audiences.

Magazines, which are already very specialized, will probably continue to get the lion's share of "image" advertising, and network television will lose ground to cable networks, according to Paul Alvarez, chairman of Ketchum Communication, Inc.

There are several types of public relations advertising. At times, the distinctions between categories can become blurred; however, for the purposes of this discussion, we will deal with five basic types: imagine building, investor and financial relations programs, public service messages, advocacy, and announcements.

Image Building

The purpose of image-building advertising is to strengthen an organization's reputation, change or reinforce public perceptions and create a favorable climate for selling the organization's goods and services.

A good example of an image-building campaign is one by NYNEX, the telephone company serving New York State and New England. The company decided to put a human face on high technology with a series of ads that focused on its employees working for and with customers to solve their telephone problems.

The attempt to humanize and personalize the company came after research indicated that people were turned off by advertisements that emphasized the cold, impersonal imagery of fiber-optic networks, microchips and other high-technology hardware. Indeed, companies too often emphasize the wonders of technology without really paying attention to showing how it improves the quality of life for the consumer.

The NYNEX campaign had an internal component as well. By featuring typical employees and distributing glossy brochures about the campaign to the entire staff, it improved morale among employees.

Another example of corporate image advertising is Chevron, which has produced a series of ads on its commitment to the environment. One ad, titled "The little house at the bottom of the sea," tells how used gas storage tank cylinders are used to create artificial reefs for fish, which is "good for the environment and the local fishing industry."

Trade groups, whose membership consists of companies in a particular industry, also use image-building advertising to create awareness or to combat negative public perceptions. For example, the American Plastics Council spent $18 million on a campaign urging consumers to "take another look at plastic" when research showed that consumers had a negative image of plastics as a major contributor to environmental pollution and the problems of waste disposal.

One ad for the plastics council showed a blurred picture (to show motion) of a mother and son in the front seat of a car as air bags inflated to cushion the impact of an accident. Here are the headline and copy:

Some Benefits of Plastic Last for Only Half a Second.

A very important half-second, though. But while the lifesaving benefits of automotive air bags are well-known, what isn't well-known is that many components, including the bag itself, are all made of plastic.

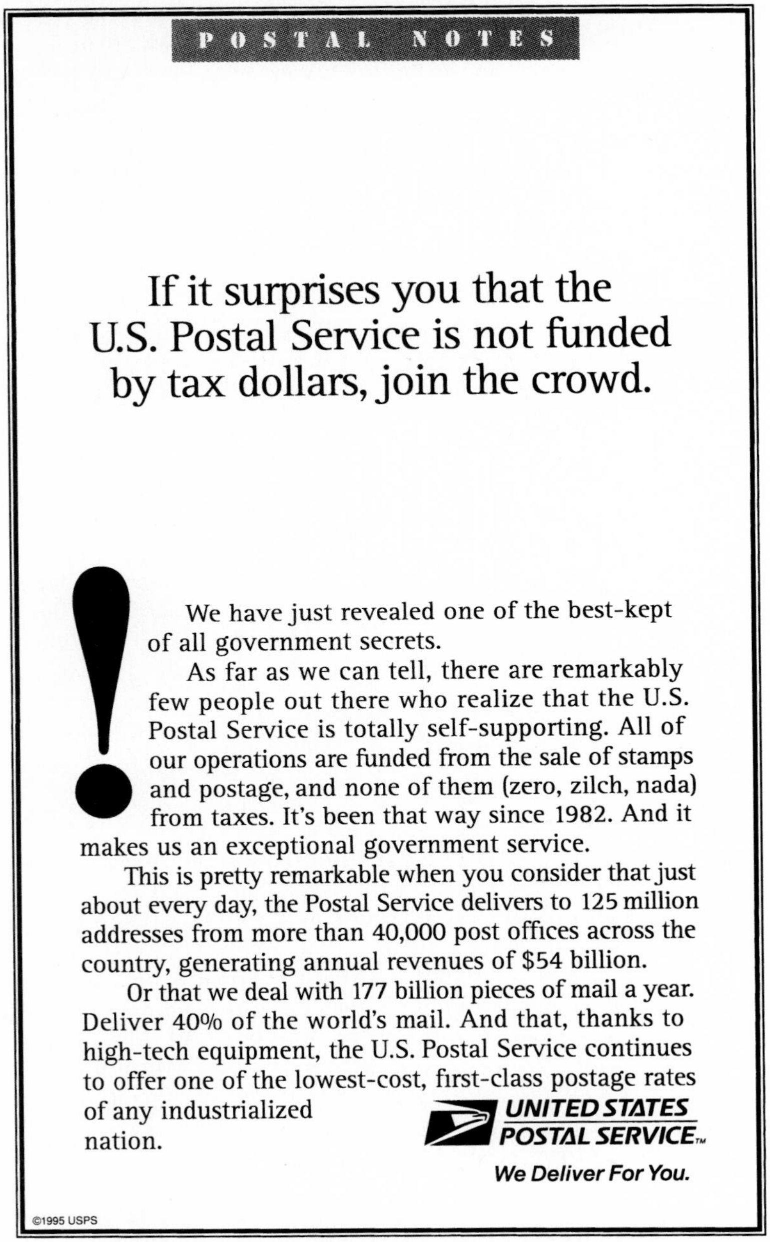

P O S T A L   N O T E S

If it surprises you that the U.S. Postal Service is not funded by tax dollars, join the crowd.

! We have just revealed one of the best-kept of all government secrets.

As far as we can tell, there are remarkably few people out there who realize that the U.S. Postal Service is totally self-supporting. All of our operations are funded from the sale of stamps and postage, and none of them (zero, zilch, nada) from taxes. It's been that way since 1982. And it makes us an exceptional government service.

This is pretty remarkable when you consider that just about every day, the Postal Service delivers to 125 million addresses from more than 40,000 post offices across the country, generating annual revenues of $54 billion.

Or that we deal with 177 billion pieces of mail a year. Deliver 40% of the world's mail. And that, thanks to high-tech equipment, the U.S. Postal Service continues to offer one of the lowest-cost, first-class postage rates of any industrialized nation.

UNITED STATES POSTAL SERVICE™

We Deliver For You.

©1995 USPS

Figure 14.2 Image building. This advertisement has the objective of building consumer trust and creating favorable opinions about the efficiency of the organization. (*Courtesy of United States Postal Service.*)

Of course, plastic makes a lot of things safe. Like packaging that keeps medical equipment sterile. And harmful medicines out of the hands of children. Plastic wraps and trays that keep food fresh and safe. And shatter-resistant plastic bottles.

To learn more about how plastic can make a world of difference in our lives, just call 1–800–777–9500 Ext. 42, and the American Plastics Council will gladly send you a free booklet.

Because even though some benefits of plastic, like the air bag, may last a mere split second, it may be one your family will remember for a long time.

Take Another Look at Plastic.

More recently, the National Fluid Milk Processor Promotion Board spent about $30 million on a national campaign to promote the drinking of milk. The campaign featured a number of celebrities such as Vanna White, Christie Brinkley, and Steve Young with milk moustaches, giving endorsements. The copy on the Steve Young ad:

32–16–43 hike. And before you blink, 350 lbs. of solid mass is heading straight for your bones. What can you do? Well, besides pray someone's open—drink lots of skim milk. Not just for calcium but the eight other essential nutrients that keep your body strong in case you do get sacked. Man, I hate when that happens.

Milk

What a surprise!

Investor and Financial Relations

A different type of public relations advertising is targeted to the financial community—individual and institutional investors, stock analysts, investment bankers and stockholders. Such advertising often has the objective of informing and reassuring investors that the company is well managed, worthy of investment and has bright prospects for the future.

Such advertising is used extensively during proxy fights for control of companies, when a company is undergoing some major reorganization or when a company believes it is being unfairly attacked by consumer groups or regulatory agencies. A variety of these ads appear in financial publications, notably the *Wall Street Journal*.

In one instance, Honeywell placed a full-page ad in the *Wall Street Journal* to announce that it had won a major lawsuit against the Minolta Camera Company for infringing on its patents. The winning of the suit and the protection of its patents assured the financial community that Honeywell would continue to make profits on its technology. Apple Computer, to cite another example, also took out several ads to bolster investor confidence when the company reported a quarterly loss of $68 million and the price of stock plunged to a new low.

Sears also had to reassure the financial community after its stock prices dropped following charges by several state regulatory agencies that the company defrauded customers at its auto repair centers. In a full-page *Wall Street Journal* ad, Sears laid out the steps it was taking to restore consumer confidence in the company: eliminating incentive compensation and goal-setting systems for employees, upgrading the company's quality control program, cooperating with state attorneys to investigate the charges and helping organize a joint industry-government-con-

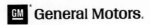 General Motors.

"GENERAL MOTORS IS RATED HIGHEST IN SATISFACTION; RIGHT FROM THE START."

Among the top-ten volume corporations
selling 1995 cars and trucks in the U.S.*

– J.D. Power and Associates

This ad is made possible by all the hard-working men and
women of General Motors, its dealers, retailers, and suppliers.

*Including General Motors Corporation, Chrysler Corporation, Ford Motor Company, American Honda Motor Company, Hyundai Motor of
America, Mazda Motor of America, Mitsubishi Motor Sales of America, Nissan Motor Corporation, Toyota Motor Sales U.S.A., Volkswagen of
America. (Based on J.D. Power and Associates 1995 New Vehicle Sales Satisfaction Index Study,℠ which includes measurement of owner satisfac-
tion with sales experience, delivery and initial vehicle condition after the first 90 days of ownership.)

Figure 14.3   Image building. This is an institutional ad for a corporation. It
focuses on GM as an organization of quality instead of touting the merits of a
particular car model. (*Courtesy of General Motors.*)

sumer effort to establish uniform car repair industry standards. The Sears ad, like
many of these announcements, was written in the form of a letter signed by the corporation's chief executive officer.

Other forms of financial advertising are more routine. You can use an ad to announce the appointment of a key executive, the acquisition of another company or a new stock offering. Some announcements, as outlined in Chapter 2, are required by the SEC or other government regulatory bodies. Releasing news to the media may be adequate, but many corporations also use advertising to make sure that there can be no question about disclosure.

Public Service

Public service advertisements provide information, raise awareness about social issues, and give how-to suggestions. A number of nonprofit and charitable organizations, as well as governmental agencies, use such advertising for public education. For example:

- The American Cancer Society gives information about vegetables and fruits that can reduce the risk of cancer.
- The American Heart Association informs people about the warning signs of a heart attack.
- The American Red Cross gives information about limiting the spread of AIDS.
- The American Lung Association warns people about the dangers of smoking.
- EarthShare, funded by the federal government, tells people how to conserve energy and resources in the workplace.
- Women in Communications raises awareness about sexual harassment in the workplace.
- The Century Fund, funded by the alcohol industry, promotes programs that educate teenagers about the dangers of drinking.

In many instances, the Ad Council prepares public service ads for national nonprofit groups. The Council, an association of advertising agencies, does this as a public service.

Corporations also do public service kinds of advertising to generate goodwill. In most cases, it is related to their products and services. For example:

- The Pacific Gas & Electric Company provides helpful hints on how to reduce energy costs during the winter months.
- The Shell Oil Company gives motorists hints on how to get better gasoline mileage.

Advocacy

Although it can be argued that advocacy is an element in all public relations advertising—whether it's the American Cancer Society telling you to stop smoking or a company telling you it's all right to buy its stock—the term "advocacy advertising" has a more exact meaning.

It usually means advertising designed to motivate voters and to influence legislation. For example, during the national debate on health care reform, any number

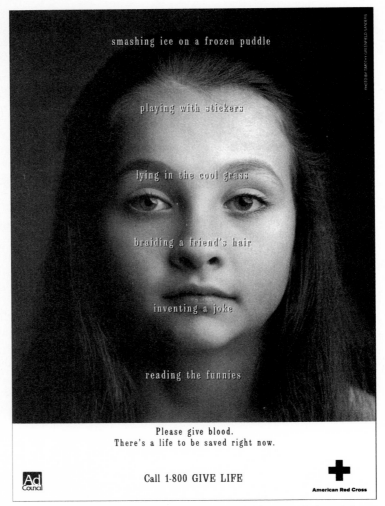

smashing ice on a frozen puddle

playing with stickers

lying in the cool grass

braiding a friend's hair

inventing a joke

reading the funnies

Please give blood.
There's a life to be saved right now.

Call 1-800 GIVE LIFE

American Red Cross

Figure 14.4 Public service. This ad, available in English and Spanish, points out the need for blood donations. It is part of a national campaign, which also includes radio and television PSAs. See Chapter 8 for examples. (*Courtesy of the American Red Cross.*)

of businesses and special interest groups sought to influence legislation through a barrage of advocacy advertisements.

The pharmaceutical industry, for example, ran a series of ads countering President Clinton's assertion that prescriptions cost too much. The American College of Surgeons warned the public about "retaining the right of patient choice," and even Delta Dental made the case that any change in dental insurance plans would seriously reverse the progress made in dental care.

Other public issues, subject to legislation, have also spawned massive advertising campaigns. A good example is a campaign by the American Association of Railroads. Millions of Americans watched one of its commercials in which a woman and her two children are almost run off the road by the impatient driver of a triple-trailer truck.

What the viewers may not have known is that the American Association of Railroads was waging a campaign to discredit the trucking industry. The objective was to generate public opposition to congressional legislation that would allow the trucking industry to use larger and heavier vehicles on the nation's highways. Such legislation would, of course, make the trucking industry more competitive with the railroad industry.

The National Cable Television Association, facing public pressure for Congress to pass a bill to regulate cable television rates, also used an extensive advertising campaign to change public attitudes about the industry. One series of ads, designed for placement by local cable companies, concentrated on the multiple benefits of cable television. The ads did not directly discuss the impending legislation (which ultimately passed); rather, they concentrated on improving the image of the cable industry. The objective was to mute public criticism and, ideally, stem the flow of angry letters to legislators about high rates.

Here is the text of one ad, which had cups in different shapes and sizes as its graphic element:

Not every cable channel is everyone's cup of tea. That's the whole point.

At any given time on any given day, your local cable company offers television designed for individuals rather than for the masses. There are channels for kids. Channels for country music fans. Even channels for people who speak Chinese. And best of all, the average basic channel costs less than two cents a day. So being able to find one that satisfies your individual taste is one of the basic values of your subscription to cable.

Cable contributes to life.

Mobil Oil is probably the best example of a corporation using advocacy advertising. For many years, it has run a campaign expressing its views on a variety of issues that affect the oil industry. The ads, in the format of editorials, appear on a regular basis in magazines that have high readership among opinion leaders and people interested in public policy.

An example of the Mobil approach is how it countered criticisms about the "high cost" of gasoline. Mobil, in its ad, pointed out that taxes averaged 40 cents on a gallon of gasoline, so the industry shouldn't take all the heat for gasoline prices. The ad, in part, said, "So, occasionally, we point out that we are not the only ones profiting from what motorists pay at the pump. In fact, a constantly larger chunk of what motorists pay at the pump goes directly to the tax collectors—federal, state, and local."

A number of consumer, environmental and human rights groups also use advocacy advertisements to persuade the public and motivate citizens to take action. One such group, the Asian Immigrant Women Advocates, took out full-page ads in several major metropolitan dailies to urge a consumer boycott of Jessica McClintock, a manufacturer of expensive women's clothes. The group charged that the clothes were being made in sweatshops where Asian women were exploited and poorly paid.

Ask Katie's parents what they think of the asthma drug that's saving her trips to the emergency room.

When asthma medicine can save Katie and her parents from anxious races to the hospital, it's obviously a good thing. What's not so apparent is how dramatically the same drugs reduce health-care costs.

A study in the use of just one anti-asthma drug showed it reduced trips to the emergency room by 96%, and hospital admissions by 62%.

As a result, while the cost of Katie's drug over a year's time can be sizable, it's still projected to save America up to $3 billion annually.

America's healthcare crisis calls for this kind of cost-saving power. And new prescription drugs are our best hope for providing it. For more information on how new medicines improve lives and save

New medicines not only prevent Katie's asthma attacks, they save America billions in emergency room expenses alone.

money, write or call The Pharmaceutical Manufacturers Association, 1100 15th Street, N.W., Box T, Washington, D.C. 20005. 1-800-538-2692.

PHARMACEUTICALS
Saving Lives. Saving Money.

Figure 14.5 This low-key advocacy ad, one of a series, was placed by the pharmaceutical industry after President Clinton criticized the high cost of prescription drugs. The ads attempted to change public perceptions by explaining how new medicines actually reduce national health care costs.

Another group, Stop Teenage Addiction to Tobacco (STAT) placed an ad that featured mug shots of prosperous media CEOs and accused them of taking "blood money" for helping promote a harmful and addictive product. In this case, the ad got plenty of news coverage when it was disclosed that the *New York Times* and the *Los Angeles Times* refused to run the ad.

Indeed, one side benefit of advocacy ads is that they often create controversy and additional news coverage. The health care debate ads, for example, generated news coverage worth many times the cost of the ad placements themselves.

In the case of the McClintock advertisement, the *Wall Street Journal* ran a full story on the manufacturing practices of Jessica McClintock and other apparel manufacturers. Other media, in turn, picked up the story. This is a good illustration of an activist group, with few resources, being able to place an issue on the public agenda for discussion and perhaps, ultimately, government regulation.

Charitable groups also do a form of advocacy advertising when the purpose of the ad is to solicit contributions. The City of Hope, for example, used a full-page ad in *Time* magazine to solicit contributions. The ad said, "You can make sure patients everywhere continue to benefit from our work by donating time and money. Just call 800–835–5504 today."

Announcements

Announcements can be used for any number of situations. The primary purpose is to inform the public promptly about something that affects them. Recalling a product, explaining a failure of service, announcing a new policy or even reinforcing an organization's commitment to quality and service are appropriate uses of announcements. Here are a few examples:

- Sears told auto owners how to apply for rebates if they believed they were charged too much or paid for replacement parts they did not need.
- Jack-In-The-Box reassured customers that it was taking precautions to make sure its restaurants met new health standards after an outbreak of food poisoning at several locations in the Seattle area.
- Denny's Restaurants reaffirmed their commitment to quality service and racial equality after the Justice Department charged them with discrimination.
- Tylenol announced a policy of adding a warning on its labels about the use of the product with other medications and alcohol.
- Two drug companies, Pharmacia and Upjohn, announced that they had merged.
- State Farm Insurance placed ads telling residents of a disaster area how to file claims.

An interesting and somewhat controversial ad was used by the University of Calgary to announce that it would admit an additional 720 students. The ad, shown in Figure 14.6, announced that the high school entrance requirements had been lowered from 73 to 65 percent. The ad ran in major Canadian newspapers and generated additional publicity because it wasn't a usual college recruitment ad. The result, however, was gratifying—enrollment went from 16,641 students to 18,004 students.

Figure 14.6 Announcement ads can motivate people. This advertisement, by the University of Calgary, caused some talk but it accomplished the purpose of increasing enrollment. (*Courtesy of Rod Chapman, director of public affairs, University of Calgary.*)

THE BASICS OF A PRINT AD

There are several key elements in a print advertisement. They are headline, text, artwork and layout.

THE ELEMENTS OF A GOOD AD

After you write an advertisement, evaluate it using the following criteria:

- **Distinctiveness** People are exposed to hundreds of ads every day. What makes yours different?
- **Interest** Does it grab attention? Will people look at it?
- **Brevity** Is the message short and meaningful?
- **Personal Touch** Does the ad speak to people as individuals?
- **Credibility** Will people believe your message, or is it hype?

Source: David Hill, *Potentials in Marketing.*

Headline

Advertising expert John Caples says, "The headline is the most important element in most ads—and the best headlines appeal to the reader's self-interest or give news."

Headlines should be specific about a benefit, or they can be teasers that arouse interest. Here is a headline about a specific program: "The Phoenix Mutual Insurance Retirement Income Plan." Caples thought this was all right, but he created a headline that sold much more successfully: "To Men Who Want to Quit Work Some Day." This was accompanied with an illustration of a smiling senior citizen fishing in a mountain stream.

Caples gives these suggestions for writing an advertising headline:

- Include the interests of the audience.
- Use words such as "introducing," "announcing," "new," or "now" to give the headline a newsworthy appeal.
- Avoid witty or cute headlines unless they include reader interest and appear newsy.
- Present the headline positively. Don't say "Our competitors can't match our service" when you can say, "Our service surpasses that of our competitors."

Text

The headline is followed by what is known as *text* or *body copy*. These are the words that persuade the reader to do something. In general, copy should be limited to one or two major points. Sentences should be short and punchy. A declarative sentence is much better than one that includes a dependent or an independent clause.

The copy should evoke emotion, provide information of value to the reader and suggest a way that the reader can act on the information. You might include a toll-free telephone number, an address to write for more information or a suggestion that people visit a local dealer. A review of the ads featured in this chapter will give you some idea about copywriting.

Artwork

An ad can consist of just a headline and copy, like the Mobil Corporation example, but ads usually have a strong graphic element. This may be a striking photo, a line drawing or a computer-generated design. Artwork attracts the reader to the ad and breaks up large blocks of type.

Artwork and graphics are doubly important if the ad is to appear on the Internet. In this case, text is secondary and graphics are primary. Web sites were discussed in Chapter 10, but the guidelines also apply to advertising. The graphics can't be too complex, and the ad needs to be interactive with buttons to click and so forth.

Layout

The headline, copy and graphic elements need to be integrated into an attractive, easy-to-read advertisement. A layout can be a mock-up of the planned ad, or it can be a detailed comprehensive that includes the actual type and artwork that will be used.

A number of tips about layout were given Chapter 13. Many of them are also applicable to preparing an advertisement. In general, avoid all capital letters or large blocks of copy. Use serif type for body copy, avoid reverse type (white on dark color) and use plenty of white space.

USING AN ADVERTISING AGENCY

Most public relations advertising is prepared and placed by advertising agencies. The agency has people who are experts in all phases of creating the ads and getting them published or broadcast in the chosen media.

If your organization has an advertising department, it is likely to be the prime contact with the agency. However, there are some organizations in which the public relations department is the contact. In either case, the public relations people are identified as the "client," the entity that approves or disapproves the agency's recommendations.

This relationship must be one of enthusiastic cooperation. Agency and client are not adversaries but partners. In general, the public relations role is to determine broad objectives ("what to do") while the agency determines the means ("how to do it").

Advertising agencies do not normally charge anything for their services. Their compensation comes from the "agency discount" that is granted by most media. Normally this discount is 15 percent of the cost of the space or time, and it is *not* granted to advertisers. It works this way: If the space or time costs $1000, the agency bills the advertiser for the sum but remits $850 to the medium. The $150 difference is retained by the agency as pay for preparing the ad. Agencies do bill clients for the cost of materials purchased for use in preparing the advertising for publication or broadcast.

OTHER ADVERTISING CHANNELS

Other forms of advertising that have value in public relations programs are billboards, transit panels, posters, sponsored books, T-shirts, buttons and bumper stickers. Direct mail, discussed in Chapter 15, is also a valuable channel.

Billboards

Most outdoor advertising consists of paper sheets pasted on a wooden or metal background. The 24-sheet poster is standard, but there are also painted billboards, which use no paper. Outdoor advertising reaches large audiences in brief exposures. Accordingly, advertising for this medium must be eye-catching and use few words. Ten words is a rule-of-thumb limit for outdoor copy. When design and copy are approved, the individual sheets of paper that will make up the whole advertisement are printed and then pasted to the background.

Location is vital in this medium—and prices are based on the traffic that is exposed to the site. Occasionally, nonprofit organizations can obtain free or heavily discounted usage of outdoor space that is temporarily unsold. Displays are usually scheduled in monthly units, and occasionally there are gaps in the schedules, so it may pay to keep in touch with local outdoor companies.

Transit Panels

This category includes both the small posters placed in subway and commuter rail stations and the cards used in buses and rail cars. Both types of transit advertising require eye-catching graphics, but the copy can be longer than for outdoor posters. The person waiting for a train or holding a strap or a bar on a bus or rail car has some time to absorb a message. Cards in transit vehicles often carry coupons or tear-off notes allowing readers to ask for more information or respond to some sort of offer.

Posters

Posters are used in a variety of settings to create awareness and remind people of something. Many companies use posters on bulletin boards to remind employees about basic company policies, benefits and safety precautions.

A good example is the Nissan Motor Company's poster campaign to remind employees at various U.S. offices to buckle up when driving. Nissan used a series of posters with a lighthearted touch, using famous artworks and personalities. One poster draped a seat belt over a stock movie photo of Sherlock Holmes with the caption, "It's Elementary, Buckle Up Now."

Government agencies often use posters as part of public information campaigns about preventing AIDS, getting flu shots or having pets neutered. The government of New Zealand used an extensive poster campaign to warn returning citizens from abroad about the dangers of bringing fruit and other banned products into the island nation. The large poster, in full color, carried the headline "Lethal Weapon" and showed a collage of banned food products in the shape of a machine gun.

Museum exhibits and art shows lend themselves to poster treatments. The poster, often a piece of art itself, can promote attendance and can also be sold as a souvenir of the show.

Posters can also be used as mailers to business prospects and key opinion leaders. The American Management Association regularly sends posters to businesses promoting its services and conferences; they are mailed in the hope that the recipients will display them on bulletin boards so that additional people are informed.

To be effective, a poster must be attractively designed and have strong visual elements. It should be relatively large, convey only one basic idea and use only a few words to relate basic information. A poster is a small billboard.

Posters, if done properly, can be expensive to design and produce. Therefore, you need to assess how the posters will be used and displayed. Costs can be controlled, often by buying ready-to-use posters from printers and having the organization's name or logo printed on them. Local chapters of national organizations, such as the American Cancer Society, also get posters from the national organization that can easily be localized.

Sponsored Books

Sponsored books may be written by anyone on your organization's staff. They may also be put together by freelance writers. If you should become involved in engaging such a writer, be sure that you read some of his or her work first. One large national corporation once hired a famous writer to put together a biography of the founder. It was so bad that extensive rewriting had to be done by a member of the company's staff.

A sponsored book can be published by the organization. In fact, most such books are produced in this way. It is simply a matter of hiring a printer to print and bind the necessary number of copies.

If the book is of such importance that it should be produced by an established book publisher, the usual procedure is to guarantee the purchase of a sufficient number of books to give the publisher a profit. After the sponsor buys the guaranteed number, the publisher is free to market the book through its regular channels.

The New Arabians is a book that was underwritten by the Bechtel Corporation. It is no coincidence that the company has extensive engineering contracts in the Middle East. *From Three Cents a Week* is the official history of the Prudential Life Insurance Company, and *The Truth About Energy* was written by the staff of the Mobil Oil Corporation.

Books that relate directly to a company's product are also often underwritten by the company. General Mills has long been producing Betty Crocker cookbooks for Random House. *Creative Cooking with Aluminum Foil* was published for Reynolds Aluminum, and *Protect Yourself* is from Master Lock and Dell Publishing. Of course, one can also purchase certain airlines' travel guides or *How to Get Lost and Found in New Zealand* by Air New Zealand.

Figure 14.7 Bright and colorful posters can call attention to special events and contests. This poster, by Visa International, was sent to schools in 20 nations. See Figure 5.2 for a news release about the contest. (*Courtesy of Visa International, San Francisco, CA.*)

T-shirts

T-shirts have been described as "walking billboards," and some people, including sociologists, lament the fact that people are so materialistic that they willingly become walking ads for products, services and social or political issues. Why people do this remains unresolved, but the fact is that they do spend their own money to advertise things with which they may or may not have any direct connection.

Because so many people are willing to serve as billboards, you may find an opportunity to use this medium, which is particularly convenient for causes such as environmental protection. Often such groups make sizable incomes from the sale of T-shirts.

Corporations don't usually sell T-shirts, but they do distribute them to attendees at conferences, sales meetings, picnics and other events. In these situations, the T-shirts contribute to a feeling of belonging to a team.

Almost every town and city in America has at least one shop where you can order T-shirts. You can specify just about anything you can imagine—slogans, corporate logos, symbols and so on. The process is simple and fast, and the costs are low. At some time, almost any organization may find T-shirts useful.

Buttons and Bumper Stickers

Akin to T-shirts are buttons. They are widely used in political campaigns and at special events. They are also useful in fund raising, when they are distributed to people who make donations. In San Francisco one year, money was raised for the ballet by selling "SOB" ("Save Our Ballet") buttons to pedestrians in the downtown area.

In general, buttons have a short life span. They are worn by convention delegates for or by sales representatives during a trade show. Outside of these areas, people don't generally wear buttons unless they are highly committed to a particular cause.

Bumper stickers are another specialty item. They are often used to support political candidates and various political causes, but they can also be used to promote a special event or a scenic attraction or membership in an organization. In recent years, the use of bumper stickers has declined, but window decals are still popular.

SUMMARY

1. Advertising is an important communication tool in public relations.
2. Public relations advertising does not sell products directly, but it can create a supportive environment for the selling of products and services by enhancing public perception of an organization.
3. Advertising enables you to deliver a message exactly as written to a chosen audience at the precise time you prefer and as emphatically as you choose.

4. Advertising has the disadvantage of high costs and lower credibility than publicity.

5. There are five kinds of public relations advertising: image building, financial, public service, advocacy and announcement.

6. When you plan advertising, you must make sure that it fits into the public relations plan. Within that plan, you must determine the objective, the target audience, the appropriate media and the message.

7. Writing an effective ad requires considerable skill and imagination. You must think about the headline, text, artwork and layout and how they all relate.

8. Effective advertising copy is short and punchy. Copy must be oriented to the self-interest of the reader, viewer or listener.

9. Most public relations advertising is created and placed by advertising agencies.

10. Other channels for public relations advertising include billboards, transit panels, posters, sponsored books, T-shirts, buttons and bumper stickers.

EXERCISES

1. Collect samples of various public relations advertisements that appear in magazines or newspapers. Select examples that illustrate the five basic categories of (a) image building, (b) investor and financial relations, (c) public service, (d) advocacy and (e) announcements. Critique the ads from the standpoint of headlines, text, artwork and layout. Which ads do you think are effective? Explain your reasons. (For this exercise, you may want to review the persuasion techniques outlined in Chapter 3.)

2. The local water company wants to produce a public service advertisement that would give tips on conserving water during the summer months. Do some research, and write the copy for this ad. In addition, make a rough sketch of what the ad would look like in print.

3. The city council is thinking about closing the city libraries on Saturdays and Sundays as a cost-cutting measure. You and other concerned citizens don't want this to happen. Write an advocacy ad that will motivate other citizens to oppose the closing.

4. Prism Industries, a manufacturer of precision engineering equipment headquartered in Dallas, has contributed $100,000 to help underwrite the cost of the city's symphony orchestra's upcoming season. In addition to issuing a news release, the company wants to place a full-page advertisement in the *Dallas Morning News* to tell the community about its support of the arts. Write the advertising copy, and make a rough sketch of what the ad would look like in print.

5. The local art museum will host a major traveling exhibition of French Impressionists during the month of March. This is the year's most elaborate exhibition, and only ten museums in the country were selected to present it. The local

art museum wants a large attendance and has decided to expend money on ads, billboards, posters and buttons to promote the exhibit. Decide on a central theme for this promotion, and plan how it could be carried out in the media mentioned. The finished assignment should contain copy and rough layout for a print ad, a billboard, a poster and a button.

15 *Letters, Direct Mail and Reports*

*T*he public relations writer doesn't always communicate with a large, impersonal audience. In many cases, he or she must also communicate on a more personal level by writing a letter, sending an E-mail message or an interoffice memo.

Letter writing in any of these forms requires thought and craft. Writing a proposal or report also requires clear thinking and organization. The ultimate report, of course, is the annual report—a requirement of any publicly owned corporation.

This chapter covers these topics, and gives tips on using voice mail and the etiquette of sending E-mail messages.

GENERAL GUIDELINES

All mass media have gatekeepers who control what is delivered to the audience. With personalized and controlled communication, you are the gatekeeper. This places the burden on you to follow the basic guidelines of clarity, completeness, conciseness, correctness, courtesy and responsibility.

Completeness   Whether you are writing a 10-line memo or a 32-page annual report, you must be certain that it contains the information needed to serve its purpose. Ask yourself why you are writing and what your reader wants or needs to know. Supply that information. If more information will aid the reader's understanding, provide it—but don't give your reader a mass of irrelevant material just because you have it on hand. An outline will help to ensure that your message is complete.

Conciseness   Conciseness means brevity in form but completeness in content. Use enough words to make your meaning clear—don't use more, but don't cut out anything that is necessary, either. Your objective is to be both complete and brief, to give the most information possible in the fewest words, but not to the point of telegraphic phrasing or choppy sentences.

Correctness   You must be accurate in everything you write. If an item in the mass media contains an error, the blame may be spread among many people, but an error in a personalized communication reflects solely on you and your abilities. Beyond the matter of blame is that of pride in successful accomplishment. Be sure that what you prepare is accurate, and you will get credit for doing things right.

Courtesy   These are *personal* communications. Personal names are used extensively, and both senders and receivers have considerable interest in the material. You might suppose that it would be advisable to make the messages as personal as possible, but don't go overboard. The writing should be polite but not effusive, personal but not overly familiar.

Responsibility   Be especially prudent with letters. A letter is a highly visible record of what you say, so be careful. You must know and understand organizational policies and attitudes. You must be aware of the FCC and the SEC and how easily something you say can cause trouble. A simple letter to a stockholder, a competitor or a customer may not be nearly so simple in the hands of a lawyer in court. (See Chapter 2 for further guidance.)

LETTERS

A letter is a written communication sent to an individual. It is usually composed for one person only; in some cases, however, where the same message may be pertinent to numerous readers, a form letter (a standardized letter in which only the name and address of the recipient varies) may be appropriate.

Purpose A letter may be used to give information, to ask for information, to motivate, to answer complaints, to soothe or arouse, to warn, to admit or to deny. In short, a letter can carry almost any sort of message to any individual. It is a written substitute for personal conversation. As a substitute, it is not as friendly as face-to-face conversation, but it has the advantage of allowing the writer to get facts in order and to phrase the message better than is likely in conversation.

Content The most important part of any letter is the first paragraph. It should concisely state the purpose of the letter so the reader immediately knows what the letter is about. This is the same principle that was discussed in Chapter 5 for the first paragraph of a news release.

From a writing perspective, a declarative statement is best. Instead of writing, "I am writing you to let you know that our company will be contacting you in the near future about your concerns regarding product reliability," you can simply say, "A company representative will be contacting you about our product reliability."

The second and succeeding paragraphs can elaborate on the details and give relevant information. The final paragraph should summarize the important details, or let the recipient know you will telephone if something needs to be resolved through conversation.

Writing a business letter requires clear thought and thorough editing to reduce wordiness. Every time you use the word "I" to start a thought, think about how to remove it. In most cases, starting a sentence with "I believe," "I feel" or "I think" is unnecessary.

Format As a general rule, letters should be written on standard business stationery. The letterhead should be printed and should carry the name, address and telephone number of the organization.

Letters should always be word processed. Usually they are single-spaced. Each paragraph should be indicated either by indention or by a line space. One page is the preferred length. A two-page letter is acceptable, but it runs longer than that, consider putting the material in another format that is introduced by a letter of transmittal.

The full name, title and address of the receiver are obvious inclusions, but how do you address the reader? The usual approach is to write "Dear Mr. ——" or "Dear Ms.——." The latter avoids the "Miss" or "Mrs." dilemma and is common in business correspondence. You should not use just a first name, such as "Dear Susan," in a greeting unless the person already knows you.

On occasion, you will need to write a letter to an organization on some routine matter and won't know the name of the person. This often occurs when you are requesting information or inquiring about a billing. You can use the traditional "Dear Sir," but this is increasingly inappropriate now that more than half the workforce is female. A better approach is to put your letter in the form of a memo. For example, a letter about a bill might be addressed, "To: Manager, Accounting Department."

Closing a letter is easy: You can write "Yours truly," "Truly yours," "Sincerely" or "Sincerely yours." Some bold correspondents omit both the salutation and the close, since they aren't really necessary.

HANDLING CORRESPONDENCE EFFICIENTLY

A personal letter is a labor-intensive effort. Here are some ways to increase your efficiency and still keep the personal touch.

- Produce courteous and effective printed forms for repetitive correspondence, such as requests for printed material or acknowledgments of inquiries.
- Develop standard replies for often-asked questions or often-solicited advice where this is a part of the organization's routine business.
- Develop standard formats for certain kinds of common correspondence to enable inexperienced writers to handle them easily and effectively.
- Prepare a correspondence guide containing hints and suggestions on keeping verbiage and correspondence volume down to reasonable and effective levels.
- Place a brief heading on the letter after the salutation, indicating the letter's subject. The heading will give the reader an immediate grasp of the letter's substance and will also facilitate filing.
- Use subheads if the letter is more than two pages long, thereby giving the reader a quick grasp of how the subject is treated and where the major topics are discussed.
- To personalize printed materials, attach your card with a brief, warm message.
- If a letter requires a brief response, it is acceptable to pen a note on the original letter and mail it back to the sender. Retain a photocopy for your files.

E-MAIL

Electronic mail, commonly called E-mail, is rapidly replacing printed letters and memos in many organizations. It virtually eliminates the traditional and somewhat cumbersome interoffice mailing system, and it considerably shortens the communication cycle time.

According to a survey of communicators in *Fortune* 100 corporations, E-mail also (1) reduces the cost of employee communications, (2) increases the distribution of messages to more employees, (3) flattens the corporate hierarchy and (4) speeds up decision making.

E-mail, as previously discussed, is also a way that public relations writers can send media advisories and news releases to the media, disseminate employee newsletters and even chat with colleagues around the world. Organizations with global operations, for example, find E-mail to be the most cost-effective way of communicating internationally.

E-mail, however, is not suitable for all person-to-person communications. A telephone call or a fax may be just as fast. Keep in mind that a person can't really cope with 80 or 90 E-mail messages that might accumulate in a day's work. Delays on E-mail are increasingly a problem as computer switching capacity gets swamped with sorting E-mail messages.

You also should be aware that E-mail is best suited for internal communications. E-mail is not available in all organizations, nor can the majority of the population be reached via E-mail.

If your organization has E-mail, you should be aware of some Do's and Don'ts about sending E-mail messages. The following tips are adapted from an article in *Communication Briefing* by Dr. Martha S. Shull of the University of Maryland:

- E-mail has the immediacy of a phone call but the formality of a document. Use the same care in spelling, punctuation and grammar that you would use with a printed document.
- Messages can be accessed by many people, including management. Be careful what you say about people and situations. If you want privacy, telephone the person or schedule a meeting.
- Blunt words and statements assume more importance in electronic form than in a telephone conversation. Temper your language.
- Be concise. Messages should fit on one screen (about 10 or 12 lines) so receivers don't have to scroll up and down to grasp all that you've said.
- Use standard English and abbreviations. Don't use a lot of cryptic symbols as shorthand.
- Don't be an E-mail junkie. Don't clutter up electronic mailboxes with nonurgent chitchat; it's irritating to receivers.
- Use bullets, numbers, underlining, boldface and so on to highlight key points.
- Don't let E-mail become a substitute for phone conversations and personal meetings. They are important for maintaining personal relationships.
- Always reread an E-mail message before sending it. Will the tone or choice of words offend the receiver? Are you coming across as friendly and courteous, or brusque and pompous?
- Always respond to E-mail messages in a timely manner.

DIRECT MAIL

Standardized letters sent to large groups of people are commonly called *direct mail*. Using an organization's own address database or a list from a national mailing house, you can mail letters to thousands of people who may be interested in your message.

By using lists, you can reach everyone from avocado growers to zoology professors. For example, if you wanted to reach the nation's public school principals (all 103,938 of them), you could get such a list on labels or diskette.

Purpose   Direct mail has one basic purpose: to get the recipient to do something. He or she may be asked to vote, to send money, to buy something, to write to a political figure, to attend a meeting or to take some other action. Whenever a number of people can be identified as potential supporters for any cause or action, it is logical to reach them with direct mail.

Content   A direct mail letter has three basic elements: (1) an introduction, which tells the recipient why the letter is being sent; (2) a body, which gives the facts—often with strong emotional overtones; and (3) a summary or conclusion, which calls

---

HOW TO WRITE A DIRECT MAIL LETTER

Here are several techniques that have proved effective over the years.

1. *Define the audience.* Know exactly who you want to reach and why they should respond. The more you know about the demographics of the members of your audience and their motivations, the better you can tailor a letter to them. Don't waste time and money sending your material to people who can't or won't respond.
2. *Get the envelope opened.* There is so much junk mail nowadays that many letters go directly into the trash without ever being opened. Put a teaser headline on the outside of the envelope that makes the recipient want to know what's inside. The opposite approach, which also raises curiosity, is to use a sender's address but not the name of the organization. Using stamps instead of a postal permit number also increases envelope opening.
3. *Keep the idea clear and pertinent.* State the offer or request in the first two or three sentences. Tell what the advantages or benefits are—and repeat them throughout the letter. At the end of the letter, summarize the message. You cannot be too clear.
4. *Make it easy for people to respond.* Tell the recipient exactly what to do and how to do it. Include a postage-paid reply card or envelope. Design forms that require only a check mark to place an order or make a pledge.
5. *Pretest the campaign.* Conduct a pilot campaign on a limited basis. Prepare two or three different appeals and send them to a sampling of the target audience. By doing this, you can find out what appeal generates the greatest response before doing an entire mailing.

---

for some action. There are often additional enclosures, and there is always something to help the reader respond. This may be an order blank, a return card, a telephone number or a form with a suggested amount to contribute. When charitable groups ask for money, it is standard to suggest various amounts—and to state that even the smallest contribution will be appreciated.

Figure 15.1 on page 370 is an example of a direct mail letter from UNICEF. The letter is from Hugh Downs, a television personality with major name recognition. In addition to the letter, the mailing included (1) a short pamphlet on the UNICEF "catalog" of seeds and agricultural tools that a contributor could "purchase" with his or her donation, (2) a card suggesting amounts from $26 to $422 with instructions for how to pay by credit card and (3) a self-addressed mailing envelope.

Format   Direct mail letters usually look like other business letters, and computer technology has made it possible for most of them to be personally addressed, even saying "Dear Mrs. Jones." Letters may even include a yellow Post-it with a computer-generated handwritten note (as in Figure 15.1 on page 370) that makes it look even more personalized.

Fund-raising letters often start with an attention-getting technique. One common technique is a story. Figure 15.2 on page 371 from The Marine Mammal Cen-

WRITING FUND-RAISING LETTERS

A large percentage of fund raising for charitable institutions is conducted through direct mail. The purpose of the letter, of course, is to elicit a response—a donation. Writers of fund-raising letters have learned to use these approaches.

1. Make use of an attention-getting headline.
2. Follow this with an inspirational lead-in on why and how a donation will be of benefit.
3. Give a clear definition of the charitable agency's purpose and objectives.
4. Humanize the cause by giving an example of a child or family that benefitted.
5. Include testimonials and endorsements from credible individuals.
6. Ask for specific action and provide an easy way for the recipient to respond. Postage-paid envelopes and pledge cards are often included.
7. Close with a postscript that gives the strongest reason for the reader to respond.

ter is an example. At the end of the letter, there is often a postscript—or even several—that summarizes the crucial need for donations.

If you plan to use direct mail, you should consult a direct mail specialist. Such organizations are listed in the Yellow Pages under "Advertising-Direct Mail." There are usually several in any sizable community, and most of them are quite knowledgeable about the mechanics of computerized mailings and the preparation of effective appeals.

MEMORANDUMS

A memorandum—*memo* for short—is a brief written message, usually half a page or less in length. A memo is an internal message; that is, it is directed to one or more people inside the organization. Normally it is informal.

Purpose A memo can serve almost any communication purpose. It can ask for information, supply information, confirm a verbal exchange, ask for a meeting, schedule or cancel a meeting, remind, report, praise, caution, correct an earlier statement or memo, state a policy or perform any other function that requires a written message.

Content A memo should be brief—the very name suggests that it is a reminder, an aid to memory, a condensed message that eliminates every extraneous idea and word. In writing a memo, remember that even though it is internal and informal, it is nevertheless a record of what you have said. Accordingly, when you write a memo, take a little time to look it over and think about its effect. Also, although the memo is internal and informal, it might be seen by anyone inside the organization.

(*text continues on page 372*)

United States Committee for

unicef 🌐

United Nations Children's Fund
333 East 38th St., New York, NY 10016

Hugh Downs
Chair

Dear Friend,

I've enclosed a Life or Death Seed Catalog for you.

I call this the Life or Death Seed Catalog because what you do after looking through this catalog could help save the life of a small child ... a child like Youssouf.

Youssouf is a little boy who lives in Mali, a landlocked nation of the African Sahara. Mali was once called the "granary of Africa" because its farms were so productive.

But the horrible droughts of the 1980s destroyed Mali's agriculture. In some areas 80 percent of all livestock perished during those years. People were so hungry that many farmers like Youssouf's father were forced to eat their seed stocks -- the very seeds they need to plant new crops. They destroyed their futures -- in a desperate attempt to keep their families alive!

Now Mali's farmers face the nearly impossible task of trying to rebuild their harvests and livestock herds while trying to feed millions of hungry people ... without good seeds.

They may lose the battle ... and as always, the children will suffer most.

Youssouf's memories of the worst years of the drought are surprisingly vivid for a child who was only a toddler at the time. But I suppose that's understandable since he nearly died of starvation, and two of his sisters did die during the drought.

Even now, though the rains have returned, <u>one</u> <u>out</u> <u>of</u> <u>five</u> <u>children</u> <u>die</u> <u>before</u> <u>their</u> <u>fifth</u> <u>birthday</u>.

Youssouf is now old enough to help his parents in the fields ... and old enough to know that without good seeds there will be no harvest ... and his family will again go hungry.

That's why UNICEF needs our help to provide seeds. We must help the farmers of Mali rebuild their crops of millet, sorghum, maize, rice, groundnuts, and bourgou.

Bourgou is a perfect example of the help that's needed. It's a plant that once grew in most of the rivers and streams of

over, please

Figure 15.1 Fund-raising letters have only a few seconds to interest a reader. This letter has a strong beginning and continues to make the case by humanizing the problem instead of giving a lot of statistics. *(Courtesy of UNICEF, New York.)*

When our rescue team reached this badly injured sea lion stranded on a rocky shoreline, they were shocked at the sight of her injuries. Both of her shoulders were broken, one badly shattered, the result of a shotgun blast to her upper body. It was a miracle she even made it to the beach.

The rescue team carefully transported her back to our hospital. Intravenous fluids, round the clock care, and <u>five</u> surgeries to remove bone fragments and gunshot from her shoulders, helped Pauline pull through.

Not that Pauline appreciated it. Not one bit. She fought us through every injection, blood test, surgery. Even the volunteers who cleaned her pen and fed her weren't safe from her wrath. But months of physical therapy helped her regain almost 100% of her original mobility. We credit her feisty attitude as much as our intensive treatment.

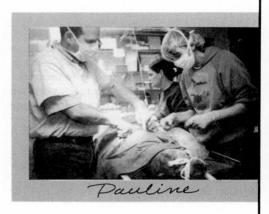

Pauline

Five months later, on a blustery January day, our release team drove Pauline out to a remote spot on the Pacific coast. She leapt out of her cage and raced the one hundred feet to the oceans' edge... Pauline was home free.

Dear Friend,

Pauline is a very special patient at one of the world's largest and most unique wild animal hospitals, **The Marine Mammal Center.** <u>And her species is endangered – in a very unfortunate sense of the word.</u> Every year thousands of sea lions are found dead from gunshot wounds. Whether competing for a fisherman's catch or just being friendly, these innocent creatures have the misfortune to be in the wrong place at the wrong time. But what makes Pauline's story different is that it has a happy ending.

Figure 15.2 Dramatic stories pique reader interest. This letter begins with a story before the actual letter begins. In succeeding pages, the letter continued in a brochure format with subheads and photos. *(Courtesy of The Marine Mammal Center, Sausalito, CA.)*

VOICE MAIL AS A MEMO SYSTEM

Memos aren't only in written form. Organizations also use sophisticated computerized telephone answering systems that allow a person to send a voice memo to one, several or thousands of persons in the organization. It is called *voice mail.*

Advantages

Voice mail speeds the process of getting information; a call is quicker than a memo delivered by interoffice mail. It eliminates "phone tag" because you can leave messages in someone's "mailbox" and that person can respond by leaving a message in yours. Messages are accessed by giving the code number that opens the mailbox—thus, confidentiality is maintained. Another feature of voice mail is the group conference call, which often eliminates the need for meetings.

Disadvantages

Although voice mail has many advantages for internal communication, it often frustrates people from outside the organization who wish to speak to someone. People are also alienated by complicated instructions involving pushing buttons as they work their way down the voice mail tree, trying to reach the proper department or individual.

Another frustration is leaving repeated messages but receiving no return call. Also, the answering message on voice mail can be long and tedious, giving more information than is really needed.

Making Voice Mail Work

Every voice mail system should be individually designed for the organization that will use it. Employees should be taught how to use the system and how to record an answering message that is short, concise and clearly enunciated. Every system should make it possible for a caller to talk to a real person immediately at the push of a button. It also is suggested that you update your answering message frequently. People also show good manners by letting callers know if they are traveling or when they can reasonably expect a return phone call. In any event, it is common courtesy to return calls as soon as possible.

Format   Every memo should identify its sender, recipient, subject and message. Printed forms are often used, but a memo can also be sent by E-mail. If it includes the essentials listed in the first sentence of this paragraph, it's a memo. One might look like this:

Monday, November 1

To: Public Relations Committee
From: Susan Parker
Subject: Meeting on Monday, November 15

Please bring some ideas on how to publicize and promote the company's annual employee picnic. The president wants to encourage the families of all employees to attend.

PROPOSALS

A proposal is a written, formal suggestion or recommendation that something be done. In most situations, a proposal calls for a major decision by top management. Almost anything can be proposed, but to give you a starting point, here are some possible subjects of proposals: to move the office, to adopt a 10-hour workday or a four-day workweek, to provide a childcare facility at the plant, or to modify the employee benefit plan.

Purpose   The purpose of a proposal is to get something accomplished—to persuade management to approve and authorize some important action that will have a long-lasting effect on the organization or its people. By putting the proposal in writing, you let management know exactly what is proposed, what decisions are called for and what the consequences may be. A verbal proposal may be tossed around, discussed briefly and discarded, by contrast, when the idea is in writing and formally presented, it forces management to make a decision.

Before writing a proposal, author Randall Majors says you should ask yourself questions like these:

70% *advertising*

- What is the purpose of the proposal?
- Who will read the proposal?
- What are the pertinent interests and values of the readers?
- What specific action can be taken on the basis of the proposal?
- What situation or problem does the proposal address?
- What is the history of the situation?
- How much information, and what kinds of information, will make the proposal persuasive?
- What format is most effective for the proposal?
- How formal in format, tone and style should the proposal be?

Organization   A proposal may be presented in a few pages or multiple pages, depending on the size of the organization and the scope of the proposal. A major proposal could include the following components:

1. *Transmittal*—a memo, letter or foreword in a booklet that summarizes why the proposal is being made.
2. *Table of contents*—a list of all items in the proposal.
3. *Tables and exhibits*—a list of illustrative elements and where they can be found.
4. *Summary*—a condensation of the proposal, which gives readers the basic information and enables them to appraise the idea before they go on to the details.

5. *Introduction*—giving the scope, the approach, how information was obtained and evaluated, limitations and problems to help the reader understand the idea and weigh its impact.
6. *Body*—a complete, detailed statement of what is proposed.
7. *Recommendation*—a clear, concise statement of just what is suggested and how it is to be implemented.
8. *Exhibits and bibliography*—items substantiating the statements in the proposal and assuring the readers that the proposal is based on thorough study of the problem or the opportunity.

A more informal proposal, one that is project-oriented, might have the following organizational structure:

1. *Introduction*—stating the purpose of the proposal.
2. *Body*—providing background to the problem situation, criteria for a solution, the proposed solution, a schedule for implementation, personnel assignments, budget and perhaps some background on the proposers.
3. *Conclusion*—requesting approval or the signing of a contract.

A more thorough discussion of how to write proposals for comprehensive public relations programs appears in Chapter 19.

SPECIAL REPORTS

A special report is usually prepared in response to a request from management; however, such a report can also be initiated at a lower level. A special report usually covers only one subject. It is normally an ad hoc, one-shot production. Almost always, it covers a problem or an opportunity. Such reports are also called *white papers*.

There are many kinds of reports, including analytical reports, progress reports and periodic reports. All of them take a somewhat different format, but a common guideline is to make them long enough to do the job but short enough to be easily digested.

In general, you should put the most important information first. This can be done in the basic summary or abstract that precedes the body of the report. Other good techniques are to use headings to divide the report and to use graphs or charts to summarize data. With desktop publishing, it is now relatively easy to make a report visually attractive and easy to read.

A large, formal report could take the basic format used for proposals, with some variation. But a great many reports are briefer and more informal. A progress report on public relations activities for a client or an employer might include the following:

1. *Introduction*—a brief statement of purpose or background.
2. *Body*—current status of the project, progress compared to plan, problems or situations encountered.
3. *Conclusion*—recommendations.

By contrast, a monthly or quarterly report on public relations activities to your supervisor might include the following:

1. *Introduction*—brief orientation.
2. *Body*—current status of work, significant developments since last report, problems or new opportunities.
3. *Conclusion*—recommendations or what will be accomplished by next report.

ANNUAL REPORTS

The most expensive and time-consuming report prepared by an organization is the annual report. Corporations, whose stock is publicly traded, are required by law to issue these reports. Most nonprofit organizations do the same because it is a good way to communicate with members and donors. In both cases, the report is a visible manifestation of an organization's culture, aspirations, and accomplishments.

Annual reports are usually drafted by the public relations department, but in many corporations the director of investor relations is responsible.

Purpose   The primary purpose of an annual report is to tell the stockholders and investment community what the organization has done in the past year and where it is going in the future. It is also sent to a variety of other audiences, including prospective employees, community opinion leaders and other businesses who have dealings with the company. In sum, it is a marketing and public relations tool of the organization.

REPORT-WRITING GUIDELINES

- On a cover page, use a title that tells exactly what the report is about.
- If the report is ten pages or more, use a table of contents or an index.
- Include, at the beginning of the report, a succinct summary of the report's findings or recommendations (often called an "executive summary"). It enables busy readers to rapidly understand the crux of the report.
- Avoid cluttering up the basic report by placing supporting materials and exhibits in the appendix at the end of the report.
- Use subheads, boldfacing, underlining throughout the report to break up blocks of copy.
- Use simple graphs, bar charts, pie charts to present key statistical information.
- Be concise. Don't use excessive words. Check for repetitious information.
- Check for clarity. Is it clear what you want the reader to do with the report?

Content   The successes and failures of a profit-making organization can be measured largely in dollars and cents. Nonprofit organizations must use different methods of appraisal, but the more numbers and facts that can be included, the more informative the report will be. The reports of nonprofit organizations have no specified requirements. The writer includes whatever is believed necessary. With profit-making firms, there are some musts.

Every corporation whose stock is publicly held must prepare and distribute an annual report to its shareholders. Basically, this is a financial document, but management usually tries to give shareholders something more than the figures required by the Securities and Exchange Commission. The figures are compiled by the financial staff of the company (nominally, the treasurer) and include assets and liabilities, earnings, financial condition of the company, dividends, stock prices, the nature of the business, trends of the business and names of directors. The goal is to supply all the information needed to appraise the value of the stock. The complete SEC regulations can be obtained from the SEC or from many public accounting firms.

If you work on an annual report, you will be primarily involved with the nonfinancial part. The report may consist largely of tables, but it is more interesting if it contains items such as a letter from the CEO or details about the products or services and the people who make or perform them. Other topics include plans, problems, opportunities and prospects. Predictions are dangerous, but calling attention to something that is likely to affect the organization in the future is certainly reasonable. For example, a lumber company might report a change in U.S. Forest Service policies, which could alter the lumbering operations; an oil company could discuss changes in rules for offshore drilling, which could modify the supply situation. Other subjects that could be included are construction plans and progress, supplies of raw material, labor and legal problems, manufacturing, personnel, taxes, tariffs, marketing, advertising, social responsibility and public relations.

Format   Most annual reports are prepared in booklet or brochure form. A few have been printed in a newspaper format and annual reports are increasingly being posted on company web sites. These innovations have merit, but few organizations go far from the tried-and-true publication that is so widely used.

The readers of annual reports are of two sorts: the nonexpert individual and the sophisticated financial analyst. The amateur is mainly interested in the quality of the management, earnings, dividends, stock appreciation and the outlook for the industry. The experts—who advise investors or manage large holdings—want much more information, which they feed into their computers. This difference in information needs presents the organization with a problem. A few hundred people want great masses of data, while thousands don't want the detail. There are several solutions to this problem. One approach is to design an annual report that gives the financial highlights in easy-to-read format at the beginning. Apple Computer, for example, used 16 pages of 24-point type and color photos at the beginning of its 1995 annual report to give key information about finances, markets and its business strategy for the coming year. The next 32 pages, however, were in 8-point type and crammed with all the statistics that a financial analyst would need.

Figure 15.3 An annual report is the most expensive and time-consuming publication of a corporation. It can run 48 pages and includes numerous color photos and computer graphics. It satisfies the requirements of the Securities Exchange Commission (SEC) but can also serve as a capabilities brochure for the organization. (*Courtesy of Apple Computer Company, Cupertino, CA.*)

A second approach is to do a summary annual report of several pages for employees, individual stockholders and other key publics who are interested in the financial health of the organization but don't want masses of detail. Hughes Aircraft Company, for example, took the innovative approach of producing an artist's version of a reservoir that represented the firm's total assets. The three outflow pipes from the dam represented current liabilities, long-term debts and other liabilities. (See Figure 15.4 on page 379.)

Preparing an Annual Report

An annual report usually covers every department of the organization. Consequently, every department head may want input, and each may have different and emphatic ideas. The task of the public relations people involved is to coordinate, plan, consult, write, design and produce the report. Tact, perseverance and determination to get the job done are essential.

Work on the report may start six months before the date of issue. The first step is to try to anticipate the socioeconomic and political climate that will prevail when the report is issued. This requires continuous monitoring of public and owner attitudes to know what is going on and coming up. It also necessitates frequent briefing of management on these trends.

With this program established, you can start planning the report. First, you should look at the last report; compare it with those of other organizations; criticize it; think of ways to make it better, more informative, more understandable, more useful.

There are many sources of information that should be tapped for possible use in writing the report. Especially critical are internal reports, planning documents, market research findings and capital budgets. You should also review the 10-K (annual) and 10-Q (quarterly) reports filed with the SEC.

When you are thoroughly informed about the situation, you can start consulting the key executives and establishing the theme of the report. Basically, the objective is to inform, but the theme makes the report more interesting. Usually it focuses on some aspect of the business—people, products, global markets, the future. The theme will have to be approved by management.

When the theme is established, it is time to think of design—how the report will look, what will be included, how the various elements will be treated. You can get some useful ideas by studying the reports that are cited each year by the Financial Analysts Federation.

Trends in Annual Reports

Annual reports change with the times. They are considered the most important single document a public company can produce, so a great amount of attention is given to content, graphics and overall design. The objective is to assure that the annual report reflects corporate culture and external economic conditions.

In the late 1990s, seven trends in corporate annual reports are discernible:

1. *Candor and frankness.* Global competition has caused the shrinkage of corporate profits and massive downsizing in many industries. Consequently, many corporations are more candid in their annual reports and "tell it like it is." There is more emphasis on such topics as specific issues facing the industry and the company's strategy for meeting future business challenges.
2. *More emphasis on marketing.* Annual reports used to be primarily for stockholders, securities analysts and portfolio managers. Today, the annual report is also used as a marketing tool to increase consumer loyalty and

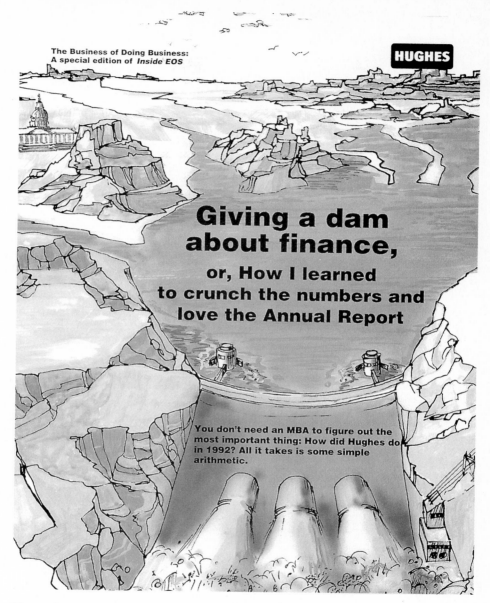

Figure 15.4 A summary of a corporate annual report is often the best way to inform employees about the organization's fiscal health. This innovative report, by Hughes Aircraft Company, explains financial details in an easy-to-understand manner. (*Copyright Hughes Aircraft Company, Los Angeles, CA.*)

TIPS FOR WRITING ANNUAL REPORTS

1. *Use a theme.* Focus the entire report on a central idea such as quality measurement, productivity, innovation, technical innovation or employee dedication. Each section should explain how the subject matter contributes to the central theme.

2. *Use headings that say something.* Instead of labels such as "Innovation," "Finance" and "Research," use newspaper-type headlines such as "How We Develop New Products" or "Where the Money Goes." For example, IBM used the following headline in one of its annual reports: "Helping Customers with Service and Solutions."

3. *Keep the report understandable.* Don't let lawyers and accountants fill the pages with turgid, pompous prose or technical jargon. Remember that an annual report is for stockholders who need simple explanations in common English.

4. *Make the shareholder letter say something.* Let the CEO write it in his or her own words. If things are good, say so. If things are bad, don't weasel. Simply say, "This year resulted in lower-than-expected earnings" or "This year was a disappointment."

5. *Humanize executives.* Brief biographies can make key people more human and can build confidence in management.

6. *Stress uniqueness.* Tell the shareholders what is different about the company. What makes it good or profitable? Why is the company a good investment? How does it compare to competitors, and what is its position in the industry?

---

build the company's image. Model Cindy Crawford adorned the annual report of PepsiCo as a "typical investor."

3. *Desktop publishing.* New innovations in desktop publishing, coupled with shrinking budgets, are causing more companies to design and produce reports without extensive use of outside writers and designers.

4. *Readability.* Annual reports are becoming more magazine-like with summary headlines, easy-to-understand charts and graphs, simple question-and-answer sections and more conversational prose. This reflects the growing trend of distributing the annual report to a variety of publics—customers, current and prospective employees, suppliers, community opinion leaders and others.

5. *Environmental sensitivity.* In their continuing efforts to portray themselves as environmentally conscious, many organizations use recycled paper and soybean-based inks for annual reports. In addition, annual reports are becoming shorter, saving more trees.

6. *Global approach.* Corporations now have global operations and the annual report functions as a capabilities brochure that markets a company on a worldwide scale. Some companies even translate parts of their annual report into several languages. The chairman's letter in Nike's annual report was translated into French, Spanish and Chinese.

7. *CD-ROM and the Internet.* Although the printed annual report will remain dominant, an increasing number of companies are also making their annual

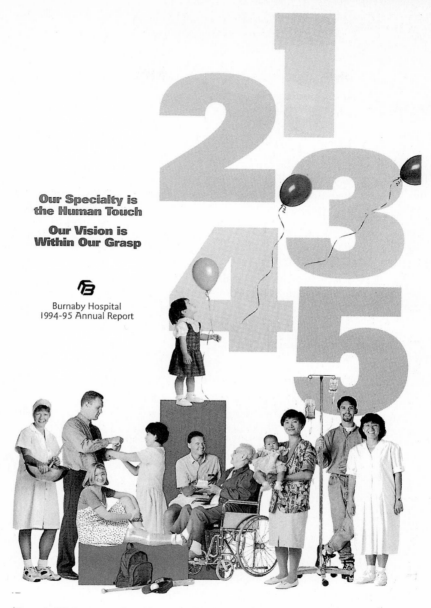

Our Specialty is
the Human Touch

Our Vision is
Within Our Grasp

Burnaby Hospital
1994-95 Annual Report

Figure 15.5   Annual reports aren't always slick and glossy. This annual report, for a Canadian Hospital, was only eight pages long and was written in an easy-to-understand style. Many nonprofit organizations publish annual reports even though they are not legally required to do so. This is one way of building consumer confidence in the institution. (*Courtesy of the KJ Lee Group, Burnaby, British Columbia.*)

reports available on CD-ROM and the Internet. One advantage of these distribution methods is savings on postage and paper costs. However, the new technology will force companies to create annual reports that are highly visual, entertaining and interactive.

SUMMARY

1. Letters are personalized communication that should be well organized, clear and concise. They can prevent misunderstandings and provide a record of an agreement or a transaction.

2. E-mail (electronic mail) has the advantage of instant delivery through a computer network. Take care to format E-mail messages correctly.

3. Direct mail makes it possible to reach many people with a personalized message using database publishing. It requires specialized writing that can motivate and persuade the receiver.

4. Memos convey brief messages clearly and accurately. E-mail and voice mail are efficient vehicles for delivering memos rapidly.

5. Proposals and reports must follow a logical, well-organized format. They are prepared in response to a management request for information in connection with a problem or an opportunity.

6. Reports should put the most important information first. This can be done by providing an abstract or executive summary at the beginning of the report.

7. An annual report is the most expensive and most time-consuming publication released by any organization. For corporations, it satisfies SEC regulatory requirements. However, most organizations use it as a public relations tool.

8. Today's annual reports are designed with a number of audiences in mind. They are more magazine-like, more environmentally correct and more global in outlook.

EXERCISES

1. The chapter contains the first pages of two fund-raising letters, from UNICEF and The Marine Mammal Center. Get some additional samples from local charitable organizations or even what you personally receive in the mail. Analyze them from the standpoint of effective writing and persuasion (you might want to review Chapter 3 again).

2. A customer has written to your company complaining about the quality of service in one of your retail outlets. She claims that the clerks were busy gossiping among themselves and oblivious to her requests for assistance. She further states that the company's advertisements about "friendly service" are dishonest and encloses her cut-up credit card, saying she will never shop at your store again. Draft a letter to this irate customer with the objective of winning back her confidence in the store.

3. As a director of public relations, you must write a memo to the company's executive vice president requesting approval for upgrading the company's quarterly publication to a monthly periodical. Although no increase in staff is necessary, another $20,000 will be needed to cover increased publication expenses for the next year. Write a persuasive one- or two-page memo that succinctly states your case.

4. Write a fund-raising letter on behalf of the local humane society. In addition, design and write the response card that would accompany a contribution.

5. Get some samples of corporate annual reports. Analyze their format and content. What do they have in common? To what extent do they reflect the current trends in annual reports that are outlined at the end of the chapter.

16 *Speakers and Speeches*

The United States is a society of speakers and audiences. An executive of Ruder Finn, a public relations firm, once estimated that companies and associations convene close to a million meetings annually, all of them focusing on speakers in endless succession.

Speakers and speeches are important tools in public relations. During your career, you will be asked to handle speakers, give speeches and write speeches for others.

This chapter will tell you how to train executives and employees in your organization; how to find placement opportunities; how to prepare for a speech, a panel or a media interview; the fundamentals of speech-writing; and how to get publicity mileage out of a speech.

SPEAKER TRAINING AND PLACEMENT

Giving talks and speeches is an important part of an organization's outreach to its key publics. A talk by an executive or an employee is a highly personal form of communication and adds a human dimension to any organization. It's a form of face-to-face communication, and it offers the chance for interaction between the speaker and the audience.

Speech giving should be an integral part of an organization's overall public relations program. Indeed, public relations personnel are often involved in training speakers and seeking appropriate forums where key publics can be reached.

Executive Training

Today the public is demanding more open disclosure and accountability from organizations, which is forcing many executives to mount the speaker's platform. *PR Reporter,* in one survey of executives, found that over half spend 10 or more hours each month meeting with outside groups. In addition, the majority average 20 speeches a year, about two-thirds spend time on press conferences and another third appear on TV.

As a consequence, more executives are taking courses designed to improve their public speaking skills. Cincinnati Gas & Electric holds seminars of this kind for both managers and line employees. Levi Strauss & Company teaches "effective presentation skills" to middle managers. Other companies have also rushed into speech training for executives, creating a major boom for consultants who train employees at all levels to represent their firms in public forums or media interviews.

Because the costs of such training sessions often run into thousands of dollars, organizations with limited budgets may not be able to afford them. Therefore, the public relations department is often given the responsibility of training executives in media interview and speech skills.

Top executives who serve as spokespeople for the organization need media training, in particular. In most cases, executives don't know much about the techniques that reporters use to interview people. It is your responsibility, as a public relations professional, to train them.

First, you must get a commitment from the executive to spend some time learning how to give effective interviews. You can teach the person many of the basics that have been discussed in previous chapters and that will be discussed later in this chapter.

You can also play the role of the reporter and ask questions. Expected questions should be supplemented by others, such as "trick and trap" questions. Charge the interviewee with ducking questions, and try in every way possible to make your student lose his or her temper.

Although your student may become somewhat irritated with you, such a session will build confidence in handling a real question-and-answer situation. If you feel uncomfortable in the role of reporter, another technique is to hire a local reporter or editor as a consultant to spend an hour or two in a simulated interview with your spokesperson. This will give your student a chance to meet a real reporter in a controlled situation.

The session should be videotaped so that executive can actually see how he or she comes across in an interview. Witnessing oneself blushing, floundering, mumbling, getting defensive or seeming incompetent is a powerful stimulus to do better next time.

Videotaping is also done to help an executive see how he or she comes across giving a speech. It's a powerful educational tool that almost always has more impact than telling a person how to give an effective speech.

Speech training can be divided in two parts: what to say and how to say it. Public relations personnel are most effective at helping executives crystallize what they want to say. Both of you should review the context of the speech from the standpoint of location, expected audience and what information would be interesting to them.

Another consideration is what you want to say that will advance organizational objectives—to position the organization or industry as a leader, to plant the perception that the organization is successful or simply to show that the organization is environmentally conscious and a good community citizen. All speeches should have one to three key messages.

There are entire courses and many textbooks on how to give a speech. The ideal speaker is one who knows about the subject, whose voice and appearance will make a good impression and who is comfortable standing in front of an audience. Ronald Reagan was successful as the "great communicator" because he had an amiable personality, a sincere manner, great vocal delivery and was photogenic.

Not every executive is a Ronald Reagan but, with practice, almost anyone can give an acceptable speech. Additional tips are given later in the chapter.

Employee Training

Executives aren't the only ones who give speeches. Many organizations also effectively use rank-and-file employees on a systematic basis to extend the organization's outreach and presence in the community.

In most organizations, there are people who are able and willing to make speeches. Some of the would-be speakers will be known; others may need to be found. This can be done by recruiting volunteers or by asking people to suggest the names of individuals who might be willing to serve in a speaker's bureau.

A speaker's bureau is more than just a list of employees who are willing to speak. It is a training center that also prepares organizational materials such as slides and overheads that speakers can incorporate into their talks (see Chapter 17 on audiovisual aids).

Public relations staff also work with the volunteers in developing key messages about the organization that should be included in any presentation—whether it be a presentation to the local chapter of the American Association of Chemical Engineers or the local Rotary Club.

Figure 16.1 Southern California Edison uses posters and advertisements in various ethnic publications to promote its multilingual speaker's bureau. Volunteers are fluent in English and one other language—Spanish, Mandarin, Cantonese, Cambodian or Vietnamese. The speaker's bureau is an effective tool for community outreach and reaching a variety of customers. *(Courtesy of Southern California Edison.)*

Ideally, a speaker's bureau will have volunteers who are expert on a variety of subjects. A person in finance may be an expert on worker's compensation, and a engineer in the research department may have an expertise in lasers.

Placement

Once executives and employees have been trained, your job is finding opportunities for them to speak.

An organization usually publicizes the existence of a speaker's bureau by preparing a simple pamphlet or brochure and sending it to various clubs and organizations in the community that regularly use speakers.

The public relations department also encourages calls from various organizations who need speakers on various topics. At other times, you have to be more proactive and contact the organization to offer the services of a speaker on a particular topic. One of the most difficult jobs in any club is that of program director, and they welcome any suggestions that make their lives easier.

The placement of the organization's top executives, however, tends to be more strategic. Top executives often get more requests for speeches than they can ever fulfill, so the problem is selecting a few of the invitations that are extended.

The criteria, at this point, become somewhat pragmatic and cold-hearted. Public relations staff are often charged with screening the invitations on the basis of such factors as the venue, the nature of the group, the size of the audience and whether the audience is an important public to the organization. If most or all of these factors are positive, the executive will most likely consent to give a speech.

Media requests for interviews are treated in much the same way. Busy executives consent to media interviews only if the publication is influential, has high circulation and reaches key audiences. A business executive, for example, rarely turns down an interview with a reporter from the *Wall Street Journal, Fortune,* or *Forbes.*

In other words, just because a reporter wants an interview with the chief executive doesn't necessarily mean that you automatically grant the request. One alternative is to ask the reporter if he or she would be willing to interview someone else in the organization.

At other times, public relations staff are proactive in seeking placement opportunities. If the chief executive officer wants to become a leader in the industry, for example, the public relations staff actively seeks out speech opportunities before prestigious audiences and tries to convince influential media to do profiles and feature stories on the person.

THE NATURE OF A SPEECH

It is important to know the basic structure of an effective speech and imperative to incorporate these concepts into every speech you prepare.

A Speech Is Heard, Not Read

The average speech has only one brief exposure—the few minutes during which the speaker is presenting it. There is no chance to go back, no time to let it slowly digest, no opportunity for clarification. The message must get across now or never.

You may be an accomplished writer, but you must realize that speaking is something else again. As Louis Nizer once said, "The words may be the same, but

---

LOOKING FOR A SPEAKER?

There are literally thousands of clubs and organizations looking for speakers. To help them with the process, there's the *Yearbook of Experts, Authorities and Spokespersons* published by Broadcast Interview Source, Washington, D.C.

The 864-page book lists speakers on a multitude of topics including: dressing down, genius, dumb jocks, PT Boats, affluence, Arizona cactus, doubtful medical devices, deep breathing, Cyberlove and puns.

the grammar, rhetoric and phrasing are different. It is a different mode of expression—a different language."

One major difference is that you have to build up to a major point and prepare the audience for what is coming. The lead of a written story attempts to say everything in about 15 to 25 words right at the beginning. If a speaker used the same form, most of the audience probably wouldn't hear it. When a speaker begins to talk, the audience is still settling down—so the first one or two minutes are devoted to giving unimportant information: a humorous comment, remarks on how nice it is to be there and so on.

You should also be aware that people's minds wander. As your speech progresses, you must restate basic points and also summarize your general message.

One platitude of the speaking circuit, but still a valid one, is to "tell them what you are going to tell them, tell it to them and then tell them what you have told them." In this way, an audience is given a series of guideposts as they listen to the talk.

Some concepts used by writers are of course transferable to speaking. The words you use should be clear, concise, short and definite. Use words that specify, explain and paint pictures for the audience.

A Speech Must Fit the Audience

Because every speech is aimed at a specific audience, you must know as much as possible about yours. Who are they? Such factors as age, occupation, gender, religion, race, education, intelligence, vocabulary, residence, interests, attitudes, group memberships, knowledge, politics and income may bear on what they will find interesting.

A talk before a professional group can also end up being more relevant if you prepare for it by doing some audience analysis and basic research. Talk to members of the profession. Get an idea of the issues or problems they face. If you don't know anyone in the profession, at least go to the local library and read five or six issues of the group's professional journal. This will give you some insight and perhaps even provide you with some quotations from leaders in the field.

In summary, most audiences have a core of common interests; this should help you to prepare a speech that will appeal to them. A talk to the stockholders of a corporation should be considerably different from one to employees or to a consumer group.

A Speech Must Be Specific

People remember only a small part of what they hear. You must therefore make sure that they hear things they can remember. A vague generality has little or no chance of being understood, let alone remembered. The speech must be built around specific ideas phrased in clear and memorable language.

A vague statement—for example, "We ought to do something about illegal immigration"—has no chance of being effective. If it were more specific—say, "We should stop illegal immigration by requiring everyone to carry a tamperproof identification card"—it would offer the audience an idea that is definite and understandable.

A Speech Must Have an Objective

This is probably the most important requirement of all. There is no point in making speeches unless they accomplish something. In preparing a speech, the first step is to determine what you want the audience to know or do. In other words, what attitude do you want the audience to have after listening to the speech?

A speech may inform, persuade, activate or celebrate. It may also amuse or entertain. That particular kind of speech will not be considered here, but this does not rule out the use of *some* humor in the other kinds of speeches.

An informative speech is one that tells the audience something it does not know or does not understand. An informative speech might tell the audience about how the new local sewage system works, the results of the latest United Way campaign, the expansion plans of a major local corporation, or budget problems facing the state's system of higher education.

A persuasive speech is designed to convince the audience about the merits of some idea. Such a speech could try to convince people that the tamperproof ID card previously mentioned could easily be adopted and implemented. A similar speech

---

HOW TO USE NONVERBAL COMMUNICATION

A speaker doesn't communicate to an audience with voice alone. The audience also receives a great deal of nonverbal communication from the speaker. Veteran speaker Jack Pyle offers this acronym method to help you appear confident and become a better communicator:

S = Smile. It's one of your best communication tools, always helps make a good first impression, and helps make others want to listen to you.

P = Posture. How you stand or sit makes a big difference. Your physical stance tells others how you feel about yourself. Confident people stand tall and sit straight.

E = Eye contact. A person who is believable and honest "looks you right in the eye." Don't stare, but look at a person's face for at least 3 seconds before moving on to look at another person. If you are talking to a group, give your message to one person at a time.

A = Animation. Show your interest in your subject with your energy and animation. Be enthusiastic. Animate your voice by speeding up and slowing down, talking louder and softer at times. Make your face animated. "A" is also for attitude. Make sure you feel good about yourself and what you are doing.

K = Kinetics (motion). Use your arms to make gestures that support your words. Use two-handed, symmetrical gestures, and hold your hands high when gesturing—at about chest level.

Source: Jack Pyle, "How to Control Nonverbal Communication and Train Others." *PR Reporter,* Oct. 19, 1992, p. 3.

could convince people of the need for a higher sales tax or better funding for the police force's crime-fighting efforts.

An activating speech is designed to get the listener to do something. Direct and specific action is suggested and urged. A basic principle of persuasion is that a speaker should provide an audience with a specific course of action to take: write to a congressional representative, vote for a candidate, purchase a product, take steps to conserve energy.

A celebratory speech is designed to honor some person or event. Such speeches are often trite and boring, but they don't have to be. If a person is being honored for lifetime professional achievement, why not start out with an anecdote that best exemplifies the feats being honored? This is much better than a chronological account of the person's life as if it were being read from an obituary.

Events such as grand openings, anniversaries and retirements usually have friendly, receptive audiences. In such cases, you can be more emotional and get away with some platitudes, which will probably be warmly received. When you prepare such a speech, however, keep it brief. Five minutes should be ample.

A Speech Must Get a Reaction

If a speech gets no response from the listeners, it is a waste of the speaker's breath and the audience's time. Regardless of the subject, a speech must convey ideas and arouse some emotion in the audience. At least the listeners must feel that they have received new information and insight on a topic that concerns them.

In most cases, the person who is asked to speak is perceived as an expert on a given subject. Consequently, the audience wants the benefit of that person's thinking and analysis. They don't want platitudes or statements that are self-evident. An economist should offer more than the flat statement that the economy is in trouble; he or she should explain why it is in trouble and what the solution might be.

Speech Length

Regardless of the nature and the objective of a speech, it must be interesting *now*. It must include up-to-date facts and information; it does no good to talk about a situation that is no longer current or has no present interest for the audience. If the topic is an old one, it is imperative that the speaker talk about it in a new way. For example, everyone knows that dinosaurs are extinct, but their demise retains current interest as scientists argue over the reasons for it.

If the speech is one of several in a general program, it is wise to learn what others will be talking about. This will provide a context for your talk and add interest by reference to the other topics and speakers. It will also help you avoid saying the same thing as other speakers.

Another dimension of timeliness is the length of the speech. In general, shorter is better. For a meeting that has no other business, the talk should be about 20 minutes long.

It is a typical practice in many organizations to put the speaker on after a half hour of organizational announcements and committee reports. In such a situation, since the audience will already be getting tired, the talk should last no more than 10 to 15 minutes. If it is one of several speeches, the limit should be 10 minutes.

Figure 16.2 Speeches can inspire. General Colin Powell gives a commencement address at Harvard University. (*Photo by Sarah Putnam/The Picture Cube.*)

The time of day is very important. A morning speech generally finds the audience most alert and receptive. At the end of the day, with the cocktail hour only minutes away, a speaker is at an extreme disadvantage. The latter situation calls for more skill on the part of the speaker; he or she must be more enthusiastic, more forceful and more attention-getting than his or her morning counterpart.

SEMISPEECHES

A speech is controlled by the speaker. He or she knows what is going to be said. The subject matter is complete and well organized. At the end, the speaker may be asked a few questions, and if the talk runs long, the chairperson may try to speed the closing. Still, the speaker is the boss.

Control passes to others when the speaker participates in semispeech activities such as panels, debates, talk shows and media interviews. Here someone else is directing the action, and other people may be talking to the same audience. Even so, these semispeech opportunities are valuable aids to public communication and should be used whenever possible.

Panels

A panel usually consists of a moderator and several people, each of whom makes an opening statement on the subject and then answers questions from the audience.

Opening statements should not last longer than five minutes. The number of questions that are answered depends on the time available. Often the moderator of the panel will prepare a sizable list of questions, which are distributed to the audience. The questions are numbered. Someone who wants an answer to a question merely says, "I'd like an answer to question 16," whereupon the moderator asks a member of the panel to give the answer. Usually there are more questions than can be answered, but this procedure does permit answering the ones of most interest to the audience. In preparing for this situation, it is necessary to decide in advance who will answer which questions. It is your job to give your speaker the answers to the assigned questions, unless the answers are already known.

Debates

In high schools and colleges, a debate is generally conducted by teams of several speakers. Most debates in the world of public relations are not team efforts. They pit two opponents against each other, and each carries the burden of making the case of his or her side and rebutting the statements of the opponent. The so-called debates of American political campaigns are not really debates; they are merely presentations during which the rivals offer their answers to the same questions.

The management of political debates is not within the purview of this book. That is best left to the political specialists. But any reader of this volume may at some time have to handle a debate on some public issue. Aside from the need to know something about debating, in general there is one special warning worth heeding. This involves the situation in which a moderator may try to split the debate into two parts, with each speaker being allowed a brief period for rebuttal. A toss of the coin determines who will be first.

It is very advantageous to speak *last* in such a situation because the last speaker may have ten or more minutes in which to try to demolish the statements of the opponent. The rebuttal period may be only a minute or two, and this is hardly adequate to overcome the effect of a long windup statement. The audience is left with a much stronger impression of what the last speaker said. To avoid being caught at such a disadvantage, you should insist that the debate be broken into short segments—five minutes would be a good length. Then the debate would consist of several five-minute statements by each speaker and a short summary rebuttal.

MEDIA INTERVIEWS

There are two types of media interviews. The first is the informal interview that a reporter conducts with you on the telephone, at an event or in your office. The second type of interview is when you appear on a radio or television talk show.

Both types are classified as semispeeches because it is necessary to do advance preparation and give some thought to what you want to say. As noted in Chapter 9, it's important to interview the reporter first before he or she interviews you. Find out what story the reporter is working on and what kind of information they want from you.

To get the best results from an interview, you should follow these tips:

- Most reporters merely want information, but some will be looking for headlines. To appreciate this, just watch a presidential press conference. Note the kinds of questions asked and visualize the headlines that might result from an injudicious reply.
- Conversely, it may be desirable to make headlines. If you do want to see special attention paid to something, say it in a way that can be quoted or even headlined.
- Watch for loaded questions. Take time to think. Don't repeat a derogatory remark; shift to another subject.
- Prepare for the worst. Think of every question that might possibly be asked, reasonable or unreasonable. Then prepare an answer for each.
- Be sure to state your key points early in the interview. Use examples and anecdotes. Don't tell half-truths. Don't exaggerate. Don't brag about your organization or its products or services.
- Watch your attitude. Don't be arrogant, evasive or uncooperative. Don't argue. Admit mistakes—and tell how you have corrected them. Don't use jargon. Don't lose your temper.
- Don't memorize your statements, but do use notes for reference. Speak from the public viewpoint; it's the public's interest that is important. Look at the interviewer when he or she is asking a question, but face the audience or the television camera when you are answering.
- Be cooperative, but don't surrender. Watch for presumptive questions: "Why are you resisting the efforts to control pollution?" "Why do you charge such outrageous prices?" Deny the statement and shift to another topic.
- If a question is unfair or too personal, say so and refuse to answer. You aren't required to answer any question. Decline with a smile, but don't say "no comment."
- Never speak "off the record." Anything you say is on some sort of record—videotape or the reporter's notes.
- Don't challenge figures unless you *know* they are wrong. Remember that there are many ways to cite statistics.
- Be as relaxed and informal as possible. A humorous remark may be used if it is appropriate, but don't be facetious; you might be misunderstood.
- Discuss only activities and policies that lie within your area of responsibility.

- Admit you don't know the answer if that's the case. If you promise to provide more information, deliver.
- If the situation permits, tape the interview yourself.

There are additional tips that apply to interviews on broadcast talk shows. Ketchum Public Relations gives the following advice:

- Say it in 60 seconds.
- Deliver your message with sincerity.
- Know your facts.
- Rehearse your message.
- Stay alert.
- Participate in discussion.
- Get your message across.
- Don't get mad.
- Don't look at the camera.

Grooming and dress are also important in a television program. Men should wear conservative suits. A sports jacket might be permissible in some cases, but it must not be loud. Wild plaids or violent colors won't do. Suits should be dark; if there is a pattern, it should be so subdued as to be almost invisible. Men should avoid white shirts. Pale blue, gray or tan with no noticeable pattern is best. Flashy rings, large cuff links, and big belt buckles are unacceptable. If a man has a dark

Figure 16.3 Broadcast interviews provide information and entertainment. Here, comedian Lily Tomlin is interviewed by Tom Berseron on "People Are Talking." (*Courtesy of Bob Kramer Studio/Stock, Boston.*)

beard, a shave just before the appearance is a good idea. For any television appearance, the producer may suggest some makeup. This should not be resisted; even the nation's presidents have used it.

Women should dress conservatively in dresses or suits. Makeup should be the kind that is normally worn for business. Any jewelry that dangles, jingles, or flashes is taboo.

Another important point is that the speaker is "on stage" at all times. A surreptitious scratch or adjustment of clothing may be seen by some members of the audience or picked up by a TV camera. A speaker should assume that an inelegant gesture will be seen.

SPEECHWRITING

The good speechwriter has the ability to stand in the shoes of the person who must give the speech. Sociologists call this empathic ability—the ability to think and feel much as the person who will give the speech. In a sense, you become your client's alter ego.

Such understanding and empathic ability do not arise in a vacuum. They can develop only after a great deal of research and thorough discussion with the person for whom you are writing.

Researching Audience and Speaker

If you are given a speechwriting assignment, the first step is to find out everything possible about the audience. Who? Where? When? How many people? What time of day? Purpose of meeting? How long a talk? Purpose of talk? Other speakers and their topics? To find the answers to these questions, it might be necessary to talk with a number of individuals. Don't necessarily trust the information you get if it appears to be only a guess. Too many speakers have innocently blundered because they received bad information about their audience.

Next, learn everything you can about the speaker. Listen to the speaker talk—to other groups, to subordinates, to you. See how his or her mind works, what word phrases are favored, and what kinds of opinions are expressed. In addition to listening, it is also a good idea to go over material that the client has written or, if written by others, that the client admires in terms of style and method of presentation.

Laying the Groundwork for the Speech

Ideally, a writer should have lengthy conversations with the speaker before beginning to write a rough draft of the talk. In a conversational setting, you and the speaker should discuss the speech in terms of objective, approach, strategy, points to emphasize, scope and facts or anecdotes the speaker would like to include.

Objective   First you must determine the objective. What is the speech supposed to accomplish? What attitude should the audience have when the speech is concluded?

REMEMBER YOUR AUDIENCE

1. *Know your listeners.* You can hardly know too much about the members of your audience: age, sex, occupation, education, socioeconomic status and any other facts—and especially why they are listening to this speech.
2. *Use their language.* Use terms and expressions that are familiar. Similes, metaphors and anecdotes are valuable only if they are pertinent.
3. *Use visuals.* Your audience will remember much more if you show *and* tell than if you only tell.
4. *Use humor carefully.* Avoid side comments and jokes that may offend the opposite sex or various racial and ethnic groups.
5. *Watch your facts.* Be absolutely certain that you are giving listeners information that is reliable. Check and double-check your information.
6. *Focus on the benefit.* Any speech must tell listeners why they will gain from the ideas being expressed.

Everything that goes into the speech should be pertinent to that objective. Material that does not help attain the objective should not be used. Whether the objective is to inform, persuade, activate, or commemorate, that particular objective must be uppermost in the speechwriter's mind.

Approach The approach might be described as the tone of the speech. A friendly audience may appreciate a one-sided talk, with no attempt to present both sides of an issue. For example, a politician at a fund-raising dinner of supporters does not bother to give the opposition's views. An executive talking to the company's sales force does not need to praise the competitor's product.

Many speaking engagements, however, take place before neutral audiences (Rotary, Lions, Kiwanis and any number of other civic or professional organizations) where the audience may have mixed views or even a lack of knowledge about the topic.

In such a case, it is wise to take a more objective approach and give an overview of the various viewpoints. The speech can still advocate a particular position, but the audience will appreciate the fact that you have included other points of view. From the standpoint of persuasion, you also have more control over how the opposition view is expressed if you say it instead of waiting for an audience member to bring it up. When someone stands up and says, "What you say is fine, but you didn't consider the problem of . . .," you have lost control. If you have included the "problem" in your talk—and perhaps have even admitted that this is a valid point—it takes the wind out of audience opposition.

Hostile or unfriendly audiences present the greatest challenge. They are already predisposed against what you say, and they tend to reject anything that does not square with their opinions. Remember the old saying "Don't confuse me with the facts—my mind is already made up." The best approach is to find some common ground with the audience. This technique lets the audience know that the speaker shares or at least understands some of their concerns.

A WRITER'S APPROACH TO SPEECHWRITING

Writing a speech for someone requires the writer to thoroughly understand the intended audience, the objectives of the speech and what key messages must be delivered. Melissa Brown, a free-lance speechwriter in St. Joseph, Michigan, compiled this outline in consultation with her client.

The assignment: Write a speech for the president of the Grocery Manufacturers of America (GMA) on the topic, "The Changing Challenges Facing the Food Industry."

The audience: The International Food and Lifestyles Media Conference, Cincinnati.

Speech objectives:
- Give food writers useful, research-based information on the lifestyles of American consumers, thus positioning GMA as a good source of statistics/information.
- Neutralize misinformation presented by opponents of biotechnologically developed food products, presenting the industry's side of the story and exposing the lack of credentials of a major voice in the opposition.
- Provide information on the good work the industry has accomplished in addressing environmental issues, in particular, packaging and solid waste.
- Demonstrate to GMA board that GMA is speaking out on the issues that affect their businesses.
- Frame the arguments other food industry spokespeople can use in other opportunities, within their companies and with the press.

Key messages:
- The profile and purchasing habits of the American consumer have changed significantly.
- We enjoy the safest and most abundant food supply in the world, despite what you hear from a small but vocal group of opponents.
- The grocery industry has surpassed government regulations and everyone's expectations in the rapid progress made on environmental issues.

Strategy   This is the *how* of speechwriting. Once you've determined the objective and the approach, your next step is to decide what ideas and information will be needed to convince the audience.

Alex Osborn, the famous advertising man, was once asked how he got so many brilliant ideas. He replied, "By constantly thinking about the problem." This prescription applies well to speechwriting. By constantly thinking about the problem of convincing the audience, you will come upon many ideas that will help you reach this goal.

At this stage, it is advisable to start making notes. As you think of ideas or examples you want to use, jot them down somewhere, perhaps on a pocket-sized note card. Don't rely on your memory; often, many of our best ideas are no more than fleeting mental flashes that are quickly crowded out by more immediate problems.

The idea of thinking about the problem also applies to the material—newspapers, reports, magazines—that you read. Many successful speechwriters are great article clippers. When they see an article on some topic of interest, they clip it and put the story in an appropriate file. It may be a broad topic such as "higher education" or something more specialized such as "residential applications of solar energy."

Writing the Speech

Writing the speech is a multistep process involving a finely honed outline and several drafts.

Outline Having gathered the material you need, you must prepare an outline. The outline for a speech has three main parts: the opening, the body and the closing.

The opening is the part of the speech that must get the audience's attention, establish empathy and point toward the conclusion. It is wise, in the opening, to tell the audience what the topic is, why it is important to them and the direction you plan to take in addressing it.

The body of the speech presents the evidence that leads to the conclusion. The outline should list all the key points. In this section, you will use quotes from acknowledged experts in the field, facts and figures and examples that drive home your point of view.

The conclusion summarizes the evidence, pointing out what it means to the audience.

The outline should be submitted to the speaker, and once it has been approved, you can go on to the next step.

Drafts The next step is to write a rough draft for the speaker. The speaker should use this draft to add new thoughts, cross out copy that doesn't seem to fit and rewrite sentences to reflect his or her vocabulary and speaking style.

Don't feel rejected if the first, second or even third draft comes back in tatters. It is only through this process that the speech becomes a natural expression of the speaker's personality.

This is the ideal process. The most successful speakers take the time to work with their speechwriters. Unfortunately, too many executives fail to understand this simple concept.

A report prepared by the Burson-Marsteller public relations agency discussed several reasons why business people have trouble explaining themselves to the public. The report noted:

> All too often the chief executive expects a speech to appear magically on his desk without any contribution on his part. He feels too busy to give the speech the attention it deserves. In the end, he becomes the victim of his own neglect. He stumbles through a speech which, from start to finish, sounds contrived. And then he wonders why nobody listened to what he said.

Words A speech talks *to* listeners, not *at* them. Your choice of words can either electrify an audience or put it to sleep. As someone once said, "The best idea in the world isn't worth a damn if it cannot be expressed well." Here are some tips about wording:

- Use personal pronouns such as "you" and "we." This makes the talk more conversational and lets your listeners know that you are talking to them.
- Avoid jargon. Do not talk about the "acquisition range" of the F-16 jet fighter—talk about an F-16 jet that can shoot down another plane 10 miles away.
- Don't use long figures. Don't say "243,629,384 Americans"; say "more than 240 million Americans."
- Use simple words to communicate. Don't say "print media" when you mean "newspaper." Don't say "perish" when "die" says the same thing. Don't say "possess" when "have" is what you mean.
- Use active verbs. Say "I think," not "It is my conviction that . . . ."
- Avoid modifiers such as "very" or "most"—these are crutches.
- Avoid empty words such as "of the nature of." Instead, say "like." Don't say "in the event of"—say "if." Don't say "at that point in time"—say "then."
- Use short sentences. Don't use clauses between the subject and the predicate of a sentence. Don't put a clause at the end of a sentence; start a new sentence.
- Use direct quotes. You could say, "Here is what my friend Allan said," and then quote him.
- Use questions—for example, "Does anyone know how many refugees there are in the world today?"
- Use comparisons or contrasts. Compare exotic locales with others that are familiar. ("New Zealand has about the same land area as California, but it has only 3 million people as compared to California's 33 million.")

The Final Draft

In addition to writing the speech to suit the speaker, there may be a need for coaching. Whether the speech is memorized, partially read or read entirely, it should be voiced enough times for the speaker to become familiar with it and to permit improvements in its delivery. Tone of voice, emphasis given to certain words or phrases, pauses, gestures, speed—all are important.

Some speakers prefer to have certain phrases underlined and to have detailed cues in the script such as "pause," "look at audience," and "pound on lectern." Others don't want such cues. It is a matter of individual preference.

Format is also a matter of personal preference. Some people prefer double spacing; others want triple spacing. A few like to have the speech typed entirely in capital letters, but most prefer the normal upper- and lowercase format that is used to present most material that is to be read. There are also speakers who like to have capital letters used in the words that are to be stressed. All of these formats are acceptable.

The speaker should be sufficiently familiar with the note cards or prepared text to permit abridgment on brief notice. Such advance thinking is particularly important for a speaker at a luncheon meeting. All too often, the meal is served late or the group takes an excessive amount of time discussing internal matters or making general announcements, leaving the speaker far less time than originally planned.

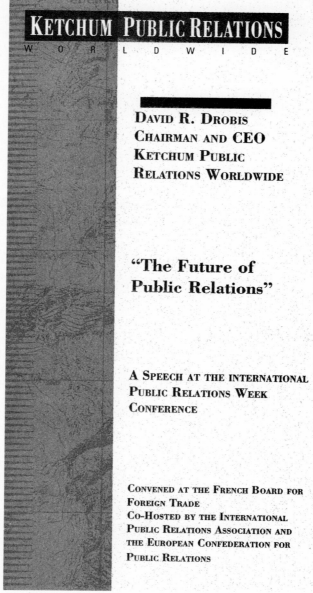

KETCHUM PUBLIC RELATIONS
W O R L D W I D E

DAVID R. DROBIS
CHAIRMAN AND CEO
KETCHUM PUBLIC
RELATIONS WORLDWIDE

"The Future of
Public Relations"

A SPEECH AT THE INTERNATIONAL
PUBLIC RELATIONS WEEK
CONFERENCE

CONVENED AT THE FRENCH BOARD FOR
FOREIGN TRADE
CO-HOSTED BY THE INTERNATIONAL
PUBLIC RELATIONS ASSOCIATION AND
THE EUROPEAN CONFEDERATION FOR
PUBLIC RELATIONS

Figure 16.4 Packaging a speech in pamphlet form and sending it to current and prospective clients is one way of getting more publicity mileage out of a speech. Another method is to convert the speech into an op-ed article. *(Courtesy of Ketchum Public Relations, New York.)*

The same thing can happen at an evening banquet. The awards ceremony takes longer than expected and the speaker is introduced at 9:15 p.m., three hours after everyone has sat down to dinner. In this instance, the most applause is for the person who realizes the hour and makes a five-minute speech.

PUBLICITY OPPORTUNITIES

The number of people a speech or a presentation reaches can be substantially increased through publicity.

Publicity Before the Event

Whenever anyone from your organization speaks in public, you should make sure that the appropriate media are notified in advance. This often takes the form of a media advisory, discussed in Chapter 9.

An advisory is simply a short note that gives the speaker's name and title, the speech title, and details about time and place. In a brief sentence or two, describe why the speech is important and of interest to the publication's audience. If it is available and it is a major policy speech, you can also send an advance copy of the speech to selected reporters. Make sure they realize that they should not report the details of the speech until after it has been given.

Reporters attending the speech should be seated near the podium, and arrangements should be made for accommodating photographers and television camera technicians. Reporters should also be provided with a press kit that gives the background of the organization and the speaker. A copy of the speech is also enclosed.

Publicity After the Event

After a speech has been given, your work is just beginning. You must write and distribute news releases about what was said so that the speech can be reported in appropriate trade and professional periodicals.

The speech can be shortened and excerpted as a possible op-ed article in daily newspapers. (How to write and place op-ed articles is discussed in Chapter 9.)

If a speech is particularly important, it can be printed in some attractive format and mailed to selected opinion leaders. Another outlet is *Vital Speeches,* which reprints selected speeches. You can also ask a member of the U.S. House of Representatives or the U.S. Senate to insert the speech in the *Congressional Record.*

SUMMARY

1. Speakers and speeches are outstanding public relations opportunities for organizations to increase their visibility and reach key publics.

2. Executive and staff speech training is often the responsibility of the public relations professional.

3. A speaker's bureau is a good way to organize an effective program of community outreach.

4. Top executives of an organization must be selective about what speech invitations they accept. Factors such as the sponsoring organization, the size of the audience and whether the venue advances organizational objectives must be considered.

5. A speech is a powerful communication tool. It must be prepared for listeners, not readers. It must fit the audience, be specific, get a reaction, have a definite objective and be timely.

6. Semispeeches—panels, debates and media interviews—follow the same basic principles as speeches. However, they also involve special preparation for dealing with opposition, interruptions and hostile questions.

7. Nonverbal communication is important in a speech. Speakers should be enthusiastic, make eye contact with the audience and use gestures that support their words.

8. The recommended length of a speech at a luncheon or dinner meeting is 20 minutes.

9. Speeches should be designed with one to three key messages.

10. Answers to media questions should be 60 seconds or less.

11. Speechwriting requires a clear objective, effective organization of relevant facts and key messages and a knowledge of the audience.

12. Speeches provide opportunities for additional publicity by preparing news releases, converting the speech to an op-ed piece or reprinting it in a leaflet or brochure.

EXERCISES

1. This chapter provides guidelines for giving an effective speech. Attend the meeting of a campus or community organization where someone is scheduled to give a speech. Write a critique of the speaker and assess the overall effectiveness of his or her speech according to these guidelines.

2. It is important for speakers to know the composition and background of an audience if they are to tailor their remarks to the occasion. Select an organization that regularly has a speaker for its monthly meeting. Compile a short memo that would help the president of the university prepare for a talk before this group. Include some brief background on the organization, a profile of the membership, the time and place of the meeting, the format of the entire meeting and the requested length of the talk.

3. Speechwriting is a highly refined skill. Imagine that the president of a local company hires you to write a 10-minute speech that he plans to present at the monthly meeting of the American Marketing Association. This group, consisting of people who work in marketing, wants to hear the president's views on

protective legislation that would restrict the import of Japanese goods to this country. The president is a busy man, but he does tell you that he thinks protective legislation is a bad idea. Taking the audience into consideration, do some research and draft a speech for the president.

4. The president of your company has been asked to appear on a TV public affairs show to discuss the company's plans to initiate mandatory drug testing of all potential and present employees. This is a controversial subject. You are expected to coach the president on how to answer specific questions from the show's host or members of the live audience. Compile a list of possible questions that he may have to deal with.

17 | *Audiovisual Aids*

*T*oday's culture is highly visual. That is why you, as a public relations writer, should constantly think in terms of audiovisual aids in all your communication activities.

This chapter, as a follow-up to Chapter 16 on speeches, covers the type of audiovisual aids that you can prepare to accompany a talk or a presentation. They include basic flip charts, overhead transparencies, slides, CD-ROM, video, and film.

THE IMPORTANCE OF AUDIOVISUALS

A number of research studies have confirmed that audiovisual aids enhance learning, productivity and message absorption. Consider the following findings:

- Sight accounts for 83 percent of what we learn.
- When a visual is combined with a voice, retention increases by 50 percent.
- Color increases a viewer's tendency to act on the information by 26 percent.
- Use of video increases retention by 50 percent and accelerates buying decisions by 72 percent.
- Group consensus in meetings is reached 21 percent more often when visuals are used.
- The time required to present a concept can be reduced by up to 40 percent with visuals.
- The average meeting length with visual aids is 19 minutes, compared to 28 minutes without them.

It is important to understand the advantages and disadvantages of each audiovisual technique and to determine what would be most effective in a given situation. Large amounts of money have been wasted on audiovisual materials because someone didn't take the time to consider the purpose, the audiences to be reached and the function of the audiovisual in the communication process.

Audiovisual aids are always planned to serve a specific audience. In addition to the general questions about who constitutes the audience and what these people know, there are other specific questions to be asked.

One major question is the projected size of the audience. If you have a small audience for a seminar or a workshop, overhead transparencies or charts are appropriate. A larger audience, listening to a speech or a formal presentation, might require slides or perhaps a video.

Another question is whether the audiovisual aid will be used for one meeting or for a number of meetings. Charts are all right for one meeting but are cumbersome to haul around to a series of meetings. By contrast, overhead transparencies, slides and videocassettes are extremely portable. If you plan to use the audiovisual materials many times, it becomes cost-effective to spend more money on them and have them professionally prepared.

In the following sections, we will examine the use of charts, overhead transparencies, slides, CD-ROM, video and film.

CHARTS

In Chapter 7 the word "chart" described drawings used to make numbers and statistics more understandable. They were identified as pie charts, bar charts and graphs.

For the purposes of this chapter, charts are large sheets of paper or cardboard used to help a speaker explain something to the audience. The content of these charts may be diagrams, pictures or words.

Advantages

Charts are the simplest and most economical visual aids. They can be made quickly, even on the spot, and they can be prepared by anyone who can do simple, bold lettering with a thick felt-tip pen. Transfer type can also be used.

Charts are particularly good for small workshops and seminars. They can be used as an outline to show key points in a talk or to convey statistical findings in the graphic form of pie, bar or graph charts.

Blank charts are used to generate ideas from an audience. The presenter engages audience members in discussion and writes down their ideas on a large-sized piece of paper. This enables the audience to see all the ideas, and it also serves to record the ideas generated. It is not uncommon for a workshop of active participants to generate 10 or 20 sheets of ideas, which can cover whole walls of the seminar room.

Preparation

Charts may take two basic forms: either soft sheets of paper that are fastened together across the top and turned over the back of an easel one by one, or stiff cards that are all placed on an easel and removed as they are used, one by one.

Every chart must be readable by everyone in the audience, so the size of the audience determines the size of the chart. For a group around a conference table, a small chart may be adequate. For a big meeting, it may be necessary to go to the largest practical size. It is a good idea to pretest readability.

Most charts are done in black ink on a white background, although a yellow background gives the highest possible visibility. Other colors can be used, but they should provide good contrast. Never use a dark color for a background.

CREATING VISUAL AIDS BY COMPUTER

The ability to create attractive visual aids has been vastly increased by the computer. With a few keystrokes and the click of a mouse, almost anyone can make attractive and colorful handouts, overhead transparencies and slides.

Basic word-processing software such as *Microsoft Word* or *WordPerfect* have basic clip art and other symbols that can be integrated with text. *Lotus Suites* and *Microsoft Office* include presentation software. *Freelance Graphics, Powerpoint, Persuasion* and the multimedia program *Astound* are the better known packages.

You should use clear, bold fonts in colors that contrast starkly with the background. Font size should be 24 to 48 points. As for background, dark blues convey a corporate approach, greens work well when feedback is desired and reds motivate an audience to action. Yellows and purples are not recommended for most business presentations.

If you need sophisticated materials, commercial firms such as Chartmasters and Genigraphics specialize in creating and producing charts, graphs and text material.

For a small meeting around a conference table, the letters should be at least an inch high. If the distance from the chart to the most distant member of the audience is 25 or 30 feet, you should use letters at least 3 or 4 inches high. For a larger audience, it will be necessary to test letter size for legibility from the rearmost seat. Remember that not everyone has 20/20 vision. Too big is never a problem, but too small is. Never use script or italic lettering. The individual letters must be strong and bold.

In preparing a chart presentation, the first step is to print all charts by hand on ordinary 8 1/2- by 11-inch paper. If the finished charts are to be vertical, the layout should be vertical. The size of the finished charts may be as small as 11 by 17 inches or as large as 34 by 44, depending on audience size.

When the layouts are complete and the proper sizes have been determined, the finished charts can be made. If a commercial artist is to make them, he or she should be asked for suggestions that may improve impact or readability. Discussion of the purpose to be served and estimation of the costs involved will yield a better set of charts at a more reasonable price.

Presentation

Soft sheets must be fastened securely to a stiff board backing in such a way that the sheets can be turned over easily and will stay in position. When too many sheets are used, the roll at the top may get so thick that previously used sheets keep slipping

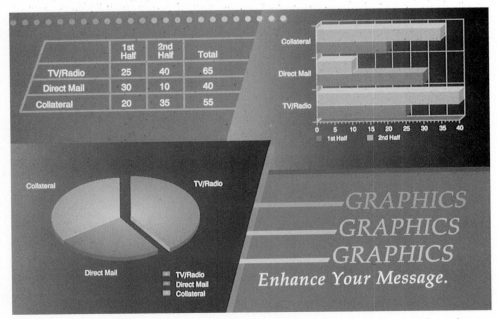

Figure 17.1 Computer graphics can produce interesting and varied charts and graphs. This representation was produced using *Aldus Persuasion*. Although presented here in black and white, the original was multicolored. *(Courtesy of Chartmasters, San Francisco.)*

back into view. It is also essential that the back of the easel be low enough to permit the sheets to hang properly behind it after their use.

With cards, you may use a double-faced easel that lets you stack the used cards on the back. If such an easel is not available, the used cards can be stacked on a nearby table. Because the cards are not fastened together, they may get out of order. To avoid this, each must be numbered. Then, if the easel collapses or someone inadvertently drops the cards, they can easily be put back in order.

A pointer is very helpful in chart presentations. The easel should be placed to the right of the speaker if he or she is right-handed or to the left if he or she is left-handed. This permits the speaker to use the pointer without turning his or her back to the audience. The listeners' attention will be held better if the speaker can always look at them, except for a brief glance at the chart now and then in order to place the pointer.

OVERHEAD TRANSPARENCIES

Overheads are inexpensive and can easily be adapted at a moment's notice. Overhead projectors are quite common; almost every meeting room has one. In fact, studies show that overhead transparencies are considered the number one choice for a visual aid.

The overhead projector is a simple device. A transparent sheet is placed on a ground-glass plate. A powerful bulb sends light upward through the plate and the sheet; the image is reflected by a mirror and projected through the lenses to a large screen.

TRANSPARENCY MISTAKES ARE APPARENT

If you're using an overhead projector for a presentation, remember these common mistakes:

- Transparencies with information printed too small to be read in the back of the room.
- Speakers moving back and forth across the path of light projection, causing repeated shadows.
- Too much information crammed onto one transparency.
- Transparencies positioned crookedly, which distracts the audience.
- The speaker reading from the screen with his or her back to the audience. Speakers should read from the transparency on the projector.

Source: *Communication Briefings,* August 1995.

Advantages

Overhead transparencies have several advantages, which make them the workhorses of the meeting circuit:

- The projector and the transparency sheets are relatively inexpensive.
- The projector is small, lightweight, and easily portable. Some are the size of a briefcase. Transparencies, like papers, can be carried in a file folder.
- Black-and-white transparencies can be produced on any photocopier.
- Transparencies can be shown in a semidark room where the speaker and the audience can see each other. Slides require a dark room.
- Transparencies can be used for small audiences or for groups of several hundred, depending on the size of the screen.

Production

Acetate (or plastic) transparencies are easy to produce. All you need do is take your paper copy, load it into a photocopier stocked with acetates, and run off the transparencies. You can also use a variety of acetate sheet colors—blue, green, yellow—so that your black-lettered transparency will have a more interesting background.

Don't make your transparencies too detailed or cluttered with too much art. A common mistake is to include too much copy. Follow the four-by-four rule: Use no

MEETING AGENDA

1 OLD AND NEW BUSINESS

2 SALES SEMINARS

3 MARKETING STRATEGY

This is an untouched reproduction of a plot created with HP's Drawing Gallery software and an HP 7550A plotter.

Figure 17.2 A few words and simple graphics are effective for a slide or overhead transparency. This transparency was quickly formatted using a word-processing program. *(Courtesy of Hewlett-Packard Company, Palo Alto, CA.)*

more than four bullets, and no more than four words for each bullet. Some people advise that there should be no more than 10 lines of copy on a transparency or a slide; others say no more than 20 words. A standard rule is a minimum of 24- or 28-point type for all words. Anything smaller would be difficult to see from the back of the room.

Presentation

A person using an overhead transparency should stand by the projector, facing the audience. A common mistake is turning your back on the audience to read from the projected image on the screen. This is not necessary, as you can easily read the transparency on the projector itself. This will keep you facing the audience and maintaining eye contact.

There are four techniques that will add to the effectiveness of your presentation:

1. Use a pointer to draw attention to some item on the chart.
2. Use a felt-tip pen to underline or circle key points or to add a word or two for emphasis. Be sure to pretest the pen to make sure that it will write on the acetate sheet. Some inks are oil-based and merely bubble up on the sheet. If you use a pen with water-soluble ink, it will work satisfactorily— and the marks can be removed after the presentation by running water over the sheet.
3. Use a blank sheet to conceal a part of the chart. This enables you to uncover points as you discuss them and keeps the audience from reading the entire list while you are still talking about the first item.
4. Use overlays by placing a colored strip on your chart to emphasize major points or by implementing a "building block" approach to expand a basic diagram. Thus you can add fenders, doors and bumpers to the skeleton of a car, or you can start with the president of the company and, with successive overlays, build an entire organization chart.

SLIDES

Slides are especially suited to reporting or explaining something. A charitable organization might show how its activities affect its beneficiaries. A manufacturer might show how a product should be used. A director of training could use slides to show new employees how to do their jobs. The slides are always described and explained, either by the speaker or by an audiocassette or a record. The purpose of the slides is to clarify and amplify a voiced message.

Advantages

Slides have several advantages. Portability is one—a single person can carry the reel, projector and screen. Thus a slide presentation makes a much more usable package than a stack of large charts and an easel.

Flexibility is another advantage. Slides can be arranged and rearranged. It is possible to use a few or many. Slides can be used in one presentation and then reused in another. Slides can be omitted or additional slides inserted. A slide can be held on-screen as long as necessary; conversely, it is possible to show a number of slides in rapid succession. It is also feasible to go backward and reshow one or more slides or an entire sequence.

Slides can show words, photographs, charts or diagrams or any combination of visual materials. Remember, however, that slides are aids. They can't tell the story alone. They are used to illustrate and explain what someone is saying.

Production

The first step in producing a slide presentation is to write a script. One way of doing this is to use a two-column format. On the right side, write the narration that will be used. The left side is reserved for listing the slides by number and identifying subject matter that will illustrate the narration.

Every important point in the message should be illustrated. This means that the narration should be written before the slides are prepared or selected from an already existing stock. Keep in mind that what appears on the screen and what you're talking about have to be coordinated and smoothly integrated. In planning a slide presentation, keep the following matters in mind:

1. *Length.* Industry research has shown that 15 to 30 minutes is the optimum length for audience attention.
2. *Sentence structure.* Keep the message short. Avoid complete sentences when possible, and use accepted abbreviations. It's better to have a slide read "Houston Profits Up" than "Profits at Our Houston Facility Have Increased Substantially."
3. *Word count.* Ten words per slide should be the maximum. Use only one point or idea per slide.
4. *Big, bold lettering.* Use standard type fonts that are easy to read.
5. *Statistics.* Use statistics judiciously. Use bar charts, pie charts or graphs that give the "bottom line."
6. *Variety.* Intersperse pictures with charts or words.
7. *Human interest.* Show people doing things, not just buildings and equipment.

The length of a slide presentation depends on its purpose. It is possible to make a good presentation with only a few slides—provided that the story can be told briefly. Conversely, a presentation can use 100 slides if they are pertinent. One example is a presentation on the potential market for American food products in Japan. The presentation showed scores of scenes in food stores. The presentation was not too long because no one in the audience had ever been to Japan, and all were unfamiliar with the marketing procedures there.

Authorities differ radically on the rate of projection. Some say it should be about four slides per minute; others say it should be 10 or 12. Your guide should be to use enough time for each slide to permit the audience to see and understand it.

FMC Overview Presentation
Page 5

21

In fact, the orange juice that you had with breakfast this morning was most likely extracted by FMC machinery.

22

FMC is the world's largest specialized machinery manufacturer of airline loading equipment. Other specialized machinery include material handling and automotive services equipment.

23

FMC manufactures wellhead equipment loading arms and valves which serve the petroleum industry.

24

Last year, Machinery and Equipment accounted for 22% of the company's total sales, 18% of its R&D expenditures and 10% of its capital expenditures.

25

Today, you are visiting the headquarters of the **Defense Systems Group** (DSG).

Marketing Communications

Figure 17.3 The text for a slide presentation is concise and supports the visual image. The slides are numbered on the left, and the copy appears on the right side of the page. *(Courtesy of FMC Defense Systems Group, San Jose, CA.)*

Some slides may stay on the screen for 10 or 20 seconds; others, especially in a related sequence, may be shown even more briefly. The pictures of the Japanese food stores were shown at the rate of about 10 per minute.

In preparing or selecting slides for use in a presentation, make sure that they are all visually clear and uniform. They should be in color. If charts or diagrams are to be used, it is desirable to have the basic charts or diagrams prepared using computer graphics. Black and white can be used, but the slides will be more attractive if the background is colored. If the slides are likely to be reused, they should be placed in metal frames. This protects the slides and ensures better feeding through the projector.

FIVE SLIDE MISTAKES TO AVOID

1. *The unrehearsed slide show.* Don't wait until you're up there at the podium to find the kinks in your slide presentation. Go through the entire presentation—with your slides—beforehand. Rehearse every move you're going to make. You don't want any surprises.

2. *Relying on a slide operator.* Always check your slides yourself. Be sure to consider the projection format. Rear-screen projection requires that the slides be stacked differently for front-screen projection.

3. *The slide surprise.* An upside down or backwards slide does very little to help you look professional. Always check your slides yourself to make sure they're correctly positioned.

4. *The awkward anecdote.* Keep your remarks concise and reflective of key points. Avoid unrelated remarks so as to keep your presentation moving along. If you feel that a particular part of your presentation will stimulate unrelated remarks, put in a blank slide so that the screen goes black.

5. *Treating your slide like a script.* Don't read your slides verbatim off the screen. Try to use the same terminology, but speak in complete sentences and in a conversational tone.

Source: Genigraphics Corporation, Liverpool, New York.

Projection

All slides are upside down when projected. If you are not familiar with the projector you plan to use, test the first slide for correct placement by actually projecting it. Once you are sure of the right placement, the other slides can be placed into the reel in the same position. Most slide processors suggest that the shiny side of the slide be toward the light bulb. When all slides are loaded, the entire reel or tray should be projected to be sure that all slides are properly placed.

If the slide presentation must be used in the field without the help of a qualified spokesperson, it is often best to place the narration on an audiocassette. By using a sound-slide synchronizer (available for rental through camera stores), you can insert electronic signals into the tape so that it automatically trips the projector to the appropriate picture.

A dissolve unit is another piece of equipment that can make the slide presentation look more professional. Instead of the normal split-second change from one slide to the next, this device makes the slide dissolve off the screen while another takes its place. At this stage, you are getting very close to multiple projection, which will be discussed shortly.

Another device that can improve a slide presentation is the light pointer, which projects a luminous arrow onto the screen. This allows the presenter to indicate items of importance. Such equipment can be rented from the same sources as those providing other audiovisual rental equipment.

Before the presentation, place the projector in the correct position in relation to the screen. Check the focus and have a spare bulb at hand. In some cases the speaker will operate the projector. If someone else does this, cues for changing the slides must be established. "Next slide please" is distracting, so try to devise some signal, such as the use of a clicker or a low-pitched electric signal. Even better is a system whereby the projector operator has the full script of the speech, with notes as to when to change the slide. With careful rehearsal, this can result in a very smooth presentation, free from distracting sounds.

Multiple Projection

By using a number of slide projectors, it is possible to make a multiple-screen presentation. The results can be anything from amateurish to spectacular. The best results will depend on careful planning, accurate projection and tight control. Presentations of this sort may use anywhere from two or three projectors to as many as eight or 10. Generally, there is one sound track, which must be synchronized with the projectors.

Productions of this sort are relatively costly; they require several projector operators and a room large enough to accommodate the necessary screens. Obviously, such a presentation would be mounted only for a sizable audience. Because the objectives of such productions vary so widely, there are few guidelines.

It is possible to transfer slides to videotape. These can then be shown on monitors or on wide-screen projection equipment. Slides on a compact and readily available videotape can easily be moved and shown. And there is never the problem of slides getting out of order. Slides can also be placed on a compact disk (CD).

CD-ROM

CD-ROM (compact disc, read-only memory) is increasingly being used in public relations activities as a powerful audiovisual tool. A CD holds the equivalent of 451 floppy discs. It can supply 72 minutes of sound and 20 minutes of video—not to mention text and graphics.

Highly portable CD players are effective for one-to-one and small group presentations. A good example of its use is when Dole Food Co. launched a national campaign encouraging school children to eat fruits and vegetables. The company wanted to get the message across in a lively manner so it packaged the information on a multimedia compact disc.

Today, more than 15,000 schools across the country use the CD. Children pop the disc into their computers and cartoon characters such as Barney Broccoli and Bobby Banana jump out at them. The CD includes songs and movies.

Public relations personnel have also found CD-ROM players helpful on media tours when they want to show editors various kinds of information about a new product or technology.

The latest idea regarding CD-ROM is to have the technology as part of a free-standing kiosk where people can access information. Ketchum Public Relations, for example, created such a kiosk for the Potato Board. The kiosk was placed in selected grocery stores around the country so customers could interactively access dinner ideas, recipes and menu plans.

VIDEO

The use of videotape is now almost universal, and it is a highly effective audiovisual aid because it combines sight, sound, color, action and movement. Video news releases were discussed in Chapter 8, and many of the concepts are the same when discussing other uses of video.

Video has many advantages, including the following:

- It's a more dramatic illustrative medium than print or slides.
- It can be produced instantaneously, whereas film requires processing in the lab.
- It can be easily edited, spliced, duplicated and distributed at relatively low cost.

Videotape's one drawback, which has now been overcome with new technology, was its dependence on small television monitors for viewing. Now, however, large playback screens are available, so a large audience can view the same monitor. Different formats also impeded widespread use of video, but this problem has also been solved by time and a constant drop in prices.

Organizations use video for a number of purposes. According to one survey of corporations, 51 percent use video for employee training purposes. Another 47 percent use it for other types of communications with the public such as fund-raising and public service announcements. About 40 percent list the use of video for employee information while 36 percent use the medium for product information to distributors and customers.

Less than 20 percent of the organizations used in-house video for the production of video news releases (VNRs). The survey also found that the average in-house video production cost about $5,800—about one-third less than the cost of hiring an outside commercial firm to produce it.

Employee video news magazines are also popular. NYNEX, for example, mails the quarterly *NYNEX News* video newsletter to its 75,000 employees' homes. The program follows a "nightly news" format. Items include human interest, financial news and other company developments.

Videocassettes are also used in marketing. Oldsmobile sent a video on its Achieva model to potential buyers in their homes. Other organizations are using video for legislative and lobbying efforts. With a tape, lobbyists and public relations people can show legislators background material on controversial issues and even show how proposed new plants will control pollution.

Nonprofit groups also use videos to explain their programs and rally public support for various issues. The Audubon Society has even produced music videos, featuring rock stars, that are sent to television and cable outlets, schools and clubs.

Although videos can be extremely effective visual aids, either with a speaker or as a stand-alone product, their preparation and production is not a job for amateurs. Like films, videos must be done by highly trained professionals who know how to produce at the quality level of commercial television. Audience expectations demand it.

Your job is to conceptualize the proposed video and work out a rough storyboard, including location shots and dialog. Indeed, in the survey of corporations previously mentioned, scriptwriting was done by 75 percent of the corporate communicators. Another 60 percent fulfilled directing duties while 54 percent got involved in production.

FILM

Although video has become the standard in public relations, corporate communications and marketing, film has not completely disappeared. Some organizations still produce sponsored films for use by schools and various community groups. Such films are also made available on videocassette to offer users a choice.

Even if a videocassette is ultimately used as the vehicle of distribution, the original production is made on 16-mm film because the reproduction quality is excellent. Even made-for-television movies are produced on film and later transferred to video. For a feature-length presentation on a big-screen in a theater, film is still the only way to go.

Motion pictures are the most expensive kind of audiovisual aid. Production of a motion picture should therefore be approached with caution. It is possible to produce a short film for $100,000, but it is also easy to spend several million. For example, the Audubon Society commissioned a made-for-TV movie titled *The Last Elephant* that cost $4 million to produce.

However, the cost of a first-rate film can be justified if it has the potential of being seen by large numbers of people. If a motion picture costs $1 million to produce and is seen by 10 million people over a period of years, it costs only 10 cents per viewer.

THE MANY USES OF VIDEOTAPE

Most organizations find videotape an extremely useful medium for a variety of tasks. Here are some examples:

- Philip Morris distributes briefing videos to both print and television journalists.
- Carlisle Plastics use a video to introduce its Eco-Choice garbage bags, the first made from recycled plastics.
- Genentech of San Francisco, a genetic engineering firm, showed a 26-minute video about itself to potential investors as part of a financing program.
- Louisiana State University raised money for its athletic program with a video, sold commercially, in which a quartet (consisting of the governor and former governor of Louisiana as well as two LSU coaches) sang four LSU songs about football and basketball.
- Fashion designers send videos of their creations, often in a fantasy setting, to cable TV stations, talk shows and retail outlets. They are also sent to nightclubs, which use them as backdrops.
- A Massachusetts congressional candidate distributed a 15-minute videotape of himself for campaign workers to show in voters' homes.

Production

Any motion picture produced for public relations should be in color. Most of these films use off-screen narration. This means that the sound track carries the voice of an announcer who tells the viewers what is going on. If live sound is used, with actors doing the talking, the cost becomes vastly greater.

Animation is attractive and may sometimes be essential, but it is very expensive. In some cases, stop-motion photography will serve. In this procedure, the motion picture camera is set to expose one or two frames at a time. The subject matter is moved slightly after each exposure, and the resulting film, projected at normal speed, creates the illusion that the objects shown on the screen are moving by themselves.

Motion pictures can be used for several years. In fact, many users plan for five years of use before replacement. If a film is keyed to a current situation, it may be obsolete in a short time; this should be considered in planning. If the cost of the film must be charged to one year, that should be known at the outset.

When a film is approved for production, the first step is to write a script that describes every scene and specifies every word or sound that is to be in the finished film. This job should be done by an experienced scriptwriter.

After finalizing a script and signing a contract with a producer, your responsibility now becomes that of production expediter. If the film is to be shot at your place of business, you must arrange for the film crew's access. If staff members are to be filmed, they must be informed and told what is expected of them. Releases should be checked and new ones signed if they are not already on file.

SUMMARY

1. Audiovisual aids help audiences retain and understand information.
2. Audiovisual aids can reduce the time required for a meeting.
3. Each audiovisual aid has its advantages and disadvantages. You should select the appropriate visual aid for the situation.
4. Charts are cheap and easy to prepare. They can also serve to record audience ideas and suggestions.
5. Computer graphic programs are readily available and can be used to make attractive transparencies and slides.
6. Overhead transparencies are the most popular visual aid. They are cheap and relatively easy to prepare.
7. Slides are portable, flexible and useful for either small or large groups. They should be simple and colorful.
8. The key to successful visual aids is brief copy and large type.
9. CD-ROM players and portable VCRs are effective in one-to-one presentations.
10. Videotape is now universally used by organizations for public relations purposes. It can be produced instantly and duplicated at relatively low cost.

11. A large market for sponsored videos is schools.

12. Motion pictures are highly effective but costly. However, for feature-length productions, film is still preferred.

EXERCISES

1. Prepare a 10-minute talk on some subject. Develop and prepare the charts or overhead transparencies you will use in your presentation.

2. The local YWCA needs a simple slide presentation to introduce parents to its upcoming summer camp. The camp, offering one-week stays, exposes grade-school girls to a variety of outdoor activities. You are commissioned to script the slide presentation, which will last five to 10 minutes. The script should include brief descriptions of the slides that will be coordinated with the script. Use a two-column format, placing the slide descriptions on the left and the script on the right.

3. A local campus organization wants to produce a short video that could be used to recruit new members. Select a campus group that you are interested in, and write a rough script outlining the narration and video shots that could be used.

PART 4

Managing Programs and Campaigns

In this last section of the book, you will learn how to put everything to-gether. You have learned a number of writing skills and media tech-niques, all of which combine to form a solid foundation for public rela-tions program management.

Part 4 is designed to shift your thinking to planning and managing all the elements of a public relations program.

☐ *Chapter 18, "Meetings and Events,"* covers committee meet-ings, club meetings and workshops, banquets, cocktail parties and receptions, open houses, conventions, trade shows and promotional events.

☐ *Chapter 19, "Program Planning,"* explores the elements of a plan, developing a plan and working the plan.

☐ *Chapter 20, "Program Evaluation,"* discusses basic evaluation questions, news releases and features, sponsored publica-tions, events, monitoring the Internet, attainment of objectives and writing the report.

18 | *Meetings and Events*

*M*eetings and events are vital public relations tools. Their greatest value is that they let the audience participate in real time. In this era of electronic communication, information overload and mechanical voices, people have a need to gather, socialize and be part of a group activity.

Effective meetings and events don't just happen. Detailed planning and logistics are essential to assure that defined objectives are achieved. This chapter discusses various types of meetings and events that require good organizational and communication skills.

We begin with the basic committee meeting. We then discuss (1) club meetings and workshops, (2) banquets, (3) cocktail parties and receptions, (4) open houses and plant tours, (5) conventions, (6) trade shows and (7) promotional events such as grand openings and organizing a 10-K run.

COMMITTEE MEETINGS

Committee meetings are an important part of any organization, from the local garden club to the multinational corporation. Indeed, through committee meetings, club members or employees have a chance to express their views and participate in decision making.

The Wharton Center for Applied Research found that senior managers spend an average of 23 hours a week in meetings, while middle managers spend 11 hours. The study also concluded, however, that 20 to 30 percent of the meetings held could be handled better through one-on-one talks, by phone or by memo. Another study concluded that executives spend an average of 288 hours a year—five full weeks—attending unnecessary meetings.

The productivity experts, given such statistics, also weigh in against excessive and, many times, unnecessary meetings. Steve Kaye, author of *Meetings in an Hour or Less: A Complete Guide to Fewer, Shorter, More Effective Meetings,* estimates that the waste equals 20 percent of payroll, which costs U.S. companies $420 billion a year.

This is not to say that all committee meetings should be banned. It does say, however, that meetings should be held only if they are needed to accomplish a specific objectives. Kaye suggests asking what would happen if the meeting were not held. "If the answer is nothing, then cancel the meeting." Others simply ask the basic question, "Is this meeting really necessary?"

If the answer is "yes," here are some guidelines for having an effective committee meeting:

- **Limit attendance.** Only those who are directly involved should be invited.
- **Distribute the agenda in advance.** Let people know what will be discussed or decided so they can think about the issues before the meeting. Limit the agenda to a few items. It's also helpful to give a starting and ending time so attendees can better plan their day.
- **Use a round table.** Everyone has equal positional status and equal access to each other. The next best alternative is a square table.
- **Set a time limit.** A meeting should run a maximum of 60 to 90 minutes. The longer the meeting runs, the less effective it is.
- **Manage the meeting.** The chairperson must make sure the meeting stays on track. Don't let someone go off on a tangent or dominate the meeting.
- **Budget time.** Don't spend an excessive amount of time on trivial items.
- **Know Robert's Rules of Order.** It may be unnecessary in an informal, friendly meeting, but knowledge of parliamentary procedure is helpful if the debate gets heated.
- **Close with a brief overview.** At the end of the meeting, summarize what has been accomplished, what will be done and who will do it. Remember that meetings are held to make decisions, not just to discuss things.
- **Distribute a summary memo.** The chair or secretary should distribute a summary of the meeting within 24 hours after the meeting. This helps remind people what was decided.

CLUB MEETINGS AND WORKSHOPS

Having meetings seems to be part of human nature. There are literally thousands of civic clubs, professional societies, trade associations and hobby groups that have meetings that attract millions of people every year. In addition, many of these organizations sponsor workshops, seminars and symposiums on a regular basis.

Planning

The size and purpose of the meeting dictate the plan. Every plan must consider these questions: How many will attend? Who will attend? When and where will it be held? How long will it last? Who will speak? What topics will be covered? What facilities will be needed? Who will run it? What is its purpose? How do we get people to attend?

Location If the meeting is to be held on the premises of the organization, the room can be reserved by contacting whoever is responsible for such arrangements.

If the meeting is to be held at some outside location, you will have to talk to the person in charge. In a hotel or motel, that person is the catering manager. In a school, it may be the superintendent or custodian; in a church, the minister or priest. Many firms have rooms that are made available to nonprofit groups, so consider this possibility if your organization is eligible.

The meeting room must be the right size for the expected audience. If it is too large, the audience will feel that the meeting has failed to draw the expected attendance. If it is too small, the audience will be uncomfortable. Most hotels have a number of meeting rooms ranging in size from small to very large.

Having selected a room, make sure that the audience can find it. The name of the meeting and the name of the room should be posted on the calendar of events. If directional arrows are needed, they should be posted in conspicuous spots.

Seating A variety of seating arrangements can be used, depending on the purpose of the meeting. A monthly club meeting, for example, often features a luncheon or dinner. In this case, attendees are usually seated at round tables of six or eight where they first have a meal and then listen to a speaker.

Seminars, designed primarily for listening, usually have what is called "theater" seating. Rows of seats are set up, all facing the speakers. Such meetings may be held in theaters or auditoriums.

A workshop or a small seminar, on the other hand, may use what is called "lunchroom" seating. This uses long tables with chairs on one side so that attendees can take notes or set up laptop computers.

Occasionally, large meetings are broken into discussion groups. Typically, the audience starts in one large room where a speaker gives information and states a problem. The audience then moves into another room, or set of rooms, where round tables seating eight or 10 people are available. A discussion leader is designated for each table. After the problem has been discussed, the leaders gather the opinions and the audience returns to the first room where reports from each group are given to the entire assembly.

MEETING CHECKLIST

Every meeting requires its own specialized checklist, but here is a general "to do" list for a local dinner meeting of a service club or a professional association.

In Advance

- What is the purpose of the meeting? Business? Social? Continuing education? Combination?
- What date and time are best for maximum attendance?
- What size audience do you realistically expect?
- Select restaurant facility at least four to six weeks in advance.
- Confirm in writing the following: date, time, menu, cocktails, seating plan, number of guaranteed reservations and projected costs.
- Enlist speaker four to six weeks in advance. If speaker is in high demand, make arrangements several months in advance. Discuss nature of talk, projected length and whether audiovisual aids will be used that require special equipment.
- Publicize the meeting to the membership and other interested parties. This should be done a minimum of three weeks in advance. Provide complete information on speaker, date, time, location, meal costs and reservation procedure.
- Organize a phone committee to call members 72 hours before the event if reservations are lagging. A reminder phone call is often helpful in gaining last-minute reservations.

On the Meeting Day

- Get a final count on reservations, and make an educated guess as to how many people might arrive at the door without a reservation.
- Check speaker's travel plans and last-minute questions or requirements.
- Give catering manager revised final count for meal service. In many instances, this might have to be done 24 to 72 hours in advance of the meeting day.
- Check room arrangements one to two hours in advance of the meeting. Have enough tables been set up? Are tables arranged correctly for the meeting? Does the microphone system work?
- Prepare a timetable for the evening's events. For example, cocktails may be scheduled from 6:15 to 7 p.m. with registration going on at the same time. Dinner from 7 to 8 p.m. followed by 10 minutes of announcements. At 8:10 p.m., the speaker will have 20 minutes to talk followed by an additional 10 minutes for questions. Your organizational leaders, as well as the headwaiter, should be aware of this schedule.
- Set up a registration table just inside or outside the door. A typed list of reservations should be available as well as name tags, meal tickets and a cash box for making change. Personnel at the registration table should be briefed and in place at least 30 minutes before the announced time.
- Decide on a seating plan for the head table, organize place names and tell VIPs as they arrive where they will be sitting.
- Designate three or four members of the organization as a hospitality committee to meet and greet newcomers and guests.

After the Meeting

- Settle accounts with the restaurant, or indicate where an itemized bill should be mailed.
- Check the room to make sure no one forgot briefcases, handbags, eyeglasses or other belongings.
- Send thank-you notes to the speaker and any committee members who helped plan or host the meeting.

Facilities   A small meeting may not need much in the way of facilities, whereas a large and formal one may require a considerable amount of equipment and furnishings. Following are things that should be considered—and supplied if needed. You should check everything at least two hours before the meeting.

1. *Meeting identification.* Is it posted on the bulletin board near the building entrance? Are directional signs needed?
2. *Lighting.* Is it adequate? Can it be controlled? Where are the controls? Who will handle them?
3. *Chalkboard.* Is it visible? Are chalk and erasers available?
4. *Charts.* Are they readable? Is the easel adequate? Who will handle the charts?
5. *Screen.* Is it visible to the entire audience? If some seats are badly located, how do you prevent people from using them? Who will refer people to better locations?
6. *Projectors.* Are they hooked up? Focused? Is there a spare bulb? Are materials to be projected in the right order and properly loaded? Who will operate the projectors? What are the cues and signals?
7. *Monitors.* Are they in the right position? Hooked up? Are VCRs available? Who will operate them? What are the signals and cues?
8. *Seating and tables.* Are they arranged properly?
9. *Tape recorder.* Is it loaded? Set for the right speed? Hooked up? In the right position? Who will run it?
10. *Telephone.* Where is it? If in the meeting room, who will answer?
11. *Wiring.* For all electrical equipment, can wires be kicked loose or trip someone? What about switches?
12. *Speaker's position.* Is it on the stage? On the dais? Can it be seen? Is there a lectern? What about a reading light? Is there a PA system? Is it working? How many people will there be on the speakers' platform? Are there name signs for the speakers?
13. *Water and glasses.* For speakers? For audience?
14. *Audience and speaker aids.* Are there programs or agendas? Will there be notepaper, pencils, handout materials?
15. *Name tags.* For speakers? For all attendees?

Invitations For clubs, an announcement in the newsletter of the meeting—time, place, purpose and who is to attend—should be adequate. For external groups—people who are not required to attend but whose presence is desired—invitations are necessary. They should go out early enough for people to fit the meeting into their schedules—three to six weeks is a common lead time. The invitation should tell the time, day, date, place (including the name of the room), purpose, highlights of the program (including names of speakers) and anything else that makes the meeting sound worthwhile. A map showing the location and parking facilities is advisable. A return card for acceptance of the invitation is sometimes used if it is particularly important to have certain people attend. In such cases, it is necessary to check acceptances and possibly phone those who have not replied.

Registration

If everyone knows everyone else, registration and identification are highly informal, but if the group is large, it is customary to have a registration desk or table at the entrance. Here the names of arrivals are checked against the invitation lists. If there is no invitation list and the presence or absence of any of the people who were invited is not important (as at a regular meeting of a club or association), the arrivals generally sign in on a plain sheet of paper, and no one checks the membership roster.

Greeting A representative of the sponsoring organization should be at the entrance of the room. If the number attending is not too large, a personal welcome is in order. Where hundreds of people are expected, this isn't possible, but the chairperson should greet the audience in his or her opening remarks.

Name Tags Name tags are a good idea at almost any meeting. You should use labelmaking software to prepare name tags for everyone with advance reservations. Names should be printed in bold, large block letters so that they can be read easily from a distance of 4 feet. If the person's affiliation is used, this can be in smaller bold letters.

For people showing up without advance registration, you can have felt-tip pens available for on-the-spot name tags. However, a nice touch is to designate one person at the registration desk to make these tags so that they look neat and consistent. Most name tags are self-adhesive. Plastic badges can also be used, but some people object to sticking pins through their clothes.

Program

At any meeting, the word "program" has two meanings. It is what goes on at the meeting, and it is the printed listing of what goes on.

The meeting must have a purpose. To serve that purpose, it is necessary to have a chairperson who controls and directs the meeting, introduces the speakers and keeps discussions from wandering. It is necessary to have speakers who will inform, persuade or activate the listeners. If the meeting is a celebrative or commemorative occasion, the speakers must avoid the trite or boring.

The printed program that is handed out to the audience in a workshop or seminar tells them what is going to happen, when and where. It lists all the speakers, the time they will speak, coffee breaks, lunch breaks and any other facts attendees should know about the meeting. Because speakers may have last-minute changes in their plans, the programs should not be printed until the last possible moment.

Speakers   Speakers should be selected early—several months in advance, if possible. They should be chosen because of their expertise, their crowd-drawing capacity and their speaking ability. It is a good idea to listen to any prospective speaker before tendering an invitation, or at least to discuss your intention with someone who has heard the person speak before. Many prominent people are simply not effective speakers.

When a speaker has agreed to give a talk, it is essential to make sure that the speaker gets to the meeting on time. Written confirmation of the commitment, giving the specifics of time and location, is desirable. This should be followed up with a reminder a day or two before the meeting. Some public relations people go a step further and phone the speaker a few hours before the meeting, just to make sure.

If the speaker is coming from out of town, it is necessary to make hotel reservations, meet the speaker on arrival and make sure that the reserved room is still available. At the meeting, the speaker must be met at the door and introduced to the chair, other speakers and other important people.

For especially important speakers, you might consider reserving a suite instead of a room. Flowers, fruit and a stocked bar add to the cordiality of the occasion. Preregistration and a personal escort from the private room to the dais are also appropriate.

Meals   Club meetings and workshops often occur at a meal time. In fact, many meetings include breakfast, lunch or dinner.

Early morning breakfast meetings have the advantage of attracting people who cannot take the time during the day to attend such functions. A full breakfast, served buffet style, is a popular choice because it allows everyone to select what they normally eat for breakfast. People attending a half-day or full-day workshop often partake of a self-served continental breakfast—rolls, juice and coffee—during the registration period just prior to the start of the meeting.

Luncheons are either sit-down affairs with a fixed menu or a buffet. A 30- to 45-minute cocktail period often precedes the luncheon, usually during registration as guests arrive. A good schedule for a typical luncheon is cocktails, 11:30; luncheon, noon; adjournment, 1:30. In rare instances, the adjournment can be as late as 2 p.m., but it should never be later than that.

Dinner meetings are handled in much the same way as luncheons. A typical schedule is cocktails, 6:30 p.m.; dinner, 7 p.m.; speaker, 8 p.m.; adjournment, between 8:30 and 9 p.m. Speakers, as mentioned in Chapter 16, should talk only 20 to 25 minutes.

You'll need to have an accurate count of people who attend a meal function. The hotel or restaurant facility will need a count at least 24 hours in advance to prepare the food and set up table service. The standard practice is for the organization to guarantee a certain number of meals, plus or minus 10 percent. If fewer than what is guaranteed show up, you still pay for the meals.

BANQUETS

A banquet, by definition, is a fairly large and formal function. They are held to honor an individual, raise money for a charitable organization or celebrate an event such as an organization's anniversary.

A banquet may have 100 or 1,000 people in attendance, and staging a successful one takes a great deal of planning. The budget, in particular, needs close attention. A banquet coordinator has to consider such costs as (1) food, (2) room rental, (3) bartenders, (4) decorations and table centerpieces, (5) audiovisual requirements, (6) speaker fees, (7) entertainment, (8) photographers, (9) invitations, (9) tickets and (10) marketing and promotion.

When figuring food costs, many amateur planners often forget about tax and gratuity, which add about 25 percent to any final bill. In addition, there are corkage fees if you provide your own liquor or wine. In many establishments, corkage fees are set rather high to discourage you from bringing your own refreshment. At one banquet, for example, the organizers thought it was a great coup to have the wine donated only to find out that the hotel charged a corkage fee of $10 per bottle.

If the object of the banquet is to make money for a charitable cause, that also drives up the basic ticket costs. Considering all the factors involved, it is not unusual for banquet tickets to cost $50 to $150 per person.

When organizing a banquet, you usually work with the catering manager of the restaurant or hotel. He or she will discuss menus, room facilities and a host of other items with you to determine exactly what you need.

Catering departments have special menus for banquets, which are often subject to some negotiation. If you plan a banquet during the week, for example, the restaurant or hotel might be willing to give you more favorable rates because week nights aren't ordinarily booked. However, if you insist on having a banquet on Friday or Saturday night—which is the most popular time—you can expect to pay full rates.

In general, it's necessary to book a facility at least two or three months in advance, particularly for a Friday or Saturday night. After setting the date and time, you begin sending invitations to a mailing list of potential attendees.

A banquet that is open to the community, for example, operates on the general rule that for every thousand invitations sent out, only a small percentage will actually make a reservation. The actual percentage, of course, depends on the event and the speaker or honoree.

In addition to sending out individual invitations, there usually is a committee that personally asks corporations and other businesses to buy a table for employees, clients or friends. A corporate table of eight, for example, may go for $1,000 to $2,500.

CHEVRON CONSERVATION AWARDS PROGRAM BANQUET

	Event Schedule	Staff Member
9:00 a.m.	Meet with hotel catering manager/staff Confirm event arrangements	Bill/Lauren/Deb
	5:00-6:00 VIP reception & photos 6:30-7:30 general reception 7:30-8:30 dinner (see attached schedule) 8:30-10:00 program-speaker & award presentation	
12:00-3:00	Coordinate ballroom set up Staging & A/V equipment	Deb/Bob
12:00-3:00	Media interviews-award honorees	B.J.
1:00	Complete seating arrangements	Bill/Mary
2:00	Complete and organize nametags	Lauren/Gail
2:00-3:00	Rehearsal/AV run through	Bill/Deb/Bob/Clair
4:00	Award booklets/program each place setting	Gail
4:30	Lobby signs	Gail
5:00-6:00	VIP reception-coordinate honoree photos (see attached)	Lauren/Gail
6:00	Brief hotel staff re reception table staffing	Gail

Figure 18.1 Banquets require coordination of logistics on the day of the event. This is a list of activities that had to be completed before the actual banquet scheduled in the evening. (*Courtesy of Chevron Corporation, San Francisco.*)

Large banquets also require that tables be marked with an easily visible sign showing a number or the name of the group to be seated at the table. Tables should be numbered in some logical sequence; if there are many, set up a chart at the entrance of the room to show the location of each. Color coding tables can also be helpful. At a banquet with 150 tables, the person in charge divided the tables into five groups of 30. Each group was identified by different colored balloons—the first group was red, the second blue and so on. Thus, the tables were easy to find even though 1,500 guests had to be seated.

A banquet usually has a fixed menu, but you must also make a vegetarian dish available to those who request it. In general, a popular choice for a meat entree is chicken or fish. Pork may be objectionable on religious grounds, and many people don't eat red meats such as beef. Offering two entrees requires the extra work of providing coded tickets for the waiters, and the hotel or restaurant may charge more for the meal. Get the catering manager's advice before ordering multiple entrees.

CHEVRON CONSERVATION AWARDS BANQUET
JW MARRIOTT HOTEL
WASHINGTON, DC
WEDNESDAY, MAY 13

Crew Agenda

3:30–5:00 p.m.	Program agenda review-participants and staff only. Live run-through of C. Ghylin's remarks. (Grand Ballroom)
5:00–6:00	Private pre-reception for honorees, judges, Chevron staff. Honoree photo session including E. Zern and J. Sullivan. (Suite 1231)
6:30–7:15	Greetings and reception, open bar. Photo opportunities available. (Grand Ballroom Foyer)
7:15–7:30	Close bar, enter Grand Ballroom
7:30–7:35	C. Ghylin: Welcome and opening remarks.
7:30–8:20	Dinner served.
8:20–8:25	C. Ghylin: Introduces special guests at head table, introduces E. Zern.
8:25–8:30	E. Zern: Welcome, honoree toast, introduces judges, completes remarks.
8:30–8:35	C. Ghylin: Introduces J. Sullivan.
8:35–8:45	J. Sullivan: Remarks.
8:45–8:50	C. Ghylin: Introduces slide presentation.
8:50–9:25	Slide presentation. (C. Ghylin remains at podium) a) Introduces/explains professional honoree category; b) Comments on professionals. Introduces/explains citizen honoree category. c) Comments on citizens. Introduces/explains organizations' honoree category.
9:25–9:40	C. Ghylin: Comments on organizations. Invites J. Sullivan and E. Zern for plaque presentation. Plaque presentation.
9:40–9:45	C. Ghylin: Final remarks.
9:45 p.m.	America the Beautiful.

Figure 18.2 The time line for Chevron's Conservation Awards banquet. The compilation of a time line, and going over it with the master of ceremonies, helps keep the event on schedule. (*Courtesy of Chevron Corporation, San Francisco.*)

COCKTAIL PARTIES AND RECEPTIONS

A short cocktail party, as previously mentioned, can precede the start of a club's luncheon or dinner. It can also be an event in itself or part of a reception. The purpose is to have people socialize; it also is a cost-effective way to celebrate an organization's or individual's achievement, to introduce a new chief executive to the employees and the community or simply to allow college alumni to get together.

In any event, the focus is on interaction; not speeches. If there is a ceremony or speech, it should last a maximum of five to 10 minutes.

Cocktail parties can last for several hours, and the typical format is a large room where most people will stand instead of sit. This facilitates social interaction and allows people to move freely around the room. Such gatherings, like any other event, require advance planning and logistics.

It is important, for example, that food be served in the form of appetizers, sandwiches, cheese trays, nuts and chips. People get hungry, and food helps offset some effects of drinking. The bar is the centerpiece of any cocktail party, but you should make sure there are plenty of nonalcoholic beverages available, too. Urns of coffee, punch and tea should be readily available in other locations around the room.

Such precautions will limit your liability if someone does get drunk and has an accident on the way home. You can also limit your liability if you have a no-host bar, which means that guests buy their own drinks.

Most cocktail parties, however, have a hosted bar, meaning that drinks are free. This is particularly true when a corporation is hosting the cocktail party or reception; it seems tacky to invite guests and then have them buy their own drinks. In every case, it is important that bartenders be trained to spot individuals who appear to be under the influence of alcohol and politely suggest a nonalcoholic alternative.

Organizations also try to control the level of drinking by offering only beer or wine instead of hard liquor. Still others issue two or three free drink tickets to arriving guests with the understanding that there will be a charge for any additional drinks.

A cocktail party, like a meal function, requires you to talk with the catering manager to order food items and decide how many bartenders are needed. As a rule of thumb, there should be one bartender per 75 people. For large events, bars are situated in several locations around the room to disperse the crowd and shorten lines.

It is also important to find out how the facility will bill you for beverages consumed. If the arrangement is by the bottle, this often leads to the problems of bartenders being very generous in pouring drinks because more empty bottles mean higher profits for the caterer.

Starting a cocktail party is easy—just open the bar at the announced time. Closing a party is not so easy. The only practical way is to close the bar. The invitation may indicate a definite time for closing, but don't rely on this. A vocal announcement will do the job. The smoothest way is to say, "The bar will close in 10 minutes." This gives guests a chance to get one more drink.

OPEN HOUSES AND PLANT TOURS

These events are conducted primarily to develop favorable public opinion about an organization. Generally they are planned to show the facilities where the organization does its work and, in plant tours, how the work is done. A factory might have a plant tour to show how it turns raw materials into finished products. A hospital

OPEN HOUSE PLANNING CHECKLIST

PREPLANNING

Initial Planning
- Select and research the date
- Set up your committees or areas of responsibility
- Determine your budget

Open House Announcement
- Notify employees and recruit their assistance
- Invite staff and families, if appropriate
- Develop your mailing list
- Design and print invitations
- Arrange advertising
- Prepare and distribute press releases/posters
- Create radio/TV spots

Food and Beverages
- Decide on the menu
- Arrange for catering or volunteer servers
- Arrange for clean-up

Equipment/Decorations
- Determine the equipment available from your organization
- Arrange for necessary rentals such as tables, chairs, outdoor tent
- Arrange for table linens, plates and silverware
- Plan flowers in strategic locations

Specialty Advertising
- Arrange for giveaways that increase your organization's visibility such as balloons, T-shirts and mugs

Media Relations
- Invite the media personally and by mail
- Develop and distribute press releases announcing the event
- Arrange for media coverage on the day of the open house
- Arrange for a photographer to cover the event (photos can be used for publicity or internal communications)

DAY OF EVENT

Reception
- Set up a staffed reception table with a sign-in book
- Distribute information on your organization and giveaways
- Have staff explain the activities to guests

Tours
(Some preparation required in planning process)
- Develop a floor plan for tours to ensure consistency
- Arrange a regular tour schedule, such as every 30 minutes
- Offer an incentive (such as a T-shirt) to those who complete the tour
- Brief tour guides on the key points to cover and how to field questions
- Arrange for visuals such as a display or demonstrations during the tour

Activities/Entertainment
This depends on the nature of your event. It could include:
- Health education displays or screenings
- A road race
- Games, a magician or a storyteller for the children
- A local community band
- A short questionnaire to evaluate community response to the event and issues related to your organization

Ceremony
- Arrange a focal point for your open house such as a ribbon cutting, awards ceremony, music/dance performance or brief message from the company president

Source: Lorraine Bauman and Elizabeth Daniels, "Making an Open House a Special Event," *Public Relations Journal*, August 1990, p. 33.

open house could show its emergency facilities, diagnostic equipment, operating rooms and patient rooms.

Open houses are customarily one-day affairs. However, if large numbers of people are to attend, the event may be extended to more than one day. Attendance is usually by invitation, but in certain exceptional instances, the event is announced in the general media, and anyone who chooses to attend may do so. In such cases, planning and control become almost impossible, and the results are often unsatisfactory.

Many plants offer tours daily and regularly while the plant is in operation. These tours are most common among producers of consumer goods such as beer, wine, food products, clothing and small appliances. These daily tours are geared to handle only a few people at any one time, whereas the other tours generally have a large number of guests and normal operations are not feasible during the tour.

Since the purpose of an open house or a plant tour is to create favorable opinion about the organization, it must be carefully planned, thoroughly explained and smoothly conducted. The visitors must understand what they are seeing. This requires careful routing, control to prevent congestion, signs and guides. All employees who will be present should understand the purpose of the event and be thoroughly coached in their duties. Rehearsal plus much checking and rechecking is imperative.

Among the principal things to include in the plans for an open house or a plant tour are these:

1. *Day and hour.* The time must be convenient for both the organization and the guests.
2. *Guests.* These may be families of employees, customers, representatives of the community, suppliers and competitors, reporters or others whose goodwill is desirable.
3. *Invitations.* These should be sent out well in advance. A month is common.

If a plant tour is a continuing daily event, the availability of the tour should be announced by signs near the plant and possibly by advertising or publicity. For any open house or plant tour, think of these points:

1. *Vehicles.* Parking must be available, and there should be a map on the invitation showing how to get there and where to park.
2. *Reception.* A representative of the organization should meet and greet all arriving guests. If guests are important people, they should meet the top officials of the organization.
3. *Rest rooms and cloakrooms.* These facilities should be provided and identified with large signs.
4. *Safety.* Hazards should be conspicuously marked and well lighted. Dangerous equipment should be barricaded.
5. *Routing.* Routes should be well marked and logical (in a factory, the route should go from raw materials through production steps to the finished product). A map should be given to each visitor if the route is long or complicated.

6. *Guides.* Visitors must be led through the tour by guides who know the route and what the visitors are to see. Guides may lead groups of visitors, or they may stay at specified positions and send each group on to the next guide when they have explained the operation at their position.

7. *Explanation.* Signs, charts and diagrams may be necessary at any point to supplement the words of the guides. The guides must be coached to say exactly what the public should be told. Many experts can't explain what they do, so a prepared explanation is necessary.

8. *Housekeeping and attire.* The premises should be as clean as possible. Attire should be clean and appropriate. A punch press operator doesn't wear a necktie, but his overalls need not be greasy.

9. *Emergencies.* Accidents or illness may occur. All employees should know what to do and how to reach the first-aid personnel, who should be readily available.

CONVENTIONS

A convention is a series of meetings, usually spread over two or more days. The purpose is to gather and exchange information, meet other people with similar interests, discuss and act on common problems and enjoy recreation and social interchange.

Most conventions are held by associations and fraternal or social groups. Because the membership is widespread, a convention is nearly always "out of town" to many attendees, so convention arrangements must give consideration to this.

Planning

It is necessary to begin planning far in advance of the actual event. Planning for even the smallest convention should start months before the scheduled date; for large national conventions, it may begin several years ahead and require hundreds or thousands of hours of work. The main things involved in planning a convention are timing, location, facilities, exhibits, program, recreation, attendance and administration.

Timing This must be convenient for the people who are expected to attend. Avoid peak work periods. Summer vacation is appropriate for educators and after harvest is suitable for farmers. Preholiday periods are bad for retailers and mid-winter is probably a poor time in the northern states but may be very good in the South. Here, as in every area dealing with the public, it is imperative to know your audience and to plan for their convenience.

Location The location must be convenient. For a national convention, it can be anywhere in the country. A national convention in Fairbanks, Alaska, is unlikely; yet one in Honolulu could be a great success because the glamour of the location would outweigh the cost and time of travel. Many organizations rotate their conventions from one part of the state, region or country to another to equalize travel burdens.

Another factor in choosing a location is the accommodations available. There must be enough rooms to house the attendees and enough meeting rooms of the right size. Timing enters into this, because many such accommodations are booked months or even years in advance. Large cities usually have large convention facilities and numerous hotels, but early reservations are necessary. Even smaller towns are likely to require a long lead time for some accommodations.

Once a tentative location has been selected, you must find out if the convention can be handled at the time chosen. Early action on this can forestall later changes. Be sure to get a definite price on guest rooms as well as meeting rooms.

Small conventions are often held in resorts, but accessibility is a factor. If the visitors have to change airlines several times or if the location is hard to get to by automobile, the glamour may fail to compensate for the inconvenience.

Facilities   For every meeting of the convention it is necessary to have a room of the right size and the equipment needed for whatever is to go on in that room. The convention might start with a general meeting in a very large room where seating is theater fashion and the equipment consists of a public address system and a speaker's platform with the necessary accessories. After opening remarks, the convention might break into smaller groups that meet in different rooms with widely varying facilities.

One room may require an overhead projector; another may need a chalkboard or an easel for charts; still another may need a VCR and monitor. In one room the seating may be around conference tables; another may have theater seating. To get everything right, you must know exactly what is to happen, who is going to participate and when.

Exhibits   The makers and sellers of supplies that are used by people attending conventions frequently want to show their wares. This means that the convention manager must provide space suitable for that purpose. Most large convention centers have display rooms that can accommodate anything from books to bulldozers. There is a charge for the use of these rooms, and the exhibitors pay for the space they use.

The exhibit hall may be in the hotel where the convention is being held or in a separate building. For example, McCormick Place is an enormous building on the Chicago lakefront. It is an easy taxi trip from the Loop, where conventions are usually based and where the visitors sleep. Eating facilities ranging from hotdog stands to elaborate dining rooms are to be found in almost any such building. Exhibits are covered in more detail in the next section.

Program

A convention program usually has a basic theme. Aside from transacting the necessary organizational business, most of the speeches and other sessions will be devoted to various aspects of the theme. Themes can range from the specific "New Developments in AIDS Research" to the more general "Quality Management and Productivity." Some groups use an even broader theme such as "Connections" or "At the Crossroads."

With a theme chosen, the developer of the program looks for prominent speakers who have something significant to say on the subject. In addition, there may be a need for discussions, workshops and other sessions focusing on particular aspects of the general theme.

The printed program for the convention is a schedule. It tells exactly when every session will be, what room it will be in and who will speak on what subject. Large conventions often schedule different sessions at the same time. Attendees then choose which session they prefer.

The program should be small enough to fit in a pocket or a handbag. Large programs may look impressive, but they are cumbersome to carry and easy to misplace. Printing of the program should be delayed until the last possible moment. Last-minute changes and speaker defaults are common. Type changes can be made with just a few hours of warning, but it is usually impossible to reprint the entire program.

Recreation   Recreation is a feature of practically all conventions. This may range from informal get-togethers to formal dances. Cocktail parties, golf tournaments, sightseeing tours and free time are among the possibilities. Sometimes recreational events are planned to coincide with regular program sessions. These are patronized by spouses and by delegates who would rather relax than listen to a speaker.

Attendance   Getting people to attend a convention requires two things: an appealing program and a concerted effort to persuade members to attend. Announcements and invitations should go out early enough to allow attendees to make their individual arrangements. (Allow several months.) A follow-up just before the convention is in order. Reply cards should be provided, accompanied by hotel reservation forms. (Remember that hotels generally offer special lower rates for conventions.)

Administration   Running a convention is a strenuous job. The organization staff is likely to see very little of the program and a great many delegates with problems. Among the things that must be done are arranging for buses to convey delegates from the airport to the convention (if it is in a remote location) and to carry them on tours. Meeting speakers and getting them to the right place at the right time is another task.

People arriving at the convention headquarters must be met, registered and provided with all the essentials (name tags, programs and any other needed materials). A message center should be set up so that people can be informed of phone calls or other messages. (This can be as simple as a bulletin board near the registration desk.) Special arrangements should be made for the media. A small convention may interest only a few people from trade publications, but larger conventions may draw attention from the major media. In this case, a newsroom should be set up with telephones, fax machines, tables and other needed equipment.

TRADE SHOWS

A trade show is the ultimate marketing event. They are a $70 billion industry in the United States with more than 600,000 organizations exhibiting in about 10,000 shows that draw an estimated 65 million people annually.

Comdex, described by the *Wall Street Journal* as the "King Kong" of computer trade shows, is held annually in Las Vegas and occupies the space of about 30 football fields. In one recent year, there were exhibits from 2,200 companies and an estimated 200,000 attendees.

The attendees occupied most of the 94,000 hotel rooms in Las Vegas and generated about $320 million for the city's economy. The trade show's caterer also reported that the Comdex crowd consumed 10,000 cups of coffee, 50,000 sodas, 5,000 hot dogs, 9,500 bottles of water, 7,000 chicken sandwiches, 3,000 pounds of roast beef and 6,000 pounds of turkey.

All this doesn't include, of course, the numerous cocktail parties and dinners that were held off-premises by various companies seeking to impress and influence potential customers. One start-up software company, for example, spent $500,000 to hire Fleetwood Mac and gave out 13,000 free concert tickets at its exhibit booth. Another company hired The Temptations for a chili cook-off that attracted 6,000 hungry fans.

Exhibit Booths

The exhibit booth is a major cost at a trade show. At national trade shows, it is not unusual for a 30-foot booth to start at $50,000, including design, construction, transportation and space rental fees. Larger, more elaborate booths can easily cost $100,000 to $250,000.

Figure 18.3 Trade shows attract millions of people annually. It's an opportunity to see products from a number of companies, generate sales leads, and attract media coverage. (*Copyright Billy E. Barnes/Stock, Boston.*)

Any booth or exhibit should be designed for maximum visibility. Experts say you have about 10 seconds to attract a visitor as he or she walks down an aisle of booths. Here are some points to keep in mind:

- Make the display or booth visually attractive. Use bright colors, large signs and working models of products.
- Think about putting action in your display. Have a video or slide presentation running all the time.
- Use involvement techniques. Have a contest or raffle in which visitors can win a prize. One exhibitor at Comdex even offered free foot massages.
- Give people an opportunity to operate equipment or do something.
- Have knowledgeable, personable representatives on duty to answer questions and collect visitor business cards for follow-up.
- Offer useful souvenirs. A keychain, a shopping bag, a luggage tag or even a copy of a popular newspaper or magazine will attract traffic.

Most organizations feel that the large investment in a booth at a trade show is worthwhile, for several reasons. First, a trade show facilitates communication with key audiences because they are all gathered in one place. It also attracts many journalists, so it is easier and more efficient to provide press materials, arrange one-on-one interviews and demonstrate what makes the product worth a story. Second, a booth allows an exhibitor to demonstrate how its products differ from the competition. This is more effective than just sending prospects a color brochure. It also is more cost-effective than making individual sales calls.

Hospitality Suites   Hospitality suites are an adjunct to the exhibit booth. Organizations use them to entertain key prospects, give more in-depth presentations and talk about business deals.

The idea is that serious customers will stay in a hospitality suite long enough to hear an entire presentation, whereas they are likely to stop at an exhibit hall booth for only a few minutes. Although goodwill can be gained from free concerts and cocktail parties, companies use hospitality suites to get product orders and sales leads.

Press Rooms

Every trade show has a press room where the various exhibitors distribute press kits and other information to journalists. Press rooms typically have phone, fax and E-mail facilities for reporters to file stories back to their employers.

As a public relations writer, you are often responsible for preparing an organization's press kit. Remember the rules about press kits discussed in Chapter 9; keep them short and relevant, and offer newsworthy information. A common complaint of reporters at a trade show is that "press kits" are only a compilation of sales brochures.

Another important part of your job is to personally contact reporters attending a trade show and offer one-on-one interviews with key executives. The competition is intense, so you have to be creative in pitching your ideas and showing why your company should be singled out for coverage.

Planning Guidelines

A trade show requires extensive planning months in advance. Gary Allen, owner of Allen Communications in Roseville, CA, offers these guidelines:

1. *Start early.* You should start planning and developing your exhibit booth 6 to 12 months ahead of time. Exhibit designers and builders need plenty of time to develop a booth.

2. *State your goal.* It may be one or more of the following: (a) to develop sales leads, (b) to test-market a new product, (c) to position your company as the leader in the industry, (d) to launch a public relations or publicity campaign, (e) to gather demographic data on potential buyers or (f) to launch a new product.

3. *Establish a way to measure success.* Establish goals for amount of press coverage, number of people who visit the booth, number of sales leads and number of business cards collected or addresses added to your mailing list.

4. *Select the right trade shows.* There are thousands of trade shows. You must research which ones will attract the key audiences that you want to reach.

5. *Develop a compelling exhibit.* At a large trade show where there are many exhibitors, a general rule is that you have only 10 seconds to attract someone's attention. Consequently, you need large, colorful graphics and movement. Many companies use large-screen videos.

6. *Train the exhibit staff.* Use the most personable and most knowledgeable people you can find in your organization. Conduct a briefing session before the show so that they thoroughly understand what key messages should be communicated.

7. *Promote your attendance in advance.* Use direct mail announcements to your target customers, and take out ads in trade magazines. In addition, send press kits and background materials to selected reporters before the trade show. Another tactic is to telephone reporters and offer interviews with key executives who will be attending the trade show.

PROMOTIONAL EVENTS

These events are planned primarily to promote product sales, increase organizational visibility or raise money for a charitable cause.

One kind of promotional event is the "grand opening" of a new store, restaurant, shopping center or civic facility. These events are really open houses or plant tours embellished with crowd attractions and some ceremony.

Usually there are speeches, participation by civic dignitaries, possibly parades, and often special attractions to draw crowds. Special attractions can include appearances by entertainers, contests, drawings for prizes, carnival attractions and the presence of a film or television personality (see Figure 18.4). The celebrity, or a high-ranking civic official, will cut the ribbon, turn on the lights or start the machinery.

Figure 18.4   Celebrities make grand openings a special event. Here, Diana Ross cuts the ribbon to open Motown Cafe in New York City, a theme restaurant of 1960s music. (*Photo provided by Victor Malafronte Archive.*)

Events that attract crowds require the same planning as an open house. You should be concerned about traffic flow, adequate restroom facilities, signage and security. Security should also be arranged to handle crowd control, protect celebrities or government officials from being hassled and to make sure no other disruptions occur that would mar the event.

Liability insurance is a necessity, too. Any public event sponsored by an organization should be insured just in case there is an accident and a subsequent lawsuit charging negligence. If your organization doesn't already have a blanket liability policy, you should get one for the event.

Charitable organizations also need liability insurance if they are running an event to raise money. This is particularly relevant if your organization is sponsoring an event that requires physical exertion, such as a 10-K run, a bicycle race or even a hot-air balloon race.

Participants should sign a release form that protects the organization if someone suffers a heart attack or another kind of accident. One organization, which was sponsoring a 5-K "fun run," had the participants sign a statement that read in part: "I know that a road race is a potentially hazardous activity. . . . I assume all risk associated with running in this event, including, but not limited to, falls, contact with

PROMOTIONAL EVENT

The Olympic Torch Relay

An outstanding marketing tool for the 1996 Olympics was the Olympic flame cross-country run that was Olympic-sized in its logistics and promotional value.

The 84-day, 42-state event involved 10,000 runners who carried the Olympic flame 15,000 miles up and down the United States from Boston to Miami, New Orleans to Minneapolis, Dallas to Seattle, and down the entire West Coast to Los Angeles.

Although the popular image of the Olympic Torch Relay is that of a solitary runner, the 1996 runners had plenty of company. A 40-vehicle caravan tagged along, carrying security officers, an advance team, media, medical personnel and even spare flames in case the original one went out. In addition, the event required the services of 10,000 volunteers and 2,500 escort runners.

Sponsoring corporations also provided massive amounts of equipment and clothing. IBM provided computers and cellular phones; BMW provided 30 cars and motorcycles; and Hanes outfitted all 10,000 runners. NBC, the official broadcaster of the Atlanta games, also gave a nightly 20-second news report on the progress of the torch relay.

Total cost: about $20 million. The result: about 1.8 million tickets sold to soccer matches by the Atlanta Olympic Committee, high public awareness for the Olympics and its sponsors and millions of dollars in revenues from the sale of T-shirts, sweatshirts and caps.

other participants, the effects of the weather, including high heat/or humidity, traffic and the conditions of the road."

Promotional events that use public streets and parks also need permits from various city departments. If you're sponsoring a run, you need to get a permit from the police or public safety department to block off streets and you need to hire off-duty police to handle traffic control.

A food event, such as a chili cook-off or a German fest requires permits from the public health department and, if liquor is served, a permit from the state alcohol board. If the event is held inside a building, a permit is often required from the fire inspector.

You must also deal with the logistics of arranging cleanup, providing basic services such as water and medical aid, registering craft and food vendors, and posting signs. Promotion of an event can often be accomplished by having a radio station or local newspaper co-sponsor the event.

SUMMARY

1. Events and meetings don't just happen. They must be planned with attention to the slightest detail. Nothing must be left to chance.

2. Before scheduling a committee meeting, always ask, "Is this meeting really necessary?"

3. Club meetings and workshops require you to consider such factors as time, location, seating, facilities, invitations, name tags, menu, speakers, registration and costs.

4. Banquets are elaborate affairs that require extensive advance planning. In additional to the factors necessary for a club meeting, you have to consider decorations, entertainment, audiovisual facilities, speaker fees and seating charts.

5. Cocktail parties and receptions require precautions about the amount of alcohol consumed, and the availability of food and nonalcoholic drinks. Possible liability is an important consideration.

6. Open houses and plant tours require meticulous planning and routing, careful handling of visitors and thorough preparation of all personnel who will be in contact with the visitors.

7. Conventions require the skills of professional managers who can juggle multiple events and meetings over a period of several days. A convention may include large meetings, cocktail parties, receptions, tours and banquets.

8. Trade shows are the ultimate marketing events that attract millions of attendees annually. Exhibit booths may cost from $50,000 to $250,000.

9. A promotional event may be a "grand opening" of a facility or a 10-K run sponsored by a charitable organization. It is important to consider such factors as city permits, security and liability insurance.

EXERCISES

1. Successful events require extensive planning and attention to every detail. Select a campus organization or a community group that has just completed an annual awards banquet or convention. Arrange to interview the person in charge of the event in order to write a case study analysis. Detail the steps taken to plan and organize the event. Include (a) budget, (b) time elements, (c) arrangements with hotels or restaurants, (d) speaker arrangements, (e) registration packets or invitations sent to potential attendees, (f) publicity vehicles used and (g) unexpected problems that occurred that should be considered in next year's planning.

2. The school of business at your university has scheduled its annual awards banquet for about six months from today. This banquet, held at a local hotel, usually draws about 500 guests, including alumni, students, faculty and members of the local business community. The usual pattern is to have a nationally known business executive give the major speech. You are charged with coordinating this event. Prepare a detailed outline of what must be done to plan the banquet, including a time line or calendar of what must be done by certain dates.

3. Contact the catering manager of a restaurant or a hotel. Discuss the costs of food and beverage for (1) a cocktail party, and (2) a dinner meeting for 150 people. Armed with this information, prepare a list of costs for having your events. Given the total costs (which would include other considerations such as invitations, postage, decorations, speaker fees and so on), how much would you have to charge per ticket to break even on the event.

19 | *Program Planning*

All public relations writing and other techniques described in this text are applied within a planned framework. We call it a public relations program or plan because multiple activities—news releases, press kits, news conferences, talk shows, brochures, newsletters, speeches and so on—are coordinated to achieve specific results.

Planning is imperative for any public relations campaign. It improves effectiveness. By using multiple communication tools together, you ensure a greater overall impact. A plan is the blueprint. It explains the situation, analyzes what can be done about it, outlines strategies and tactics and tells how the results will be evaluated.

Assuming that you've mastered the individual public relations skills discussed so far, it is now time to transfer them to the broader canvas of program planning.

ELEMENTS OF A PLAN

There is no standard description of the elements that go into a campaign. Different organizations designate these elements in different ways, combining or dividing them as seems appropriate. Nevertheless, any good plan will cover situation, objectives, audience, strategy, tactics, timing, budget and evaluation.

Situation

An organization's situation can be determined by summarizing the organization's relations with its public or publics. This tells why the program is needed and points out problems and opportunities. This may be the most important part of the plan. Unless management is convinced that a campaign is necessary, it is not likely to approve spending money on it.

Problem situations that require remedial programming include situations such as these:

- The beef industry experienced a decline in the per capita consumption of beef because consumers perceived the product to be high in fat and not as healthy as chicken or fish.
- The state of Florida experienced a major decline in European tourism after considerable negative publicity about the murder of several foreign tourists in drive-by shootings or at rest stops on the interstate highway.
- Apple Computer, after losing $68 million in one quarter and going through major disarray at the top management level, needed to reassure customers and the financial community that the company was still sound.

Most public relations situations, however, are not problems that must be solved in a hurry. Instead, they are opportunities for an organization to increase public awareness, advance its reputation or attract new customers and clients. Here are some examples:

- Dole Food Company conducted a major public relations campaign to inform children and parents about the importance of fruit and vegetables in a balanced diet.
- Friskies PetCare Company increased brand awareness by sponsoring a national canine Frisbee competition.
- The New York State Canal System launched a campaign to make citizens more aware of the historic canal system as a first-class tourist destination.
- The County Hospital Council in Columbus, Ohio, conducted a campaign that significantly increased the number of fully vaccinated children.

Objectives

Years ago, one of the authors of this book returned from a disastrous meeting with a client who had rejected every recommendation. With the door shut and his feet on top of the desk, he pondered the problem. Why had he failed to secure approval?

Finally the answer came: Neither he nor the client had a clear idea of the campaign's objectives.

The next step was to ask the question, What are we trying to accomplish? This led to considerable research and ultimately to a determination of the objectives. With the client in agreement on the objectives and the campaign revised to fit them, it was approved and carried out to the satisfaction of both parties.

The lesson from this case is that neither employers nor clients are likely to approve a campaign without clear objectives. Furthermore, even if a campaign is approved, it will surely fail without objectives.

Within any campaign, there may be multiple objectives. Smaller campaigns may have only one target and one objective, but in any planning you must be sure that you thoroughly understand what you are trying to accomplish.

It's also important that you don't confuse objectives with the "means" instead of the "end." Novices, for example, often set an objective such as "Generate publicity for the new product." Publicity, however, is not an end in itself. The real outcome is to create an awareness among consumers about the availability of the new product and motivate them to purchase it.

There are basically two kinds of objectives: informational and motivational.

Informational Objectives A large percentage of public relations plans are designed primarily to increase awareness of an issue, an event or a product. Here are some possible informational objectives:

- To inform people about the kinds of food needed for good nutrition
- To tell people that cigarette smoking is a major cause of cancer
- To proclaim the virtues of raisins
- To alert people to the fact that aerosol sprays damage the ozone layer

Although informational objectives are legitimate and are used by virtually every public relations firm and department, it is extremely difficult to measure how much "awareness" was attained unless before-and-after surveys are done; these are expensive and time-consuming. In addition, awareness doesn't equal action. Consumers may have been made aware of your new product, but that doesn't necessarily mean that they will buy it.

Motivational Objectives Motivational objectives are more ambitious and also more difficult to achieve. Basically, you want to change attitudes and opinions with the idea of modifying behavior.

Some motivational objectives might be:

- To get people to eat healthier foods
- To reduce cigarette smoking
- To increase the consumption of raisins
- To prevent the sale of aerosol sprays

Notice that motivational objectives are more "bottom line–oriented." The effectiveness of the public relations plan is based on making something happen, whether it be increasing sales or changing public support for some issue.

BASIC ELEMENTS OF A PUBLIC RELATIONS PLAN

A basic public relations plan is a blueprint of what you want to do and how you will accomplish your task. Such a plan, be it a brief outline or a comprehensive document, will enable you and your client or employer to make sure that all elements have been properly considered, evaluated and coordinated for maximum effectiveness.

1. **Situation** You cannot set valid objectives without understanding the problem. To understand the problem: (a) discuss it with the client to find out what he or she expects the publicity to accomplish, (b) do your own research and (c) evaluate your ideas in the broader perspective of the client's long-term goals.

2. **Objectives** Once you understand the situation, it should be easy to define the objectives. To determine if your stated objectives are the right ones, ask yourself: (a) Does it really solve or help solve the problem? (b) Is it realistic and achievable? and (c) Can the success be measured in terms meaningful to the client?

3. **Audience** Identify, as precisely as possible, the group of people to whom you are going to direct your communications. Is this the right group to approach in order to solve the problem? If there are several groups, prioritize them according to which are most important for your particular objectives.

4. **Strategies** The strategy describes how, in concept, the objective is to be achieved. Strategy is a plan of action that provides guidelines for selecting the communications activity you will employ. There are usually one or more strategies for each target audience. Strategies may be broad or narrow, depending on the objective and the audience.

5. **Tactics** This is the body of the plan, which describes, in sequence, the specific communications activities proposed to achieve each objective. Discuss each activity as a separate thought, but relate each to the unifying strategy and theme. In selecting communication tools—news releases, brochures, radio announcements and so on—ask yourself if the use of each will really reach your priority audiences and help you accomplish your stated objectives.

6. **Calendar** It is important to have a timetable, usually outlined in chart form, that shows the start and completion of each project within the framework of the total program. A calendar makes sure that you begin projects—such as brochures, slide presentations, newsletters or special events—early enough that they are ready when they are needed. A program brochure that reaches its target two days after the event is not an effective publicity tool.

7. **Budget** How much will implementation of the plan cost? Outline in sequence the exact costs of all activities. Make sure that you include such things as postage, car mileage and labor to stuff envelopes. In addition, about 10 percent of the total budget should be allocated for contingencies.

8. **Evaluation** Before you begin, both you and the client or employer must agree on the criteria you will use to evaluate your success in achieving the objective. Evaluation criteria should be (a) realistic, (b) credible, (c) specific and (d) appropriate to the client's expectations. Don't show stacks of press clippings if only sales results are important.

By contrast, informational objectives merely inform or educate people. Take the informational objective of making people aware of cigarette smoking as a major cause of cancer. This might be achieved successfully enough, but people who are "informed" and "aware" often continue to smoke. A better gauge of the American Cancer Society's success in its efforts would be an actual increase in the number of people who stopped smoking.

In setting objectives, you must be sure that they are realistic and achievable. Furthermore, they must be within the power of the campaign alone to attain. Sometimes the unwary set objectives such as "to increase sales" without realizing that sales may be affected by such things as product quality, packaging, pricing, merchandising, advertising, sales promotion, display and competitive activity.

In establishing objectives, you must state exactly what you want the audience to know (a new product is now on the market), to believe (it will cut utility bills) and to do (ask for a demonstration). Objectives must be measurable. At some point the people who pay for the campaign are likely to ask, What did you accomplish? Many practitioners rely on general feedback—random comments and isolated examples that indicate public reaction. True professionals give facts and figures.

Evaluation is covered in detail in Chapter 20; at this point, however, you must start thinking about setting objectives that can be measured with figures. In an informational campaign, it is easy to state an objective such as: "To increase the number of people who believe that carpooling is a good way to save energy."

A motivational objective in this situation could be "To increase the number of people who use carpooling." However, it would be far better to put it this way: "To increase carpooling by 50 percent."

As you think about these numerical goals, you should realize that there must be a base point for such measurements. To know how many people have been convinced by your campaign, you must know how many people believed in carpooling before you began your campaign. With this figure in hand, you can prove that your efforts have increased awareness. When you then get figures on current carpooling, you will be able to prove that the campaign has increased utilization and by how much. Finding these base points require research, which will be discussed later.

Audience

Public relations programs should be directed toward specific and defined audiences or publics. If you define the audience as the "general public," you're not doing your homework.

In most cases, you are looking for specific audiences within a "general public." Take, for example, the Ohio vaccination program for children under the age of two. The primary audience for the message is parents with young children. A secondary audience is pregnant women. This knowledge should provide guidance on the selection of strategies and tactics that would primarily reach these defined audiences.

Increasing the use of carpooling is another example of an objective for which you can define the audience more precisely than saying "the general public." The primary audience for the message on carpooling is people who drive to work. A secondary audience might be parents who drive their children to school.

PUBLIC RELATIONS PLANNING AND MARKETING STRATEGY

Public relations programs, particularly product publicity, can make a substantial contribution to fulfilling the marketing objectives of a business organization.

- It can develop new prospects for new markets, such as inquiries from people who saw or heard a product release in the news media.
- It can provide third-party endorsements—via newspapers, magazines, radio and television—through news releases about a company's products or services, community involvement, inventions and new plans.
- It can generate sales leads, usually through articles in the trade press about new products and services.
- It can pave the way for sales calls.
- It can stretch the organization's advertising and promotional dollars through timely and supportive releases about it and its products.
- It can provide inexpensive sales literature for the company because articles about it and its products can be reprinted as informative pieces for prospective clients.
- It can establish the organization as an authoritative source of information on a given subject.
- It can help sell minor products. Some products are too minor for large advertising expenditures, so exposure to the market is more cost-effective if product publicity is utilized.

A third example might be a company that wants to increase the sale of a CD-ROM program on home improvement for do-it-yourselfers. Again, the primary audience is not the "general public" but only those who actually have CD-ROM players and enjoy working around the house. Such criteria exclude a large percentage of the American population.

Another common mistake is defining the "mass media" as an audience. In nine out of 10 cases, selected mass media serve as channels to reach the audiences that you want to inform, persuade and motivate. On occasion, in programs that seek to change how mass media reports an organization or an issue, editors and reporters can become a primary "public" or audience.

Gaining a thorough understanding of your primary and secondary audiences, which are directly related to accomplishing your objectives, is the only way that you can formulate successful strategies and tactics.

Strategy

Strategy is the broad concept on which the campaign will be based. Strategy must be keyed directly to the objective, and it must be formed with a thorough knowledge of what the primary audiences perceive as relevant and in their self-interest.

The vaccination program for children, for example, was based on the idea that parents love their children and want them to be healthy. Thus, the strategy was to tell parents how important vaccinations were in keeping their children out of danger. In fact, the theme of the campaign became "Project L.O.V.E." with the subhead "Love Our Kids Vaccination Project."

The program to increase carpooling was based on research showing that commuters were interested in saving time and money. Thus, the strategy was to show how people using designated carpool lanes could cut the time of their commute. A second strategy was to show how much money a carpooler would save annually in gasoline, insurance and maintenance costs.

The strategy on the CD-ROM home improvement product was to let people know that multimedia visual instruction would help the do-it-yourselfers complete their jobs more competently and with fewer hassles. The 2,200 full-color illustrations and 50 how-to narrated videos also appealed to those who wanted to do home improvements but didn't have much experience.

These examples illustrate two basic concepts about strategy. First, the strategy must reflect the audience's self-interests. Second, the strategy must be expressed in simple terms as a *key selling proposition.*

The key statement is the message of the communication process. It must be reiterated throughout the campaign in various ways, but the concept should remain clear and simple. Every campaign has what is called *key copy points,* which are ex-

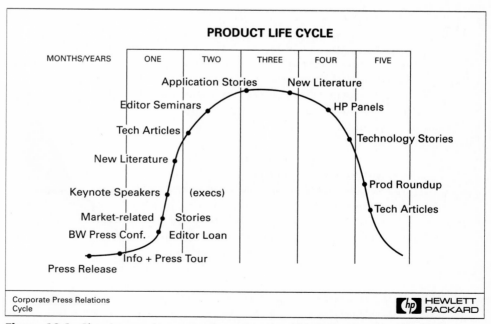

Figure 19.1 Planning requires strategies and tactics. This bell curve shows a product's life cycle and the kinds of public relations activities needed at each stage. Note that numerous tools are used at the beginning to launch the product. (*Courtesy of Hewlett-Packard Company, Palo Alto, CA.*)

pressed in every activity—whether it be in a news release, a feature article, a media interview or even a VNR.

Indeed, one of the criteria for an effective public relations program is whether the audience was exposed to your key copy points and absorbed them. One way of determining this is a content analysis of media mentions, which will be discussed under evaluation and in the next chapter.

Tactics

This is the "how to do it" portion of the plan. In the communication process, it is described as using the tools of communication to reach primary and secondary audiences with your key messages.

The children's vaccination project, for example, used a variety of tactics, including:

- Posters in child-care centers and doctor's offices
- PSAs on radio stations that had audiences of childbearing age
- Articles in newspapers and magazines catering to parents
- Pamphlets sent to child-care service providers
- Booklets mailed to every new mother explaining vaccination and the schedule of shots
- Letters to doctors reminding them to ask about vaccinations when a child has a checkup
- Corporate and hospital sponsorship of two week-long "Shots for Tots" promotional events
- Endorsements by governmental leaders and child-care experts
- Information advertisements in community newspapers
- Stories about the L.O.V.E. Project on television and in the city's daily newspaper

The campaign on carpooling also used a variety of tactics. One tactic was to enlist the support of drive-time DJs on popular radio stations who promoted carpooling as part of their early morning and late afternoon banter between songs. Billboards along major highways were also used. There was also a concentrated effort to distribute posters and pamphlets that businesses could post and distribute to employees. Editors of employee newsletters and magazines were given background information on carpooling for possible stories. Another successful tactic was the compilation of a kit for employers telling them how to organize car pools for their employees.

The CD-ROM program, because of budget, was primarily a media campaign. The public relations firm worked to place articles and product reviews in (1) publications that reached relatively affluent households that would most likely have a CD-ROM player, (2) publications that catered to home improvement do-it-yourselfers and (3) publications that covered new titles on CD-ROM.

Calendar

Two aspects of timing must be considered: when the campaign is conducted and what the sequence of activities will be.

A campaign must be timely; it must run when the key messages mean the most to the intended audience. Some subjects are seasonal; hence publicists release information on strawberries in May and June when a crop comes to market They talk about insulation and roofing in the summer when these projects can be done. And a software program on doing your own taxes attracts the most audience interest in February and March, just before the April 15th deadline.

At times, the environmental context is important. A campaign on carpooling might be more successful if it follows a price increase in gasoline or a government agency report that traffic congestion has reached gridlock proportions. A charitable campaign to provide for the homeless is more effective if the local newspaper has just run a five-part series on the human dimensions of the problem.

Other kinds of campaigns are less dependent on seasonal or environmental context. The L.O.V.E. vaccination program, a Red Cross drive for blood donations, and even the selling of a CD-ROM on home improvements could be done almost anytime during the year. The Christmas season, however, would be great for selling the CD-ROM but it would be a bad time for running a vaccination project.

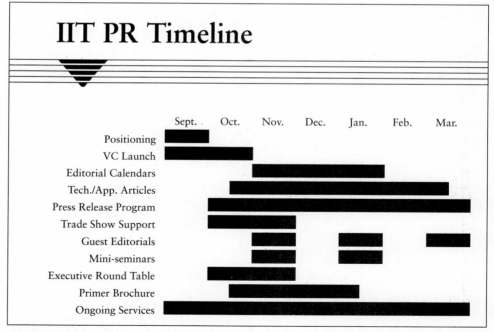

Figure 19.2 A campaign requires precision scheduling. This is a simplified timeline showing the duration of various activities. Some activities, such as news releases, are ongoing; others are phased in during the campaign. (*Courtesy of Hoffman Agency, San Jose, CA.*)

The second aspect of timing is the scheduling of activities during a campaign. A typical pattern is to have a concentrated effort at the beginning of a campaign where a number of activities are implemented. This is the launch phase of an idea or concept and, much like a rocket, takes a concentration of power just to break the awareness barrier. After the campaign has achieved orbit, however, it takes less energy and fewer activities are needed to maintain momentum. A good example of this is the product life cycle shown in Figure 19.1.

You must also think about advance planning. Monthly publications, for example, often need information at least six to eight weeks before an issue. If you want something in the August issue, you have to think about placing it in May or June. A popular talk show may work on a schedule that books guests three or four months in advance. The main idea is that you must constantly think ahead to make things happen in the appropriate sequence.

Organizing a calendar of activities, and their timing is discussed later in Working the Plan.

Budget

A budget can be divided into two categories: staff time and out-of-pocket (OOP) expenses. Staff and administrative time usually takes the lion's share of any public relations budget. In a $100,000 campaign done by a public relations firm, for example, 70 percent of more will go to salaries and administrative fees.

A public relations firm has different hourly rates for the level of personnel involved. The head of the agency, which would oversee the account, might bill at $200 per hour. The account supervisor might bill at $120 per hour, and the account executive at $100 per hour. Account coordinators, those who do a lot of the clerical work, might bill at $55 per hour.

A public relations firm, when submitting a plan, has usually constructed a budget based on the number of estimated staff hours it will take to implement a plan. Let's say that the plan calls for a press kit, the development of five news releases, the writing of a slide script and a news conference. The public relations firm might estimate that all this work will take at least 150 hours of staff time divided as follows:

> President, 20 hours × $200 = $4,000
> Vice President, 40 hours × $180 = $7,200
> Account Executive, 50 hours × $100 = $5,000
> Account Coordinator, 40 hours × $55 = $2,200
> TOTAL STAFF COSTS: $18,400

The other part of the budget is what is called out-of-pocket expenses (OOP), which includes payments to various vendors for such things as printing, postage, graphics, production of VNRs, travel, phone, fax, photocopying and so on.

You can do a reasonable job of estimating out-of-pocket expenses by making a few phone calls. You would call a printer, for example, to get an estimate of how much 10,000 copies of a pamphlet would cost. If you're doing a media tour, you would decide what cities would be visited and then find out the cost of airline fares, hotels, meals and ground transportation costs. The Internal Revenue Service even has a guide to daily living expenses in major cities around the world.

One method of doing a budget is to use two columns. The left column, for example, will give the staff cost for writing a pamphlet or compiling a press kit. The right column will give the actual OOP for having the pamphlet or the press kit designed, printed and delivered. Internal public relations departments, where the staff is already on the payroll, often compile only the OOP expenses.

Budgets should also have a line item for contingencies; that is, unexpected expenses. In general, allow about 10 percent of the budget.

Evaluation

Evaluation relates directly back to your stated objectives; it's the process in which you determine whether you have met your objectives.

If you have an informational objective, such as increasing awareness, a common procedure is to show placements in key publications and broadcast stations that reached the intended audience. Related to this is a content analysis of whether the news coverage included your key messages. A more scientific approach is doing a benchmark study of audience knowledge and perceptions before and after the campaign. In many cases, "before" activity has already been documented through marketing studies so all you have to do is a post-campaign survey.

Motivational objectives, such as increased market share or sales, are much easier to determine. The Ohio campaign had the objective of increasing vaccinations—and it succeeded by raising the vaccination rates by 117 percent in public clinics over a two-year period. A campaign by Ketchum Public Relations on behalf of prune producers caused a 4 percent increase in sales after several years of decline.

Increased sales, however, may be the result of other factors such as the economy, the additional use of advertising or a reduction in prices. Because of this, it's often wise to limit your objectives to something that can be directly related to your activities. For example, you may get feature placements in various magazines that also give an address for a free brochure. Success could then be declared when there are 10,000 requests for the brochure.

Chapter 20 expands on methods of evaluation in public relations.

DEVELOPING A PLAN

The first step in developing a plan is to consult with the client or with management. There are two purposes in this. First, it gets these people involved; if they are interested, they are likely to support the effort. Second, it is likely to give you the basic information you need to start making a plan.

In talking with the people who will pay for the campaign, you strive to identify the problems and opportunities confronting the organization. In some cases, these will be apparent to all. At other times, one party will have ideas that have not occurred to the other. Out of this discussion should come an agreement as to the general nature of the problems or opportunities and a preliminary establishment of objectives. All of this, of course, is subject to change when more information is gathered.

A good example is the California Avocado Commission. It faced the problem of selling Haas avocados on the East Coast. Sales were not good, and with a bumper crop of 600 million avocados, the California growers realized that they had a problem. Some informal research found that New Yorkers were not acquainted with avocados that turned jet black when ripe; they thought the fruit was rotten. The objective, then, was to inform consumers that Haas avocadoes were supposed to have black skins so that they had excellent flavor. The campaign succeeded because it was based on sound information and analysis.

Gathering Information

You cannot know too much about the subject you intend to promote. Don't be satisfied with a cursory investigation—dig and keep on digging until you have the whole story. There are several sources from which you can get the facts and figures that will enable you to plan an effective campaign.

1. *Organization.* Much basic information should be available within the organization. Ask for marketing plans, public relations plans and the research on which they are based. Talk to the people who deal with the public. Get an overall picture of the organization's successes and failures. Find out why things have happened or have been done.

2. *References.* Go through all the information in your files. Consult other files. Use libraries and on line databases. Read Chapter 1; many sources of information are cited there.

3. *Questions.* Ask colleagues for their ideas. Review the experiences of others in similar situations. Read any case histories you can find. The trade press is a good source.

4. *Analysis of communications.* Field reports from representatives of the organization, inquiries on telephone hot lines and consumer complaints should be checked and studied.

5. *Brainstorming.* Get a group of six to 10 people together and ask for suggestions. Many of the suggestions will be irrelevant, but some may contain the kernel of a good idea or point out areas where more information is needed.

6. *Focus group interviews.* Assemble a group of people who are representative of the audience you will want to reach. These interviews are not quantitative research, but they may point to a need for detailed research in a specific area.

7. *Surveys.* In many situations, you will need to conduct a formal survey to ascertain the attitudes and perceptions of target audiences. Doing a survey takes a lot of time and money. If the organization does not have the relevant data on hand, you must either do the survey yourself or hire someone to do it for you.

8. *Media directories.* To plan your tactics, you need to know which channels of communication will be most efficient. A number of media directories, including *Bacon's* and *Media Map,* give you profiles of various media outlets and their audiences.

9. *Demographics.* The *Statistical Abstract of the U.S., American Demographics* and the comprehensive *Simmons Index* provide insights into the characteristics of an audience. *Simmons,* in particular, will give you detailed information on consumer buying habits and their major sources of information. There are even lists that give you the demographics of people in various zip codes.

Analyzing the Information

Having gathered all pertinent information and conducted one or more surveys (if they are needed), your job is to analyze all the facts and ideas. You must consider the reliability of what you have found out. If there are contradictions, you must eliminate erroneous elements and confirm the credibility of what remains.

Now, with reliable information, you can start to draw conclusions. The situation, with its problems and opportunities, and the reason for the situation should be apparent. The objectives should be obvious and the strategy, after careful thought, should start to take form.

At this point, you should prepare an outline of your findings and discuss them with management or the client. You can say, "These are the facts that I have, this is the situation as I see it, these are the objectives I think we should select and this is the strategy I suggest."

This discussion may result in an approval in principle. If it does, you can start preparing the plan. If the general idea is not approved, you must find out what is wrong and make the needed corrections or gather additional information and try again.

Pretesting the Plan

Before you submit a written plan for final approval, you should pretest it. Ask some knowledgeable person whose opinion you respect to read the plan and then discuss it with you. Check these points:

1. What is the spontaneous reaction—is the person enthusiastic? If not, why not?
2. Is the situation clearly stated?
3. Is the audience the right one? Is it clearly defined?
4. Are the objectives attainable and measurable?
5. Is the strategy logical and effective?
6. Is the message persuasive and memorable?
7. Are the tactics sound and effective?
8. Is the timing right?
9. Are the costs reasonable and justified?
10. Will the proposed evaluation really measure the results?

11. Is the plan practical, palatable and appropriate?

12. Is the plan logical, strong and clearly written?

13. Are there any additions or deletions that should be made?

Ask yourself the same questions. Be sure to allow enough time for deliberate and unhurried review and for making changes if they are needed. Do this several days before the actual presentation.

WORKING THE PLAN

There's an old expression, "Plan your work, and work your plan." To carry out a multifaceted public relations program, you must have a precise list of steps for every activity and a schedule for when each step will be completed.

A brochure may be needed on March 29, but you must start the brochure long before that date. To determine the starting date, you must know every step in the production process and how long it will take.

This activity, as well as the scheduling of other public relations tactics, should not be trusted to your memory or to jottings on your desk calendar. It is important that the entire public relations team working on the program has a single source of information for the schedule of the entire campaign.

The easiest way to keep everything on schedule is to prepare a working calendar for detailed planning and internal use. The brochure example, cited above, might look like this:

Activity	Date Due	Responsibility
BROCHURE	March 29	J. Ross, G. Jones
Outline	January 11	J. Ross, G. Jones
Writing	January 18	J. Ross
Photos and artwork	January 25	A. Peck and N. Lopez
Design and layout	February 8	A. Peck and N. Lopez
Final client approval	February 15	B. Boss
Printer prep and proofs	February 28	Ace Printers. G. Jones, supervising
Printing and binding	March 10	Ace Printers. G. Jones, supervising
Delivery	March 15	United Parcel Service. G. Jones, supervising

Other entries planned using this kind of format might be preparing news releases, drafting speeches, writing pitch letters, scheduling spokespeople on radio talk shows, arranging media tours and commissioning a camera-ready feature article.

You can also map activities by listing the activities at the left of a chart with days or weeks across the top. Lines or bars graphically show when various steps are being worked on. This is often called a Gantt chart.

The main idea is that you should have a systematic means of tracking activities throughout the public relations program so everything stays on schedule. If a brochure or a press kit is delayed, it can delay other activities such as a media tour or a news conference that is dependent on having the materials available. All activities in a public relations program are interrelated for maximum effectiveness.

A MODEL PLAN: GETTING DRUNK DRIVERS OFF THE ROAD

An excellent example of a well-planned public relations program is one conducted by Aetna Insurance Company, which received a Silver Anvil award from the Public Relations Society of America (PRSA) in the category of public service conducted by a business.

Problem   Skyrocketing auto insurance rates have caused various state legislatures and the media to look critically at what could be done to reduce rates. Aetna, long active in driver safety programs, examined the issue of road safety to determine what factors had the greatest effect on the underlying cost of auto insurance.

Aetna began by reviewing studies compiled by the National Highway Traffic Safety Administration (NHTSA) and the National Safety Council. From this research, a prominent element of the problem was defined: drunk driving.

For example, it was found that half of all traffic fatalities (22,000) and about 534,000 injuries every year involved drunk drivers. It was also found that accidents from drunk driving cost $16 billion a year—a bill paid by taxpayers and insurance policyholders. Aetna's claims for alcohol-related car crashes came to $200 million annually.

Once the drunk driving problem was isolated, Aetna conducted primary research to identify public relations needs. Interviews were conducted with local police, prosecutors and anti–drunk driving groups. They also found that police funds for combating DUI ("driving under the influence") had been cut in many communities.

Figure 19.3   Planning a public relations campaign takes a lot of meetings, brain-storming, and delegation of responsibilities. (*Courtesy of Superstock, Inc.*)

Objectives   The research helped Aetna to establish four measurable public relations objectives:

1. To increase enforcement of drunk driving laws
2. To increase public awareness of the drunk driving problem
3. To create awareness about enforcement to help deter drunk driving
4. To differentiate Aetna from other insurance companies by positioning it as working to improve driver safety

One of Aetna's long-term objectives was to reduce auto insurance costs. Aetna also began a quantitative national public opinion study to establish benchmarks that would permit it to determine if public awareness changed during the course of the program.

Audience   The target audience was the general adult population and community leaders throughout the United States. Metropolitan areas, where there were a concentration of media outlets, were primary geographic targets.

Strategies   The program was named Aetna's EYE on DUI. Strategies included the donation of video cameras to local police departments, publicity about these donations and about the ill effects of drinking and driving, one-year anniversary events and the involvement of a leading anti–drunk driving group in each community.

The idea of donating video cameras to local police departments was based on research showing that convictions for drunk driving increased dramatically when arresting officers could videotape the proceedings while detaining suspects and conducting sobriety tests. Police also confirmed that publicity about this new enforcement effort acted as a public deterrent to drunk driving.

Tactics   A pilot program was run in Houston to permit debugging before using it in other markets. Aetna donated 16 video cameras at a press event in Houston two days before the fourth of July holiday weekend to dramatize the high incidence of drinking and driving during holidays and to achieve maximum publicity.

The police chief and the mayor participated in the news conference, and Aetna also arranged support from the local chapter of Mothers Against Drunk Driving (MADD). Media coverage was abundant, and local officials praised the camera program as a powerful new tool in the fight against drunk driving. This pilot program provided the basis for the tactics used in other cities:

- Conduct a news conference with local officials to announce the donation of video cameras to the police department.
- Hold the news conferences in dramatic locations, such as gritty jail cells or central booking rooms of police stations.
- Stage mock DUI arrests, and use the arrest footage from the local police on local television stations, accompanied by testimonials from surviving victims of drunk drivers.
- Arrange for local reporters to ride in camera-equipped police cars on busy weekend nights to witness the EYE on DUI program in action.

- Book surviving victims of drunk drivers and MADD representative on local radio and TV talk shows.
- Provide press kits and bylined op-ed articles to local media.
- Stage anniversary events to generate ongoing publicity about drinking and driving.

Using these tactics, Aetna's EYE on DUI program was adopted by 231 law enforcement agencies in 32 states over a three-year period.

Calendar   This is an ongoing annual program that is conducted throughout the year. However, events such as the donation of video cameras and annual anniversaries are planned around the holidays, such as New Year's Eve, when drunk driving is more prevalent.

Budget   The budget increased every year as the EYE on DUI program gained acceptance and popularity. It started at $240,000 and rose to $800,000 by the end of the third year.

Evaluation   Each objective of the program was evaluated. The first, stepped-up DUI law enforcement and a higher conviction rate, was measured by compiling the number of guilty pleas for drunk driving in various cities. In Orlando, for example, 100 percent of the taped cases resulted in guilty pleas without going to trial. In Dallas, after one year, 95 percent of the taped arrests resulted in convictions, compared to 80 percent of untaped arrests.

The second and third objectives, both involving creation of public awareness, were measured by news coverage in various cities. Almost 13 hours of television coverage and more than 14,000 column-inches of print coverage were tabulated. Aetna's public opinion tracking research showed a 33 percent increase in public awareness of the dangers of drunk driving after the program was launched.

The fourth objective, increasing Aetna's visibility, was shown by a content analysis of news coverage. In most cases, the insurance company was identified as the sponsor of the EYE on DUI program. Another study reported that consumers perceived that Aetna outperformed its competition in the use of its "influence and resources to improve public safety."

SUMMARY

1. Most public relations activities occur within the framework of a program plan.
2. A program plan has the elements of situation (problem statement), objectives, audience, strategies, tactics, calendar, budget and evaluation.
3. Objectives can be informational or motivational, depending on the kind of results expected.
4. Creating publicity is not a valid objective; it is a means to an end.
5. For public relations purposes, audiences must be clearly defined. In most cases, a specific audience is defined by income, interest, geography, lifestyle and a host of other variables.

6. A strategy is a broad conceptualization that gives direction to a public relations program. A good strategy is based on research and reflects audience self-interests. It can also be expressed as the program's key selling proposition.

7. Tactics are the "how to do it" part of the program plan. They list the communication tools and activities that will be used to support the strategy.

8. Timing of activities and messages is important. They must occur within a broader context of public interests and must be scheduled in advance.

9. A detailed budget is an integral part of a public relations plan. Staff and administrative expenses usually consume more of the budget than out-of-pocket expenses.

10. A program is evaluated as a success if it meets the set objectives of the campaign. Objectives must be measurable for evaluation methods to be effective.

11. Working a plan means that you must have a detailed calendar of activities and who is responsible for carrying them out.

EXERCISES

1. A new computer software company has started to manufacture sophisticated educational programs for children and adults. Officers of the firm believe that their products represent the next generation of software programming in terms of graphics, ease of use and versatility. From a public relations perspective, how would you write the objectives of a consumer publicity program? After doing this, write a list of strategies to accomplish the objectives.

2. The Almond Advisory Board, a trade group of almond growers, is gearing up for a major marketing effort to increase almond consumption by the American public. Write three informational and three motivational objectives for this campaign.

3. The University Theater opens its season on September 15. Before that date, however, a number of public relations materials must be prepared, including a direct mail brochure outlining the season and soliciting purchase of season tickets, a press kit about the theater and its personnel, posters for bulletin boards, a variety of news releases for the news media (including community calendars) and an opening night reception for university and civic officials. Prepare a timeline for these activities.

4. A large developer has decided to build a 40-story office building in a key downtown area. This is a major event for the downtown area, which has suffered a decline over the years due to the rising numbers of suburban shopping malls and office complexes. Because of this, a gala groundbreaking ceremony is planned in three months. Prepare a public relations plan for this ceremony. The plan should include (a) background of the situation, (b) objective, (c) publics to be reached (d) strategies, (e) action plan, often called tactics, (f) timeline, (g) budget and (h) evaluation method.

20 | *Program Evaluation*

*T*he final step in any campaign or program is evaluation. Was the program effective? It is important to ask this question for two reasons.
First, you must show your client or employer that the money, time and effort devoted to the program were well spent and actually contributed to the attainment of organizational objectives. Second, you need to know what worked and what didn't work so you can do a better job next time.

This chapter describes a number of techniques for evaluating a public relations program. Some are quite simple, such as counting news clippings. Others, however, require the extra effort of systematic content analysis or doing benchmark studies. Also included are techniques for evaluating events and organizational publications such as newsletters and brochures.

BASIC EVALUATION QUESTIONS

Here are some questions that you should ask yourself upon completion of a public relations program:

- Was the program or activity adequately planned?
- Did recipients of the message understand it?
- How could the program strategy have been more effective?
- Were all primary and secondary audiences reached?
- Was the desired organizational objective achieved?
- What unforeseen circumstances affected the success of the program or activity?
- Did the program or activity stay within the budget set for it?
- What steps can be taken to improve the success of similar future activities?

Answering these questions requires a mix of evaluative methods, many borrowed from advertising and marketing, to provide complete evaluations. To evaluate a public relations program fully, you must use formal and more systematic research methods to document message exposure, accurate dissemination of the message, acceptance of the message, attitude change and change in overt behavior.

Message exposure and accurate dissemination of the message are fairly easy to evaluate by keeping track of the messages sent, compiling the resulting news clips and broadcast mentions and performing a content analysis to determine if key messages were included.

Acceptance of the message by the audience and change of attitude are more difficult to evaluate and require systematic public opinion polling. Change in overt behavior can be documented by looking at sales figures, attendance, audience feedback, and so on.

NEWS RELEASES AND FEATURES

For many public relations practitioners, the sum and substance of evaluation revolves around the production and dissemination of news releases. Katherine Paine, president of The Delahaye Group, estimates that 85 percent of public relations programs use press clippings to measure program success.

Although press coverage is an element of evaluation, it is important to remember that publicity is a means, not an end. It is the means to accomplish such organizational objectives as increased sales, visibility and market share.

Production

One elementary form of evaluation is simply to give your client or employer a count of how many news releases, feature stories, photos and such were produced in a given time period. This kind of evaluation is supposed to give management an idea of your productivity. However, this approach is not very meaningful because it em-

FACTORS OF PROGRAM SUCCESS

What factors are important in judging the effectiveness of a public relations program? A survey of corporate communicators and marketers conducted by CDB Research & Consulting and Thomas L. Harris & Associates found that 99 percent of the respondents rated "increase in awareness" as the most important factor. Other findings:

- Delivery of message points (95 percent)
- Enhancement of company image (88 percent)
- Placement in key publications (87 percent)
- Increase in awareness of company or issue (85 percent)
- Change in attitudes (84 percent)
- Response to program (83 percent)
- Overall audience reach (72 percent)
- Increase in reported purchasing (59 percent)
- Bottom-line sales increase (58 percent)
- Number of placements (47 percent)
- Number of gross impressions (40 percent)
- Advertising equivalents (24 percent)

phasizes quantity instead of quality. It also encourages the public relations writer to send out more news releases than necessary, many are worthless as news, in an attempt to meet some arbitrary quota.

It may be more cost-effective to write fewer news releases and spend more time on preparing truly newsworthy stories that are tailored to specific publications. Is it better to do 15 routine news releases in a week or to spend the same amount of time pitching one story to the prestigious *Wall Street Journal*?

Distribution

Closely aligned to the production of materials is their dissemination. Thus it may be reported that a news release was sent to "977 daily newspapers, 700 weekly newspapers and 111 trade publications." Such figures are useful in terms of evaluating how widely a news release or feature is distributed, but sending out vast quantities of news releases just to impress management with big numbers is futile. For example, a large media mailing may be a waste of time and money if the news release in question has true news value only to the 50 daily newspapers in a region or if the release is so technical and specialized that only five trade publications would be interested in it.

Large mailings are not necessarily the fault of publicists. Often management has a skewed view of what is newsworthy and wants everyone in the world to know that the company has a new vice president of research and development. In addition, many organizations figure that sending a news release is a relatively cheap proposition involving only postage, so why not do a blanket mailing to increase the press clipping file and impress management?

As a professional public relations practitioner, you should document distribution but not succumb to sending out reams of news releases just to impress the boss. A better approach is to use targeted mailings that generate a high percentage of media placements.

Coverage

The most common way of evaluating coverage is to collect press clippings and broadcast mentions. You can do this yourself, or you can use a clipping or broadcast monitoring service.

There are regional and national news clipping services that can be hired to review large numbers of publications and clip all the articles about your client or employer. Two of the largest companies are Burrelle's and Luce Press Clippings. The latter has a staff that reads every daily newspaper and virtually every weekly newspaper and magazine published in the United States—over 15,000 publications. Luce also has affiliate coverage of the major press in 66 nations.

Burrelle's has similar scope. Both services can provide clients with clips giving the name of the publication, date, frequency and circulation. Clients can also have the clipping service evaluate clips on such variables as article size, advertising cost equivalent, audience, editorial slant of the article, subject, number of keyword mentions, type of article and byline.

The main purpose of systematically gathering press clippings is to find out if your news releases have been used by the media. By doing this, an organization can determine if the public was exposed to its message. It can also find out, by analyzing the press clippings, if the message communicated was accurate. The creation of public awareness is the first step in the diffusion process leading to acceptance of the message and modification of attitudes and behavior.

Another purpose of press clippings is to monitor trends and the competition. AT&T may ask its clipping service to clip any articles pertaining to keywords such as "telephone," "fiber optics" and "information technology" to keep track of industry trends and developments. It may also have the clipping service send clips on MCI and Sprint just to see what the competition is doing and saying.

Broadcast mentions can also be tabulated, but less reliably because this has to be done exactly at the time of the broadcast. Here, too, there are national companies that provide monitoring services.

One of the largest is Video Monitoring Services (VMS), which records all news and public affairs programs on local television stations in more than 130 markets, local radio stations in 14 markets and all national broadcast and cable news and talk shows. VMS logs the shows on computer and, like the clipping services, will send you a summary of news or talk show segments on the subjects you've specified.

New technology has also made video news releases easier to track. The old way, still used extensively, was to call up the television or cable outlet and ask if it used your VNR. However, the A. C. Nielsen Company has now developed the

VIDEO MONITORING SERVICES OF AMERICA, INC

Page: 5

INTEL REPORT
Continued....

17) **News/Ask An Expert**
WFBT-TV (Ind) CH 23 Chicago   1/5/96   1:00-1:30 PM
13:38 Market Talk with Jack Taylor. TZ;I; Bill Hummer, of Wayne Hummer & Co. Discussion of the budget talks in Washington and it's effect on lack of market data. He is recommending Intel, Motorola, and Microsoft. 18:10

18) **News/Ask An Expert**
WFBT-TV (Ind) CH 23 Chicago   1/5/96   1:30-2:00 PM
06:22 Stocks in the News with Curt Renz. >Intel is claiming that it found a new bug in a betta compiler (?). >Bethlehem Steel has raised prices for steel. >Hooper Homes is upgraded by Smith Barney. >Cowan & Co. downgraded DSC Communications. >Alex Brown downgraded Genesis. 08:49

19) **Good Morning San Jose**
KNTV-TV (ABC) CH 11 San Jose   1/5/96   6:00-7:00 AM
47.38 hi-Tech. GR; Listed. SI; Veronica Guerrero, analyst says Intel Corp has just announced a new computer chip for it Pentium processors. 50.15

20) **Evening Drive Time**
KGO-AM (ABC) Freq. 810 San Francisco   1/5/96   4:00-6:00 PM
6.34 Business report. > Stocks report. > Intel and Advanced Micro Devices signed 5 year cross-license deal to use each others patents. > Apple Computer says it'll unveil its Internet strategy at MacWorld Expo next week. > The Gap store sales rose 6% last month. > Esprit Du Cour has been told to find a buyer fast or debt holders will take over. 6.35

21) **WTOP News Radio 15**
WTOP-AM (CBS) Washington   1/5/96   6:00-7:00 AM
53.26 Jack Spear reporting; Business; >Disappointing holiday retail sales. >Disney will acquire Cap Cities/ABC. >Intel markets faster Pentium chip. >Market reports. 54.29

22) **WTOP News Radio 15**
WTOP-AM (CBS) Washington   1/5/96   4:00-5:00 PM
23.33 Jeff Claybaugh reporting; Business; >Compaq wants a computer in every room. >Advanced Micro Devices and Intel reach patent agreement. >Market reports. 24.48

23) **Eyewitness News At 5:30 AM**
WUSA-TV (CBS) CH 9 Washington   1/5/96   5:30-7:00 AM
19.16 TZ; Business report. > Retailers declared sales decline including JC Penny. Sears had a rise. > Disney one step closer to acquiring ABC. > Intel has faster version of pentium chip. Dell, Hewitt Packard have newer models to go with chip. > Stocks.

Figure 20.1 Commercial monitoring services give clients a list of television programs where the organization or its products were mentioned. This helps organization track publicity placements. Videocassettes or transcripts of any of the placements can be ordered separately. (*Courtesy of Video Monitoring Services, Inc., New York.*)

Sigma system, which inserts an electronic signature (something like bar coding on grocery store items) on a video news release at the time it is produced. When the VNR is used, Nielsen's electronic decoding devices pick up the code and record the time, date and place. Nielsen scans TV stations in 200 markets on a 24-hour basis in search of the codes. Arbitron, another monitoring service, has developed a digital character recognition system that does the same thing.

The Sigma system is not perfect in that television systems can strip the code off the VNR, but the technology is an improvement over the time-consuming task of calling stations to ask, "Did you use my piece?"

Impressions

Clipping services and broadcast monitoring firms tell clients the circulation of publications and the audited audience size of a radio or television program. This helps you determine the number of people who may have been exposed to your message. In the advertising and public relations industry, this is known as compiling *gross impressions,* or just *impressions.*

For example, if a story about the company appears in the local daily with a circulation of 130,000, the number of impressions is 130,000. If the story appears in a number of publications, you simply add up the circulation of all the publications to get *total impressions.*

A story appearing in 15 or 20 national publications can easily generate several million total impressions. A public relations campaign for Underground Atlanta, for example, reported that the total impressions for the 12-month period, excluding radio coverage, was 200 million.

Gross or total impressions are used in advertising and publicity to illustrate the penetration of a particular message. However, high impression figures don't guarantee that the message was effective.

Advertising Value

The numbers game is also played by converting stories in the news columns or on broadcast news and talk shows into the equivalent of advertising costs. For example, the public relations department of a major corporation might give top management the following report: "When print inches are calculated as advertising space, the company received exposure worth $158,644 this year—a 27.5 percent increase over last year."

Converting space received in the news columns or in broadcast time to the cost of space or time in advertising rates, say many experts, shows management that the time and effort have paid off. After all, the coverage received has given the company $158,000 worth of "free advertising." This is particularly impressive to vice presidents of marketing who are constantly looking for ways to get around the high costs of advertising.

COMPILING IMPRESSIONS

A simple way of estimating print and broadcast exposure is to multiply the number of message placements by the publication's circulation or the station's audited listening audience. Each exposure is reported as an "impression" because the same person may read or hear the message several times. Here is a sample impression report:

Radio	Placements		Impressions		Total
KGO-AM	6	×	109,000	=	654,000
KCBS-AM	1	×	60,000	=	60,000
KYA	2	×	30,000	=	60,000
KMEL-FM	10	×	35,000	=	350,000
Total Gross Impressions					1,124,000

It is true that product publicity is more cost-effective than paid advertising, and a good case can be made that publicity can give a better return on investment than high-priced ads.

Daniel Edelman, president of a major U.S. public relations firm, once told the Public Relations Institute of Australia (PRIA) that five public relations campaigns carried out for a single client generated publicity worth $12 million when measured against equivalent costs for advertising space. And a San Francisco practitioner boasted that his hotel client, featured in the *New York Times,* got $36,000 in equivalent advertising space.

Such comparisons, however, are not really valid because you're comparing apples and oranges. First of all, in advertising, you control the exact wording, graphics and placement of your message. By contrast, news releases and features are subject to the whims of media gatekeepers who decide what is published and in what context. There is no guarantee, as there is in advertising, that your message will be communicated in the way you wish.

Second, a mystery remains as to what is actually being counted. If a 10-inch article in the local daily mentions your company along with several competitors, is this equivalent to 10 inches of advertising space? Does the university football team reap "millions of dollars of comparable advertising" if its losing season gets extensive media coverage?

Third, the practice of equating news stories and publicity with advertising is not particularly beneficial for promoting effective media relations. Editors often suspect that all that publicists seek is "free advertising," and this impression is reinforced when public relations people themselves take great pains to convert story placements to comparable advertising costs.

Although many public relations departments and public relations firms still measure press clips by converting them to advertising rates, the practice is fading among professionals. Very few winners of the Silver Anvil awards competition sponsored by the Public Relations Society of America exclusively use comparable advertising rates to demonstrate the success of their programs. Instead, they use end results such as increased sales, public awareness and contributions to overall organizational objectives.

Content Analysis of Press Clippings

Press clippings are still measured by the pound and the inch, but a more systematic content analysis can now be done thanks to the computer and various software programs.

A more systematic analysis can pay dividends in terms of determining exactly what news releases are used and by what media, what key messages are included, whether the story is favorable or unfavorable, the degree to which the message penetrates key markets and how your coverage compares to that of your competitors.

In the first area, a content analysis may show that 45 percent of your company's news releases are management and personnel stories, but that these releases account for only 5 percent of the stories published about the company. By contrast, stories about new product developments may constitute only 10 percent of the news releases but account for 90 percent of the press coverage. Given these data, a logical step might be to send our fewer personnel stories and more product development articles.

A systematic tracking system also identifies which publications receiving the news releases are using them. Your mailing list may include 500 different periodicals, but by the end of a 12-month period, you may find that only half of these used your releases in any way. Given this information, you would be wise to prune your mailing list.

Computer analysis of press clippings, now done routinely by many large organizations, is a valuable way to make sure that key copy points are being included in the published stories. For example, a company may wish to emphasize in all its press coverage that it is a manufacturer of high-quality professional audio and video recording systems or that it is a well-managed company. Analysis may show that 87 percent of the stories mention the high-quality products but that only 35 percent mention or imply that the company is well managed. Such feedback can help you structure your news releases so that the more important points receive greater emphasis.

PR Data Systems of Norwalk, Connecticut, pioneered the computer analysis of press clippings and can even tell a company if the media in key urban markets are being reached effectively. Other systems are also now available, but the fundamental purpose is the same. A computer profile shows whether your news releases are being published by the media in prime market areas. If they are not, it means that you will have to revamp your publicity strategy for greater market penetration.

A systematic tracking mechanism like the one just described is especially valuable for making specific changes in publicity activities to increase cost-effectiveness. The public relations staff of the Ampex Corporation made the following recommendations to management after a yearlong analysis of its press clippings.

1. Division should be discouraged from sending our releases on relatively small contracts because the media don't show much interest.
2. Press conferences do not generate as much publicity for new products as pre–trade show publicity does.
3. There is slight media interest in stories about personnel promotions at the group manager or regional sales manager level. Such stories should be discouraged in the interest of economy and effectiveness.
4. The company's second largest division is not getting its share of product publicity (only 17.5 percent), so more news releases should be distributed about this division.
5. Media interviews with Ampex executives are given good coverage, so it would be in the company interest to make executives accessible for additional interviews.

Gatekeeper Surveys

An alternative to systematic analysis of press clippings is surveying periodical editors and broadcast news and program personnel to ascertain exactly what kinds of information they find most usable.

**Typical News Management System charts
demonstrate your success.**

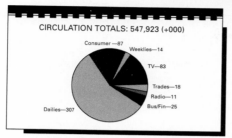

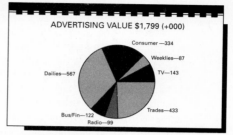

Prove the success of your publicity program quantified by clip totals, circulation/audience, key media, media category, key markets, and also measured by time period.

Prove the dollar value of your publicity by comparing space and time received with the cost of advertising for that same space and time. You'll look very good indeed.

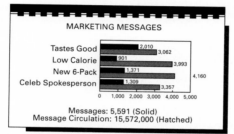

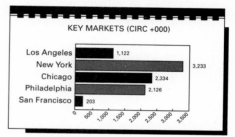

Prove that the media delivers your message by comparing the content of your clips to your message objectives. Tracking individual releases also shows which messages work best.

Prove your media coverage in key markets or in any defined region: ADI's, state, county, city, zip cluster, shareholder concentration, sales territory, or regional office.

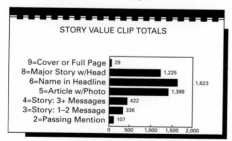

Prove the quality of your media coverage showing how the media has used and featured your material.

Prove the excellent return on investment. Total PR cost often can be less than a dollar per thousand circulation.

Figure 20.2 The ways of measuring success are varied. This illustration, from a sales brochure of a measurement service, gives at least six ways. (*Courtesy of PR Data Systems, Norwalk, CT.*)

Prepare a questionnaire—but don't make it too long (25 questions maximum)—written in such a way that respondents can answer with check marks. Here is an example:

MEDIA ANALYSIS BY THE NUMBERS

Systematic content analysis of media stories is now possible through computer software and on-line access to services such as Nexis/Lexis. There are also vendors that provide monitoring services and sophisticated data analysis.

Burrelle's, for example, now has a "paperless" clipping service that electronically delivers clips about clients and employers directly to your PC. Other firms, such as The Delahaye Group, specialize in computer analysis of clippings to give a statistical picture of whether the coverage was positive or negative and whether it carried key messages, and even a box score on the stories written by individual reporters.

As Katharine Delahaye, owner of the firm, says, "The world doesn't need more data. What it needs is analyzed data." Listed below is a sample of the kind of data that The Delahaye Group generates for clients:

Total Coverage	Total
Total impressions	89,641,378
Percent of positive impressions	26.98%
Percent of negative impressions	19.85%
Total articles	1,049
Percent of positive articles	35.65%
Percent of negative articles	16.02%
Percent of articles containing one or more positive message	52.43%
Percent of articles containing one or more negative message	18.78%

Check the three major types of information sources that would help you cover the microprocessor industry and Millennium Systems in particular:

_____ Interviews with top officers

_____ Mailed releases and product photos

_____ Press kits

_____ Feature articles

_____ Story-line synopses

_____ Brochures, data sheets

_____ Other _____

You can also assess what kinds of information an editor would most likely publish about a company. For example, a checklist might include the following categories:

- New products
- Technology breakthroughs
- Annual earnings of parent company

- Corporate personnel changes
- Profiles of top executives

SPONSORED PUBLICATIONS

If you are an editor of a newsletter or an employee magazine, it is wise to evaluate its readership on an annual basis. This will help you ascertain reader perceptions of layout and design, the balance of stories, kinds of stories that have high reader interest, additional topics that could be covered, the publication's credibility and whether the publication is actually meeting organizational objectives.

Systematic evaluation, it should be emphasized, is not based on whether all the copies are distributed or picked up. This is much like saying that the news release was published in the newspaper. Neither observation tells you anything about what the audience actually read, retained or acted on. If all newsletters or printed materials disappear from the racks in a few days, it may simply mean that the janitorial staff is efficient.

The following discussion focuses on periodical publications, but the same methods can be used to evaluate leaflets, booklets and brochures. Since many of these may be used externally, you also need to study the reactions and opinions of people who are not employees. Informal questioning of readers, monitoring of mail and requests for additional information can all show whether the material is being read and whether it is doing its job or needs improvement.

There are a number of ways in which a newsletter, newspaper or magazine can be audited. These include content analysis, readership interest surveys, readership recall of articles actually read, application of readability formulas and use of advisory boards or focus interview groups. An informal appraisal can be made by simply walking around the office or plant and learning if employees are talking about items in the publication.

Content Analysis

Select a representative sample of past issues and categorize the stories under general headings. You may wish to cover such subjects as management announcements, new product developments, new personnel and retirements, employee hobbies and interests, corporate finances, news of departments and divisions and job-related information.

A systematic analysis will quickly tell you if you are devoting too much space, perhaps unintentionally, to management or even to news of a particular division at the expense of other organizational aspects. For example, you may think that you have a lot of articles about employee personnel policies and job advancement opportunities only to find, on analysis, that less than 10 percent of the publication is devoted to such information.

By analyzing organizational objectives and coupling the results of a content analysis with a survey of reader interests, you may come to the conclusion that the publication's contents require some revision.

Readership Interest Surveys

The purpose of such surveys is to obtain employee feedback on the types of stories they are most interested in reading.

These are relatively simple surveys. Merely provide a long list of generic story topics and have employees rate each one as "very important," "somewhat important," or "not important." In such a survey, you may be surprised to find employees expressing limited interest in personals (anniversaries and birthdays) but great interest in the organization's future plans.

A readership interest survey becomes even more valuable if you can compare it to the content analysis of what your publication has been covering. If there are substantial differences, it is a signal to change the editorial content of your publication.

FAX YOUR FEEDBACK!

Please take a few moments to fill out this questionnaire, and fax it to us by Oct. 9. Your answers will help guide Corporate Communications efforts to continually improve the usefulness to you of the company's varied communications publications and other media. Results will be published in an upcoming issue of Praxair News. *Thanks for your time, and we look forward to hearing from you!*

1. My primary sources of information about Praxair's business and strategies are (check 3):

_____Praxair News	_____"The Grapevine"
_____Electronic Bulletins	_____Telephone Conferences
_____Immediate Supervisor	_____Bulletin Board Postings
_____Group Meetings	_____Local Publications
_____Other (specify)_____	

2. Please indicate how strongly you agree or disagree with the following statements:

	Strongly Disagree	Disagree	No Opinion	Agree	Strongly Agree
Praxair communicates clear company goals.	_____	_____	_____	_____	_____
Praxair communicates clear strategies to achieve its goals.	_____	_____	_____	_____	_____
Praxair communications are believable.	_____	_____	_____	_____	_____
The information I receive helps me do my job better.	_____	_____	_____	_____	_____
My supervisor does a good job of communicating useful information.	_____	_____	_____	_____	_____

3. Please circle the number for each phrase that best describes your opinion of *Praxair News.* **You may circle any number from 1 to 5:**

It's all old news to me	1	2	3	4	5	I learn a lot
The articles are boring	1	2	3	4	5	It has interesting articles
The stories are trivial	1	2	3	4	5	The stories have substance
The design is unappealing	1	2	3	4	5	The design is attractive
It is poorly written	1	2	3	4	5	It is well-written
It's too management-oriented	1	2	3	4	5	There's something for everyone

Additional comments:_____

Figure 20.3   Employees publications need reader feedback to evaluate effectiveness. This is part of a questionnaire that was included as an insert in an issue of a company newspaper. (*Courtesy of Praxair, Inc., Danbury, CT.*)

Article Recall

The best kind of readership survey is done when you or other interviewers sit down with a sampling of employees to find out what they have actually read in the latest issue of the publication.

Employees are shown the publication page by page and asked to indicate the articles they have read. As a check on the tendency for employees to tell you that they have read the publication from cover to cover (often called a "courtesy bias"), you also ask them how much of the article they read and what the article was about. The resulting marked copies of the publication are then content-analyzed to determine what kinds of articles have the most readership.

The method just described is much more accurate than a questionnaire asking employees to tell you how much of the publication they read. You do not get accurate data when you ask questions such as "What percentage of the newsletter do you read? All of it? Most of it? Some of it?" In this case, employees know that the company expects them to read the publication, so you get a preponderance of answers at the high end of the scale. Very few people will want to admit that they don't read it at all.

It is also somewhat fruitless to ask rank-and-file employees to evaluate the graphic design or the quality of the photographs. Most employees don't have the expertise to make such judgments. It would be much wiser to ask these questions of individuals who are versed in graphic design and printing quality.

A variation of the readership recall technique is individual evaluation of selected articles for accuracy and writing quality. For example, an article on a new manufacturing technique might be sent (before or after publication) to the head of plant engineering for evaluation.

On a form with a rating scale (excellent, good, fair, deficient), the person may be asked to evaluate the article on the basis of factors such as:

- Technical data provided
- Organization
- Length
- Clarity of technical points
- Quality of illustrations

Such a systematic evaluation enables you, as an editor, to make sure that the articles are accurate and informative.

Readability

Every publication should be evaluated for readability at least once a year. This can be done in several ways. An informal method is to ask people during a reader recall survey if they think the articles are clear and understandable. Comments "I don't know what they're talking about" and "I don't get anything out of some articles" might indicate that there is a readability problem.

Also available are various readability formulas that quantify reading level. Rudolf Flesch was one of the first educational researchers to develop a formula, now commonly called the Flesch formula. There are also the Gunning formula, the Dale-Chall formula, the Fry formula, and the Cloze procedure.

Basically, all these formulas allow you to determine how difficult a given piece of writing might be to read. They depend on measuring mean sentence length and counting the average number of multisyllabic words. Some also include the number of personal pronouns used. In general, writing is easier to read (is accessible to readers at a lower educational level) if the sentences are simple and short and there are many one- and two-syllable words.

If a randomly selected sample of 100 words contains 4.2 sentences and 142 syllables, it is ranked at about the ninth-grade level. This is the level that most daily newspapers strive for.

If you are writing for an employee publication, ninth-grade level is usually a good starting point. However, if a large percentage of the employees are recent immigrants and English is their second language, you might want to strive for six or seven sentences and 120 syllables per 100 words.

For news releases to the general media and publications geared to all employees, you should write at a ninth-grade level. News releases to trade publications with a primary audience of scientists and engineers as well as publications geared to managers can be written at a higher level. For example, readability formulas show that a college-educated audience can readily cope with 3.8 sentences and 166 syllables per 100 words.

Advisory Boards and Focus Groups

Periodic feedback and evaluation can be provided by organizing an employee advisory board that meets several times a year to discuss the direction and content of your publication. Between meetings, members of the advisory board would also be able to relay employee comments and concerns to the editor. This is a useful technique in that it expands the editor's network of feedback and solicits comments that employees may be hesitant to offer the editor face to face.

A variation of the advisory board is to periodically invite a sampling of employees to participate in a general discussion of the publication and its contents. It is important that all segments of the organization's employees be represented and that these sessions not become forums for charges and countercharges. The purpose is to share information, generate new ideas and mutually work to make the publication more valuable as an instrument for obtaining organizational objectives.

EVENTS

Speeches, meetings, presentations, tours, grand openings and other such activities have one important thing in common: They all involve group audiences to which the same message is given at the same time. All events can be evaluated in the same way.

A first step in evaluating these activities is to count the number of such activities and the number of people who are exposed to the message. This can indicate the amount of work done and the size of the audience reached. Poor attendance at any event may show that people were not interested or that there was not enough advance information.

The numbers are not conclusive. You must do more than count noses; you must find out whether anything was accomplished. A standing ovation at the end of a speech, spontaneous applause, complimentary remarks as people leave, even the "feel" of the audience as expressed in smiles and the intangible air of satisfaction that can permeate a group of people will give you an idea as to the success of the session.

Conversely, if people are unresponsive, if they ask questions about subjects that were supposedly explained or if they express doubts or antagonism, the effort has not succeeded.

Some people stop here and think that they have evaluated a given activity, but this is not enough. Your management or client may accept your report that the meeting or presentation was a great success, but your claim will be much more convincing if you can provide some proof.

A good way to obtain such proof is to ask each person attending the event to fill out an evaluation form and turn it in at the door when leaving. A simple form might look like this:

YOUR EVALUATION OF THIS MEETING (Please check each item)			
	Excellent	Good	Average	Could Be Better
1. Location	____	____	____	____
2. Costs	____	____	____	____
3. Facilities	____	____	____	____
4. Program	____	____	____	____
5. Speakers	(These should be listed by name.)			

Why did you attend? _____

How did you learn about it? _____
Suggestions for future events: _____

MONITORING THE INTERNET

Measuring the reach and effectiveness of your messages on the Internet seems like an impossible task, but it can be done.

An organization's home page, also called a web site, is the easiest the monitor. Determining the circulation, or impressions, that a news release or piece of information receives is measured by the number of "hits" (users accessing the home page).

You can get additional information about users by asking them to answer some demographic questions before they use the site or as they leave it. For best results, offer free software or something similar that must be mailed to users; this entices people to give their names and addresses. Marketers, for example, use this technique to compile databases of potential customers.

Chat groups, forums and bulletin boards on the Internet should also be monitored to determine what people are saying about your products or organization. There are literally thousands of chat groups, so you have to determine what groups are most important to you. If you have a widely recognized product, consumer chat groups may be worth monitoring.

Gripe groups should also be monitored. For example, there is one chat group called *McSpotlight* that is anti-McDonald's and anti-multinational corporations. Another chat group is more explicit about its purpose; it's called *The Mart Sucks Page* (anti-K-mart).

Monitoring chat groups is increasingly important in issues management. It gives you direct feedback about what people are thinking. While the people expressing their views may not represent the majority public opinion, their comments often give organizations a "wake up call" about potential problems and issues.

ATTAINMENT OF OBJECTIVES

It is imperative to report how the program has helped to reach organizational objectives. For example, Ketchum Public Relations won a Silver Anvil Award from the Public Relations Society of America (PRSA) by showing that its extensive campaign for the California Prune Board resulted in sales gain of 4 percent for the year (with no advertising involved) following more than five years of declining sales.

Ketchum's simple objective was to increase prune sales. The strategy was to generate positive awareness among women aged 25 to 49 through a campaign on the theme "Prunes . . . Just Plum Good." By using a credible spokesperson and introducing prunes as a snack food for people interested in health and fitness, Ketchum attained the objective. The agency also tabulated the numerical counts to show dissemination and coverage.

- 1,189 consumer magazine and newspaper articles generating 143 million total impressions
- 7,000 *Feeling Energetic* booklets distributed as a result of TV and radio publicity
- 22,000 copies of basic fact booklet distributed

But the bottom line was the fact that the agency met its objective—it was able to increase prune sales. You must never forget that publicity in itself is not the objective. Publicity is merely a tool used to achieve objectives.

Benchmark Studies

It is difficult to evaluate whether you have changed a person's perceptions about something, but it can be done. One way is to sample the opinions of the target audience before and after the campaign. This means conducting *benchmark studies*—studies that graphically show percentage differences in attitudes as a result of increased information and persuasion. (The Aetna case study in Chapter 19 showed how the company used benchmark surveys to measure increased public awareness about the dangers of drunk driving.) Of course, a number of possible intervening variables may also account for changes in attitudes, but a statistical analysis of variance can help pinpoint to what degree the attitude change is attributable to your efforts.

U.S. Steel conducted a benchmark study of its image among American business leaders and major educators. The company then sent a number of speech reprints and other publications to a selected sample of these opinion leaders while making sure that a control group did not receive the materials. At the end of the year, it was found that the group receiving company publications was considerably more positive about U.S. Steel as a progressive and well-managed company that spoke on behalf of the entire steel industry. By contrast, the control group still retained its original low-level image of the company.

Mobil Oil, General Electric and AT&T regularly use benchmark surveys to measure the effectiveness of publicity promotion campaigns. Surveys conducted after particular campaigns go a long way toward documenting their impact on the public. Surveys show, for example, that Mobil's sponsorship of *Masterpiece Theater* on the Public Broadcasting System (PBS) has gained the company a reputation for corporate leadership and social responsibility.

Feedback

Benchmark surveys are only one way to measure results. You can also do evaluations on a less sophisticated level by keeping complete and thorough tabs on telephone calls logged and letters received and by conducting focus group interviews with cross sections of the publics being reached. Analysis of telephone calls and letters is very important in the area of consumer affairs. If a pattern can be ascertained, it often tells the company that a particular product or service is not up to standard.

The readership of product publicity features is often monitored by offering readers an opportunity to write for a brochure or for more information. In this way, for example, Air New Zealand has measured the value of sending travel features to daily newspapers throughout the United States. Inquiries through toll-free telephone numbers are also monitored to find out where a person first heard about a particular product. Such monitoring often shows top management that product publicity generates more sales leads than straight advertising.

WRITING A REPORT

When you have finished evaluating a campaign, you must report the results to the people who paid for it. In some cases, it may be necessary to report on individual events or activities immediately after they have occurred. Even if an immediate report is unnecessary, an overall report on the entire program must be made—usually annually. Budgets and programs are generally reviewed at least once a year, and this is the time when you must convince management or the client that what you have done is worthwhile and that the program should be continued and improved.

To prepare the report, you should refer to the original plan and state what you accomplished under each heading. Answer the following questions:

1. *Situation.* Was the situation properly appraised? While the program was under way, did you learn anything that forced changes? What happened, and what did you do?

2. *Audience.* Was it properly identified? Did you reach it? How effectively did you reach it (numbers reached, response, feedback)?
3. *Objectives.* Did you achieve what you planned to achieve? Provide figures. You should have set numerical goals; now tell how well you did in reaching them.
4. *Strategy.* Did it work? Did you have to modify it? Should it be continued or changed?
5. *Tactics.* Did all the tools accomplish what they were supposed to accomplish? Were changes made? Why? Here again you can give numbers: news items published, feature stories published, printed items distributed, response of readers or viewers, TV and radio appearances and so on.
6. *Timing.* Was everything done at the right time? Should changes be made next year?
7. *Costs.* Did you stay within the budget? If not, why not? This is the point at which you set the stage for the next budget and perhaps explain why more money would have permitted greater accomplishment.

SUMMARY

1. Evaluation is absolutely essential. You must tell what was done, how well it was done and what good it did. Quantify whenever possible.
2. Don't just count news items and features. Find out where they were used, who used them, whether they reached the right people and whether they were effective.
3. Through research, you can find out who your publicity reached and how effectively.
4. Newsletters, house magazines and printed materials can all be evaluated by content analysis, reader interest surveys, article recall and readability tests. Advisory boards and focus groups may also be used.
5. Events can be evaluated through informal study of response and postevent surveys.
6. Attainment of objectives can be measured in some cases by counting noses or studying sales figures. More often, you will use benchmark studies, feedback, pretesting and monitoring the competition.
7. Evaluation isn't complete until you have given a comprehensive report to your management or client.

EXERCISES

1. During a one-week period, clip all articles about your school in the community daily newspaper, including all general news items and sports. Find out the average cost of advertising per column-inch and multiply it times the number of col-

umn-inches found. Given the dollar value of the publicity, do you think the coverage was actually worth this amount? Why or why not?

2. During a period of several weeks, follow the news coverage of a major company in your area. After compiling the news clippings, do a content analysis of each clipping. What percentage of these, in terms of the information provided, probably originated with the company? Indicate the percentage of clippings in which reference was made to the following: (a) the size of the company, (b) its product lines, (c) its competitive position in the marketplace and (d) the quality of the product.

3. Design and write a short questionnaire, for use by a company or an organization, to determine the attitudes of media gatekeepers about the kinds of news releases and other informational material they receive from the organization. The questionnaire should be designed in such a way as to gather information that will help the company do a better job of providing media gatekeepers with useful material.

4. Design and write a questionnaire to determine the readership of the campus newspaper. You could also conduct the readership survey.

5. Do a content analysis of a company newsletter or magazine. Articles, and the number of column-inches, should be placed in general categories: messages from management, employee features, news of departments and divisions, personals, recreational activities, retirements and so on. Given your findings, do you think the publication is accomplishing such corporate objectives as (a) building employee loyalty and morale, (b) informing employees of opportunities for advancement and (c) informing employees about company policies and procedures?

6. The national tourism office of Thailand has launched a major public relations campaign in the United States to promote Thailand as a vacation destination. Some of the activities include placement of travel articles in leading publications, exhibits of Thai culture at local art museums in major cities, advertisements in leading travel publications and demonstrations of Thai dancing on local television shows. A toll-free number is widely advertised and promoted as a way for people to order booklets and brochures about vacationing in Thailand. After one year, how would you evaluate the success of this promotional program?

A Glossary for Public Relations Writers

actuality A recorded statement by an identified person used in a radio newscast.

advertising Mass communication controlled and paid for by a sponsor. Paid space in a publication or broadcast.

annual report A report that details the financial aspects of a business or a nonprofit organization during the past year. Publicly held corporations are required to file such reports with the Securities and Exchange Commission (SEC).

assignment editor A person at a radio or television station who assigns reporters to cover stories.

audiotape A sound tape recording that is used to carry information to a broadcasting station and may be used on the air.

backgrounder A compilation of information about an organization, a problem, a situation, an event or a major development. It is given to the media to provide a factual basis for news to be published or broadcast.

benchmark study A study of public attitudes and opinions at a definite time, typically before and after a public relations campaign.

bio Short for *biography*. A brief biography, often supplied in a press kit or as part of the printed program for an event.

blueline Also *dylux*. The final proof before something is printed, usually by offset press.

booker A publicist whose assignment is to place clients on talk shows and in other public events.

b-roll Only the video portion of a tape without interviews or an announcer.

browser Software designed to view documents created for the Internet's World Wide Web.

camera-ready Suitable for duplication through offset or laser printing.

clip art Line art and other graphic designs in the public domain that can be used for a variety of purposes. Such material is available in print form or on diskette.

clips Also *clippings*. News stories and publicity placements cut from newspapers and magazines.

column A regular feature in a publication written by a columnist; also, a vertical stack of text, separated from the next by white space.

copy point A key message in public relations materials such as a news release or a brochure.

copyright Statutory protection to keep others from using a person's literary, musical or artistic work without proper permission.

copy testing Exposing several messages about the same subject to find out which particular set of words is most effective.

cu Close up video shot of a person or object. An *MCU* is a moderate close up.

cyberspace Refers to the unreal world in which information passes between computers.

database Indexed information held in computer storage, from which a computer user can call up selected information, usually for a fee. Also called *databank*.

demographics Classification of people by physical characteristics such as age, race, occupation, sex or state of health.

desktop publishing The use of computer software programs to format and lay out camera-ready materials such as newsletters, brochures and leaflets.

direct mail A means of reaching the public with letters that are mass produced. They are often individualized to give the appearance of being personally written.

editor The person on the staff of a publication who decides what to publish. The job often includes supervision of reporters.

editorial A statement of opinion by the publication or broadcast outlet about a current issue or situation. Also, the space devoted to news and information in a publication, as opposed to space used to display paid advertising.

electronic mail Messages transmitted from one computer terminal to another rather than delivered by telephone or messenger. Also referred to as *E-mail.*

electronic publishing The transmittal of news releases and reports via computers linked in a network.

E-mail Short for electronic mail. A message sent via computer networks.

external publication A publication designed to be read by persons not employed by the sponsoring organization. (Compare *internal publication.*)

facsimile Electronic method of transmitting exact reproductions of printed matter over telephone lines. Commonly called *fax.*

fact sheet A written summary about some event or situation that is given to reporters so that they will have the basic facts at their fingertips. Often a fact sheet will give information in the journalistic format of *who, what, when, where, why,* and *how.*

feature story A message giving detailed information about some subject such as a company, an association, a product, a service, a situation or a problem, the objective of which is to educate and entertain readers. The focus is often on human interest instead of late-breaking news.

film Motion picture footage, often used to convey information to audiences.

flack A derogatory and contemptuous term used by journalists to belittle public relations people.

gatekeeper A person at a publishing or broadcasting institution who decides whether to use news or features supplied by outsiders, typically public relations personnel sending material on behalf of their clients or employers.

gross impressions Total circulation or estimated listening audience of the print and broadcast media that use a news release.

home page Electronic "pages" on the World Wide Web where organizations post information. See *web site.*

hot line A toll-free telephone line used by organizations who want the public to call them for information.

hype Exaggerated publicity about a product, a service or a celebrity. Often characterized by flowery adjectives and inflated claims.

internal publication A document intended primarily for employees of an organization.

Internet A vast network of interconnected computers that can instantly access other computers anywhere in the world.

invasion of privacy Releasing personal information about someone that the person does not want the public to know.

libel A false and defamatory statement that is published about someone. (Compare *slander.*)

logotype A stylized drawing or lettering used to identify a product or service. Often the logotype is a trademark.

magazine show A television show that gives viewers information about special interest subjects. Neither news nor pure entertainment, these shows are comparable to the feature stories in newspapers or magazines.

marketing The management function that plans and produces goods or services to meet public desires and then tries to sell them to the public. Often a company or an organization will use public relations techniques (product publicity) to advance marketing objectives.

mechanical Type, photos, line art and so on assembled on a single board used for reproduction by a printer.

media Publishers and broadcasters. The media can be divided into various categories: trade media, special interest media, national media, local media and so on.

media advisory A short memo to a publication or broadcast outlet announcing an opportunity for news coverage. Such a memo often gives the date and time of an event and describes the possible interview or photo opportunities.

medium Any one of the media; a single publication or station.

monitor A television screen that can be used to convey messages via live broadcast or videotape. Monitors are used in meetings and to reach employees in a workplace. Also, a computer screen.

mug shot *(slang)* A head-and-shoulders photograph of an individual for newspaper publication.

news hole The space available in a publication for the placement of news and features.

news release Information sent to a medium in the hope that it will be published or broadcast.

offset A common printing method using the process of film negatives to make the printing plates. Materials for offset printing must be camera-ready.

on-line Describing a computer database that can be accessed directly through a device called a *modem* to tap information no matter where the database or the user is located.

op-ed Short for *opposite the editorial page*. The op-ed page contains the views and opinions of individuals who are not on the staff of the newspaper.

out-of-pocket Amounts paid to outside vendors by a client or public relations firm. Often called *OOP*.

pitch letter A letter urging a gatekeeper to publish or broadcast a specific story. This letter, persuasive by definition, should convince the gatekeeper that the material is newsworthy.

placement The act of getting a story to the right gatekeeper and having it published or broadcast.

planter A publicist who delivers news releases to media offices and urges their use. The term is often used in the entertainment industry.

political correctness Taking care not to offend through statements or actions that demean or stereotype on the basis of sex, race, religion, ethnic background, sexual orientation or physical characteristics. Often referred to as *PC*.

position paper A statement by an organization about some problem, situation or issue.

press agent A person, also called a publicist, that tries to get stories in the mass media. The term is often used in the entertainment industry.

press conference A meeting between reporters and one or more people representing an organization. The purpose of a news conference is to announce news and to answer reporters' questions.

press kit A folder containing information for reporters about some event, product or service. Press kits usually contain several pieces of information, including photos.

press release See *news release*.

psychographics A system for classifying people by mental attitudes and values rather than by physical characteristics, income level or place of residence.

publicity Communication that is uncontrolled and not paid for, as opposed to *advertising*. An organization may *seek* publicity (send information out) and *get* publicity (obtain coverage by the media).

public relations The management function that plans and establishes policies and actions to meet with public approval and endeavors to get that approval.

public relations advertising Advertising that supports a public relations program, in contrast to advertising that tries to sell goods or services.

publisher The principal executive of a newspaper or magazine who oversees all functions of the operation. In broadcast media, the chief executive is usually called a *general manager*.

report A compilation of information about a particular subject.

reporter A person who gathers news and prepares it for publication or broadcast.

reverse type Copy where the ink is reversed, as in white type on a black background.

satellite transmission A method of transmitting text, pictures and sound by beaming an electronic signal to a transponder on a satellite orbiting 22,300 miles above the earth, from which it bounces back to receiving dishes on the ground.

semantics The study of meaning, of what words actually mean to the people who see or hear them.

slander Oral communication that tends to defame the character of some person. (Compare *libel*.)

slide A piece of photographic film mounted in a paper or metal frame. A projector is used to show it on a screen before an audience.

SOT Sound on tape. Usually refers to an interview.

sound bite A short but complete statement that may be incorporated into a news broadcast.

sponsored film or video A film or video paid for by an organization to deliver information or a message, usually shown free of charge. There also are *sponsored publications*, which charge no subscription fee and contain no advertising.

stock footage Television tape or film that can be used to provide background visual material for newscasts.

talent release A document authorizing the use of a person's name, picture, skill or other aspect of identity in advertising or publicity.

talk show A television or radio program on which a host chats with guests or telephone callers.

teleconference A meeting using television monitors and satellite facilities to bring together people in various locations.

trademark A name, symbol or other device identifying a product, officially registered for exclusive use by its creator or manufacturer.

trade press Newspapers and magazines designed and edited for a special interest commercial or professional group.

transparency A sheet of clear plastic or photographic film on which text or graphic material is placed, for showing on an overhead projector. Transparencies are often referred to as *overheads*.

videocassette A small cartridge of videotape that can be inserted in a playback machine for projection on a monitor or television set.

video news release A piece of videotape containing a news story, sent to broadcasters for possible use in newscasts. Commonly referred to as a *VNR*.

voice mail A computerized telephone answering system that allows callers to leave messages.

v/o Voice-over. Someone off camera reading a portion of a story video.

web site A place on the World Wide Web where an organization has its home page.

white space The space in a publication's layout where no text or graphics appear.

word processor A computer workstation used for putting ideas into words. A word processor does the work of a typewriter and has a number of other functions. Word processing is done on a personal computer, often referred to as a *PC*.

World Wide Web A section of the Internet. The format can accommodate graphics, photos, sound and video.

Index